A Political Biography of
Maharaja Ripudaman Singh of Nabha

Dear HS and Sunaina
Hope you enjoy Reading
this piece of History
fondly
Jai Nabha
30.6.2018.

Dastār bandī (coronation) of Maharaja Ripudaman Singh (1912)
Source: Bhayee Sikandar Singh and Roopinder Singh, *Sikh Heritage: Ethos and Relics* (New Delhi: Rupa, 2012), p. 156.

A Political Biography of Maharaja Ripudaman Singh of Nabha

Paramountcy, Patriotism, and the Panth

J.S. GREWAL
and
INDU BANGA

OXFORD
UNIVERSITY PRESS

Oxford University Press is a department of the University of Oxford.
It furthers the University's objective of excellence in research, scholarship,
and education by publishing worldwide. Oxford is a registered trademark of
Oxford University Press in the UK and in certain other countries.

Published in India by
Oxford University Press
2/11 Ground Floor, Ansari Road, Daryaganj, New Delhi 110 002, India

© Oxford University Press 2018

The moral rights of the authors have been asserted.

First Edition published in 2018

All rights reserved. No part of this publication may be reproduced, stored in
a retrieval system, or transmitted, in any form or by any means, without the
prior permission in writing of Oxford University Press, or as expressly permitted
by law, by licence, or under terms agreed with the appropriate reprographics
rights organization. Enquiries concerning reproduction outside the scope of the
above should be sent to the Rights Department, Oxford University Press, at the
address above.

You must not circulate this work in any other form
and you must impose this same condition on any acquirer.

ISBN-13: 978-0-19-948135-4
ISBN-10: 0-19-948135-0

Typeset in ScalaPro 10/12.5
by The Graphics Solution, New Delhi 110 092
Printed in India by Replika Press Pvt. Ltd

To
Dr Gurcharan Singh Kalra
A cardiologist who cares

CONTENTS

List of Illustrations	ix
Preface	xi
Introduction: Paramountcy and Its Historiography	xiii

1.	A Mixed Heritage	1
2.	Tikka Ripudaman Singh	23
3.	Installation and Investiture	48
4.	The Maharaja, Michael O'Dwyer, and the World War	69
5.	Government and Politics	93
6.	Government Prepares Grounds for Deposition	118
7.	Removal from Nabha under Duress	140
8.	Issue of Restoration and the Jaito Morcha	160
9.	Attitude of the Congress and Its Leaders	181
10.	Defiance and Deposition	199
11.	The *Indictment of Patiala* Turned into an Indictment of Nabha	221
12.	The Maharaja Loses Custody of the Tikka	244
13.	The Nabha Issue in the House of Commons	264
14.	Last Bid and the Last Days	285

In Retrospect	301
Maharaja Ripudaman Singh in Photographs	315
Glossary	323
Select Bibliography	330
Index	342
About the Authors	354

ILLUSTRATIONS

Photographs

Frontispiece image: *Dastār bandī* (coronation) of
Maharaja Ripudaman Singh (1912)

1. Maharaja Hira Singh (1871–1911) — 315
2. The Coat of Arms of Nabha, with a crown at the top — 315
3. Raja Hira Singh with Tikka Ripudaman Singh — 316
4. Seated, left to right: Raja Hira Singh, Tikka Ripudaman Singh, and Bhai Kahn Singh Nabha. Standing, left to right: Sardar Nihal Singh and Munshi Faiz Bakht — 316
5. Seated, left to right: Tikka Ripudman Singh, Lord Curzon, Raja Hira Singh, and Dunlop Smith (1903) — 316
6. Maharaja Ripudaman Singh outside the Nabha Fort after *dastār bandī* (coronation) — 317
7. Seated, left to right: Bhai Arjan Singh Bagrian, Maharaja Bhupinder Singh of Patiala, and Maharaja Ripudaman Singh of Nabha. Standing, left to right: Raja Gurdit Singh of Retgarh and Bhai Kahn Singh Nabha — 317
8. Maharaja Ripudaman Singh with his courtiers — 318
9. Maharaja Ripudaman Singh and his infant son, Tikka Partap Singh, seated on a hunted tiger — 318
10. The young Maharaja Partap Singh at the time of his installation (1928) — 319
11. A signed portrait of Maharaja Ripudaman Singh at Kodaikanal (September 1929) — 319
12. Maharaja Ripudaman Singh and Maharani Gurucharan Kaur with their children at Kodaikanal — 320

13. Maharani Gurucharan Kaur and her children with
    Sardar Kharak Singh and others 321
14. Maharani Gurucharan Kaur and her children with
    Master Tara Singh and others 322
15. Maharani Gurucharan Kaur in conversation with
    Master Tara Singh at his residence in Amritsar 322

Maps

I.1 Princely States under British Paramountcy	xiv
1.1 The Phulkian States	3
5.1 Administrative Divisions of Nabha	95

PREFACE

Maharaja Ripudaman Singh of Nabha (1883–1942) has been a much misunderstood figure in the history of the early twentieth-century India. This volume reconstructs Ripudaman Singh's public career in terms of his relations with the paramount power, his increasing interest in nationalist causes, and his growing involvement in issues related to the Sikh Panth.

A vast corpus of unpublished archival sources enables us to see the life of the Maharaja as a continuous and more or less consistent whole, informed by certain ethical values and guided by certain political ideas. What comes out clearly in this study is his sympathy with the Singh Sabha movement, appreciation of the struggle of the Akalis for Gurdwara legislation, and his association with the political movements and causes of his time. Probably no other Indian ruler showed so much resistance to the paramount power, and sacrificed so much in pursuit of his convictions, as the Maharaja of Nabha.

Consistently challenging the paramount power with his own interpretation of treaty rights, Maharaja Ripudaman Singh sought to undermine the importance of symbols, rituals, and the semantics of paramountcy. He could enlist active support of the British Left against the diehard imperialists, exemplifying a complex form of resistance to colonial rule. Its complexity was heightened by a deep sense of patriotism, strengthened by his strong Sikh identity, and informed by his consistent concern for reform.

Thus, this political biography of Maharaja Ripudaman Singh is placed in three overlapping contexts: paramountcy, patriotism, and the Sikh Panth. In other words, this book has equal relevance for an integrated history of British colonialism, Indian nationalism, and Sikh politics.

In the pursuit of this study for over a decade we became indebted to a number of institutions and individuals, including the persons at Nabha and Kodaikanal whom we interviewed. We are thankful to them all.

Among the institutions where we consulted materials, we may specifically mention the British Library, London, UK (particularly for the India Office Records), the Cambridge University Library, University of Cambridge, UK (for the Crewe Papers), the National Archives of India, New Delhi, India, the Punjab State Archives at Patiala and Chandigarh, India, the Bhai Kahn Singh Nabha Library at the Punjabi University, Patiala, A.C. Joshi Library at the Panjab University, Chandigarh, the library of Indian Council of Historical Research and the Nehru Memorial Museum and Library, both at New Delhi, and the library of the School of Oriental and African Studies, London.

We may particularly mention the late Professor Christopher A. Bayly of St Catharine's College, Cambridge, and Lionel Carter, former librarian, Centre of South Asian Studies, University of Cambridge, who were extremely helpful to us in getting access to the India Office Records, which were in the process of being transferred to the British Library. Three scholars were formally associated with this project at different times: Dr M.P. Singh (a retired brigadier), Dr Karamjit K. Malhotra, and Dr Kuldip (Grewal). We would like to add that Dr Malhotra, presently Assistant Professor, Punjabi University, Patiala, continued to take active interest in this study till its completion. We are grateful to them.

The manuscript was typed with great care by Komal. Maps were drawn by S. Mohan Singh of the Department of Geography, Panjab University, Chandigarh, India. The sources for photographs have been acknowledged elsewhere in this work.

We really appreciate the concern with which the Oxford University Press processed this book for publication.

J.S. Grewal and Indu Banga

INTRODUCTION
Paramountcy and Its Historiography

Biographies are placed within specific contexts, unravelling 'multiple layers of historical change'.[1] The present volume is not a traditional biography in the sense of reconstructing details of personal life. It treats the history of an exceptional ruler and of his response to a changing political context. His consistent resistance to British colonialism illustrates what a prince could do in a crucial period of Indian history. Out of the three contexts relevant for his political biography—Indian nationalism, Sikh resurgence, and British paramountcy—the last is the least known and also the most important. To understand Maharaja Ripudaman Singh, it is necessary to understand paramountcy and its historiography.

Paramountcy at Work

Paramountcy under the British was a continuation of the suzerain–vassal relationship, which was an old feature of Indian polity. Known widely in the seventh century, it was systematized by the Mughal emperor Akbar (1556–1605), who gave considerable autonomy to the vassal chiefs. The British adopted this political arrangement in the late eighteenth and early nineteenth centuries, and allowed nearly 600 subjugated Indian rulers to continue as protected chiefs (Map I.1). Their role during the Mutiny of 1857 earned them a permanent position in the British Indian empire. Their relations with the paramount power were defined by treaties or *sanads*. However, the British

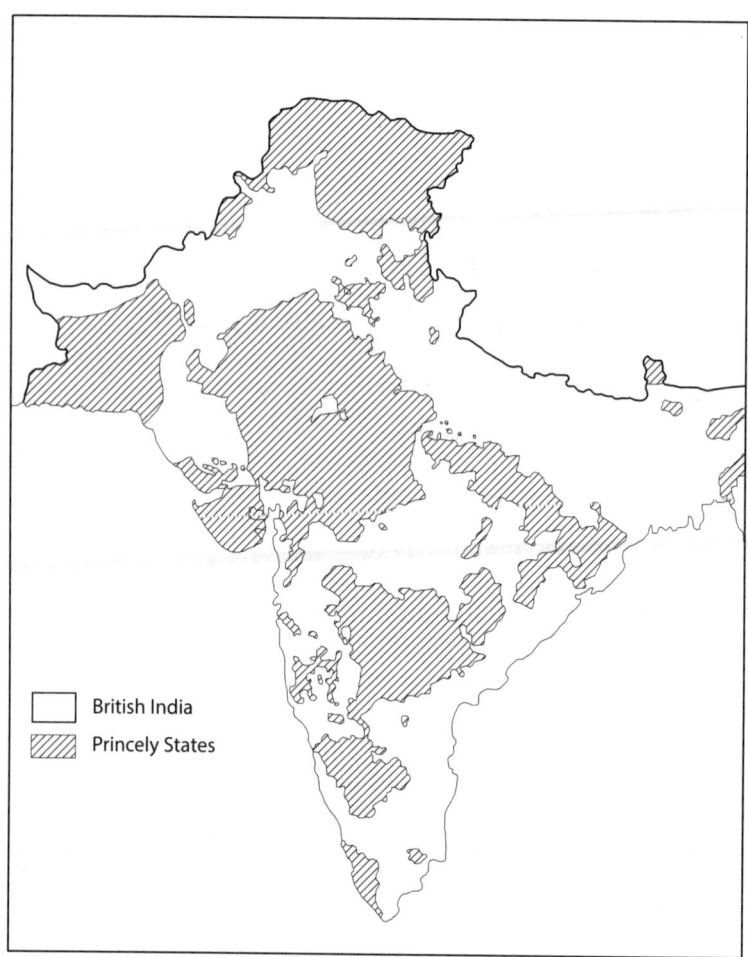

Map I.1 Princely States under British Paramountcy

Source: Adapted from Map in A.P. Nicholson, *Scraps of Paper: India's Broken Treaties, Her Princes and the Problem* (London, 1930).

interpreted the treaties in accordance with their own interests. This process culminated in the claim of the paramount power to exercise unfettered authority over a subordinate ruler.[2]

The system of controls devised by the British increasingly restricted princely options but enhanced the formalities of their relationship with the British monarch and her representatives in India. British officials formulated a hierarchy of the princely states and kept a table of salutes ranging from 9 to 21 guns. In due course, salutes became coveted and contentious. Appropriate banners with coats of arms were also created for the princes. The notions of feudal hierarchy of royal knighthoods were reinforced with an elaborate system of honours for various classes and categories to strengthen the princes' loyalty for the British monarch. David Cannadine in his *Ornamentalism: How the British Saw Their Empire* (2001) highlights that bonds of class and status linked the empire to the metropole through salute tables, royal orders, and imperial rituals such as the grand assemblage of 1877 when Victoria was declared the Empress of India. The spectacle and precedence in the viceregal Darbar, honorary military ranks, judicial powers, and visits of British officials to the states also acquired meaning in the intricate symbolism of the empire. Only the princes with 11-gun salute were styled 'His Highness'. Like the princes with unrestricted judicial powers, they became entitled to the full membership of the Chamber of Princes established in 1921.[3]

This so-called rationalization of paramountcy was based on enunciation of theory and codification of precedents to guide British policies. Sir Charles Aitchison edited the *Collection of Treaties, Engagements and Sanads Relating to India*. Originally published in 1865, its fifth edition appeared in 1929–33 in fourteen volumes. Sir Mortimer Durand, a Foreign Secretary, compiled the *Leading Cases* as a selection of past decisions in disputes between the British and the individual states to cover issues on which treaties were silent. Sir Henry Maine, Law Member of the supreme government under Lord Mayo, argued that the British had exclusive control over war and foreign relations as the only 'independent' sovereign while the Indian princes had the right to collect revenues and administer justice within their states. This principle of the divisibility of sovereignty, or 'dual sovereignty', enabled the British to give a legal cloak to their political alliances with princely states.

The treaties and precedents did not cover all the situations on the ground. The concept of 'usage' was evolved on the assumption that toleration of practices by the princes implied consent. Usage enabled the paramount power to serve current strategic needs by re-interpreting inconvenient clauses. Because of its built-in flexibility, 'usage could rationalise breaking promises made in treaties and sanads'. Sir Charles Lewis Tupper produced four volumes of the *Indian Political Practice*, published in 1895 for the use of British political officers.

William Lee-Warner's *The Protected States of India* (1899) highlighted the role of the British political officers (mostly recruited from the army) in moulding the relations with the princes. As projected by the British political officials, variously styled Resident, Agent to the Governor General, and Political Agent, paramountcy gave the right to confirm all successions to the *gaddī* (throne) in princely states, to advise the princes on the need for improving their administration, and to intervene in conflicts between princes and their feudatories or neighbouring states. In due course, the paramount power extended its jurisdiction over railway lines that crossed the borders of states. Lord Dufferin prevailed upon them to maintain Imperial Service Troops, which siphoned off a substantial chunk of the state revenues. Each prince stood alone in his relations with the paramount power. Protests against British interference in the internal affairs of the state could be made only individually by the ruler. In theory, the British political officers represented both the empire and the princes, but they fell increasingly in line with the policies of the Foreign and Political Department, because the avenue to promotion lay through conformity to the policy from above.

The British gradually came to claim that no succession was valid without their consent. The minority administrations provided a welcome opportunity for 'forceful intervention'. The education of a minor prince was seen as the prerogative of the paramount power, and a means of political control. The so-called rationalization of administration at the instance of the British officials affected the position of the traditional nobility and resulted in tensions between the ruler and his officers and courtiers. The paramount power renounced annexation but insisted on good conduct of the princes. Misconduct could include financial irregularities and oppressive treatment of subjects. Recalcitrance and resistance constituted a much greater crime that invited a serious notice. Indeed, even serious misconduct could be overlooked if a prince had political value for the British. The ultimate sanction of a recalcitrant prince was deposition. In the rarest of rare cases, the Bengal Regulation III of 1818 was applied to intern a prince.

In the first decade of the twentieth century Lord Curzon initiated the practice of conferring with the princes on issues of common concern such as the ailing Chiefs' Colleges. European travel by some princes was also beginning to dismantle the barriers of isolation and they were beginning to look beyond the narrow confines of their own states. Some English-educated princes such as Sayajirao Gaekwad of

Baroda could attempt to modernize the state's administration, though the rulers educated at the Chiefs' Colleges, such as Bhupinder Singh of Patiala, tended to be more Westernized and distanced from their subjects. In the backdrop of the rise of extremist nationalism following the partition of Bengal in 1905, Lord Minto decided to woo the princes collectively by announcing in 1909 a policy of non-interference in state affairs. The prompt offers of support from the princes in World War I convinced Lord Chelmsford that they could now be formally brought on a single platform. He convened the first Princes' Conference in 1916. More such meets followed eventually to take the constitutional form of the Chamber of Princes, inaugurated in 1921. The gathering momentum of the national movement increased the possibilities of political partnership between the British and the princes. When they became more vocal and assertive, Lord Reading reasserted the claims of paramountcy in no uncertain terms by deposing two inconvenient princes (one of whom was Maharaja Ripudaman Singh of Nabha) and publicly snubbing the Nizam of Hyderabad, the foremost prince of India.

Under the direct or indirect influence of developments in British territories, administrative and economic changes began to occur in the princely states. Gradually, social change and political awakening in the states resulted in formation of groups to struggle for greater share in power and economic resources. The first phase of popular political activity in the states related to specific local grievances. The second phase started in the late 1920s and the early 1930s under the aegis of the States' People's Movement, with the demand for popular representation. Peasant movements constituted the third phase in the late 1930s and the early 1940s.

In the 1930s, there was a certain degree of collaboration between Indian princes and Indian politicians sympathetic to the idea of a Federation. There was division within the princely ranks, and there was increasing opposition to Federation in British India. Desultory negotiations between the British and the Indian princes from 1935 to 1939 were ultimately suspended after the outbreak of World War II. After the war, it became clear that the British would transfer power to Indians. Princes lost their relevance for the paramount power.

The Indian National Congress had deliberately distanced itself from political mobilization in the Indian states after an initial interest in the princes as financial benefactors. Mahatma Gandhi articulated a policy of non-intervention in overt political mobilization within the princely states, though individuals from the princely areas were allowed to join the Congress. In 1939, however, several Congress leaders, notably Gandhi himself and Vallabhbhai Patel, became seriously involved in key agitations in the states. After the war, the Congress became increasingly interested in making princely India a part of independent India.

Historiography

A substantial chunk of historical writing was produced by British administrators with a focus on relations between the paramount power and the princely states. The stereotypes emerging from their studies present the 'native princes' (the generic term used in the 1858 proclamation of Queen Victoria) as collaborators but obstacles to progress as relics of oriental despotism. The territories of 600 odd princes, covering two-fifths of the subcontinent and with one-third of its population, were supposed to be under the 'indirect rule' of the paramount power.[4] The notion of 'indirect rule' to describe the relations between the Government of India and the princely states can now be seen as a conceptual tool of the colonial mode of historiography to justify the ever-increasing encroachments on the internal autonomy of the politically subordinate chiefs.

Recent historical studies have questioned the stereotypes created by the British, and attempted to rehabilitate the princes and the states' people as historical subjects for a rounded history of colonial India. Some general studies cover a phase or period to deal with various dimensions of paramountcy. Examples of works of this nature are the *Princely States and the Paramount Power, 1858–1876* by Mihir Kumar Roy; *Princely India and the British: Political Development and the Operation of Empire*, covering the period from 1858 to 1909, by Caroline Keen; *British Policy towards the Indian States 1905–1939* by S. R. Ashton; *British Policy towards the Punjab States 1858–1905* by A. C. Arora; *The Princes of India in the Twilight of Empire* by Barbara N. Ramusack; and *The Princes of India in the Endgame of Empire 1917– 1947* by Ian Copland. Some refreshing essays appear in anthologies, such as the *People, Princes and Paramount Power: Society and Politics in the Indian Princely States* edited by Robin Jeffrey, and *India's Princely States: People, Princes and Colonialism* edited by Waltraud Ernst and Biswamoy Pati. A recent work providing an overview of the princely states while also taking into account much of the literature produced on the subject is *The Indian Princes and Their States* by Barbara N. Ramusack. Its annotated bibliography provides a comprehensive view of the present state of understanding about paramountcy.[5]

Given the built-in difficulty of studying all the states, some works tend to focus on particular clusters of states or regions such as Rajputana, western India, Orissa, and south India. The examples of studies related to a group of states are *The British Raj and the Indian Princes: Paramountcy in Western India 1857–1930* by Ian Copland, and *Sovereignty, Power, Control: Politics in the States of Western India* by John McLeod. Case studies of important states such as Hyderabad, Mysore, and Baroda are taken up for detailed investigation. *Political Change in an Indian State: Mysore 1917–1955* by James Manor is an example of a large state in the south; *The Princely States: British Paramountcy and Internal Administration 1858–1948 (A Case Study of the Kapurthala State)* by Anju Arora represents a small state in the north. Manu Bhagwan's *Sovereign Spheres: Princes, Education and Empire in Colonial India* is a study of two states: Baroda and Mysore. Then there are studies related to one or another aspect of the history of the states' people, such as the *State, Community and Neighbourhood in Princely North India, c. 1900–1950* by Ian Copland. *Communalism and Indian Princely States* by Dick Kooiman, *People's Movements in the Princely States* edited by Yallampalli Vaikuntham, and *Praja Mandal Movement in East Punjab States* by Ramesh Walia focus on the 1930s. All these books are relevant also for an understanding of paramountcy as a political system and its bearing on the administration and politics of the Indian states.

Reservations about the policies and measures of the paramount power were occasionally expressed by individual rulers, but no serious attention has been paid to this aspect of the situation. The movements for socio-religious reform and political freedom are seen as relevant for the states, but the issue of the possible influence of such movements on the princes has been largely ignored. This silence may be due simply to the somewhat erroneous assumption that the princes were generally immune to such influences.

Some of the recent studies of individual princes show that the princes are the subject of a diverse range of books: 'Biographies ranging from authorised to sensational, adulatory to vituperative, empirical to post-modern, collections of essays, lavishly illustrated volumes designed for coffee tables, and perceptive scholarly articles and monographs.'[6] Notable among these are the biographies of Maharaja

Ranjitsinghji of Nawan Nagar, Ganga Singh of Bikaner, Madhav Rao Scindia of Gwalior, Sawai Man Singh II of Jaipur, Sayajirao III of Baroda, and Nizam Osman Ali Khan of Hyderabad. Two biographies were written by family members: *Sayajirao of Baroda: The Prince and the Man* by his great-grandson, Fatesinghrao Gaekwad, and *The Magnificent Maharaja: The Life and Times of Maharaja Bhupinder Singh of Patiala* by his son-in-law, Kanwar Natwar Singh. A comparison with the last two princes, almost representing the opposite poles, is particularly illumining for the present study.

Sayajirao was adopted at the age of 13 from a village some 300 miles away from Baroda, from a family of farmers very distantly related to the Gaekwads. He started his formal education very late and at home but he was ready to take up rulership in just five years. The British got annoyed with him when Sayajirao hobnobbed with their known 'enemies'. Among other restraints put on him, he was not allowed to go abroad for some time. In 1911, in a lavish Darbar held at Delhi in honour of George V, the then heir to the British throne, Sayajirao wore no jewellery, carried a walking stick instead of a bejewelled sword, and wore a plain white Indian long coat (*achkan*). When his turn came to pay his respects, he got up from his seat, walked up, made a cursory salutation and, instead of taking two steps backwards, made an about turn and walked towards his seat. An uproar followed and there were demands for his deposition, even deportation and so on. Sayajirao reluctantly offered an apology. His gesture of defiance was an expression of his nationalist sentiment; he cherished the idea of India's freedom. However, he gave no serious offence to the British during the rest of his reign.[7]

Maharaja Bhupinder Singh of Patiala was a staunch supporter of the British. He was educated at the Chief's College at Lahore and his administration was supervised by the British during his minority. Invested with full powers in November 1910, he was selected to captain the first Indian cricket team to tour England in 1911. At the Delhi Darbar, he was made a Knight Grand Commander of the Order of the Indian Empire (GCIE). During World War I, Patiala made the largest contribution in proportion to its size and resources. The Maharaja attended the Imperial War Conference in 1918, sitting with world-renowned statesmen of the empire in London. His elevation to the honorary rank of Major General was announced in the *London Gazette*. He gave full support to the government during the disturbances following the Jallianwala Bagh massacre and during the Akali movement in 1920–5. In 1929, he attacked the Congress resolution demanding complete independence. As Chancellor of the Chamber of Princes from 1926 to 1931, he helped the paramount power as much as himself. In 1930, when he was seriously indicted of grave crimes by the States Peoples' Conference, the paramount power bailed him out. 'The Raj stood by the Maharaja, as he had stood by the Empire almost all his life...'[8]

Though not mentioned by Ramusack, a biography of Maharaja Ripudaman Singh of Nabha had also been published by Munnalal Syngal, a 'trusted official' of Maharaja Ripudaman Singh, who had remained associated with him even after his 'so-called voluntary abdication'. After his retirement from the service of the state, Syngal collected materials for the biography and published it as 'part of the History of Freedom Movement'. His story of the Maharaja was based not only on his own experience and observation but also on written materials, including official correspondence. In Syngal's view, the Maharaja deserved a national memorial as 'the patriot prince' who died as a political martyr.[9] Significantly, the foreword to this book was written by Raja Mahendra Pratap, who knew Maharaja Ripudaman Singh personally. There is evidence of their interaction and correspondence in confidential British records. According to Mahendra Pratap, 'The British took steps against him when he actively supported Indian National Congress.'[10] As may be expected, the Maharaja's association with a known revolutionary was also held against him by the paramount power.

Maharaja Ripudaman Singh's forced abdication, but generally not his career before and after, has engaged the attention of historians who have taken almost contradictory positions. In a discussion of his abdication as 'Incident at Nabha', and on the basis of British sources, Barbara Ramusack gives primacy to 'bitter personal feud' between the rulers of Nabha and Patiala because of which Ripudaman Singh 'volunteered' to abdicate. She goes on to say that 'a myth' of the Maharaja's nationalist and Panthic concerns was subsequently created. In her view, it was just one more instance of deteriorating administration in an Indian state, and one more instance of strong control exercised by the government. Ramusack postulates a type of patron–client relationship between the government and the Indian states, with privileges and duties on both sides. She maintains that Patiala had performed numerous helpful services for the government during World War I and during the post-war political turmoil, while Nabha had neglected his duties and even argued openly with the patron. 'Therefore, Patiala was entitled to more sympathetic treatment than Nabha.'[11] In her later work, a general history of princely India referred to earlier, Ramusack dismisses Ripudaman Singh in a sentence or two, finding 'nothing remarkable' in his career. Broadly accepting Ramusack's position in his *Princes in the Endgame of the Empire,* Ian Copland attributes Ripudaman Singh's abdication essentially to a policy reorientation on the part of the paramount power and the Maharaja's maladministration.[12]

However, having access to both English and Gurmukhi sources, Indian historians view Ripudaman Singh's abdication differently. Mohinder Singh attributes Ripudaman Singh's abdication to the background of a prolonged confrontation with the government which led to a certain amount of ill-feeling against him among the Punjab officials who utilized the 12-year-old dispute between Nabha and Patiala to pressurize him to abdicate.[13] In his *Sikh Politics, 1920–40,* K. L. Tuteja lays emphasis on Ripudaman Singh's 'independent nature' and Akali sympathies as the basic causes of his deposition.[14] Harbans Singh regards Ripudaman Singh's removal as 'inevitable', because of his 'independent and nationalistic outlook', and his close association with the leaders of the National movement.[15]

Notes

1. Barbara Caine, *Biography and History,* Theory and History Series (Hampshire, UK: Palgrave Macmillan, 2016 [2010]), p. 2.
2. Much literature has been generated on the construction and practice of 'indirect rule'. For example: Sir William Lee-Warner, *The Protected States of India* (London: Macmillan, 1899, revised as *The Native States of India* [London: Macmillan, 1910]); Sir Charles Lewis Tupper, *Indian Political Practice* (New Delhi: B.R. Publishing [1895] 1974), vol. I. For a scholarly study of the period until 1858, see Michael H. Fisher, *Indirect Rule in India: Residents and the Residency System, 1764–1858* (New Delhi: Oxford University Press, 1991). For developments during the later period, see Ian Copland, *The British Raj and the Indian Princes: Paramountcy in Western India 1857–1930* (Hyderabad: Orient Longman, 1987).
3. For a discussion of the 'honours system' in princely India, see John McLeod, *Sovereignty, Power, Control: Politics in the States of Western India (1916–1947)* (New Delhi: Decent Books [1999] 2007), pp. 245–63.
4. Barbara N. Ramusack, *The Indian Princes and Their States* (The New Cambridge History of India, III. 6) (Cambridge: Cambridge University Press [2004] 2008), p. 283.

5. For an annotated bibliography, Ramusack, *The Indian Princes and Their States*, pp. 281–93.
6. Ramusack, *The Indian Princes and Their States*, p. 286.
7. Fatesinghrao P. Gaekwad, *Sayajirao of Baroda: The Prince and the Man* (Bombay: Popular Prakashan [1989] 1997).
8. K. Natwar-Singh, *The Magnificent Maharaja* (New Delhi: Harper Collins Publishers India, 1998), p. 190.
9. Sardar Munnalal Syngal, *The Patriot Prince, or the Life Story of Maharaja Ripudaman Singh of Nabha Who Died as a Martyr* (Ludhiana and Delhi: Doaba House, 1961), preface.
10. Syngal, *The Patriot Prince*, 'A Word', pp. ix–x. For further details on Raja Mahendra Pratap, see p. 112 of this volume.
11. Barbara N. Ramusack, 'Incident at Nabha' [1969], in *The Panjab Past and Present: Essays in Honour of Dr. Ganda Singh*, edited by Harbans Singh and N. Gerald Barrier (Patiala: Punjabi University, 1976), pp. 433–4.
12. Ian Copland, *The Princes of India in the Endgame of Empire 1917–1947* (Cambridge: Cambridge University Press, 1997), pp. 54–5.
13. Mohinder Singh, 'Abdication of Maharaja Ripudaman Singh of Nabha', *Proceedings Punjab History Conference*, Punjabi University, Patiala, 1973, pp. 169, 174.
14. K. L. Tuteja, *Sikh Politics (1920–40)* (Kurukshetra: Vishal Publications, 1984), pp. 89–90.
15. Harbans Singh, 'Maharaja Ripudaman Singh—His Involvement in Popular Causes', *The Panjab Past and Present* IV, no. 2 (October 1970): 416–17.

1

A MIXED HERITAGE

At the time of Maharaja Ripudaman Singh's accession to the throne of Nabha in 1912, the state was nearly 150 years old. His predecessors had left a mixed legacy of absolute autonomy, willing acceptance of political subordination to the British, defiance of the British authorities, feeble resistance to encroachments, and dignified insistence on their own rights. Maharaja Ripudaman Singh responded to his heritage selectively. He resisted the increasing encroachments of the paramount power on the autonomy of his state with a tenacity rare in the history of princely India.

Foundation of the Nabha State

Nabha was one of the three states founded by the descendants of Chaudhari Phul in the eighteenth century. The other two were Jind and Patiala. The rulers of these three states cherished their association with Guru Gobind Singh.[1] In a signed *hukamnāma* (written order) of Guru Gobind Singh, dated 2 August 1696, addressed to Bhai Tiloka and Bhai Rama, the sons of Chaudhari Phul, the Guru asks them to come with armed horsemen and calls their house as his own (*terā ghar merā hai*). They were later initiated into the Khalsa order by the Guru himself as Tilok Singh and Ram Singh.[2]

Tilok Singh was succeeded by his elder son, Gurdit Singh, who began initially to extend the area of his jurisdiction as the collector of revenues on behalf of the Mughal authorities. In the midst of new villages brought under his control, he built the fort of Dhanaula and founded the town of Sangrur. Gurdit Singh's only son died during his lifetime and his elder grandson died issueless. His younger grandson, Hamir Singh, succeeded Gurdit Singh on his death in 1754. Hamir Singh founded the town of Nabha in 1755, which later became his capital and the state also came to be known as Nabha. In 1764, he joined the combined forces of the Khalsa to sack the city of Sirhind and occupy the *sarkār* (an administrative unit) of Sirhind. The area of Amloh was occupied by Hamir Singh.[3] According to Griffin, he struck the same coin at Nabha as the one struck by the Khalsa at Lahore in 1765. It was a declaration of his sovereign status (Map 1.1).[4]

Meanwhile, Ala Singh, the youngest son of Rama, had become the ruler of Patiala and acquired territories much larger than those of Hamir Singh. Following his father's example, Ala Singh became a collector of revenues and proved to be far more successful than all his collaterals in enlarging his jurisdiction, and eventually founding the town of Patiala. Before his death in 1765, he received from Ahmad Shah Abdali the title of Raja. Ala Singh's grandson, Amar Singh, was made 'Raja-i-Rājgān' by Ahmad Shah.[5]

The state of Jind was founded by Gajpat Singh. He was the elder son of Sukhchain Singh, the younger brother of Gurdit Singh. Though Gajpat Singh was closer in relationship to Hamir Singh than to the rulers of Patiala, his relations became hostile towards Hamir Singh. Gajpat Singh's daughter was married to Mahan Singh Sukerchakia (father of Maharaja Ranjit Singh). At the time of this marriage in 1774, Yakub Khan, the right-hand man of Hamir Singh, insulted some members of the marriage party. Soon after the marriage, Gajpat Singh imprisoned Hamir Singh by a ruse, and occupied his territories around Sangrur, Bhadson, and Amloh. Hamir Singh was released through the intervention of Patiala, and all his territories were restored except Sangrur. The rulers of Nabha never forgot this usurpation.[6]

Raja Jaswant Singh 1783–1840

At the time of Hamir Singh's death in 1783, his only son, Jaswant Singh, was eight years old.[7] He assumed full powers as the ruler of Nabha in 1790. His primary concern was to retain his independence against his ambitious neighbours, both Sikh and non-Sikh. The Irish adventurer George Thomas had established himself at Hansi to encroach upon the territories of his neighbours. Jaswant Singh became a party to the settlement of the Phulkian chiefs with Mahadaji

A Mixed Heritage 3

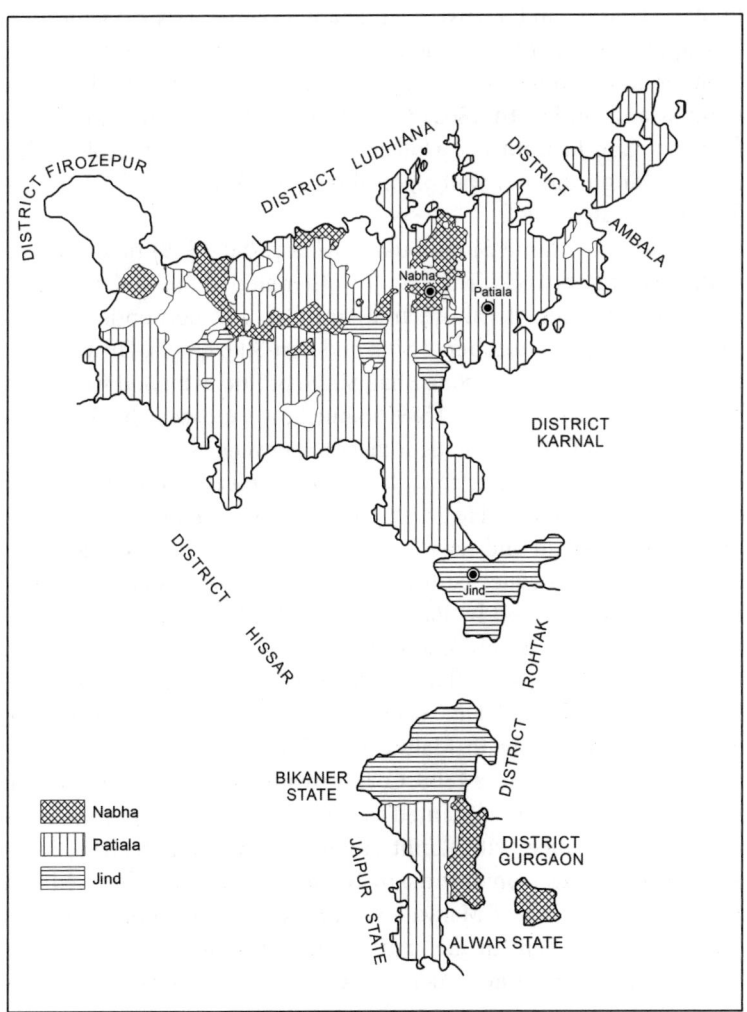

Map 1.1 The Phulkian States

Source: Adapted from Map 2, in Kuldeep, 'Modes of Colonial Control: A Case Study of Nabha under Maharaja Hira Singh, 1871–1911', MPhil dissertation, Panjab University, Chandigarh, 1999.

Scindhia, the Maratha ruler, who had become dominant in Delhi, to decimate George Thomas in 1801. In 1803, General Lake of the East India Company defeated the Maratha army under its French commander, extending the political control of the British to Gurgaon,

Rohtak, Hissar, and Hansi. Lieutenant Colonel David Ochterlony was appointed British Resident in Delhi to administer the newly conquered territories and to deal with the chiefs between the rivers Jamuna and Sutlej. In 1805, General Lake came in pursuit of the Maratha chief Jaswant Rao Holkar of Indore. As the ruler of Nabha, Jaswant Singh did not wait upon the General, nor did he help the fugitive Maratha chief.

By this time, Ranjit Singh Sukarchakia (1780–1839) had emerged as the pre-eminent Sikh ruler on the other side of the Sutlej. He had occupied the cities of Lahore and Amritsar, and befriended, subjugated, and ousted a number of Sikh and non-Sikh chiefs. On a request from his maternal uncle, Raja Bhag Singh of Jind, who had succeeded his father Gajpat Singh in 1789, Ranjit Singh crossed the Sutlej for the first time in 1806 to settle a dispute between Nabha and Patiala. He used this opportunity to dislodge petty chiefs of the area and to occupy their territories. He gave a large number of conquered villages to Raja Bhag Singh and Raja Jaswant Singh, who were aligned with him. Ranjit Singh collected tribute from the other important chiefs. In 1807 he was invited by Rani Aas Kaur for help in a dispute with her husband, Raja Sahib Singh of Patiala. Ranjit Singh returned to Lahore after sacking several places and occupying territory worth over 300,000 rupees a year.[8] His aim was to establish his overlordship in the Sutlej–Jamuna Divide, Malwa, and Sirhind.

Before the end of June 1808, C. T. Metcalfe, Assistant to the British Resident at Delhi, was appointed as envoy to explore the possibility of a 'defensive alliance' with Ranjit Singh in view of a perceived threat of an overland invasion of India by Napoleon. Metcalfe observed that almost all the chiefs of Malwa and Sirhind, or their representatives (*vakīls*), were present in the camp of Ranjit Singh. He crossed the Sutlej for the third time to demonstrate his virtual sovereignty over the region. On his insistence that recognition of his sovereignty over this region was an essential condition for a 'defensive alliance', Metcalfe agreed to refer the matter to the Governor General at Calcutta. By then, however, the possibility of a French invasion of India seemed rather remote. Metcalfe was now instructed to assert that the chiefs of Malwa and Sirhind were under British protection. Metcalfe delivered a note to this effect to Ranjit Singh at Amritsar on 12 December, and British troops marched towards the Sutlej under the command of Lieutenant Colonel Ochterlony. A proclamation (*ittila'nāma*), dated 9 February 1809, was issued by him at Ludhiana on 18 February. It was meant to tell Ranjit Singh in no uncertain terms that the British were determined to confine him to the other side of the Sutlej. Ranjit Singh yielded with reluctance and eventually signed the Treaty of Amritsar on 25 April 1809. Ratified by the Governor General in Council on 30 May, this treaty placed Ranjit Singh 'on the footing of the most favoured powers', and left him free to do whatever he liked as a sovereign ruler 'to the northward of the river Sutlej'.[9]

In his proclamation of 3 May 1809, Colonel Ochterlony confirmed that the chiefs of Malwa and Sirhind were under the protection of the British Government. The Treaty of Amritsar bound Ranjit Singh against 'any encroachment on the possessions or the rights of the Chiefs'. The protected chiefs were 'exempted from all pecuniary tribute to the British Government'. They were assured that they 'shall remain in the exercise of the same rights and authority within their own possessions which they enjoyed before they were taken under the British protection'. However, all European articles brought by merchants for the use of the army were to be allowed to pass 'without molestation or demand of duty', and all horses purchased for the cavalry regiments were to be allowed to pass freely.

Two other clauses of the proclamation imposed the most important obligations. Whenever a British force marched through the country of the protected chiefs, 'every Chief within his own possessions shall assist and furnish the British force to the full of his power, with supplies of grain and other necessaries which may be demanded'. The other clause stipulated that if the country was invaded by a foreign power, the chiefs were duty bound to 'join the British Army, with their force, and exert themselves in expelling the enemy' and 'act under discipline and proper obedience'.[10] Under these two clauses the British forces could pass through the territories of the chiefs, and their resources in men and materials were to be placed at the disposal of the British.

Not satisfied with proclamation of 3 May 1809, Raja Jaswant Singh sought a separate document from the British Government. The Governor General, Minto, affirmed in November 1810 that no tribute or *nazrāna* 'will ever be demanded' from Nabha, and Raja Jaswant Singh 'shall continue' to exercise the same power and authority within his own territories which he had enjoyed 'since he has been received under the protection of the British Government'. He was to remain in occupation of 'all the lands' which he possessed at the period of the last expedition of Ranjit Singh. Raja Jaswant Singh could rely with confidence on the continuance of its favour and protection 'so long as his conduct shall continue to be regulated by the principles of attachment and obedience'.[11] The Nabha House appears to have cherished this special sanad from Lord Minto as a charter of its rights in relation to the paramount power.

On 22 August 1811, Ochterlony issued another proclamation which stated that several Sardars had wrested estates of others. Therefore, it was declared that if such properties were not restored to their lawful owners, 'the revenues of the estate, from the date of the ejection of the lawful proprietor, together with whatever other losses the inhabitants of that place may sustain from the march of troops, shall, without scruple, be demanded from the offending party'. Furthermore, 'a penalty be levied for disobedience of the present orders by the British Government'.[12] This proclamation became a prelude to the ever-increasing intervention of the British in the disputes among the chiefs and between them and the other claimants to revenues from land.

The rulers of Nabha, Jind, and Patiala lost jurisdiction over their own collaterals. The ancestors of Phul used to live in the village Mahraj. Their descendants came to be called Mahrajke. In the early nineteenth century, they used to go to Nabha or Patiala for arbitration in their disputes, which were often fed by the rivalries of the two chiefs. To save themselves from this contentious jurisdiction the Mahrajke Sikhs approached the British authorities. The Government of India offered these villages to the ruler of Patiala for a fixed term on certain conditions, but he insisted on unconditional jurisdiction. Instead of making the same offer to any of the other two Phulkian chiefs, the paramount power chose to place these villages under its own jurisdiction in August 1833.[13]

The keenness of the British to regulate the relations of the Phulkian chiefs with their feudatories encouraged the latter increasingly to approach the paramount power against their overlords. The Sardars of Lidhran and Saunti complained to the British Political Agent against Raja Jaswant Singh for demanding constant service of 50 horsemen from Lidhran and 70 horsemen from Saunti. Raja Jaswant Singh was directed to demand their services or presence only in time of actual war, or on occasions of birth, marriage, and death.[14]

Not missing any opportunity for intervention, the British authorities supported Tikka Ranjit Singh against his father, Raja Jaswant Singh. Unhappy with his refractory ways, Raja Jaswant Singh proposed to disinherit the heir-apparent in favour of his younger brother, Kanwar Devinder Singh. The Governor General was not convinced that the Tikka (heir apparent) was involved in any serious crime. He was wild and extravagant, disorderly and immoral, but there was no credible evidence that he had tried to get his father assassinated. Tikka Ranjit Singh died in 1832.[15]

Raja Devinder Singh (1840–6)

At the time of Raja Jaswant Singh's death in May 1840, his only surviving son, Devinder Singh, was 18 years old. At the formal ceremony of his accession to the gaddī of Nabha on 5 October, the Political Agent to the Governor General brought a khil'at (robe of honour) of seven pieces, including an elephant with trappings, a horse with a silver saddle, a sword, and a shield. This was the first installation of a ruler of Nabha by a superior power.

Devinder Singh appears to have been brought up and educated as a Sikh prince. Griffin called him a 'bigoted Sikh'. The disaster met by the British force in the first Afghan war in 1842 appears to have encouraged Raja Devinder Singh, like several other Indian rulers, to believe that the British were not invincible. He did not conceal his disapproval of the British Government escheating in 1843 the territory of Kaithal worth 400,000 rupees after the death of Bhai Udai Singh, who did not have a son.[16] Another decision of the Government of India was resented even more by Raja Devinder Singh. Raja Jaswant Singh had given the village Mauran to Maharaja Ranjit Singh so that he could assign it to his favourite General Dhanna Singh who hailed from Mauran. Raja Devinder Singh occupied Mauran after General Dhanna Singh's death in May 1843, with the consent of the then Political Agent. Later on, the British Government took the view that Nabha had no right over Mauran. In October 1844, the disputed village was annexed by the British. Furthermore, Raja Devinder Singh was directed to pay the equivalent of the property worth lakhs (one lakh equals one hundred thousand) of rupees alleged to have been taken away by his men from the fort of Mauran a year earlier.[17]

Meanwhile, tension between the British and the Lahore Darbar had been mounting. On 3 December 1845, the Governor General, Lord Hardinge, severed diplomatic relations with the Lahore Darbar, and his Political Agent, Major Broadfoot, sent 'stringent orders' to Nabha to provide supplies to the British troops on the Kalka–Khanna road. On 10 December when war was formally declared by the British, Broadfoot ordered Raja Devinder Singh to make a road from Latala to Bassian. The Raja treated these orders with 'silent contempt', and on 13 December, Broadfoot confiscated the Nabha estates of Daheru and Amloh. On 15 December, he ordered Raja Devinder Singh to come personally to the British camp on that or the following evening. If he did not, he would be considered an enemy to the British'.[18]

Raja Devinder Singh regarded Broadfoot's order to personally report outside the Nabha territories as illegal and chose not to comply. The British officers complained that the Nabha contingent present in their camp at the battles of Mudki (18 December) and Pherushahr (21–22 December) took no part in these or the subsequent actions. Raja Devinder Singh's open defiance could not be tolerated even though the Governor General was aware of the general 'disaffection to the British power'. One-fourth of the territory of Nabha was confiscated. Territory worth 28,766 rupees was retained by the British on the plea that now they would maintain a contingent of 100 horse and 133 foot on behalf of Nabha, exempting the state from sending any contingents in similar situations in future. The remainder, worth 71,224 rupees, was given in equal shares to the chiefs of Patiala and Faridkot in reward for their services in the war. Devinder Singh of Nabha was the most important among the 'protected' chiefs to be punished for recalcitrance.[19]

Raja Devinder Singh was deposed and a pension of 50,000 rupees was allowed to him from the revenues of Nabha. He was to reside in British territory to the south of Delhi or Meerut. He chose to reside at Mathura, and 'gave as much trouble as he could' to the British authorities who finally decided to shift him from Mathura to Lahore and live in the palace of the late Maharaja Kharak Singh (son of Maharaja Ranjit Singh). Raja Devinder Singh lived there under the watchful eyes of the British administrators till his death in November 1865.[20]

Raja Bharpur Singh (1846–63)

Raja Devinder Singh's elder son, Bharpur Singh, was only seven years old when he was installed as Raja in January 1847 by the British Commissioner of the Cis-Sutlej States. Rani Chand Kaur, the surviving widow of Raja Jaswant Singh, was made his guardian, and a Council of Regency was appointed to look after the administration of the state. During the mutiny and civil rebellion of 1857–8, the youthful Raja Bharpur Singh helped the British enthusiastically. He moved to Ludhiana with horse, foot, and guns, and stayed there for six months. A detachment of Nabha men assisted the Deputy Commissioner of Ludhiana to destroy the bridge over the Sutlej and to obstruct the passage of the Jalandhar mutineers. A detachment of 300 men of Nabha did 'good service' at Delhi. Carriage and supplies were furnished by the Nabha ruler in addition to a loan of 250,000 rupees. The services of Raja Bharpur Singh were 'as distinguished as those of the other Phulkian Chiefs'.[21] Land worth over 100,000 rupees was given to Nabha in Bawal and Kanti, and in liquidation of a loan of 950,000 rupees to the British, villages worth about 48,000 rupees a year were added to the Nabha territory in Kanaud. The Raja's visit to the Governor General was to be returned by the Foreign Secretary. A salute of 11 guns was awarded, and his customary robe of honour (khil'at) was increased from 7 to 15 pieces.[22] The Viceroy appreciated the services of Raja Bharpur Singh in a Darbar held at Ambala in January 1860.

Raja Bharpur Singh joined the chiefs of Patiala and Jind to make a number of 'requests' to the Governor General. On 5 May 1860, the Governor General signed a sanad for the ruler of Nabha. Its first clause embodied the most important assurance which went beyond the earlier sanad of Lord Minto to Raja Jaswant Singh:

> The Raja and his heirs for ever will exercise full sovereignty over his ancestral and acquired dominions, according to the annexed list. All the rights, privileges, and prerogatives which the Raja enjoys in his hereditary territories, he will equally enjoy in his acquired territories. All feudatories and dependants of every degree will be bound to render obedience to him throughout his dominions.[23]

The second clause of the sanad reaffirmed that the government 'will never demand from the Raja, or any of his successors, or from any of his feudatories, relations, or dependants, any tribute on account of revenue, service, or any other plea'. The third clause of the sanad gave to the Raja of Nabha the right of adoption. If at any time a ruler of Nabha died without a male issue and without adopting a successor, it would still be open to his collaterals, the Maharaja of Patiala and the Raja of Jind, in consultation of course with the British Political Agent, to select a successor from the Phulkian family. In all such cases, a nazrāna 'equal to one-third of the gross annual revenue of the Nabha State shall be paid to the British Government'.

The fourth clause restored to Raja Bharpur Singh the power to inflict capital punishment which had been withdrawn in 1847, but 'the Raja will exert himself to execute justice, and to promote the happiness and welfare of his people'. The Raja also engaged to prohibit sati, slavery, and female infanticide throughout his territories and 'to punish with the utmost vigour those who are found guilty of any of these crimes'. The fifth clause of the sanad clearly laid down that 'the Raja will never fail in his loyalty and devotion to the Sovereign of Great Britain'. The obligation of the Raja to oppose the enemy of the British Government 'in his neighbourhood' was laid down in the sixth clause: 'He will exert himself to the utmost of his resources in providing carriage and supplies for the British troops, according to requisitions he may receive.' Understandably, there is no mention of troops for which the Nabha territory had been annexed after the deposition of Raja Devinder Singh. The seventh clause of the sanad embodied the assurance that the government 'will not receive any complaints from any of the subjects of the Raja, whether *māfidārs*, *jāgīrdārs*, relatives, dependants, servants or other classes'. The eighth clause gave the further assurance that the British would 'respect the household and family arrangements of the Raja, and abstain from any interference therein'. The last two clauses carried the assurance that the unpleasant experience of Raja Jaswant Singh vis-à-vis his feudatories and his wayward son would not be repeated. A new obligation was embodied in the ninth clause: the Raja was to furnish at current rates the necessary materials required for the construction of railroads, railway stations, and imperial roads and bridges; he was also to 'freely give the land required' for these purposes.

The sanad of March 1862 repeated the assurance given in May 1860 regarding the adoption of an heir from amongst the members of the Phulkian family. Reiterating the condition of nazrāna in the case of failure to adopt an heir, the sanad repeated the assurance that, 'nothing shall disturb the engagement thus made to you so long as your house is loyal to the Crown and faithful to the conditions of the treaties, grants, or engagements which record its obligations to the British Government'.[24]

Maharaja Narinder Singh of Patiala died in November 1862 when his only son, Mahinder Singh, was ten years old. A Council of Regency was formed without reference to the British authorities. In response to the objection raised by the Agent to the Cis-Sutlej States, the Patiala ministers argued that the sanad of May 1860 granted by Lord Canning gave them 'full' power to make such arrangements. They were told that the term 'full sovereignty' in the sanad was a conventional term which signified independence compatible with the claim of the paramount power to general control, active loyalty of the chiefs, and all previous arrangements! A new Council of Regency had then to be formed.[25]

However, due regard was shown to the sanad of 1860 in the case of Raja Bharpur Singh's relations with his feudatories. Aware of the old antagonism between the Sardars of Saunti and the Nabha rulers, Lord Canning thought of 'a friendly compromise' without impairing any of Nabha's recognized rights. The Commissioner of the Cis-Sutlej States, G. C. Barnes, was able to persuade Raja Bharpur Singh to pay 5,000 rupees a year to the Sardars in lieu of their share in the revenues of 36 villages. The Raja was assured that if the Sardars refused to accept the settlement of 5,000 rupees a year, the government would not interfere on their behalf in future. When the Sardars of Saunti appealed to the Secretary of State for India, he upheld the decision of Lord Canning. To reopen the case, he thought, would have meant that the words of the Governor General had 'no value', and to order an enquiry would have meant that the sanads of 1860 were 'waste papers'.[26]

The Raja of Jind was given precedence over Raja Bharpur Singh in the Governor General's Darbar of 1860. Raja Bharpur Singh made a representation for reconsideration of the case, arguing that he represented the senior branch of hereditary *chaudharīs* since the time of Chaudhari Phul, and the revenues of Nabha were larger than those of Jind. But, in contrast with the recalcitrant attitude of Nabha in the past, the loyalty of Jind went in its favour. Even in 1860, the two chiefs were considered 'as precisely equal in dignity' and both were regarded 'with equal favour' by the government. Yet, in respect of address, titles, khil'ats, salutes, and *nazars* (a kind of tribute), precedence was given to the chief of Jind. The Viceroy, however, thought well of Raja Bharpur Singh. He was nominated on the Imperial Legislative Council in place of the deceased ruler of Patiala.[27]

Raja Bhagwan Singh (1864–71)

Raja Bharpur Singh was only 23 years old when he died in November 1863. He had no son and he had adopted no heir. In accordance with the terms of the sanads of 1860 and 1862, his younger brother,

Bhagwan Singh, was selected as his successor, subject to the payment of one-third of the gross revenue of Nabha as nazrāna. He was formally installed on 17 February 1864 by the Agent to the Lieutenant Governor of the Punjab in the presence of a number of ruling princes, with fifteen trays, three jewels, two arms, one horse, and one elephant constituting the khil'at.[28] This was an improvement upon the two earlier installations of the rulers of Nabha.

Contrary to the letter and spirit of the earlier sanads, the reign of Raja Bhagwan Singh (1864–71) was marked by interference in the affairs of Nabha. Sir John Lawrence, who succeeded Lord Elgin as Governor General (1864–8), was not much concerned with the formal assurances given to the chiefs of Nabha through the sanad of 1860. He believed that the Sardars of Saunti as the feudatories of Nabha had been 'grievously ill-treated'. The Commissioner of Cis-Sutlej States, Major General R. G. Taylor, was directed in September 1864 to effect a compromise on the lines suggested previously by the Secretary of State for India. The Saunti Sardars represented that instead of cash they should be paid in villages. Eventually, in December 1868, an exhaustive report submitted by Taylor and approved by the authorities gave 12,997 rupees (in place of 5,000 rupees given previously) a year to the Sardars of Saunti. They were still dissatisfied. As a final settlement, Raja Bhagwan Singh was obliged to instruct the *patwārīs* (accountants) of the villages concerned to pay the share of the Sardars directly to them and to clear their arrears. This reversal of the decision of Lord Canning affected the position of Nabha state rather adversely. Sir H. M. Durand, the Foreign Political Secretary, regarded the position taken by the Government of India as a practical breach of the sanad-rights of Nabha.[29]

The Punjab Government also chose to interfere in the internal matters of Nabha on the basis of allegations brought up by a Nabha subject, resulting in 'the most remarkable enquiry' in the Punjab states since 1809. Sardarni Mehtab Kaur, a widow of Raja Bhagwan Singh's maternal uncle, was murdered early in January 1864. Raja Bhagwan Singh instituted a judicial enquiry, which revealed that the crime was committed by a man named Mehtaba who had been released from the Nabha jail prematurely by a minister, Gurbakhsh Singh, who made counter allegations. The Punjab Government appointed Major J. E. Cracroft, with Lepel Griffin as his assistant, to investigate. They came to the conclusion that Gurbakhsh Singh had instigated the murder. Mehtaba was sentenced to death, which was later commuted to transportation for life. Sardar Gurbakhsh Singh was acquitted but banished from Nabha.[30]

Nevertheless, in April 1867, the British Government chose to entrust the administration of Nabha to a Council for two years. During this period, and even after the assumption of full powers by the ruler in April 1869, Taylor did not desist from interfering in the administration of Nabha and disregarding the Raja's wishes.[31] Taylor's active intervention obliged the Punjab Government, now under Sir H. M. Durand as the Lieutenant Governor, to appoint a committee to investigate Taylor's dealings with Nabha and Patiala. On the basis of its report, and despite Taylor's explanation, the Lieutenant Governor came to the conclusion that Taylor's interference in the affairs of Nabha and Patiala had been 'excessive' and 'undesirable'. Some senior British officials also found his partisan and unscrupulous behaviour distasteful. Taylor was transferred and, with the approval of the higher authorities, the Punjab Government assumed direct control of the Phulkian states, abolishing the Agency at Ambala in 1870.[32]

Maharaja Hira Singh (1871–1911)

Raja Bhagwan Singh died on 3 May 1871 without a male heir and without adopting a successor. In accordance with the terms of the sanads of 1860 and 1862, Sardar Hira Singh of the estate of Badrukhan, a feudatory of Jind, and a direct descendant of Raja Gajpat Singh, was selected as the successor. Seventh in descent from Chaudhari Phul through his elder son, Tiloka, the 27-year-old Hira Singh was considered the most competent candidate from amongst the closest collaterals.[33] He was installed as Raja on 10 August 1871 by the Commissioner of Delhi in the presence of an Under-Secretary of the Punjab Government who placed a necklace round Hira Singh's neck while he was sitting in a chair. Raja Hira Singh then offered '*itar* (perfume) and *pān* (betel leaf) to the Commissioner who sat on an identical chair. This procedure signified that the Raja was in his own *darbār* (court).

The long reign of Raja Hira Singh proved to be important for the military, political, and economic integration of Nabha and the other Phulkian states with British India. In the very first year, he was called upon to provide military assistance to suppress the Namdhari followers of Baba Ram Singh, popularly known as the Kukas.[34] Raja Hira Singh sent infantry, cavalry, and guns to Malerkotla under the command of Bakhshi Wazir Ali. The conduct of the Nabha troops in this local crisis was appreciated by the Governor General.[35]

Raja Hira Singh attended the imperial assemblage held by Viceroy Lytton at Delhi in the beginning of 1877 to proclaim the assumption of the title of 'Empress of India' (Kaisar-i Hind) by Queen Victoria. Nabha's salute was raised from 11 to 13 guns. Towards the end of 1878, Raja Hira Singh sent field guns, horsemen, and infantry for the Kabul campaign under the overall command of the Bakhshi of the state. In 1879, the Raja was conferred a Grand Commander of the Star of India (GCSI). In 1887, he offered 400,000 rupees for the defence of the north-western frontier which the Government of India wanted to strengthen for 'maintenance of peace in the country'. In 1888, he responded enthusiastically to the scheme of Imperial Service Troops, announced by Viceroy Dufferin at Patiala.[36] With a total strength of 1,720, the Nabha army cost the state about a third of its total revenues in 1888. The British inspecting officers found the Nabha squadron up to full strength, the Nabha Lancers exceedingly well officered, and their horses kept in extraordinarily good condition. The 1st Nabha Infantry, likewise, was reported to be 'a very fine well set up regiment'. In 1893, Raja Hira Singh received the title of Rājā-i Rājgān for his 'good administration'.[37] The Imperial Service Troops of Nabha were employed in war for the first time in 1897. The Raja's personal salute was now raised to 15 guns. In 1903, he attended the imperial Darbar held at Delhi to mark the coronation of Edward VII as the King Emperor. On this occasion, Raja Hira Singh was invested with the insignia of a Knight Grand Commander (of the Order) of the Indian Empire (GCIE), and appointed Honorary Colonel of the 14th Ferozepore Sikhs.

Throughout his long reign, Raja Hira Singh studiously cultivated the Lieutenant Governors of the Punjab from Sir Henry Davies to Sir Louis Dane, and the Viceroys from Lord Mayo to Lord Hardinge. All ceremonial occasions connected with the Crown and the Empire were celebrated in Nabha. The Raja was courteous and considerate towards all British officers whom he generally appreciated for their integrity and efficiency. Lord Lansdowne visited Nabha in the early 1890s. Lord Curzon visited Nabha in 1903. Raja Hira Singh had the honour of meeting the Prince of Wales (later King George V) at Lahore in 1905 when he offered 25,000 rupees as *sarwārna* (cash rotated round the head of a person and given in charity for his safety). Lord Minto visited Nabha towards the end of November 1906.[38] Lady Minto observed that Raja Hira Singh was very proud of his Sikh soldiers and intensely loyal. He was 'a typical Indian Ruling Chief of the old school, an autocrat in excelsis who runs his state admirably'.[39]

Raja Hira Singh's loyalty to the Crown did not mean that he welcomed every decision of the British Government. Lepel Griffin, officiating Secretary to the Punjab Government, came to Patiala in 1876 to inaugurate the Council of Regency during the minority of its Maharaja, Rajinder Singh. In the course of his speech, Griffin remarked that the Lieutenant Governor might recommend the appointment of a British officer to superintend the administration of Patiala. Raja Hira Singh was quick to point out that if any member of the Council proved to be unfit, the advice of the chiefs of Nabha and Jind was again to be sought for appointing a more competent person. The Council of Regency continued to function till Maharaja Rajinder Singh reached the age of 18 in 1890 and was invested with full powers by the Viceroy.[40]

In 1900, Viceroy Curzon decided to establish an exclusive Political Agency for the states of Nabha, Jind, and Patiala under the Government of India. Significantly, the Lieutenant Governor, Sir Mackworth Young, favoured the idea but not for Nabha during the lifetime of its 'fine old Chief'. The Government of India appointed Major J. R. Dunlop-Smith as the Political Agent for all the three states, and authorized the Lieutenant Governor to instruct the new Political Agent to desist from functioning actively in Nabha during Raja Hira Singh's lifetime. Raja Hira Singh, nevertheless, made a representation against the appointment of a Political Agent on the argument that placing an intermediary between the states and the Punjab Government, with his residence in a state capital (in this case, Patiala) would diminish the respect and dignity of the states. In his view, a 'Political Secretary for the Phulkian States' under the Punjab Government located at Lahore could achieve the objects of the government and also maintain the 'rights, respect, regard and honour' of the three states. Since Raja Hira Singh himself used to invoke the sanad of 1860 to support his propositions, the Punjab Government pointed out that no clause in the sanad of 1860 was infringed by this decision. Raja Hira Singh had to accept it as a 'disagreeable necessity'.[41] Later events proved that his fears were not unfounded and the stationing of the Political Agent at Patiala worked against the interests of Nabha in general and its ruler in particular.

An issue that Raja Hira Singh pursued with great tenacity for three decades had a close bearing on the interests and honour of the Nabha state. In March 1901, the Raja sought the Punjab Government's permission to make a representation to the Government of India for the restoration of the Nabha territory confiscated in the reign of his uncle, Raja Devinder Singh. The issue had been raised with the Lieutenant Governor for the first time in 1880, that is, within a decade of Hira Singh's installation. It was repeated in 1887, 1888, 1894, and 1895. However, the Government of India took the same view as the provincial government that the decisions once taken should not be reopened. Not giving up, Raja Hira Singh broached the subject differently in 1906. He wrote to the Political Agent that the past was not quite dead. The alleged 'misdemeanours' of Raja Devinder Singh remained operative in the relationship of Nabha with the paramount power. The sanad granted by Lord Canning to Raja Bharpur Singh on 5 May 1860 mentioned the name of his grandfather, Raja Jaswant Singh, but not the name of Raja Bharpur Singh's father, Raja Devinder Singh. Both truth and justice demanded that this blot on Nabha should be erased. Therefore, Raja Hira Singh requested that his appeal of March 1901 be submitted to the Secretary of State for India for favour of a decision 'on the merits of the case'. The Secretary of State appears to have agreed to a cash *jāgīr* (an assignment of land revenue in lieu of salary) of 28,000 rupees a year in lieu of the territory of Nabha confiscated in 1846, but Raja Hira Singh asked for land which was more honourable, with the assurance that the stain attached to the name of his uncle was wiped out for ever. The case was not reopened even though Lord Minto was keen to help him before leaving India. Raja Hira Singh declined the offer of the cash jāgīr, which he considered as no compensation for the blot on the Nabha House.[42]

Raja Hira Singh was also sensitive about his position in relation to Jind. In 1880, the government decided that the Raja of Jind would be received first and the Raja of Nabha would receive the Viceroy's return visit first. Apparently, this was not a satisfactory arrangement from Raja Hira Singh's viewpoint. He felt convinced that the only reason for placing Nabha after Jind was the government's annoyance with the conduct of Raja Devinder Singh in 1845–6.

While the paramount power respected Raja Hira Singh for his sagacity and loyalty, it felt obliged to encroach upon the rights and authority of Nabha, as of all other princely states in the name of political security and economic integration. The existing treaties and sanads were increasingly violated in both letter and spirit in the course of the construction and management of the railways and the Sirhind canal project, as well as in working out a comprehensive postal and currency arrangement with British India. The authority of the states was steadily lowered in the process. They suffered economic losses too in the form of payment of duty on the salt imported and the restraints imposed on opium trade. The Foreign Jurisdiction and Extradition Act of 1879 became the basis of an agreement with the states to ensure a different treatment of the British subjects committing crimes within state territories. The Government of India, however, claimed the right to take notice of unjust or inhuman punishments given to their own subjects by the states, and to intervene in what the British considered miscarriage of justice.[43] Significantly, in the time of Raja Hira Singh, there was no such intervention in Nabha. All along, and as the oldest and most respected Phulkian chief of his day, Raja Hira Singh tried to strike a balance between interests of the paramount power and the dignity of the Phulkian states as assured by the sanads of 1860.

Nabha generally figured favourably in the Annual Reports on the Administration of Native States, which the chiefs were directed to send and which served as an indirect check on them. The chiefs of Patiala and Jind appear to have complied, but Nabha probably was not required to do so. Further interference of the paramount power was obviated by Raja Hira Singh's lack of interest in going abroad unlike that of several princes of his day. Moreover, he was not keen to employ Europeans in his civil administration. It is important to note that the revenues of Nabha rose from about 700,000 rupees in 1881 to more than 1,700,000 rupees in 1911, which was a proof of good governance by all standards.[44]

Raja Hira Singh was well regarded also in the context of princely India. He was one of the five Indian chiefs to be invited to the coronation of Edward VII in 1902. Elaborate arrangements were made for his trip to England, including the transportation of his cow as he was on a milk diet. His visit, however, had to be cancelled at the last moment due to his ill health. By the time of the coronation of George V in 1911 Raja Hira Singh was deemed to be too old. The young Maharaja Bhupinder Singh of Patiala was in England at that time as the captain of the cricket team and he was invited as a chief who happened to be present. An infantry unit of Patiala, Nabha, and Kapurthala represented the Imperial Service Troops of the Punjab princely states.[45]

All the Indian chiefs were invited to the coronation of George V in Delhi. Raja Hira Singh was among 'the old class of Ruling Chiefs' who preferred to stand before the King-Emperor.[46] He was not in good health at this time. Having suffered from 'chronic amoeboid dysentery' for some three months since September, he was hardly able to move by the end of November 1911. According to Colonel Mulroney, who had been treating him, he was a wreck, with hardly an ounce of reserve power. By 5 December, however, he had sufficiently recovered to leave for Delhi. On 7 December, he paid an official visit to His Majesty and received the Viceroy in his own camp darbār. On 9 December, dysentery relapsed and it was complicated by a feverish chill. This precluded him from taking any further part in the ceremonies. On 15 December, he returned to Nabha after receiving the hereditary title of 'Maharaja'.[47]

Maharaja Hira Singh is said to have reverted to the *hakīm*'s treatment at Nabha. This was followed by a return of the dysentery, which weakened him further. Insufficiently clothed, he exposed himself to the cold morning air on 23 December. This brought an attack of bronchitis and aggravated the bowel disorder. He succumbed to exhaustion at 6.45 p.m. on 25 December. The Maharaja of Patiala performed 'the duties of the nearest relative' in the absence of Tikka Ripudaman Singh who was in Europe.[48]

The Foreign Minister of Nabha sent a telegram to the Private Secretary to the Viceroy that the Maharaja had breathed his last. The Viceroy expressed 'great distress' over the death of His Highness and conveyed 'his deep and sincere condolences' to the family.[49] The Nabha Darbar sent a telegram also to the Lieutenant Governor, Sir Louis Dane, who sent his condolences. King George had enquired after the Maharaja's health. He was informed of the event. The Nabha Darbar sent a cable to Tikka Ripudaman Singh who was in Paris. The Tikka expressed his deep regret at being absent at the time of his father's death, enjoined the Darbar to observe all the funeral ceremonies, and confirmed his full confidence in his father's officials. He proposed to take the first available steamer to reach Nabha in 20 days or so.[50]

Appendix 1A: Ancestors and Predecessors of Maharaja Ripudaman Singh

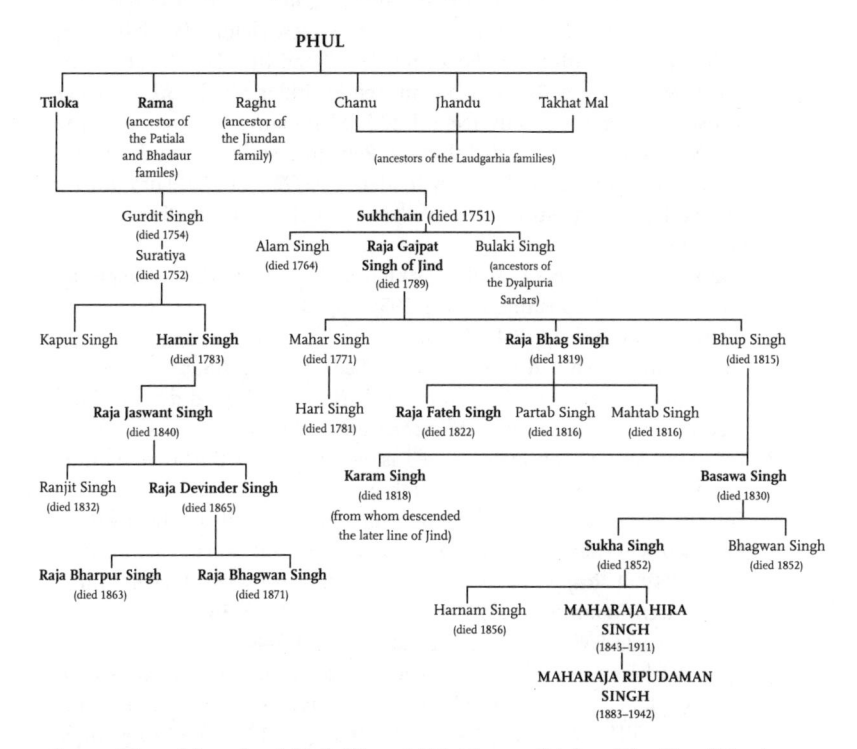

```
                                    PHUL
    ┌───────────┬───────────┬─────────┬─────────┬──────────┐
  Tiloka      Rama       Raghu     Chanu    Jhandu    Takhat Mal
          (ancestor of (ancestor of
          the Patiala  the Jiundan
          and Bhadaur  family)
          families)              (ancestors of the Laudgarhia families)

        Gurdit Singh              Sukhchain (died 1751)
        (died 1754)        ┌──────────┬──────────────┬──────────┐
          Suratiya      Alam Singh  Raja Gajpat    Bulaki Singh
          (died 1752)   (died 1764) Singh of Jind  (ancestors of
                                    (died 1789)    the Dyalpuria
                                                   Sardars)

  ┌──────────┬──────────┐    Mahar Singh    ┌──── Raja Bhag Singh ────┐    Bhup Singh
Kapur Singh  Hamir Singh   (died 1771)           (died 1819)              (died 1815)
             (died 1783)
                         Hari Singh   Raja Fateh Singh  Partab Singh  Mahtab Singh
        Raja Jaswant Singh (died 1781)  (died 1822)    (died 1816)    (died 1816)
        (died 1840)
                                   Karam Singh                    Basawa Singh
  ┌──────────┬──────────┐           (died 1818)                   (died 1830)
Ranjit Singh  Raja Devinder Singh   (from whom descended
(died 1832)   (died 1865)           the later line of Jind)     ┌──────────┬──────────┐
                                                              Sukha Singh  Bhagwan Singh
  ┌──────────┬──────────┐                                     (died 1852)  (died 1852)
Raja Bharpur Singh  Raja Bhagwan Singh
(died 1863)         (died 1871)
                                              Harnam Singh    MAHARAJA HIRA
                                              (died 1856)     SINGH
                                                              (1843–1911)

                                                          MAHARAJA RIPUDAMAN
                                                              SINGH
                                                            (1883–1942)
```

Source: Adapted from Lepel H. Griffin and C.F. Massey, *Chiefs and Families of Note in the Punjab* (Lahore, 1911), vol. III, p. 227.

Notes

1. For the genealogical table of the Nabha House, see Appendix 1A.
2. Ganda Singh, *Hukamnāme: Guru Sāhibān, Mātā Sāhibān, Bandā Singh, Ate Khalsa Jī De* (Patiala: Punjabi University, 1969), no. 43, pp. 146–7.
   According to tradition, the Phulkians had also been associated with Guru Hargobind and Guru Har Rai, the sixth and seventh Gurus respectively. Shiromani Gurdwara Prabandhak Committee (SGPC), *Truth about Nabha* (Amritsar: SGPC, 1923), pp. 2–4.
3. Lepel H. Griffin, *The Rajas of the Punjab* (Patiala: Languages Department, Punjab [1870] 1970), p. 382.

4. The inscription on the Nabha rupee may be rendered as: 'Bounty and power and unlimited victory are the gifts received by Guru Gobind Singh from [Guru] Nanak' (Indu Banga, *Agrarian System of the Sikhs: Late Eighteenth and Early Nineteenth Century* [New Delhi: Manohar, 1978], p. 36 and nn. Griffin, *The Rajas*, pp. 286–9 and nn). For the argument that Jaswant Singh struck this coin, see Surinder Singh, *Sikh Coinage: Symbol of Sikh Sovereignty* (New Delhi: Manohar, 2004), pp. 100, 132, 137–8, 164. It may be added that the Persian inscription on the Patiala and the Jind rupees can be freely rendered as: 'The Eternal Lord ordered Ahmad Padshah to strike coin in silver and gold from the Pisces [fishes] to the moon.'
5. Ganda Singh, *Ahmad Shah Durrani: Father of Modern Afghanistan* (Bombay: Asia Publishing House, 1959), pp. 303, 317.
6. Griffin, *The Rajas*, pp. 284–90, 382.
7. Hamir Singh also had two daughters, Sada Kaur and Sabha Kaur, who were married, respectively to Gurbakhsh Singh Kanhiya and Sahib Singh Bhangi, two leading Sikh chiefs across the Sutlej.
8. For Ranjit Singh's conquests as well as incursions into the Sutlej–Jamuna Divide, there is plentiful information in published works.
9. For the texts of Ochterlony's proclamation as well as the treaty of Amritsar with Ranjit Singh, see Bikrama Jit Hasrat, *Anglo-Sikh Relations 1799–1849: A Reappraisal of the Rise and Fall of the Sikhs* (Hoshiarpur: V. V. Research Institute, 1968), Appendices 2 and 3, pp. 365–7.
10. Hasrat, *Anglo-Sikh Relations*, Appendix 4, pp. 367–8.
11. C. U. Aitchison, *A Collection of Treaties, Engagements and Sanads Relating to India and Neighbouring Countries* (Calcutta: Government Printing, 1909), vol. VIII, pp. 286–7. Earlier, in September 1810, the British diplomats stationed at Delhi had helped Raja Jaswant Singh receive the title of 'Brar Bans Sirmaur Malvinder Bahadur' from the Mughal emperor to whom Jaswant Singh sent two guns and four bows as present. Griffin, *The Rajas*, p. 386.
12. Hasrat, *Anglo-Sikh Relations*, Appendix 5, pp. 368–9.
13. Griffin, *The Rajas*, p. 160.
14. Griffin, *The Rajas*, pp. 160–3, 392–6.
15. Griffin, *The Rajas*, pp. 382–92.
16. Griffin, *The Rajas*, pp. 181, 184–5.
17. Griffin, *The Rajas*, pp. 323–5, 402–9.
18. Griffin, *The Rajas*, p. 411–12.
19. Griffin, *The Rajas*, pp. 413–18; also pp. 183, 185, 189, 192, 193. It may be added that the possessions of the Raja of Kapurthala to the south of the Sutlej were confiscated. The chiefs of Ladwa and Ropar were banished as prisoners and their estates were confiscated. The Sodhis of Anandpur also lost their possessions.

20. Griffin, *The Rajas*, pp. 418–19.
21. Griffin, *The Rajas*, pp. 207–9, 421–3.
22. For the text of the sanad of 1860, see Griffin, *The Rajas*, pp. 425–7.
23. Griffin, *The Rajas*, pp. 425, 427. The additional title—*farzand-i arjmand, aqīdat-paivand-i daulat-i Inglisia*—made Raja Bharpur Singh the exalted and faithful son of the British Empire.
24. For the text of the sanad of 1862, Griffin, *The Rajas*, pp. 427–8.
25. Griffin, *The Rajas*, pp. 228–43. See also C. L. Tupper, *Indian Political Practice* (New Delhi: B. R. Publishing, 1974, reprint), vol. I, pp. 47–8.
26. Griffin, *The Rajas*, pp. 446–8. For further details, see A. C. Arora, *British Policy towards the Punjab States 1858–1905* (Jalandhar: Export India Publications, 1982), pp. 148–54, 164.
27. Griffin, *The Rajas*, pp. 370–2 and nn.
28. Griffin, *The Rajas*, pp. 434–48.
29. Arora, *British Policy*, p. 154.
30. Griffin, *The Rajas*, pp. 439–45.
31. Arora, *British Policy*, pp. 51–2.
32. Arora, *British Policy*, pp. 52–7. According to Tupper, this change was largely, if not entirely, due to the sympathies of the Commissioner with one of the parties in the Patiala state during the minority of its chief (*Indian Political Practice*, vol. II, p. 189).
33. See Appendix 1A for the genealogical table.
34. The Namdharis represented a reformist sect among Sikhs originating in the 1840s under Baba Balak Singh who laid stress on the importance of Name (*nām*) for salvation. The Namdharis also came to be called 'Kukas' because they emitted shrieks (*kūk*) in a state of ecstasy. Their second Guru, Baba Ram Singh, politicized the sect and entertained millenarian hopes of the re-establishment of Sikh rule. He greatly resented the lifting of prohibition on kine killing by the British in 1849 after they annexed the Punjab. Kine killing and Muslim butchers became identified with British rule. The more irate among his followers struck at the butchers at different places, including Malerkotla, a Muslim principality, to overawe the kine killers all over the Punjab. Terrified of a possible repeat of 1857–8, the British initially hanged some Kukas, and blew another 63 of them from guns later. Baba Ram Singh was exiled to Burma under the Bengal Regulation III of 1818 where he died after some years. Incidentally, Maharaja Ripudaman Singh, too, was exiled under this archaic Regulation. For some detail on the Namdharis, see J. S. Grewal, *The Sikhs of the Punjab*, The New Cambridge History of India II.3 (Cambridge: Cambridge University Press [1999] 2014), pp. 142–4. See also Joginder Singh, *A Short History of Namdhari Sikhs of Punjab* (Amritsar: Guru Nanak Dev University, 2010), pp. 37–54.
35. For the services rendered by Raja Hira Singh to the Government of India and the rewards he received, see *Punjab States Gazetteers*, vol.

XVII, A., *Phulkian States: Patiala Jind and Nabha, 1904* (Lahore: Punjab Government, 1909), p. 343. Punjab State Archives, Patiala (PSA), President, Council of Regency, Nabha State (PCRNS) Records, File no. 523/E, 1929.
36. Quoted in Arora, *British Policy*, p. 267. See also Tupper, *Indian Political Practice*, vol. I, pp. 150–4, 158–9.
37. National Archives of India, New Delhi (NAI), Foreign Department, Native States, no. 321/6, 322/6.
38. Kuldeep, 'Modes of Colonial Control: A Case Study of Nabha under Maharaja Hira Singh, 1871–1911', MPhil diss., Panjab University, Chandigarh, 2006, pp. 50–93.
39. Mary, Countess of Minto, *India: Minto and Morley 1905–1910* (London, 1934), pp. 69, 316.
40. As a matter of fact, as a special case, Maharaja Rajinder Singh had begun to conduct his administration eight months earlier (Tupper, *Indian Political Practice*, vol. II, p. 189).
41. Arora, *British Policy*, pp. 60–7.
42. Punjab States Archives, Patiala (PSA), Office of the Nabha State, File no. 10002 E. This file is wrongly entitled 'Indian National Congress' but it contains copies of Raja Hira Singh's letters. Also related to the same subject are PSA, Foreign Department–Secret 1, Proceedings, June 1911, nos 30–32.
43. Arora, *British Policy*, pp. 179–245. *Punjab States Gazetteers*, vol. XVII, A., *Phulkian States* pp. 371–2. Tupper, *Indian Political Practice*, vol. I, pp. 17, 178, 182, 183, 187, 189, 192; vol. III, pp. 81–2, 88–9.
44. *Punjab States Gazetteers*, vol. XVII, A, *Phulkian States*, pp. 355–7.
45. NAI, *Hardinge Papers*: Coronation of King George V in England, pp. 3, 9, 12, 13.
46. NAI, *Hardinge Papers*, Correspondence Regarding 'Coronation Durbar' at Delhi, 1911, no. 499a (N. 471), vol. III, no. 610.
47. Punjab Government Records (PGR), Political Department–1913, Annual File no. 3, p. 3. See also Kirpal Singh, *Hardinge Papers Relating to Punjab* (Patiala: Punjabi University, 2002), pp. 80–1.
48. PGR, Political Department–1913, Annual File no. 3, p. 2, 'Death of Maharaja Hira Singh and Recognition of His Son Tikka Ripudaman Singh' (Telegram no. 408, *Hardinge Papers*, p. 528).
49. NAI, *Hardinge Papers*, Telegram nos. 291, 408, 430.
50. PGR, Political Department–1913, Annual File no. 3, p. 2, 'Death of Maharaja Hira Singh and Recognition of His Son Tikka Ripudaman Singh'.

2

TIKKA RIPUDAMAN SINGH

Ripudaman Singh's careful upbringing and education was markedly different from that of most other princes of his day, especially in the Punjab. Uninterested in the usual princely pursuits and trappings, he grew up to be a devout Sikh, a keen social reformer, and a staunch nationalist. In the Imperial Legislative Council as the Tikka, he forcefully raised Panthic issues of far-reaching significance, evinced serious concern for the education and uplift of women, and fearlessly criticized the Government of India and the Punjab Administration. His abiding concern for the autonomy of princely states and the protection of their rights became evident during this period. He was a suspect in the eyes of the bureaucracy before he became the Maharaja.

Early Life and Education

On 4 March 1883, a servant of the palace brought the news to the 40-year-old Raja Hira Singh that Rani Jasmer Kaur had given birth to a boy. An heir to the throne of Nabha, the newborn immediately became 'Tikka Sahib'. A salute of 101 guns was fired. The officers (*ahlkār*s) of the state brought nazars according to their status. The Raja distributed money among the people assembled in front of the fort-palace. A number of prisoners were released, and exiles were allowed to return. Telegrams were sent to the Punjab Government and the Government of India.[1]

Raja Hira Singh saw his son for the first time on 17 March after the 'inauspicious' period following birth (*sūtak*) was over. A salute of 21 guns was fired and *karhā parshād* (sacramental food) was offered at Saropa Sahib, the Gurdwara in the fort-palace. On 16 January 1884, the Tikka was taken to the *diwān khāna* (audience hall) and a salute of 17 guns was fired on his entry. The ahlkārs presented nazars to the Tikka. When he was taken back to the palace, a salute of 17 guns was fired again. A couple of days before his birthday in March 1884, the Tikka was taken to the cantonment, cash was distributed among the troops, and sweets were distributed among students of 'the camp school' established by Raja Hira Singh to further his special interest in the education of promising boys of the state.[2]

The first birthday of the Tikka was marked by another round of festivities. On 28 September 1884, he was taken to Gurdwara Saropa Sahib for permission (*vāk*) from the *Guru Granth Sahib* to wear arms. He rode an elephant on 18 October 1885 to review troops.[3] On 20 February 1887, he was taken to Saropa Sahib to start learning Gurmukhi. After performing *ardās* (a prayer) before the *Guru Granth Sahib*, Bhai Narain Singh, the Mahant of Dera Baba Ajaipal Singh (which was associated with Guru Gobind Singh), made the Tikka write the first four letters of the Gurmukhi alphabet. Bhai Narain Singh's erudite son, Kahn Singh, was appointed officer of the establishment (*deodhī*) of Tikka Sahib on 14 March. On 16 March, Tikka Sahib attended the Darbar held at the diwān khāna for the Lieutenant Governor, Sir Charles Aitchison. In April 1888, Tikka Sahib was in the Darbar where the Political Agent, Colonel Grey, expressed his delight over the prince's bearing and his ready replies.[4]

On 24 October 1890, Tikka Sahib accompanied Raja Hira Singh to receive Viceroy Lansdowne and Lieutenant Governor J. B. Lyall at the Nabha Railway Station. Five carriages formed the procession, which moved from the railway station to the Viceregal camp behind the cantonment. The dinner in the fort-palace was not attended by Raja Hira Singh as a matter of policy of not eating with Europeans. After the dinner, the Foreign Secretary to the Government of India and the Chief Secretary to the Punjab Government led His Highness to the Dining Hall, and His Excellency 'gave him seat' on his left while the Tikka Sahib sat next to the Lieutenant Governor. After the toasts, the whole party witnessed fireworks from the balcony where the state ahlkārs down to the *nāzims* (administrators) were present.[5]

The Viceroy stated on this occasion that the Government of India regarded His Highness as 'a staunch friend and ally', and referred to his well-earned and distinguished Order of the Star of India. His Highness had placed a part of his forces under special training in order to make them fit to serve with the troops of the Queen-Empress in the event of a great imperial emergency. The Viceroy assured His Highness that he greatly valued his friendship.[6] Tikka Ripudaman Singh was over six years old and is likely to have remembered this first great ceremonial occasion of his life.

Raja Hira Singh was opposed to the idea of sending his son to a Chief's College, which made the pupils lose touch with their own religion and cultural moorings. The Aitchison College at Lahore was one of the institutions set up recently to Westernize the scions of the ruling families, encourage social conformity, and inculcate an unquestioning admiration for the British empire.[7] Unlike Bhupinder Singh of Patiala and other Sikh princes of his day, Ripudaman Singh did not receive even a public school education.

The Tikka's childhood and education coincided with a period of significant resurgence and cultural reorientation in the Punjab, leading to the emergence of hundreds of voluntary associations (called Samajes, Anjumans, and Sabhas) geared to socio-religious reform and promotion of 'communally-safe' modern education among Hindus, Muslims, and Sikhs. These movements of cultural adjustment among Hindus were represented by the Brahmo Samaj, Arya Samaj, Dev Samaj, and the Sanatan Dharm, with different shades of eclecticism, radicalism, and conservatism.[8] Relatively slow to modernize, the Muslim Anjumans were oriented towards Sir Syed Ahmad's Mohammadan Anglo-Oriental Conference, or the Aligarh movement.[9] The modernizing movement among the Sikhs was represented by the Singh Sabhas.[10]

The first Singh Sabha was founded by aristocratic Sikhs at Amritsar in 1873. On the initiative of relatively radical middle class reformers, the Lahore Singh Sabha was founded in 1879. Thereafter, a number of Singh Sabhas and ancillary institutions came up in the Punjab. The Chief Khalsa Diwan was founded at Amritsar in 1902 to coordinate their activities. Broadly, the Singh Sabha movement was concerned with religious reform according to the teachings of the Gurus as enshrined in the *Guru Granth Sahib*, which included rejection of idol worship, Brahmanical rituals, and un-Sikh practices. The other major concerns of the Singh Sabhas were the uplift of women, spread of Anglo-Sikh education, and promotion of Punjabi language in Gurmukhi script. The radical elements among the reformers advocated uplift of the outcastes through purification (*shuddhī*).

With the growing articulation of a distinctive socio-religious identity of the Sikhs, the radical Sikh reformers came into conflict with the

Aryas and the Sanatanists who asserted that the Sikhs were Hindu. By the end of the nineteenth century, differences between the Sikh and Hindu reformers and also among the conservative and radical Sikhs were coming to the fore. At this stage, the Sikhs were considered by and large loyal to the government, and the leading Sikh organization, the Chief Khalsa Diwan, was regarded as politically moderate. Raja Hira Singh was personally inclined towards the conservative reformers, but he entrusted the main responsibility for the Tikka's education to Bhai Kahn Singh who aligned himself with the radical reformers.

The choice of Kahn Singh as the tutor of Tikka Ripudaman Singh was made after serious thought by Raja Hira Singh. Kahn Singh's father, Bhai Narain Singh, who was known for his selfless dedication to Sikhism, was held in high esteem by the Raja. Bhai Narain Singh did not believe in any personal Guru after Guru Gobind Singh and regarded the *Guru Granth Sahib* as the Guru. Recitation of the *Guru Granth Sahib* and its exposition was his serious concern. He maintained a regular *langar* (an open kitchen for charity), and carried on initiation of the double-edged sword at Dera Baba Ajaipal Singh, which preserved some of the arms of the tenth Guru as sacred relics and received horses as offering. It was also a centre of Sikh learning.[11]

Born in 1861, Kahn Singh had received his early education at Dera Baba Ajaipal Singh. In two years, he learnt the *Guru Granth Sahib* folio by folio. In the ten years following, he learnt Sanskrit from Maharashtrian Brahmans settled in Nabha. He also learnt to compose poetry in Braj from a pupil of Kavi Gawal who had been patronized by Raja Bharpur Singh and Raja Bhagwan Singh. Kahn Singh went to Delhi in 1880 to learn Persian. Two years later, he went to Lahore and became actively associated with the Lahore Singh Sabha, which advocated radical reform in religious and social matters, emphasizing the importance of the *Guru Granth Sahib*, the Gurdwara, and the Khalsa code of life for the Sikhs. On his return to Nabha in 1884, Kahn Singh became a courtier (*musāhib*) of Raja Hira Singh. Three years later, at the age of 26, as mentioned earlier, he was made the officer in charge of the establishment of Tikka Ripudaman Singh.[12] This office of great responsibility turned out to be of great significance for the Tikka's political outlook and concerns.

Bhai Kahn Singh recollects with a sense of gratification that Tikka Ripudaman Singh was educated to be competent in every way.[13] From 1887 to 1893, the Tikka learnt the Sikh scripture. Raja Hira Singh was so pleased with his son's early education that he made Kahn Singh the Tikka's personal secretary to make him familiar with his own views on statecraft and government.[14] For the political education of the Tikka, Bhai Kahn Singh chose the Braj version of Kavi Hirday Ram's *Hanumān Nātak*, a story of Ramchandra of Ayodhya, believed to have been rendered from Sanskrit during the early seventeenth century. Raja Hira Singh used to give his own interpretation of the verses taken up for exposition. His comments were put down in writing and became the basis of a book called *Nātak Bhāvārth Deepika*, published in 1897. Significantly, the comments of Raja Hira Singh were mostly ethical and political. His ideal ruler was adept in both *yog* (austerities and meditation) and *bhog* (used here for enjoyment of worldly pleasures).[15]

In 1898, Bhai Kahn Singh published his classic statement on Sikh identity: *Ham Hindu Nahīn*. This work was a stunning blow to those Hindus and Sikhs who were keen to establish that 'Sikhism' was a branch or sect of 'Hinduism'. They alleged that this book was meant to disturb Hindu–Sikh relations, and suggested that Raja Hira Singh should punish Kahn Singh. As a staunch upholder of amicable relations between all religious communities, Raja Hira Singh removed Bhai Kahn Singh from the service of the state. An English translation of the book was submitted to the legal adviser of the Punjab Government for his opinion and he was categorical that the book did not offend the susceptibilities of any religious community, and was not disrespectful towards Hinduism or Hindus. Furthermore, *Ham Hindu Nahīn* was warmly appreciated by Sikh scholars and religious authorities. Raja Hira Singh now realized that there was no truth in the allegations made against the author of *Ham Hindu Nahīn*. Bhai Kahn Singh was appointed as the Vakīl of the Nabha state with the Political Agent to the Governor General for the Phulkian States and Bahawalpur.[16]

The Tikka's English education had been entrusted to Lala Bishan Das, a graduate from the Forman Christian College, Lahore, and a classmate of Lala Harkishen Lal, the well-known banker, industrialist, social reformer, and a nationalist associated with the Lahore Brahmo Samaj. He had been instrumental in the founding of the Punjab National Bank and several other *swadeshī* (Indian) enterprises.[17] Raja Hira Singh probably was unaware that Bishan Das had nationalist leanings. Originally a subject of Nabha, Bishan Das had served as the Headmaster of a school in Dera Ismail Khan. He was well regarded by the Raja, and used to accompany the heir apparent to Calcutta and

Simla during 1906–8. Bishan Das later became the Foreign Minister of Maharaja Ripudaman Singh and reportedly died of shock a week after his deposition.[18]

Early Interest in the Affairs of the Sikhs

At the age of 22, Tikka Ripudaman Singh wrote to the Lieutenant Governor of the Punjab, Sir Charles Rivaz, on 30 March 1905 that he had found idols in the inner and outer circumambulatory precincts (*parkarmā*) of Sri Darbar Sahib at Amritsar. The Sikhs were not idol worshippers and the *Guru Granth Sahib* strongly prohibited idolatry. The Tikka requested the Lieutenant Governor to take 'some permanent steps' to ensure that a Sikh 'possessing force of character' was appointed to 'this most sacred and responsible post'.[19]

The Lieutenant Governor referred the matter to R. E. Younghusband, the Commissioner at Lahore, who asked C. M. King, the Deputy Commissioner of Amritsar, to verify facts and elicit advice from some of the leading Sikh Sardars. King visited the Golden Temple and saw half a dozen or more idols arranged along the outer parkarmā by Brahmans from the hill districts. The practice was at least 20 years old when the then Manager of the Golden Temple, Colonel Jawala Singh, had put a stop to it, but it was revived because of strong pressure from the wealthy Hindus of the city.[20] Commenting on King's report, Younghusband suggested some improvements in the management but no immediate change. Sir Charles Rivaz decided to leave the Tikka's letter unanswered.[21]

Due to pressure from the leaders of the Chief Khalsa Diwan, on the first of May 1905, the Manager of the Golden Temple, Sardar Arur Singh, ordered the Brahmans not to bring idols to the Golden Temple because the practice was 'opposed to the principles and customs of the Gurdwara'. After some resistance, the Brahmans agreed on 7 May not to bring their idols in future without the permission of the Manager.[22] On 16 May, Tikka Ripudaman Singh wrote to the Deputy Commissioner of Amritsar that all the Sikhs were happy over the news that idols had been removed from 'the Holy of the Holiest of Sikh shrines'. He was thankful to the Deputy Commissioner for putting an end to 'this most shameful practice'. A copy of Sewa Ram Singh's book on Guru Nanak, which was the first such work in English by a Sikh, was sent to enlighten C. M. King on Sikhism.[23]

Under the aegis of the 'Hindu Hitkari Sabha', representing Hindu 'orthodoxy' (as opposed to the Arya Samaj), the wealthy Hindus of Amritsar sent a memorial to the Lieutenant Governor against the removal of idols. The memorial claimed that Brahmans performing priestly duties for Hindu pilgrims had remained in position with their idols 'from the foundation of the Temple'. It was asserted that their removal was 'contrary to the wishes of the great majority of the Sikhs themselves', and that only the radical Sikhs called the *tat Khalsa*, who were regarded as 'outcastes' by the orthodox Hindus and Sikhs, favoured the removal of the idols.[24]

The 'Hindu Hitkari Sabha' approached Raja Hira Singh, who assured them that he was against this measure. He suspended Bhai Kahn Singh from his position as the Vakīl of Nabha for writing directly to the Deputy Commissioner of Amritsar. Raja Hira Singh also issued a public notification (*ishtihār*) to denounce the 'strange party that has sprung up among the Sikhs who say that they are not Hindus'.[25] He announced a reward of 500 rupees to anyone who could refute the substance of his statement in the ishtihār. Significantly, the person who defended the distinct identity of the Sikhs was later appointed as a Judge of the Nabha High Court by Maharaja Ripudaman Singh.[26]

The father and the son were thus ranged on opposite sides. The British administrators were inclined to accept the Tikka's view. Deputy Commissioner King maintained that the Golden Temple was 'a Sikh temple' and the property 'of the Sikhs as a whole'. Even its relatively conservative *granthīs* (functionaries in charge of a Gurdwara) and *pujārīs* (shrine attendants) were not opposed to the removal of idols.[27] The subsequent enquiries made by the administrators convinced them that the only mode of worship allowed in the Darbar Sahib until after the inception of British rule was the one in accordance with the *Guru Granth Sahib*. They chose to ignore Raja Hira Singh's keenness to know the name of 'the author of the action'.[28]

Member of the Imperial Legislative Council

On Lord Minto's arrival in India in late 1905, the Phulkian rulers were the first to send delegates with 'addresses of welcome' to hammer home the point that the first Lord Minto had protected the Phulkian states a hundred years earlier against the encroachments of Maharaja Ranjit Singh. Minto responded by referring to the Phulkian chiefs as his 'personal friends'. Within a few months, he visited their states. 'On November 28 we arrived at Nabha', says Lady Minto in her *Journal*, 'and found the old Rajah standing on the platform, covered with orders and ribands. He is a splendid old warrior, such a picturesque figure in his embroidered coat, with full white petticoats worn over long white Jodhpur breeches'.[29]

When the Viceroy was inspecting the Guard of Honour at the railway station before his departure, Raja Hira Singh asked Dunlop-Smith, the former Political Agent and now Personal Secretary to Lord Minto, to be kind to his son in Calcutta, hoping that the Tikka would learn from association with 'the wise men of the Empire'. Lady Minto observed that whereas Raja Hira Singh was 'a typical Indian Ruling Chief of the old school', Tikka Ripudaman Singh was 'rather sympathetic with the modern and moderate school of Indian politicians'.[30]

Lord Curzon (1899–1905) had contributed substantially towards the mounting political unrest in India by his policies and measures, especially the partition of Bengal in 1905. Lord Minto found a highly charged political situation in India. The agitation against the partition of Bengal was reaching out to other provinces. In the Calcutta session of the Congress in 1906 the demand for self-government (*swarāj*) through swadeshī was articulated forcefully by Bal Gangadhar Tilak, Bepin Chandra Pal, and Lala Lajpat Rai. Dubbed as 'extremists' by the British, the trio formed a new party to agitate for swarāj and swadeshī. The moderate politicians such as Gopal Krishna Gokhale and Madan Mohan Malaviya continued to have firm faith in British liberal thought and constitutional methods. A split between the moderates and extremists took place at Surat in December 1907 and the latter were expelled from the Congress. Gradually, there was a shift to individual terrorist violence in Bengal and Maharashtra in 1908. The movement for swadeshī in the Punjab was spearheaded by Lajpat Rai and Ajit Singh (paternal uncle of Bhagat Singh), and the latter was more active in the peasant agitation of 1907.[31]

Nominated to the Imperial Legislative Council (ILC) in 1906, Tikka Ripudaman Singh proved to be one of its vocal members in 1907–8. He developed friendships with G. K. Gokhale and M. M. Malaviya, among others. The record of his speeches in the ILC reveals his patriotic mettle, his Sikh interests, and princely concerns. He was embarrassingly direct and critical in the sessions of the ILC at Calcutta and Simla. Well-drafted with 'excellent' matter, his speeches were delivered in a low and solemn tone.[32] In his somewhat lengthy speeches he dwelt on many of the most important contemporary Indian concerns, including discontent over the policies and measures of Curzon and his successor. He did not miss a chance to criticize the government, but his criticism was invariably followed by constructive suggestions. His questions exposed the unsound policies of the government and administrative inefficiency and high-handedness of its local representatives. It is notable that, in the significant majority of political issues, the Tikka was generally in alignment with Gokhale whom he appears to have admired and emulated and with whom he was seen exchanging glances and 'significant smiles' in the course of the proceedings.[33] In his brusqueness, which appears to have increased with time, however, the Tikka was probably more like Tilak. Talking of 'my country' and 'my country-men', on different issues, Ripudaman Singh spoke as an Indian nationalist and social reformer, as a Punjabi and a Sikh, and as an Indian prince who was directly critical of the Raj.[34]

Tikka Ripudaman Singh's strongest opposition was directed against the new instrument of repression, the Prevention of Seditious Meetings Bill. It was 'vaguely drafted' and 'very wide' in scope, which was liable to be abused by 'the overzealous subordinate officials'. Along with Gokhale and another moderate Congressman, Rashbehary Ghosh, he actually voted against it on 1 November 1907.[35] Unlike the majority of the non-official members of the ILC, the Tikka also objected to the Explosive Substances Bill as 'vaguely drafted', and to the Newspapers (Incitement to Offences) Bill introduced on 8 June 1908, as 'ambiguous' and 'unnecessary'. He was sceptical about the government's assertion that a state of 'emergency' existed to justify the passing of the two Bills without any further discussion or delay. He advised the government to 'try to find out its causes and remove them', and to 'decide whether coercion or conciliation would be the better remedy'. Significantly, Ripudaman Singh had prefaced his comments with the tongue-in-cheek observation that, 'for good or evil, "democracy" is in the air', and India could not have escaped the 'infection' from Europe.[36]

The Tikka strongly criticized the police and judicial administration, the twin arms of the government, as oppressive. Innocent people were more afraid of the police than they were of criminals. A terror to respectable people, the police force was utterly incompetent. For example, the culprits who had burnt a certain Sikh Gurdwara in the Punjab some months ago were still at large. The image of the police as a 'shabby department' (*gandā mahkmā*) must be changed.[37]

Tikka Ripudaman Singh was not afraid to take up the most sensitive and politically charged issue of racial discrimination. In picking up themes directly reminiscent of, and even arguably related to the consequences of, the great Ilbert Bill controversy, he maintained that the image of 'British justice' was being tarnished by incidents like the 'Rawalpindi rape case' and the 'Lahore shooting case'. A European station officer and his Muslim assistant were acquitted by a European jury from the charge of dishonouring a Hindu lady. A European master who shot his servant was sentenced to only a six-month imprisonment by a European jury, treating the crime as an accident. What would have been the result if the victims in both these cases had been Europeans and the assailants natives, the Tikka asked?[38]

Objecting strongly to the treatment meted out to Indians in their own country, Ripudaman Singh pointed out that Indian gentlemen were sometimes bodily expelled from railway carriages. European officers did not show due courtesy and politeness, whether in writing or in conversation. In his view, it was their ignorance of Indian manners, customs, religions, languages, and etiquette that was increasingly resulting in strained relations with the people of the country.[39] Referring with appreciation to the speeches of the Prince of Wales and the Liberal Secretary of State, the Tikka advised the government to 'treat Indians kindly and sympathetically, encourage them and cheer them with friendly words'. He assured the British that they would find them ready 'to lay down even their lives' for them.[40] In other words, loyalty could not be assumed; it had to be earned; it would certainly not spring from discrimination and harsh treatment.

The Tikka's tenure coincided with Mohandas Karamchand Gandhi's campaign of passive resistance to the Transvaal Government's policy of harsh racial discrimination against Indians in law as in daily life. Ripudaman Singh did not hide his admiration for Gandhi's efforts, and drew the attention of the government to the plight of Indians in the Transvaal. It was freely said in speeches and writings that India was the most brilliant jewel in the British Crown but Indians were never given British protection. The Tikka reminded the government of one of its 'foremost duties': to protect the 'rights of Indians in the British colonies'. Echoing Annie Besant, he had the courage to remind the colonists that India was in 'the full glory of her ancient civilization' when their forefathers were 'no better than savages'.[41]

Tikka Ripudaman Singh was acutely unhappy with the relations of the paramount power with the Indian states which needed 'a great deal of improvement'. Reminding the government of the proclamation of the late Queen Victoria and a recent speech of the Secretary of State for India, the Tikka spoke on behalf of the princes that nothing would win their hearts more than respecting their treaty rights, and giving them independence in matters of internal administration. Probably with reference to over a dozen depositions in recent decades he suggested that where apparently at fault, the Indian princes should be tried 'only by their peers' to 'save a great deal of misunderstanding and heart-burning'.[42]

Ripudaman Singh was opposed to excessive expenditure on the Imperial Service Troops. It went up to 14 per cent of the state's income in some cases. He suggested that only a fixed percentage of the income of a state, but not exceeding 5, should be spent on the upkeep of these troops. The Tikka also wanted the government to preserve their identity rather than being 'swept into the Indian Army', or treated as 'the mercenaries of the Crown'. Furthermore, looking upon the Indian aristocracy as 'the true and natural leaders of the people', he wanted them to play a more active role in the Imperial Advisory Council and the Imperial Cadet Corps.[43]

Sharing the concern of Indian social reformers and political leaders of his day, Tikka Ripudaman Singh was equally forthright in seeking the government's intervention in social, economic, and administrative matters. He dwelt at length on the condition of women. He sought improvement in their condition through legislation and education. Women required protection of their personal ornaments and property against attachment in execution of decrees against their husbands or other male relatives. Long 'desertion' of five years should be recognized by law as sufficient to annul a marriage. The age of marriage should be raised, the practices of bride-price and slavery should be checked, and it should be ensured that young girls were not married to old men. Educated girls, even if widowed, should not be confined to the domestic walls, or subjected to veil or seclusion (*pardah*). Ignorance and early marriages of women were as harmful for 'the country and its people' as the caste system. Education of girls was as important as the education of boys.[44]

Ripudaman Singh looked upon the existing system of education as flawed because of the policy of 'religious neutrality'. An education that lacked moral and religious training could not be of any real advantage. The Tikka favoured 'denominational education'. Primary education meant for agriculturists should be made useful for their vocation.

Echoing the concern of the Singh Sabha reformers, he maintained that reading, writing, and arithmetic should be taught in Punjabi and not in Urdu, which was 'a foreign language' in the Punjab (adopted by the British after annexation in 1849). Furthermore, 'the things which merely tax the memory of the students without awakening their curiosity and training their faculties of reasoning and observation should be avoided'. The system of examinations should be made 'more elastic', and students should be allowed to pass examinations in 'compartments'. The Tikka favoured the idea of free primary education, and pleaded for enhanced budgetary provision for education as well as public health.[45]

Ripudaman Singh dwelt on the demoralizing effects of intoxicating drugs, leading to crime and pauperization. The consumption of opium and drinking of country liquor should be checked through preventive enactment. Their use should be allowed only on medical advice. He did not hesitate to say that 'the revenue from opium was collected at the expense of the cause of morality'. He reminded the government that philanthropic work by the Temperance Societies was no substitute for preventive legislation. 'Total abstinence would make the soldiers strong, healthy and courageous.' To sell tobacco to young men and women below the age of 20 should be made punishable.[46]

The Tikka pointed out that surplus from railways came at the cost of public convenience and health. To make budgetary provisions to obviate the inconveniences of the third-class passengers was to serve the cause of 'humanity and justice'. To mitigate misery and distress caused by the failure of rains called for extension of canal irrigation. Voicing one of the major concerns of economic nationalism of his day, the Tikka remarked: 'It seems a pity that grain should be allowed to be exported out of India when the children of the soil can hardly buy enough thereof to keep body and soul together.' In the context of swadeshī and the growing demand for Indianization of the services, the Tikka wanted 'the children of the soil' to be associated more and more with the higher administration of the country, both civil and military, and the existing system of education to be changed to create new avenues of employment for economic development.[47]

Tikka Ripudaman Singh pleaded for a Legislative Council for the Punjab but without reservation of seats for Muslims alone. He asked for simplification of the law and legal procedures, with clear definition of the terms like 'growing crops' and 'moveable property', and with limits fixed on the interest taken on loans. He wanted curbs to be put on the moneylenders' tendency to charge interest for an indefinite period. In his view, not much had been done by the Punjab Administration to alleviate the suffering caused by famine and plague during the past decade. He suggested that the proportion of 'partial exemption' from land revenue in case of calamities should be fixed and not left to the discretion of local authorities.[48]

As a Sikh, defence of the country was the Tikka's 'natural concern'. To keep the martial spirit of the Sikhs alive through physical and military instruction, he wanted each able-bodied Sikh youth to receive military training. Taking up some specific Sikh issues, Ripudaman Singh asked a number of questions with reference to a news item in *The Tribune* of 22 August 1907 and subsequently in the *Khalsa Advocate* of 11 January 1908, that the government had done nothing 'in connection with the burning to ashes by the local Muhammadans of a magnificent Sikh temple in the village of Udharwal in the Jhelum distinct'. Two Gurdwaras in two other villages were looted. The Tikka wanted to know what action was proposed to be taken in a matter that was 'bound to deeply wound the feelings of the loyal Sikh community'. Even when he was assured that 'the persons believed to be guilty will be brought before the court for trial', all the accused were discharged by the Magistrate on 5 December 1907. The Tikka expected the government not to allow the matter to rest there.[49]

In tune with his concern for reform in the management of Gurdwaras, Ripudaman Singh repeatedly spoke on proper utilization of the resources of 'endowed institutions'. Meant originally for charitable and educational purposes, these institutions had become the 'dens of vice'. Their funds had become the private property of the priests of the temples. Under the control of worthless, immoral, and selfish people, these institutions had become 'a veritable curse to the country'. The people in charge of these institutions should be compelled to spend considerable portions from their income for the charitable and educational purposes for which they were intended.[50]

The range of concerns articulated by Tikka Ripudaman Singh reflects his multiple self-identifications as a prince, as an Indian, and as a Sikh with a high degree of social and political awareness. In his criticism of the government and constructive suggestions, he virtually summed up the nationalist critique and reformist concerns of his times, moderated by his own education. Like Tilak, he advocated 'a radical change in the spirit of the administration'. Like him, the Tikka maintained that 'the true well-wishers of the government are those who speak the truth plainly'.[51] It was clear that the general drift of his speeches and questions was unlikely to result in anything but official disapproval. Much before Ripudaman Singh's term ended, his questions began to be disallowed by the Governor General as the President of the ILC.

The Anand Marriage Act

Tikka Ripudaman Singh managed to get the Anand Marriage Bill introduced in the Imperial Legislative Council to validate the Sikh form of marriage effectively and legally to replace the Hindu form of marriage. The records pertaining to the Anand Marriage Act show that Ripudaman Singh repeatedly broached this subject in 1907 with Erle Richards, the Law Member on the ILC. On his advice, the Tikka collected opinions of a large number of leading Sikh intellectuals, professionals, religious leaders, aristocrats, and secretaries of the Singh Sabhas from all over the Punjab. The supporters of the proposed measure included the well-known Sikh reformers like Bhai Kahn Singh of Nabha, Giani Gian Singh, Bhai Vir Singh, Bhai Takht Singh, and Bhai Arjan Singh of Bagrian.[52]

In his Statement of Objects and Reasons for introducing this measure, the Tikka emphasized that the Anand form of marriage had long been in practice among the Sikhs. However, the absence of a 'validating enactment' had created great difficulty for the concerned parties who were obliged to get involved in expensive civil suits. In such situations, the judicial officers were not certain about the validity of Anand marriage. While pleading that all doubts should be set at rest for the future, he underlined that the proposed enactment 'merely validates an existing rite and involves no new principle'.[53]

In his conversations with Erle Richards, Ripudaman Singh appears to have alluded to the attempts of the Hindus—the Sanatanis as well as the Arya Samajis—to absorb the Sikhs by declining to recognize the validity of the marriage by the Anand rite. In fact, in view of such doubts, the bride's family felt obliged often to ensure the presence of a 'Hindu priest' at the Anand ceremony. Erle Richards forwarded the Tikka's letter and the papers containing his proposal and abstracts of supporting opinions to Harvey Adamson, the Home Member. The Law Member sympathized with the Tikka's objective and emphasized that it was 'not inconsistent with our general policy of preserving the Sikhs who have been loyal to us'.

The proposal went through several stages as required under the procedures. The most crucial, politically, was the Punjab Government's approval. The Lieutenant Governor, Sir Louis Dane, had reservations initially, but all the civil officers of the province whose opinions were sought considered the Bill unobjectionable. M. W. Fenton, the Acting Chief Secretary, supported it enthusiastically. He did not want 'the principle of non-interference in religious matters' to be carried too far to deprive 'a progressive community' such as the Sikhs of the only method available in a civilized state for promoting reform. Earlier, as the Commissioner of the Multan Division, he had recommended that the Sikh faith should be fortified against the 'insidious assaults of an uncompromising Hinduism'. Yet, Dane did not relish giving in to the 'Sikh reform party', who were obviously in league with the Tikka, and had at one time even considered dropping the measure. The predicament of the Punjab Government was conveyed by its Chief Secretary to the Government of India:

> It is perhaps unfortunate that the Tikka Ripudaman Singh should have raised the question at all, but as he has done so, and as he is supported by the great body of his co-religionists, and as it would probably cause serious popular discontent if no action is taken in the matter of the Bill, the Lieutenant Governor considers that it should be passed into law.

The Tikka was permitted to introduce the Anand Marriage Bill in the Imperial Legislative Council on 30 October 1908 which, unlike his speeches in the past, he did tersely in one sentence:

> My Lord, the Statement of Objects and Reasons fully explains the object and scope of the Bill, so I need not trouble Your Excellency and my Hon'ble Colleagues with any further remarks.

Much had happened by this time to make Ripudaman Singh unhappy with the government's handling of his proposal. In view of his generally critical stance in the ILC, he did not get another term to steer his Bill through. He particularly resented the amendments suggested by Sir Louis Dane in the original proposal. Instead of 'the Sikh Marriage Act' it was to be called the 'Anand Marriage Act' so that it remained one of the forms of marriage prevalent among the Sikhs. This enabling provision changed the character of the original proposal, which aimed at making it the only valid Sikh ceremony of marriage. Furthermore, following the Christian Marriage Act 1872 (Sec. 4), Dane had insisted that the Anand marriage 'must be between parties of whom one or both are Sikhs'. The Home Member had made it clear that the attitude of the government towards this Bill was 'one of neutrality', and that the final support would depend on the opinion elicited from the Sikh community whose interests it affected.

Despite the non-renewal of his term, Tikka Ripudaman Singh continued to mobilize Sikh opinion in favour of the Bill. The Lieutenant Governor remarked in the ILC that 'the discussions about the Bill have shown how well organized is the Sikh reform party. The word goes forth and petitions practically identical in substance pour in from all parts of the world'.[54] An unprecedented mobilization of the Sikh opinion in favour of the proposed Bill obliged the government to look for a suitable Sikh member to steer it through the ILC. After nearly 10 months, and on the recommendation of the Lieutenant Governor, Sardar Sunder Singh Majithia was appointed as an Additional Member specifically for this purpose. Majithia was Secretary of the moderate and pro-government Chief Khalsa Diwan. His nomination was, therefore, seen by imperial authorities as a way by which the modified Bill could be safely steered. In the final meeting of the ILC, on 22 October 1909, Majithia informed the members that persons ranging from a Sikh ruler to the village *chaukīdar* (watchman) spoke in its favour. Over 126 Sikh public bodies had expressly written to the Punjab Government in support of the measure. In addition, a very large number of petitions containing many thousands of signatures had been submitted to the provincial government in its favour. The Chief Takhts and Gurdwaras of the Sikhs had given their warm support to the Bill. The Manager of the Golden Temple too had expressed in its favour. 'On the whole, there has never been such unanimity over a private Bill', it was reported.[55]

Ripudaman Singh's contribution as the originator of the idea and promoter of the Anand Marriage Bill was hailed by the Sikhs all over India and was somewhat grudgingly acknowledged by the government in the ILC. He came to be publicly associated with the politically radical Sikh reformers. However, he bitterly resented the dilution of his original proposal by Louis Dane and the ready acquiescence by Sunder Singh Majithia, who proved to be a poor substitute for the Tikka of Nabha.[56]

Within a month of the passing of the Anand Marriage Act, Tikka Ripudaman Singh took initiative to establish the Central Khalsa Diwan as a counterweight to the Chief Khalsa Diwan led by Majithia. Bhai Arjan Singh of Bagrian, who was held in high esteem in the

Phulkian states, was elected as President of the new body. Apart from the Tikka and his private secretary, Bhai Kahn Singh of Nabha was present in the meeting held at Bagrian on 21 November 1909. The rules for conducting the Diwan were drafted on 28 November, and the Central Khalsa Diwan was formally established on 5 December when the Tikka Sahib donated 1,500 rupees towards its funds.[57]

Contrary to Barbara Ramusack's dismissal of his tenure in the ILC as 'undistinguished',[58] Tikka Ripudaman Singh's performance was politically mature, eloquently touching on the most important political, social, and Sikh issues of his day. His concern for comprehensive social reform, with its tangible proof in the Anand Marriage Act, appears to have raised his stature in the eyes of the reformers subscribing to the idea of national regeneration.

Before the end of 1909, the Tikka was elected President of the All India Social Conference, which shared the pavilion with the Indian National Congress at Lahore in December 1909. To support regional and local causes, the Social Conference customarily elected a prominent local figure dedicated to the cause of social reform. Only five years earlier, this honour was conferred upon Maharaja Sayajirao III of Baroda, who was foremost among the progressive princes of his day.[59] S. Natarajan, editor of *The Tribune* and Chairman of the Reception Committee, praised the Tikka for his services to the country as a politician. The address presented by Ripudaman Singh dwelt at some length on social reform as the basis of national progress. He condemned caste and untouchability and appreciated Maharaja Sayajirao III of Baroda for providing education to the untouchables. The Tikka spoke at length on women's uplift and girls' education which should combine Western and traditional learning. All along, he laid emphasis on the liberating role which the Sikh movement had played in the history of the country and which could now serve as the source of inspiration for a resurgent India.[60]

Ripudaman Singh's Confrontation with the Government

Tikka Ripudaman Singh appears to have felt that the non-renewal of his term in the ILC was deliberate and rather unfair. He believed that he was kept out by the government as much to weaken his Bill as to undermine his position among the Sikhs. On grounds formally of health, Ripudaman Singh went to England in 1910 and stayed on through 1911. Not much is known about his stay there. A local paper reported that 'this cultured modern Prince' was 'an ardent student of literature, both oriental and European', having 'a specially warm corner in his heart' for Shakespeare and Tennyson.[61] Among other things, Tikka Ripudaman Singh attended the coronation of King George V at the Westminster Abbey, and visited the House of Commons.[62]

The 'Crewe Papers' dealing with the correspondence of the then Secretary of State for India, available at the Library of the University of Cambridge, provide insights into the working of the Government of India and the British Parliament in relation to Ripudaman Singh.[63] He was not given a second term in the ILC because Lord Minto was unhappy with his 'independent' attitude as a member. In a private letter written after the end of his tenure, Lord Minto told Lord Crewe on 15 August 1911: 'Between you and me I certainly would not have re-appointed the Tikka Sahib to the Legislative Council under any circumstances.' In this letter, Minto referred to the Anand Marriage Act as 'an important obsession' of the Tikka Sahib.

Minto explained to the Secretary of State that the Tikka had asked for leave to introduce the Bill at Simla within a very few weeks of the termination of his office as Additional Member of the Legislative Council. No member of the Council associated with the government could take it up and see it through, and no other unofficial member was prepared to handle the matter. Under the Rules of Business, if it had remained untouched for two years it would have been removed from the list of pending business. About 10 months after the introduction of the Bill, the Lieutenant Governor of the Punjab, Sir Louis Dane, represented to the Governor General that it was very desirable to proceed with the Bill. He suggested that Sardar Sunder Singh Majithia should be appointed ad hoc Additional Member of the Council. Minto accepted that and directed his Private Secretary, Dunlop-Smith, to write a letter to Sardar Sunder Singh, with a copy to the Tikka. This letter was in a form that was used when a Bill introduced in the Council required expert advice. Majithia was appointed, saw the Bill through, and resigned. Lord Minto also added that Tikka Ripudaman Singh had never even hinted to the Lieutenant Governor Louis Dane that he wished to be reappointed to the Council. That the Tikka was the father of the Bill was emphasized during the debate. Thus, he had not been 'passed over' in any way. 'Whatever credit may be given to the promoter of the Act, as it is now, is entirely due to him,' Minto said in his letter to Crewe.

The Secretary of State wrote to the Tikka and enclosed Lord Minto's letter of 15 August. The Tikka thanked Lord Crewe for his letter, but he was sorry to say that this letter was not likely 'to help the general public in forming a correct opinion'. Countering the Governor General's explanation, the Tikka pointed out that his letter requesting the Bill to be moved was written nine months *before* the expiry of his term. He did not receive sanction to move the Bill for seven months. He had made no speech, reserving his remarks for a meeting of the Council at which the object and reasons of the Bill were to be discussed. Another man was put in charge of the Bill and the Tikka was given no opportunity to finish his work. While he had told Political Secretary Dunlop-Smith and Sir Louis Dane that he was willing to accept an extension of his term as a Member of the Legislative Council, Dunlop-Smith's letter to Majithia carried the implication that Tikka Ripudaman Singh was not considered fit to carry the Bill through.

Lord Crewe wrote back on 1 November to assure the Tikka that at no stage of the conduct of the Anand Marriage Bill was it the intention of the Indian authorities that their action should be regarded as a slight, or in any way undervalue the services of the Tikka Sahib. The Secretary of State shared Lord Minto's regret 'for any misunderstanding that may have obtained currency on the subject'.

Ripudaman Singh replied to Lord Crewe's letter on 8 November 1911. The Tikka pointed out that Lord Minto's explanation was not substantiated by official records. His regret was not couched in 'such words as would clearly show that he is sorry for his act of omission which caused the unfortunate incident'. It was now for Lord Crewe to see that justice was done. Lord Minto's regret, it was suggested, should be so worded as to leave no doubt in the mind of the public that the Tikka continued to command the confidence of the government, and that his not being asked to finish his work in the Council was due to an official error. In December 1911, Keir Hardie, the Labour leader, told Edwin Montagu, then the Under Secretary of State for India, that the Tikka refused to accept the apology and would have a more frank expression of regret.

The Labour Party had emerged by this time under the leadership of James Keir Hardie (1856–1915).[64] Its members had remained in close contact with the Congress and its leaders like Gokhale, Lajpat Rai, and Tilak.[65] In 1907, the Indian visit of Keir Hardie was sponsored by the

Congress and aided by Gokhale. Apart from his spirited opposition to the partition of Bengal, Hardie touched upon nearly all those political, administrative, and economic issues in his speeches and writings on India that had been raised by the Tikka in the ILC.[66] According to his contemporary biographer, the Tikka developed a 'friendship' with Hardie sometime during his Indian visit.[67]

Ripudaman Singh continued to pursue this matter even after his return to Nabha and accession as the Maharaja in January 1912. On 15 February 1912, Hardie again told Montagu that Maharaja Ripudaman Singh would not accept less than what he had claimed as the Tikka Sahib. The Secretary of State remained firm that it was neither necessary nor desirable 'to take any further step'. In fact, he had a piece of friendly advice for the new Maharaja: 'It would be much better in his own interests to let the matter drop.' Neither Ripudaman Singh nor Keir Hardie gave up. Even so, Crewe wrote to Hardie on 7 May that the government found it 'hardly possible' to satisfy the Maharaja, who wanted an 'unqualified expression of official error'. Hardie saw the difficulties but suggested an amendment in the form of a pointed question, which could elicit the desired response. The government appears to have relented, finally.

On 20 May 1912, Keir Hardie asked the Under Secretary of State for India in the House of Commons:

> Whether it was due to want of confidence on the part of the Government of India that His Highness the present Maharaja of Nabha, then the Tikka Sahib of Nabha was not reappointed to the Viceroy's Legislative Council to take charge of the Anand Sikh Marriage Bill, which he introduced during his term of membership and was subsequently carried into law?

Montagu replied:

> The Secretary of State is satisfied that there was no want of confidence on the part of the Government of India in the Tikka Sahib, who had recently been installed in Nabha as the successor of His Highness the late Maharaja. Any impression to the contrary is mistaken.

Minto's letter of 15 August 1911 had been substantially improved upon in the explanation thus offered by the Under Secretary of State:

> The Anand Marriage Bill was prepared, and introduced in the Viceroy's Legislative Council by the Tikka Sahib of Nabha on the 31st [sic] of October, 1908, and lay upon the Table of the Council for some months. Meanwhile as Tikka Sahib's term of office, as an Additional Member of the Council,

had expired, in order to carry the Bill into law, the Government of India appointed Sardar Sundar Singh Majithia as an Additional Member of the Council. Thus the *Tikka Sahib, the real author* of the measure to whom is due the entire credit for its inception and introduction, and therefore, indirectly for its being finally passed into law, was unfortunately unable to superintend the final stages of the measure. Lord Minto has expressed to the Tikka Sahib his regret for any misunderstanding that may have arisen out of the circumstances in which he was prevented from carrying his Bill through all its stages, and that feeling is shared by the Secretary of State for India. [Emphasis ours.]

Maharaja Ripudaman Singh looked upon the proceedings of the House of Commons as a vindication of his firm stand, but he remained unhappy over the dilution of his original proposal. Nor did his confrontation with the government augur well for his relations with the paramount power. Already, in his communication of August 1911, Minto had confided in Crewe that the Tikka could be 'troublesome as a ruler', and that it was 'one of the reasons' why as the Viceroy he wanted the Phulkian states to be brought 'directly under the Government of India'. It is not surprising that even before Ripudaman Singh could reach India, and merely four days after his father's death, Lieutenant Governor Louis Dane was making enquiries on whether the Criminal Intelligence Department (CID) had anything on the Tikka's activities in Europe![68]

Notes

1. S. Ranga Iyer, *Diary of the Late Maharaja of Nabha* (Lucknow: Indian Daily Telegraph, 1924), pp. 249–50. See also Bhai Kahn Singh, *Gurshabad Ratnākar Mahānkosh: Encyclopaedia of Sikh Literature* (Patiala: Bhasha Vibhag, Punjab, 1974, reprint), p. 521.
2. Iyer, *Diary of the Late Maharaja of Nabha*, pp. 250–1, 253–4.
3. Iyer, *Diary of the Late Maharaja of Nabha*, pp. 254–7.
4. Iyer, *Diary of the Late Maharaja of Nabha*, pp. 214, 258–60.
5. Iyer, *Diary of the Late Maharaja of Nabha*, pp. 170–4.
6. Iyer, *Diary of the Late Maharaja of Nabha*, p. 174. *Speeches by the Marquis Lansdowne, Viceroy and Governor General of India 1884–1894* (Calcutta: The Standard Press, 1895), pp. 125–6.
7. Lord Mayo (1869–72) had inaugurated the policy of educating princes as 'partners in the imperial enterprise' by founding colleges modelled on British public schools for different regional clusters at Rajkot (1870) and Ajmer (1872), followed by Lahore (1886) and Indore (1898). But

even some Englishmen were critical of their products who 'acquired the veneer of a public school education with its addiction to sports, some unfortunate vices, and little of the substance of a classical education or commitment to duty' (Barbara N. Ramusack, *The Indian Princes and Their States*, The New Cambridge History of India, III.6 [Cambridge: Cambridge University Press, 2008, reprint], p. 111).

8. For an overview of these acculturative movements among the Punjabi Hindus, see Kenneth W. Jones, *Socio-Religious Reform Movements in British India*, The New Cambridge History of India, III.1 (Cambridge: Cambridge University Press, 1989), pp. 94–121. For more on Sanatan Dharm, see Sheena Pall, 'The Sanatan Dharm Movement in the Colonial Punjab: Religious, Social and PoliticalImensions', PhD diss., Panjab University, Chandigarh, 2008, pp. 127–315.

9. For more on Muslim Anjumans, see Ikram Ali Malik, 'Muslim Anjumans and Communitarian Consciousness', in *Five Punjabi Centuries: Polity, Economy, Society and Culture*, edited by Indu Banga (New Delhi: Manohar, 2000 [1997]), pp. 112–25.

10. For an overview of the Singh Sabha movement, see J. S. Grewal, *The Sikhs of the Punjab*, The New Cambridge History of India, II.3 (Cambridge: Cambridge University Press, 2014, reprint), pp. 144–50.

11. Devinder Singh Vidyarthi, *Bhai Kahn Singh Nabha, Jīwan te Rachnā* (Patiala: Punjabi University, 1987), pp. 13–15, 17. Pritam Singh, *Bhai Kahn Singh Nabha: Pichhokar, Rachnā te Mulānkan* (Amritsar: Guru Nanak Dev University, 1989), p. 13.

12. Vidyarthi, *Bhai Kahn Singh Nabha*, pp. 17, 19–24, 27. Pritam Singh, *Bhai Kahn Singh Nabha*, pp. 13–14.

13. Bhai Kahn Singh, *Gurshabad Ratnākar Mahānkosh*, p. 521.

14. Vidyarthi, *Bhai Kahn Singh Nabha*, pp. 28–99.

15. Pritam Singh, *Bhai Kahn Singh Nabha*, pp. 73–4. Vidyarthi, *Bhai Kahn Singh Nabha*, pp. 66, 82.

16. Bhai Kahn Singh, *Ham Hindu Nahīn* (Amritsar: Singh Brothers, 1995, reprint), pp. 12–24. Vidyarthi, *Bhai Kahn Singh Nabha*, pp. 29–31. For a brief discussion of *Ham Hindu Nahīn*, see J. S. Grewal, *History, Literature, and Identity: Four Centuries of Sikh Tradition* (New Delhi: Oxford University Press, 2011), pp. 275–97.

17. K. L. Gauba, *The Rebel Minister: The Story of the Rise and Fall of Lala Harkishen Lal* (Lahore: Premier Publishing House, 1938), pp. 13–38.

18. Sardar Munnalal Syngal, *The Patriot Prince* (Ludhiana and Delhi: Doaba House, 1961), p. 40.

19. Punjab State Archives (PSA), Chandigarh, Tikka Ripudaman Singh to Lieutenant Governor of the Punjab, 30 March 1905, nos 668/12, Confidential 1905.

20. PSA, Chandigarh, nos 668/12, Confidential 1905, C. M. King (Deputy Commissioner, Amritsar) to R. E. Younghusband (Officiating Commissioner, Lahore Division), 20 April 1905.
21. PSA, Chandigarh, nos 668/12, Confidential 1905, Chief Secretary, Punjab to Commissioner, Lahore, 27 April 1905.
22. PSA, Chandigarh, nos 668/12, Confidential 1905, Translation of the order of Sardar Arur Singh, Manager, Golden Temple, Amritsar, dated 1 May 1905.
23. PSA, Chandigarh, nos 668/12, Confidential 1905, Prince Ripudaman Singh to C. M. King, 16 May 1905.
24. PSA, Chandigarh, nos 668/12, Confidential 1905, Memorial of Sikh and Hindu Residents of Amritsar to Lieutenant Governor of Punjab, dated 5 June 1905.
25. PSA, Chandigarh, nos 668/12, Confidential 1905, Raja Hira Singh to Major Robertson, P.S. to Lieutenant Governor, 15 June 1905.
26. Bachan Singh, a pleader of the Chief Court, Punjab, refuted the Ishtihār in two pamphlets, one in English and the other in Punjabi: *Sikhs and Idols: A Reply to the Raja of Nabha* (Lahore: Civil and Military Gazette Press, n.d.) and *Na Ham Hindu Na Musalman: Nabha Da Uttar ate Khandan* (Amritsar: Wazir Hind Press, n.d.).
27. PSA, Chandigarh, nos 668/12, Confidential 1905, C. M. King to R. E. Younghusband, 10 June 1905, 17 June 1905 and 1 July 1905.
28. PSA, Chandigarh, nos 668/12, Confidential 1905, Denzil Ibbetson to His Highness Raja-i-Rajgan, Raja Sir Hira Singh, 12 June 1905; Major C. M. Dallas to Hailey, 7–8 June 1905; Raja Hira Singh to Robertson, 6 June 1905; A. H. Diack (Chief Secretary, Punjab) to H. A. B. Rattigan, 14 October 1905; C. M. King to R. E. Younghusband, 13 October 1905; R. E. Younghusband to A. H. Diack, 20 November 1905.
29. Mary, Countess of Minto, *India: Minto and Morley 1905–1910* (London, 1934), p. 69.
30. Mary, Countess of Minto, *India: Minto and Morley*, pp. 69, 316.
31. For the political fallout of the viceroyalty of Lord Curzon, see Sumit Sarkar, *Modern India 1885–1947* (Madras: Macmillan India, 1995 reprint), pp. 100–39. See also N. G. Jog, *Lokmanya Balgangadhar Tilak* (New Delhi: Publications Division, Government of India, 1974, reprint), pp. 84–126.
32. Reported in *The Bengalee*, 29 March 1907.
33. *Bande Matram*, 28 March 1907.
34. See, for example, *Proceedings of the Council of the Governor General of India Assembled for the Purpose of Making Laws and Regulations*, from April 1906 to March 1907, vol. XLV (Calcutta, 1907), pp. 78–85; *Proceedings of the Council of the Governor General of India*, from April 1907 to March 1908, vol. XLVI (Calcutta, 1908), pp. 2, 55–6, 81, 107–8, 120–4, 141–3, 179–96;

Proceedings of the Council of the Governor General of India, from April 1908 to March 1909, vol. XLVII (Calcutta, 1909), pp. 8, 16–17.
35. *Proceedings of the Council,* vol. XLVI, pp. 55–6, 81.
36. *Proceedings of the Council,* vol. XLVI, pp. 8, 16–17.
37. *Proceedings of the Council,* vol. XLVI, pp. 183–4.
38. *Proceedings of the Council,* vol. XLVI, p. 191.
39. *Proceedings of the Council,* vol. XLVI, pp. 190–1.
40. *Proceedings of the Council,* vol. XLVI, pp. 191–2.
41. *Proceedings of the Council,* vol. XLVI, p. 185.
42. *Proceedings of the Council,* vol. XLVI, p. 193; also pp. 191–2.
43. *Proceedings of the Council,* vol. XLVI, pp. 107–8; vol. XLV, pp. 80–1.
44. *Proceedings of the Council,* vol. XLV, pp. 81–2; vol. XLVI, p. 188.
45. *Proceedings of the Council,* vol. XLV, p. 83; vol. XLVI, pp. 187–8.
46. *Proceedings of the Council,* vol. XLV, pp. 83–4; vol. XLVI, p. 189.
47. *Proceedings of the Council,* vol. XLV, pp. 84–5; vol. XLVI, pp. 179–81; vol. XLVI, pp. 181–2, 186.
48. *Proceedings of the Council,* vol. XLVI, pp. 122, 183, 194–5, for example.
49. *Proceedings of the Council,* vol. XLV, pp. 79–80; vol. XLVI, pp. 184–5.
50. *Proceedings of the Council,* vol. XLV, p. 83; vol. XLVI, pp. 124, 141–3.
51. *Proceedings of the Council,* vol. XLVI, pp. 179, 191.
52. Our understanding of Ripudaman Singh's contribution towards the passing of the Anand Marriage Act is based on the voluminous record preserved at the National Archives of India [NAI], New Delhi, under 'Papers Relating to Anand Marriage Act VII of 1909 (Legislative Department)'. Cf. K. S. Talwar, 'The Anand Marriage Act', *The Panjab Past and Present,* vol. II, pt. 2 (1968): 400–10.
53. For this and the following three paras, see NAI, 'Papers Related to Anand Marriage Act of 1909, no. 427, para 17. This was reiterated in the *Proceedings of the Council of the Governor General of India,* from April 1909 to March 1910, vol. XLVIII, p. 41; vol. XLVII, pp. 45–6.
54. *Proceedings of the Council,* vol. XLVIII, p. 39.
55. *Proceedings of the Council,* vol. XLVIII, pp. 19–21, 31–7.
56. Gurdev Singh Deol, *Sardar Sundar Singh Majithia: Life, Work and Mission* (Amritsar: Khalsa College, n.d.), pp. 86–7. The author refers to *The Prem,* a paper from Ferozepur.
57. It may be added that in 1902, Bhai Kahn Singh Nabha had participated in the proceedings leading to the formation of the Chief Khalsa Diwan at Amritsar. In 1904, not only Bhai Kahn Singh Nabha but also Tikka Ripudaman Singh and Raja Hira Singh had helped Sardar Sunder Singh Majithia in the collection of funds for the Khalsa College at Amritsar. Before the end of 1909, however, neither Raja Hira Singh, who was politically conservative, nor his son, who had marked *tat-Khalsa* leanings, was happy with Sardar Sunder Singh's conduct and loyalist stance. Deol, *Sardar Sundar Singh Majithia,* pp. 33–4, 44, 60.

58. Ramusack, *The Indian Princes and Their States*, p. 126.
59. Founded in 1887 by Mahadev Govind Ranade (1842–1901) at the Madras Session of the Indian National Congress, the All India Social Conference stemmed from the same intellectual roots as the Indian National Congress. By scrupulously excluding religious reform, the Social Conference was able gradually to create a common front on social questions and act virtually as the apex body of social reformers across the country. For some detail, see Charles H. Heimsath, *Indian Nationalism and Hindu Social Reform* (Princeton, New Jersey: Princeton University Press, 1964), pp. 176–229, 241–77.
60. Tikka Ripudaman Singh, *Presidential Address to the All India Social Conference* (Lahore, 1909).

    This address was translated and serialized in the monthly *Punjābī Bhain*, January–February 1910, pp. 21–4; March 1910, pp.11–15. As a ruler, Ripudaman Singh continued to subscribe to these ideas and support reformist and educational institutions such as the Sikh Kanya Mahavidyala, Ferozepur. *Punjābī Bhain*, March 1912, pp. 19–20.
61. 'Men of the Day', *May Fair and Town Topics*, 20 July 1911, p. 853.
62. Kahn Singh, *Gurshabad Ratnākar Mahānkosh*, p. 521.

    We are grateful to the late Mr Piara Singh Khabra, Member Parliament, for obtaining the relevant papers from the Parliament Library for us.
63. Crewe Papers, Cambridge University Library, Cambridge, 'Tikka Sahib of Nabha', I/3(12) (1911–12).
64. For a scholarly biography, see K. O. Morgan, *Keir Hardie: Radical and Socialist* (London: Phoenix, 1997).
65. Prabha Ravi Shankar, *The British Committee of the Indian National Congress, 1889–1921* (New Delhi and Chicago: Promila and Co. Publishers in association with Bibliophile South Asia, 2011), pp. 70–2.
66. For a discussion of Hardie's Indian visit, activities and interests, see Jonathan Hyslop, 'The World Voyage of James Keir Hardie: Indian Nationalism, Zulu Insurgency and the British Labour Diaspora 1907–1908', *Journal of Global History*, 1 (2006): 343–54. Because of his anti-government and anti-partition stance and fiery speeches, Hardie's programme and activities were reported in local papers. See, for example, the *Amrita Bazaar Patrika*, 25, 28, and 30 September 1907.
67. Syngal, *The Patriot Prince*, p. 14.
68. Punjab Government Records (PGR), Political Department–1913, Annual File no. 4.2 (Chief Secretary, Government of India, Foreign Department), pp. 1, 2.

    Interestingly, a companion of the Tikka was suspected to be involved in the murder of John Wilkie, an Englishman in the UK. A 'strong complaint' against the Tikka for having such 'advisers' had been sent to Maharaja Hira Singh (Syngal, *The Patriot Prince*, p. 15).

3

INSTALLATION AND INVESTITURE

Tikka Ripudaman Singh's exposure to the political climate in Calcutta and England appears to have strengthened his general stance of independence and encouraged a somewhat disdainful attitude towards the Punjab Government and also, perhaps, the Government of India. The issues raised by him as the Tikka and the contacts developed during this early period stayed with him through his reign and had a bearing later on his deposition.

Succession as a Matter of Right: *Dastār-Bandī*

Tikka Ripudaman Singh landed in Bombay on 14 January 1912 and travelled to Nabha by train. He walked barefoot from the railway station to the spot where Maharaja Hira Singh had been cremated. He invoked his late father's blessings for a successful rule and declared state mourning for a year.[1] On 24 January 1912 he held a Darbar with due ceremonies, including *dastār-bandī* (lit. the tying of turban, denoting succession) in the presence of the *Guru Granth Sahib*.[2] This ceremony, performed by the venerable Bhai Arjan Singh of Bagrian,[3] formally marked the Tikka's succession to his father's position. It was 'much advertised' as reported by the government representative.[4]

In his letter of 14 January 1912, the Lieutenant Governor, Sir Louis Dane, had offered his sincere condolences to the new Maharaja on the death of his father and congratulated him on his succession. This letter referred to the last advice of Maharaja Hira Singh for his son and successor: to remain loyal to the British. 'I feel sure that you will always follow his counsel and then all will be well with you.'[5] The

Political Agent, C. H. Atkins, had also sent a letter on 13 January to inform the new Maharaja, among other things, about the administrative arrangements temporarily made in his absence. Atkins hoped that the Maharaja would carry on 'the tradition of steadfast loyalty and friendship' established during his father's long and distinguished rule.[6]

Maharaja Ripudaman Singh reacted to the tone and the implied threat in these letters. He acknowledged Atkins' letter, thanking him for his sympathy in his great loss and for entrusting management of the state to the senior officials of the late Maharaja. He reciprocated the hope for pleasant relations, adding that he would do his best to carry on the tradition of loyalty and friendship established during his beloved and illustrious father's long and distinguished reign. The tone of the letter was rather sarcastic. It carried the implication that Maharaja Hira Singh's extreme loyalty was the cause of his death. His visit to Delhi for attending the Darbar 'told upon him very heavily in his delicate state of health'.[7] In his reply to the Lieutenant Governor also the new Maharaja referred to the precarious state of his father's health before leaving for Delhi, which became worse on his return to Nabha. Maharaja Ripudaman Singh would nevertheless strive to follow the 'wise counsel and excellent advice' of his late father.[8] The dastār-bandī Darbar held on 24 January 1912, without reference to the paramount power, however, made a very different kind of statement.

As evident from his cable from Paris responding to the news of Maharaja Hira Singh's death, Ripudaman Singh appeared to have assumed that he had already succeeded his father.[9] Even the Lieutenant Governor and the Political Agent seemed to concede this in their letters sent before the ceremony.[10] Confirmation of succession, however, was crucial to the exercise of paramountcy. Over the past half a century or so, the British had evolved a two-stage protocol for public installation and investiture, following the usual period of mourning and purportedly distinct from customary accession.[11] Even when succession was undisputed, these procedures affirmed the source of authority and provided a handle to the paramount power to discipline a wayward young prince like Bhupinder Singh of Patiala.[12] Maharaja Ripudaman Singh appeared to be well aware of the political significance of this ritualized framework of subordination, and he did not miss the veiled threat particularly in the letter received from Dane. However, he was prepared to resist the provincial administration.

After some preliminary talks with the Maharaja, the Political Agent reported to the Punjab Government that the Maharaja wanted the official ceremony of installation and investiture postponed for a year due to official mourning in the state.[13] This was unthinkable for the British authorities. On 13 March 1912, Atkins wrote to the Maharaja that a formal ceremony was necessary to entitle him to exercise the powers of a ruling chief. If his filial grief did not admit of a great public ceremony, the installation and investiture could be performed by the Political Agent. Atkins added that the procedure would be generally the same as when Sardar Hira Singh was installed as Raja in 1871. The ceremony was fixed for 27 March 1912.

On 22 March, Atkins sent another letter with an informal note suggesting the procedure. The Maharaja was quick to point out the very next day that Atkins had stated earlier that the procedure to be followed would be the one adopted at the installation of Raja Hira Singh in 1871. On that occasion only a necklace was put on the late Maharaja but no *sarpech* (a jewelled headband worn over the turban), or sword, was included. Maharaja Ripudaman Singh, therefore, wanted the earlier practice to be followed on the present occasion too. 'I highly value the kindly thought of Government to show me full honours', said the Maharaja, 'but I am contented to have those that are according to the established traditions of my house.' The Maharaja would receive the Political Agent in the diwān khāna and give him a seat on his right. Since 27 March was drawing near, and should it not be possible to follow the procedure of 1871, another date could be fixed after the preliminaries were settled, added the Maharaja.[14]

Atkins had already written to the Punjab Government on 21 March that the Maharaja was anxious that the sarpech and sword, respectively marking installation and investiture, should be omitted and that only a necklace be presented. The Lieutenant Governor, on the other hand, was keen not to depart from what had become the set procedure. He felt convinced that the Maharaja wished to avoid the appearance of 'having derived his powers from the sanction of the Paramount Power'. Atkins informed the Punjab Government telegraphically on 25 March that the Maharaja 'refused to accept' the programme chalked out by the provincial government until his objections had been considered by the Government of India. It was decided to postpone the ceremony.[15]

Atkins told the Maharaja that the procedure being suggested had been followed in Patiala and Jind on recent occasions. The procedure followed in Nabha 40 years earlier, which was apparently irregular, could not form a precedent. He added meaningfully that the government 'might refuse to give him his powers or even to install him' unless he accepted the programme. Despite the threat, the Maharaja said that 'it was a matter of conscience with him'. He felt obliged to maintain the rights and customs which he had inherited. He only wished to be treated as his father was treated and promised to exceed him in loyalty and service to the empire.[16]

Both Ripudaman Singh and Atkins were aware of the symbolic difference between the two procedures. The procedure of 1871 meant that the British representative came to the Raja's Darbar to recognize him formally as the ruling chief of Nabha. The procedure suggested now meant that Ripudaman Singh was to attend the government Darbar, to be installed by its representative as the chief, and to be invested with ruling powers. Atkins felt convinced that the Maharaja would not submit to the new procedure: 'It is rooted in his mind that he owes it to his state and to his ancestors to insist on what he chooses to regard as his rights.' The only alternative was to remove him from the state if he did not comply with the government requirements, but there seemed to be no good case to justify such a strong measure. Atkins went on to point out that the government had already admitted his right 'by proposing to install and invest him'. His only contumacy was his insistence on a procedure other than the one proposed by the government. Since the Maharaja had no objection to the sarpech and sword being included in the khil'at, the former as the badge of sovereignty and the latter as the mark of full powers, and he was willing to profess formal loyalty to the government, Atkins thought that the real object of the ceremony would be served.[17]

Sir Louis Dane did not like Ripudaman Singh wanting the Government of India to consider his objections to the procedures being suggested. The Lieutenant Governor approached the Viceroy Hardinge for orders on the subject of installation and investiture at Nabha. Dane regarded the ceremony of 1871 as 'only' 'supplementary' to the selection of Raja Hira Singh. In the Lieutenant Governor's view, Ripudaman Singh wished to avail himself of this precedent to support his contention that the chief of Nabha 'succeeds by virtue of inherent right and does not stand in need of installation or investiture'. If this was conceded, similar claims would certainly be made by the other Phulkian chiefs and most of the leading states of India.

The Lieutenant Governor conceded that the sanad of 1860 gave 'a very special position' to Nabha, but there was nothing in the sanad regulating installation and investiture. Ripudaman Singh could not set up any special claim on the strength of the sanad to a special form of installation and investiture. He must be installed in the same manner as the other Phulkian chiefs.[18] Even when he had agreed to the inclusion of a sarpech and a sword in the khil'at, he had raised the issue of his position so definitely that it could not be ignored. Therefore, Dane insisted that the ruling of the government should be that 'the draft programme must be followed'. Since the Maharaja himself had asked for a ruling of the Government of India, he could hardly refuse to accept this when issued. Should he refuse, it would be necessary to consider 'whether he should not reside outside the State or what other measures should be taken'.[19]

Sensing the drift of things, the Maharaja professed hearty loyalty to the King Emperor but continued to insist that 'the Darbar shall not be an ordinary investiture Darbar held by the representative of Government, but his own'. His contention was that the government's insistence on this point would be 'an interference with the internal management of the State and an encroachment on the rights granted by the British Government in the Sanad of 1860'. In his view, a government Darbar in Nabha would be an unprecedented event and a breach of tradition. Dane hoped, however, that 'continued firmness will result in a satisfactory ending to this unfortunate controversy'.[20]

To reinforce his profession of loyalty, Maharaja Ripudaman Singh offered 5,000 pounds as 'a tribute of gratitude and true devotion' on the happy occasion of the birthday of His Majesty King George V on 3 June 1912. He asked the Political Agent to place this offer before the higher authorities for 'submission to and approval of our revered King-Emperor'. Atkins forwarded the offer at once, appreciating this mark of the Maharaja's devotion to His Majesty. The Government of India appreciated the Maharaja's generous intentions but regretted their constitutional inability to communicate this offer from him, because his status was in doubt in view of the pending issue of his 'formal investiture with Ruling Powers'. Maharaja Ripudaman Singh showed no further interest in the matter, remarking that it was 'distressing to think that a plain question about a formal procedure pending between the Government of India and the Nabha Darbar should have interfered in my showing devotion and loyalty to His Majesty the King-Emperor'.[21]

The Maharaja Takes a Firm Stand

Already, on 3 June 1912, two senior officials of Nabha had sent a representation to the Political Agent with the request that, since the matter of the installation had been referred to the Government of India, their representation too may be laid before the government. Among other things, they pointed out that the Political Agent in his letter of 13 March 1912 had intimated that 'the procedure on this occasion will be generally governed by that adopted by the Commissioner, Cis-Sutlej States, at the installation of His Late Highness Maharaja Hira Singh Sahib Bahadur in 1871'. But quite a different programme was proposed after the date had been fixed.[22] Forwarding this representation from the Nabha officials to the Officiating Chief Secretary on 6 June, the Political Agent clarified that the procedure of 1871 had been mentioned in the Chief Secretary's letter of 11 March, but he had added the word 'generally' on his own to allow for possible necessary differences. On 14 June, the representation was returned to Atkins on procedural grounds of a different kind: In accordance with the Lieutenant Governor's order of 7 June, the representation should have been made to him and not to the Government of India.[23]

On 25 June, Atkins forwarded another representation by the Nabha Darbar, addressed now to the Lieutenant Governor. This representation differed from the earlier one only in minor detail. The basic argument was the same. At the installation of Raja Devinder Singh of Nabha in 1840, which was the first occasion of installation in the state under British paramountcy, the Agent to the Governor General had come and presented khil'at on behalf of the government. This procedure was followed in 1871. If the procedure had been changed in some other states, it did not justify deviation from the tradition in Nabha. The state has been firm 'in its loyalty and devotion to the British throne'. The sanad of 1860 clearly stated that all powers shall remain vested in the Raja Sahib Bahadur and his successors 'generation after generation and descendant after descendant, in present and in future, forever and in perpetuity'. Therefore, 'the ceremonials that had been in practice in this State from ancient times' should be allowed now as in 1871.[24]

This representation was forwarded to the Government of India by the Punjab Government on 4 July 1912. In its forwarding letter, it was reiterated that the ceremony of 1871 'must have been of a supplementary and very informal character'. It was 'useless' as a precedent. No exception should be made to 'the present procedure', and Sir Louis Dane himself could perform the ceremony. The Government of India conveyed its ruling to the Punjab Government on 19 July: 'Imperfect knowledge or carelessness on the part of the British Political Officers concerned' appeared to be behind the departure from the established principles. However, the Government of India had no record of the procedure adopted in 1871, and was not bound by the action of the Commissioner in 1871. There was no reason to depart from the established practice in the present instance. The Maharaja's right to 'ruling powers' could not be recognized until the ceremony was held in accordance with the principle enunciated by the Government. The Lieutenant Governor himself might hold the Darbar if it was convenient.[25]

Furthermore, the Government of India maintained that Maharaja Ripudaman Singh had shown ignorance of the source from which he derived his authority when he held the dastār-bandī ceremony. The later correspondence also indicated a similar kind of ignorance on his part of the principles which underlie the succession to the gaddīs of native states and the exercise of ruling powers in them:

> A succession to a Native State is not complete without the formal recognition of His Majesty's Viceroy, and even after such formal recognition a Chief cannot exercise ruling powers unless and until he has been invested with the authority to do so by His Majesty's Viceroy or by an officer acting on His Excellency's behalf. To convey formal recognition to a succession and to grant authority to exercise ruling powers His Excellency is at liberty to adopt such procedure as he considers desirable. He is usually guided, not bound, by precedent and shows his recognition and grants authority at a ceremonial Durbar. But His Excellency is bound by the principle that such Durbar as may be held must be held by himself or by an officer representing him, so that there may be a clear indication to the general public of the source from which the Chief derives his right to succeed and his authority to rule.

The actual procedure at such Darbars varied from state to state but two parts of the ceremony were essential: the conducting of the chief to the *masnad* (throne) and the attachment of the sarpech and sword, respectively recognizing succession and 'the grant of ruling powers'.[26]

Sir Louis Dane was now keen to install Maharaja Ripudaman Singh. The Chief Secretary wrote to the Political Agent on 6 August 1912 that he may ask the Maharaja when he could receive the Lieutenant Governor at Nabha to have the pleasure of installing and investing 'the son of his old friend, the late Sir Hira Singh'.²⁷ Atkins conveyed the orders of the Government of India to the Maharaja on 17 August and after 20 days sent the state's Vakīl to say that the government wanted a reply. On 18 September Atkins sent a written reminder. Finally, he received only a tentative reply from the Maharaja to the effect that the matter being important, it was still engaging the attention of the Darbar. A reply would be sent after due consideration.²⁸ The exasperated Chief Secretary wrote after ten days that Atkins should ask the Maharaja to state the date. The Government of India would not endure a much longer delay.²⁹ When Atkins wrote again the Maharaja took another 10 days to reply that he had 'to procure reliable advice' and would send an answer before long. With nothing further to add, Atkins simply forwarded the reply to the Chief Secretary.³⁰

On 28 October 1912, finally Ripudaman Singh wrote to Atkins that the delay in responding to his letter of 17 August was due to the fact that he felt constrained to travel outside the immediate confines of his official surroundings in order to procure reliable advice with reference to matters which appeared to affect his own personal status, and to mark 'the starting point for further possible encroachments in the future on the rights and privileges of my successors and descendants'. Then the Maharaja reiterated his position and hoped that the Viceroy would reconsider his decision. 'If, unfortunately, His Excellency declines my entreaty, I shall feel that I have no option but to appeal, however reluctantly, to the Secretary of State for India in Council.' Ripudaman Singh matched the categorical statement of the Viceroy with an emphatic assertion of his own:

> My contention, based upon the unalterable belief of my House on precedents beyond dispute, is that my succession rests wholly, and solely, upon my Sanad, and that the gracious presentation of the khillat by the British Government is but an acknowledgement that I am where I am by virtue of my flawless right, while its grateful acceptance by myself is public admission of my holding it under a higher power. Any interpretation but this would, it appears to me, relegate my Sanad and all that it implies to the background.³¹

The Maharaja went on to add that any other interpretation of the sanad would amount to a confession that his right and the right of his predecessors and successors was based not upon an unbroken succession by inheritance, but upon repeated manifestations of recurring official grace, each installation constituting in itself almost a new assumption and a new re-grant. 'That confession I find myself unable to make, and the Darbar shares my views.' Furthermore, he had never contested the principle that he owed allegiance and fealty to the King Emperor. What he contested was the specific form in which the testimony of loyalty was sought to be clothed. A 'newly-declared policy' of the Government of India did not oblige him to 'trifle with or imperil the cherished views of those who have preceded me and of those who will succeed me'. He insisted that 'our right to rule stands based not upon investiture, but upon Sanad'. Atkins forwarded the Maharaja's reply, saying that 'no remark or opinion of mine is required'.[32]

Defending his inherent right to succeed and to rule autonomously, Ripudaman Singh took the government head-on, making a mockery of the so-called principles of 'political practice' and 'usage' that had been invoked by the British to transgress the treaties and encroach upon the sanads. Offended by his resistance to their explicit advice, the provincial authorities favoured penalizing him, but the Government of India found it difficult to disregard the cogency of his arguments.

As suspected by Dane, Ripudaman Singh had engaged Sir Eardley Norton, Bar-at-Law, with an illustrious career in Madras and Calcutta and 'a staunch supporter of the Indian National Congress movement from its start', to advise him on the matter of installation and investiture and to draft his replies. It was during his membership of the Imperial Legislative Council that he probably 'earned' Sir Eardley Norton's friendship.[33] The procedure of installation had been a sore point with princes, especially where an adult elder son had duly succeeded in accordance with his family custom.[34] However, no other prince appears to have pursued it so systematically and tenaciously, even to the peril of his throne.

The Viceroy Concedes the Essential Point

Neither the Chief Secretary nor the Lieutenant Governor had to offer any remark or opinion on Maharaja Ripudaman Singh's letter because they had already received a new ruling from the Government of India in modification of the Viceroy's rather stern ruling of 19 July 1912 quoted earlier. Representations received by the Government of India in connection with installation and investiture ceremonies had disclosed a considerable divergence of opinion on the subject of the correct procedure to be adopted. It was evident from a searching examination of the whole subject that the procedures adopted at installation to signify succession were similar throughout India 'in all essential points'. In the case of investiture with ruling powers, however, there was some divergence of practice. The government conceded that its local authorities had overlooked that the ceremony of investiture was distinct both in character and origin from that of installation. The installation ceremony was based on pre-British customs and usages, and the procedures adopted at an installation should ordinarily be in conformity with established custom and usage of the particular ruling house. With a few doubtful exceptions, the Darbars appeared to have been held by the chief who seated the political officer on his right and offered him 'itar and pān as traditional tokens of respect and honour due to his position as the representative of the Viceroy.[35]

Thus, the Government of India felt obliged to take a comprehensive view of Nabha's representation while placing it in its specific historical context. Whatever the current practice in the Punjab, it seemed eminently desirable to revert to the customary procedure. This was applicable to Nabha as much as to any other state. 'Where a Chief of mature age succeeds and it is not proposed to withhold or to limit his powers, the installation ceremony carries with it *proprio vigore* the right to exercise full powers and no question of investiture with them arises.' Therefore, it was necessary to accede to the representation of the Nabha Darbar insofar as the following items in the ceremonial programme were concerned: the Darbar will be held not by the representative of the Viceroy but by the chief; the chief will sit on the left of the British official; and 'itar and pān will be given by the former to the latter. However, despite Nabha's contention to the contrary, and to accommodate the local authorities, the government conceded that there was no reason why the chief should not be invested with more than one article of the khil'at and why he should not be conducted from a temporary seat to the throne (masnad).[36]

Sir Louis Dane did not relish the new decision of the Government of India. He felt constrained to address the Viceroy before carrying out his orders. The essence of the Lieutenant Governor's argument was that, since the paramount power confirmed succession and conferred powers, it was logical that the Darbar should be held by its representative and not by the chief. Dane tried to show that this was no 'recent innovation' in the case of the Punjab. However, the examples he could give were all post-1871. He pleaded that an installation-cum-investiture Darbar by the paramount power was fundamentally different from a dastār-bandī ceremony, which has been held separately in the

Punjab. In Nabha 'a very elaborate and rather objectionable ceremony of this nature' was held, which made it all the more desirable that the Maharaja should be regularly installed and invested. In his exasperation, Dane even suggested that the Maharaja's succession could be regularized without any ceremony at all on the basis of his presence at the State Entry of the Viceroy into the new Imperial capital of Delhi on 23 December.[37]

The Lieutenant Governor was strongly of the view that if the proposed procedure of installation-cum-investiture was modified to meet the Maharaja's wishes, the whole fabric of the existing relationship of the Protected Princes of India towards the Imperial Government would be very seriously undermined. Other chiefs would press similar claims and resistance to such claims would be extremely difficult, if not impossible, once a precedent was established. Therefore, an admittedly British ceremonial should be insisted upon. Alternatively, the Maharaja should be invested with only limited powers in view of his great reluctance to fall in with the wishes of the British Government. In this connection, Dane meaningfully referred to the rather unsatisfactory political bearing of Ripudaman Singh when he was on the Imperial Legislative Council and in England.[38]

The Lieutenant Governor was so keen to carry his point that he enclosed a copy of the Maharaja's letter of 28 October with his own comment that the letter appeared to have been composed in Europe. Dane hammered the Maharaja's contention therein that his succession rested wholly and solely upon his sanad; he was where he was by virtue of his 'flawless right'; and that he proposed to appeal to the Secretary of State for India if his view was not accepted.

The Viceroy did not modify his decision. He directed telegraphically that the ceremony should be carried out with alterations prescribed in his letter of 8 October, which did not preclude presentation of three articles of the khil'at or seating on the masnad. It was also added that the Viceroy would not recognize the status of the Maharaja until the ceremony was duly performed. If it was not carried out before 23 December, the Maharaja would not be able to take part in the Delhi ceremonies. The Punjab Government had to instruct the Political Agent accordingly: the Darbar should be held by the Maharaja; the Political Agent would sit on his right; and the Maharaja would give him 'itar and pān; the Political Agent would then conduct the Maharaja from a temporary seat to the masnad. Atkins wrote to the Maharaja on 7 December to fix the date. The programme of the ceremonial to be observed at Nabha was drawn up by the Chief Secretary on 17 December 1912, less than a week before the Delhi event.[39]

Twists in this tale were not over yet. Atkins received the orders of the Punjab Government in Bahawalpur, on its boundary with Sind, which was 40 kilometres from the nearest railway station. On account of the delay in the delivery of the telegram it was impossible for him to reach Nabha before the midnight of 19 December, the day fixed for the ceremony by Maharaja Ripudaman Singh. Atkins telegraphed to the Maharaja that he would arrive on the 20th. On reaching Bhatinda Atkins received a telegraphic reply from the Maharaja, saying that 20 and 21 December were not suitable, being respectively the tenth day of Muharram and the twelfth day of the moon (*duādashī*). If the Political Agent obtained permission from the Government of India, the Darbar could be held on either of these dates but 'under reservation of the protest already communicated'. The Punjab Government authorized Atkins to perform the ceremony on the 20th and he informed the Maharaja that he would arrive at 1.43 p.m. At Nabha, the Vakīl of the Maharaja asked Atkins for a copy of the programme laid down by the Government of India and also whether he had been ordered to perform the ceremony in spite of the objection raised by the Maharaja. Atkins gave the Vakīl a letter, saying that he had received orders from the Government to perform the ceremony on the 20th itself, and adding that he could not give a copy of the programme without permission.

The Maharaja visited Atkins at 4.20 p.m. and the Darbar was held at 5 p.m. Compared to his predecessors and contemporaries, the Maharaja was rather plainly dressed for the occasion. But he came already wearing a necklace, a sarpech, and a sword—all the symbols of installation and investiture assiduously devised by the British. Atkins had 'to put on him those sent by Government over those he was already wearing'.[40] Maharaja Ripudaman Singh's gesture of wearing a necklace, sarpech, and sword of his own was a symbolic assertion of his right to wear these emblems of royalty. This trivialized the formal ceremony of installation and investiture which, at any rate, was being held nearly a year after his accession.

In his speech on the occasion the Maharaja expressed his 'sense of allegiance to the King Emperor' and his 'loyalty and devotion to the British Throne' in the spirit of his ancestors in general and Maharaja Hira Singh in particular. This was the only 'satisfactory' statement from the viewpoint of the paramount power. The Maharaja expressed his pleasure to receive the Political Agent 'in this my Darbar' as the representative of the Viceroy who had conceded that 'the Darbar shall be the Darbar of my State'. The khil'at presented to him on behalf of the Government of India was gratefully received 'in token of my formal recognition as the rightful Ruler of the Nabha State'. The Maharaja regretted that the Government thought it proper 'to direct that the ceremony be performed today' and not on the 19th which was the only auspicious day before 23 December. He had no alternative left but to submit to the wishes of the government. He nevertheless reserved the right to appeal to the Secretary of State for India, or elsewhere. His assent under protest was given simply to enable him 'to do honour to His Excellency the Viceroy at the approaching State Entry'. The Maharaja added that he would send in due course his reply to the message of the Lieutenant Governor read on the occasion.[41]

The exalted communication (*kharīta*) of Sir Louis William Dane was meant to inform the Maharaja that the Governor General in Council had 'sanctioned' His Highness' succession as 'the Maharaja of Nabha'. It was on behalf of the Lieutenant Governor that the Political Agent had been requested to install the Maharaja as 'a Ruling Chief of the Nabha State'. Dane referred to the announced intention of the Maharaja to follow the illustrious example of his father, and he felt sure that the Maharaja could not do better. He trusted that the Maharaja would take advantage of the 'advice' of the Political Agent, who was 'a trusty counsellor and true friend'.[42] The tone as well as the content of this message was obviously not to the liking of Ripudaman Singh and he did not want to let it pass without a considered comment.

On 5 February 1913, the Maharaja responded to Dane's communication, deliberately referring to it as a 'letter' (*murāsila*), that he signified his intention to attend the State Entry at Delhi because, in his view, it was unconnected with the issue of installation and investiture. Since it would have been discourteous to dissociate himself from the historic event at Delhi, he agreed to the formal ceremonial on 20 December. However, it was his duty to repudiate views against which he had always protested:

> I maintain that our rights under our Treaties open up, *co instanti*, our predecessors' deaths, whether in the cases of natural heirs or of those adopted. To me as an heir-apparent my succession accrued and was perfected immediately upon the death of my father, when under my Sanads I became entitled to be the *de facto* and *de jure* Ruler of my State.

The Maharaja thus protested against the assumption that the Darbar held on 20 December had installed him as the ruler of his state. 'If my opinion is well founded, as I think and am advised it is, I was already in enjoyment of a status dating from its origin to a period long anterior to the date of that Darbar.' The government were placing a novel and a dangerous and unjustifiable limitation upon the ancient and guaranteed rights of the House to which he had the honour to belong. The real difficulty of the situation was that if he advanced opinions unpalatable to authority, he ran the risk of being considered ambitious, and if he defended his opinions he ran the risk of being considered irreconcilable. After expressing these candid views, the Maharaja tendered his 'grateful and sincere thanks' for Sir Louis Dane's good wishes for his successful and prosperous rule.[43] The Chief Secretary forwarded a copy of this letter to the Government of India for information, with the comment that, since the Lieutenant Governor had already expressed his views on the attitude assumed by the Maharaja of Nabha in the letter of 22 November 1912, he had nothing further to add on the subject.[44]

In their communication of 2 January 1913, the Government of India had reasons to reject the arguments advanced by the Lieutenant Governor. The views of the government had been incorrectly interpreted in many instances, and irrelevant propositions or incorrect hypotheses had been maintained. The main question at issue was whether there was evidence to show that the installation-cum-investiture ceremony observed in the Punjab in the past fifteen years or so was an innovation or had, as the provincial government asserted, the sanction of long established usage. In matters of the ceremonial, the question was not what was reasonable or unreasonable but what was customary or the reverse. The claim of the Punjab Government that its practice was more logical from the viewpoint of paramountcy, even if valid, was hardly relevant. Therefore, the Punjab Government's interpretation of the sanad of 1860 was not tenable. 'A Chief of full age', especially whose powers it is not desired to restrict or withhold, 'comes into his powers as soon as the recognition of his succession is communicated'. Ripudaman Singh pointed out that 'the present practice obtaining in the Punjab was introduced subsequent to the year 1890 and is consequently not in accordance with established usage'.[45]

Thus, the Government of India were not disposed to take the extreme view of the provincial government that 'the Maharaja wishes to assert a divine right to rule unfettered by the approval or disapproval of the Government of India'. It was conceded that he possessed an inherent right to succeed, a right which was qualified by certain obligations. A despatch of the Government of India to the Secretary of State, sent as early as 3 March 1880, had clarified the position of the paramount power: 'Where there is a natural heir, whose title to succeed is indisputable according to law and usage, he succeeds as a matter of course, unless he be obviously and totally unfit.' It was emphasized, however, that in all cases, succession required formal confirmation and recognition by the paramount power.

Much in the communication of the Government of India vindicated the views and the position taken by Maharaja Ripudaman Singh. The main point was explicitly made with reference to him. 'The whole point at issue is whether the Chief or the Political Officer should hold the Durbar. Reasons have been given for the conviction that this point should be conceded to Nabha.' What was conceded to the Lieutenant Governor was 'the remaining items of procedure'. Furthermore, it was 'to certain extent unfortunate that the decision should involve what may appear to be of the nature of concession to a Chief whose conduct may not have been all that could be desired'. But the issue of his conduct had to be considered separately from the rights or wrongs of his representation on the subject of his installation. The Government of India would be prepared to consider any recommendations which Sir Louis Dane might wish to make in the matter of Maharaja Ripudaman Singh's conduct demanding restrictions on his powers. But there was nothing to justify 'so drastic a measure on the information which the Government of India have at present received'.

As evident from the response of the Government of India on the issue of his installation and investiture, Maharaja Ripudaman Singh scored a point not only for the state of Nabha but also for the sovereignty of the princely states per se.[46] The other Punjab states, however, were not at all keen to resist encroachments on their sovereignty by provincial authorities. Far more significant, politically, was the Maharaja's insistence on the letter and spirit of the treaties and sanads as the bases for the procedure for installation and investiture as well as relations between the princes and the paramount power. He took the risk of defying the provincial government and approaching the Government of India against the local authorities; he even threatened to appeal to the Secretary of State for India.

The Paramount Power Modifies Its Practice

The issues raised by Maharaja Ripudaman Singh assumed special importance in the changing political context in India during the second decade. The whole procedure to be followed at installation and investiture of ruling princes was revised for the future. An examination of precedents relating to states in different parts of the country had revealed so much diversity of custom that it was clearly impossible to prescribe in detail any uniform procedure to be observed on the succession of these Darbars. A preliminary and private ceremony was usually held with religious or customary rites. But in a formal Darbar it was essential that the approval and confirmation of the succession was announced by a representative of the British Government. If a newly installed chief was of full age, the installation carried with it *proprio vigore* the investiture with ruling powers unless the government saw fit to restrict by special order the exercise of powers by the chief. If a chief was minor at the time of his installation, a separate ceremony of investiture was required later to mark the restoration of ruling powers. An investiture ceremony was sometimes held to mark the withdrawal of temporary restrictions imposed on the exercise of ruling powers by a chief who was not a minor as in the case of Bhupinder Singh of Patiala.

Significantly, details of procedure in each case of installation and investiture were to be settled with reference to precedent and local custom and feeling. On any doubtful point, reference was to be made to the Government of India. The basic position was clear. When the Viceroy or the head of a provincial government was present at an installation, the Darbar was held by him throughout, and the chief's seat was placed on the right of the seat occupied by the Viceroy, Governor, or Lieutenant Governor. When a political officer representing the government was present at an installation, the Darbar was not held by him and his seat was placed on the right of the chief's seat. The main outline of the procedure was that the representative of the Government of India would conduct the chief to the gaddī if this was in accordance with the custom of the state or was desired by local feeling. Where it was customary, the government's representative fastened the sarpech or sword or both and placed a necklace round the chief's neck. After the ceremony, the British representative formally announced the paramount power's approval and confirmation of the succession and presented its formal communication, if there was one, from the Viceroy, or the Head of the Local Administration.[47]

It is interesting to note that Lord Hardinge confidentially told Sir Michael O'Dwyer, Lieutenant Governor–designate for the Punjab, that Dane was 'not at all sympathetic' towards the Phulkian states. These Sikh states had 'very great importance', and needed 'careful watching and nursing'.[48] Neither Dane nor the political agents appointed by the Punjab Government had any influence whatever with the chiefs of these states. Such 'miserable specimens' of political agents, who obviously included C. H. Atkins, could not be allowed to continue.[49] Hardinge would have placed the Phulkian states directly under the Government of India, but for his 'great confidence' in O'Dwyer.[50] On the Viceroy's recommendation, the Secretary of State for India sanctioned modifications in the structure of paramount control over the Punjab states. A specially selected officer from the Political Department would be appointed as the Political Agent for the three Phulkian States to function under the Punjab Government.[51]

This change did not affect Maharaja Ripudaman Singh's attitude towards the paramount power. Much to the annoyance of the Punjab Administration, he refused to receive a farewell visit of Sir Louis Dane to Nabha. The Maharaja's stance of defiance was heightened during the war years.

Notes

1. Munna Lal Syngal, *The Patriot Prince* (Ludhiana and Delhi: Doaba House, 1961), p. 19.
2. The custom of dastār-bandī after the death of the head of the family in the Punjab entailed the tying of turban, usually given by the brotherhood or the relatives by marriage, to recognize succession, which is generally by the eldest son. Some kind of religious ritual was integral to this ceremony. Among the orthodox Sikhs all important ceremonies were performed in the presence of the *Guru Granth Sahib* (Bhai Kahn Singh, *Gurshabad Ratnākar Mahānkosh: Encyclopaedia of Sikh Literature* [Patiala: Bhasha Vibhag, Punjab, 1974, reprint], p. 615). Cf. Barbara N. Ramusack, *The Indian Princes and Their States*, The New Cambridge History of India, III.6 (Cambridge: Cambridge University Press, 2008, reprint), p. 140.
3. Special sanctity was attached to the village of Bagrian, situated at about 12 kilometres from Nabha. It was the seat of the family of Bhai Rup Chand, who had been blessed by the sixth Guru, Guru Hargobind. The establishment had relics associated with him and the tenth Guru, Guru

Gobind Singh. It maintained a regular langar supported by the jāgīrs from the Phulkian rulers, the Sikh state of Faridkot, and the British Government. As the head of the Bagrian estate and establishment, Bhai Arjan Singh was held in great esteem by the Sikh rulers (Bhai Kahn Singh, *Gurshabad Ratnākar Mahānkosh*, p. 849).

4. Punjab Government Records (PGR), Political Department-1913, no. 152-C, 'Installation of Maharaja Ripudaman Singh as Chief of Nabha State', p. 1.
5. Syngal, *The Patriot Prince*, p. 21.
6. Syngal, *The Patriot Prince*, pp. 20–1.
7. Syngal, *The Patriot Prince*, pp. 22–3.
8. Syngal, *The Patriot Prince*, pp. 22–3. The words of advice left by Maharaja Hira Singh were 'to be loyal to the British Government and to attend to the orders received from the Government as I have been doing'.
9. As mentioned in Chapter 2, the cable by Ripudaman Singh had enjoined on the Darbar to observe all the funeral ceremonies and expressed full confidence in his father's officials.
10. Not only was Ripudaman Singh addressed as the 'Maharaja' and 'Your Highness', the letters sent by the local British authorities gave the impression that he had already assumed the reins of power. For the texts of these letters, see Syngal, *The Patriot Prince*, pp. 20–1.
11. Ramusack, *The Indian Princes*, p. 137.
12. Maharaja Bhupinder Singh of Patiala (1900–38) had turned 18 in October 1909, but his investiture was delayed for over a year because the government had found both his personal conduct and administration, ironically under the close supervision of the highly paid British officers, as 'not satisfactory'. The Political Agent confirmed reports that the young Maharaja was getting addicted to wine and women. By then, he had contracted four marriages, which too the government disapproved of. However, for political reasons, Viceroy Minto had decided to make the 'gift' of 'full' powers to Bhupinder Singh on 3 November 1910. For some detail, see Kuldeep, 'Paramountcy and Patiala, 1900–1947', PhD diss., Panjab University, Chandigarh, 2008, pp. 47–50. See also, K. Natwar-Singh, *The Magnificent Maharaja: The Life and Times of Maharaja Bhupinder Singh of Patiala 1891–1938* (New Delhi: Harper Collins Publishers India, 1998), pp. 42–6.
13. PGR, Political Department-1913, Lahore, 9 May 1912, nos 6, 291, Pol. N.S.
14. Syngal mentions that the Maharaja did not want any ceremony at all (*The Patriot Prince*, pp. 25–6). See also, PGR, Political Department-1913, letter dated 23 March 1912, p. 4.
15. PGR, Political Department-1913, no. 261, Pol–N.S., 9 May 1912.
16. PGR, no. 152-C, 'Installation of Maharaja Ripudaman Singh as Chief of Nabha State', Patiala, 1 April 1912, no. 2.
17. PGR, 'Installation', 1 April 1912, no. 2.

18. PGR, 'Installation', 9 May 1912, p. 3.
19. PGR, 'Installation', 9 May 1912, p. 4.
20. PGR, 'Installation', 9 May 1912, pp. 4, 5.
21. Punjab State Archives (PSA), Patiala, *Nabha Affairs 1912–1917*, correspondence between Maharaja Ripudaman Singh and C. H. Atkins, from 27 May to 25 June 1912.
22. PGR, 'Installation', Khan Munawwar Ali Khan and Sardar Hazura Singh to C. H. Atkins, 3 June 1912, p. 1.
23. PGR, 'Installation', C. H. Atkins to the Officiating Chief Secretary to Government, Punjab, 6 June 1912.
24. PGR, 'Installation', C. H. Atkins to the Officiating Chief Secretary to Government, Punjab, 25 June 1912.
25. PGR, 'Installation', H. P. Tollinton to the Secretary to the Government of India, Foreign Department, 4 July 1912.
26. PGR, 'Installation', Secretary to the Government of India, Foreign Department, to Chief Secretary to the Government, Punjab, 19 July 1912.
27. PGR, 'Installation', Chief Secretary to Government, Punjab, to the Political Agent, Phulkian States and Bahawalpur, 6 August 1912.
28. PGR, 'Installation', C. H. Atkins to Chief Secretary to Government, Punjab, 24 September 1912; Maharaja Ripudaman Singh to C. H. Atkins, 20 September 1912; C. H. Atkins to Chief Secretary to Government, Punjab, 24 September 1912;
29. PGR, 'Installation', Chief Secretary to Government, Punjab, to the Political Agent, Phulkian State and Bahawalpur, 30 September 1912.
30. PGR, 'Installation', Maharaja Ripudaman Singh to the Political Agent, 9 October 1912.
31. PGR, 'Installation', Maharaja Ripudaman Singh to C. H. Atkins, 28 October 1912, p. 1.
32. PGR, 'Installation', 28 October 1912, p. 2.
33. Syngal particularly refers to Ripudaman Singh's long association with Sir Eardley Norton (*The Patriot Prince*, pp. 27–30). In view of the unassailable argument of Ripudaman Singh, and its fearlessness in tone, Syngal has reproduced in full the Maharaja's letter to the Viceroy.

    It may be added that Maharaja Ripudaman Singh continued to engage Sir Eardley Norton professionally until the Government was able to twist the procedures to keep him out of the judicial charade preceding the Maharaja's deposition. See also C. Hayavadana Rao, *The Indian Biographical Dictionary 1915* (Madras: Pillar & Co., 1925), pp. 307–8.
34. See John McLeod, *Sovereignty, Power, Control: Politics in the States of Western India (1916–1947)* (New Delhi: Decent Books, 2007, first South Asian Edition), p. 189.
35. PGR, 'Installation', From Secretary to the Government of India, Foreign Department, to Chief Secretary to Government, Punjab, 28 October 1912, p. 23.

36. PGR, 'Installation', From Secretary to the Government of India, Foreign Department, to Chief Secretary to Government, Punjab, 28 October 1912, p. 24.
37. PGR, 'Installation', From Secretary to the Government of India, Foreign Department, to Chief Secretary to Government, Punjab, 28 October 1912, pp. 1–6.
38. PGR, 'Installation', From Chief Secretary to Government, Punjab, to Secretary to Government of India, Foreign Department, 22 November 1912, pp. 6–8.
39. PGR, 'Installation', telegram from Foreign Secretary to Punjab, dated 3 December 1912; telegram from Chief Secretary to Government, Punjab, to Political Agent, dated 5 December 1912: 'Programme of Ceremonial to be observed at Nabha'.
40. PGR, 'Installation', C. H. Atkins to Chief Secretary to Government, Punjab, 22 December 1912.
41. PGR, 'Installation', speech delivered by His Highness the Maharaja of Nabha on the occasion of the Installation Darbar held at Nabha on 20 December 1912.
42. 'Murasila' of Sir Louis William Dane to Maharaja Ripudaman Singh, quoted in Syngal, *The Patriot Prince*, p. 33.
43. PGR, 'Installation', Maharaja Ripudaman Singh to Sir Louis Dane, 5 February 1913.
44. PGR, 'Installation', From Chief Secretary to Government Punjab, to Secretary to Government of India, Foreign Department, 27 February 1913.
45. For this and the following two paras, see PGR, 'Installation', From Secretary to Government of India, Foreign Department, to Chief Secretary to Government Punjab, 2 January 1913.
46. Cf. Ramusack, *The Indian Princes*, p. 139. Here Ramusack erroneously assumes that it was after vociferous protests in the Princes' Conference of 1916 that the British had conceded that 'installation and investiture durbars should be held in the name of the princes and that the British representative should be seated as the chief guest at the right hand of the presiding prince'.
47. Punjab Government Civil Secretariat, 'Procedure at Installation and Investiture. Annual file 20, Deputy Secretary to Government of India, Foreign and Political Department to Chief Secretary to Government, Punjab, 20 July 1916: 'Memorandum regarding the ceremonies to be observed on the occasion of Installation and Investiture Durbars in Native States'.
48. National Archives of India (NAI), *Hardinge Papers*: 'Summary of the Administration of Lord Hardinge of Penhurst, Viceroy and Governor General of India, November 1910–March 1916, Delhi, 1916'; vol. IV, 1912, pp. 188–9, private and confidential letter from Hardinge to O'Dwyer, 18 December 1912.

49. NAI, *Hardinge Papers 1913–1915*: letters and telegram from and to persons in England, Hardinge to Sir Valentine Chirol, 1 April 1913.
50. Michael O'Dwyer was known as one of the efficient 'Punjab officers' with pronounced imperialist inclinations. He started his career as a civil servant in 1885 at Lahore and held postings in Shahpur, Gujranwala, and the North West Frontier Province. His last posting before becoming Lieutenant Governor was as Acting Agent to the Governor General in Central India. He was handpicked by Lord Hardinge for the most sensitive province of the Punjab on the assumption, belied subsequently, that he understood the people well and could handle them firmly yet tactfully. For some detail about his career and general attitude, see O'Dwyer's *India As I Knew It, 1885–1925* (London: Constable & Company, 1925).

    However, Punjabis regarded O'Dwyer's regime as particularly harsh. For his ideological position and its bearing on his administration, see pp. 87–8, nn. 1–2 in this volume.
51. Through a notification dated 1 November 1913, the services of Lieutenant Colonel B. E. M. Gurdon, CIE, of the Political Department were placed at the disposal of the Punjab Government with effect from the date of his return from leave.

4

THE MAHARAJA, MICHAEL O'DWYER, AND THE WORLD WAR

The new Lieutenant Governor of the Punjab, Sir Michael O'Dwyer, was expected to improve the political situation, but his tenure (1913–19) worsened matters. Ideologically, he was an arch-imperialist,[1] and his repressive regime culminated in the Jallianwala Bagh massacre in 1919.[2] It is evident from his *War Speeches* that he was most enthusiastic about supplying human and material resources of the Punjab for the World War I. Maharaja Ripudaman Singh was the least enthusiastic of all the Indian princes about the war.

Tension had begun to develop between the Maharaja and the new Lieutenant Governor even before the outbreak of the war. O'Dwyer was keen that the Maharaja should meet him to clear 'certain misunderstandings',[3] but the Maharaja was equally keen to avoid such a meeting. In his letter to O'Dwyer, he maintained that if any 'misunderstandings' did exist, their possible cause could be his 'installation ceremonies', which was 'a subject too intricate and important to be either discussed or disposed of at a personal interview'.[4] After a contentious correspondence for over four months, the two met in October 1913.[5] O'Dwyer expressed his displeasure over the Maharaja's installation and investiture and his apparent discourtesies. At the end of his dressing down, the Lieutenant Governor reported to the Viceroy that the Maharaja seemed to be in a 'reasonable and compliant frame of mind'. Ripudaman Singh maintained, however, that he had the right of representation to the Secretary of State regarding the installation, which O'Dwyer interpreted as a face-saving device.[6] The

Viceroy was happy that the Maharaja had given up 'his attitude of contumacy'. To encourage him to conduct himself 'like other properly behaved Ruling Chiefs', Hardinge proposed to meet him in the near future. The Viceroy also liked the idea of an amicable settlement of the Nabha–Patiala differences through the good offices of the Political Agent, Lieutenant Colonel B. E. M. Gurdon.[7]

Early in 1914 the Maharaja felt constrained to question the propriety of Gurdon's order requiring the ruling chiefs to write well in advance to the Political Agent if they wished to reside in British territory for some time. The Maharaja refused to give a written undertaking for the future that he would give 'adequate notice' of his stay at Mussoorie.[8] With O'Dwyer's approval, the Political Agent met the Maharaja in Mussoorie on 4 August 1914 (the day Britain declared war on Germany) to persuade him to adopt 'a more friendly and less obstructive attitude'. At the end of the meeting, Gurdon gave him a note seeking his written guarantees about matters discussed and considered important by the government—like prompt and courteous replies to their communications, supply of information asked for, and introduction of excise reforms.[9] Ripudaman Singh, however, wanted these 'minor controversies' to be suspended for the time being as the empire had got involved in war.[10] O'Dwyer and Gurdon continued to press for written guarantees, and the Maharaja finally replied on 14 October 1914 to say that 'guarantees' in 'matters of more or less routine character' militated against the principle of autonomy. 'I have a right to act independently in the purely internal affairs of my State.' Furthermore, 'the friendly relations which have subsisted between my house and the British Government' for more than a hundred years rested on 'the solid foundation of treaties'.[11]

Nabha's Offers for War Made into a Political Issue

Within three days of Great Britain joining the war, Maharaja Ripudaman Singh sent a telegram to the Viceroy: 'Nabha beg to offer their humble services through Your Excellency to His Majesty the King-Emperor in the present crisis.'[12] The Viceroy warmly thanked His Highness in the name of His Imperial Majesty for his 'loyal offer of assistance'.[13] The offer was repeated when the Political Agent formally informed the Maharaja that war with Austria had broken out.[14] On 19 August the Maharaja informed Colonel Watson, Inspector General of Imperial Service Troops, that Nabha Infantry was ready to be mobilized.[15] However, three days later, the Political Agent informed the Maharaja that the Imperial Service Troops of the state were not fit for active service.[16] After an inspection of the troops, Colonel Watson had already written to the Political Agent that the Nabha Regiment was not fit for service.[17] Whether the Maharaja took a calculated risk or O'Dwyer wanted him to be discredited, it is difficult to say. At any rate, further correspondence by the Maharaja with the Political Agent resulted in a stalemate.[18]

In response to the King Emperor's message conveyed to the princes and peoples of India by the Viceroy, Maharaja Ripudaman Singh addressed a murāsila to him on 14 October. Assuring His Excellency of the readiness of his Darbar to make every sacrifice that the situation might demand, the Maharaja referred to his contribution to the Prince of Wales Fund and the Indian Relief Fund (25,000 rupees in all), besides the offer of troops as mentioned earlier. He made a further offer of a contribution of 300,000 rupees to defray the expenses of 'our expeditionary forces', one hundred horses for the use of the army in the war, and his own residential house in Simla and his houses in Lahore and Ambala for the accommodation of the wounded persons during the war. This communication was sent by the Foreign Minister of Nabha on 19 October to the Political Agent, who was expected to forward it without opening it.[19]

The Political Agent, however, complained to the Chief Secretary, Punjab, that neither on 7 August nor now had the Maharaja given any information of offers made directly to the Viceroy, ignoring the local authorities quite 'deliberately' to demonstrate that the institution of the Agency was 'unnecessary'. Furthermore, he refused to discuss official matters with the Political Agent. Like O'Dwyer, Gurdon took the Maharaja's acts of commission and omission as a personal affront, and maintained that if his protestations of loyalty were considered genuine as a political measure and his offer of money and horses was accepted, he would attribute 'our magnanimity to a sense of weakness' and the other Phulkian chiefs would draw the same inference. Therefore, Gurdon suggested that the Maharaja's offer of money and horses made to the Viceroy on 14 October should be politely declined.[20]

In support of the Political Agent's recommendation, the Lieutenant Governor put before the Government of India the general attitude of the Maharaja and his Darbar towards the government and its officers. The Maharaja did not seem to be hostile to the British Government, and he was personally courteous and effable.

But the root of the evil is that the Maharaja does not at present, - and it is doubtful if he ever will, - correctly appreciate his position relative to the British Government, and till he does so all appeals to adopt an attitude suitable to a feudatory of the British Government are made to deaf ears.

O'Dwyer suggested that the Maharaja looked upon himself as the head of a sovereign state established by treaty with the British Government. He talked of 'the departments of two friendly Governments' (actually 'administrations'), and 'alliances' and 'treaties'. These assumptions explained his attitude towards the various old and new issues. Therefore, the Lieutenant Governor was inclined to follow the advice of the Political Agent 'that these fresh offers should be treated in the same manner as the offer of the Nabha Imperial Service Troops'. Furthermore, a clear indication could be given to the Maharaja of 'the real reasons which have influenced the Government of India in coming to this decision'.[21]

By this time, the Government of India were inclined to accept the Lieutenant Governor's view that the offers made by the Maharaja should be 'firmly but politely declined'. The Viceroy did not propose to send any formal reply. The decision could be communicated to the Maharaja by the Political Agent through a demi-official letter. It should be sufficient to say that 'in view of His Highness' constant and persistent disregard to their expressed wishes Government regret that they are unable to avail themselves of any of his kind offers of assistance in connection with the present War'.[22]

Viceroy Hardinge supported the Lieutenant Governor unambiguously but not without showing some consideration for the Maharaja. The Government of India were not aware of the reasons underlying the obstructive behaviour of His Highness. It would be well to give him a further opportunity to unburden himself freely and disclose his real grievance.

> Any concession that His Highness might desire, the grant of which would be likely to lead to an improvement of his relations with the Government of India and their local representatives, the Governor General-in-Council would most readily make, provided that it were consistent with the maintenance of the established policy of Government in dealing with the Ruling Chiefs of India.

Even the question of his installation could be re-examined. 'His Highness should be invited to meet His Honour the Lieutenant-Governor and discuss the situation at an early date.'[23]

Accordingly, the Political Agent informed the Maharaja that in view of His Highness'general attitude, the Government of India could not accept his offers.[24] The Maharaja remarked that he expected the British Government to be just and to make allowance for differences of opinion held in good faith and not allowed to stand in the way of his loyal offers of assistance being accepted.[25] By then the issue of offers had become a political one and the Maharaja left it at that.

About a week later, in response to Gurdon's suggestion that the Prime Minister of Nabha, Sir P. C. Chartterjee, should visit him at Patiala for a 'friendly conversation',[26] Ripudaman Singh informed the Political Agent that it was for the Maharaja to decide who would represent the Darbar and not for the Political Agent to select an ahlkār for discussion.[27] When the Political Agent visited Nabha on 11 January 1915, he was met by Sir P. C. Chatterjee along with Khan Sahib Munawwar Ali Khan, Sardar Hazura Singh, Lala Tippar Chand, Lala Atma Ram, and Sardar Bakhshish Singh. After three days' stay at Nabha, Gurdon reported to the Chief Secretary that His Highness had done very little to give a better impression but there was no evidence of disloyalty. Therefore, it was hardly fair to punish the state for the eccentricities of its ruler.

> If we persist in disregarding the Darbar's offers of assistance, a very grave stigma will attach to the Nabha State, as it is probably the only State in India which has not been permitted to assist the British Government in this critical period in the history of the Empire. The Nabha Darbar rendered loyal services in 1857 and the late Chief, Raja Sir Hira Singh, was so devoted to the Crown that although he was in a weak state of health, he insisted on attending His Majesty the King-Emperor's Darbar at Delhi in 1911, and thereby probably hastened his end.

Moreover, by then Captain Anderson had made a satisfactory report regarding the Nabha Imperial Service Infantry. Gurdon was now strongly of the view that the regiment should be sent on foreign service. He suggested that the Maharaja could be told that his offers were accepted in view of the past loyalty of the Darbar and in the hope of more cordial relations with the representatives of the government.[28] However, O'Dwyer turned down this recommendation. He preferred a personal interview with the Maharaja for 'improving' relations between the Darbar and the government.[29]

The Lieutenant Governor wrote to the Maharaja that a frank personal discussion could remove misunderstandings and lead to friendly official relations. Therefore, the Maharaja could meet him in Lahore to discuss 'the matters which now give rise to controversial correspondence with the Nabha Darbar'.[30] However, the Maharaja wanted the Lieutenant Governor to receive the state officials first to explain some points.[31] O'Dwyer saw no point in meeting a deputation of officials.[32] On 6 March 1915, the Maharaja wrote to him that the Nabha Darbar had always been loyal to the British Government. He could meet him but not to discuss any official or controversial matter. In Ripudaman Singh's experience personal interviews had not been conducive to a better understanding. In October 1913, by his own admission, O'Dwyer had used 'plain and even blunt language'. Therefore, the Maharaja wanted him to keep the controversial matters separate from the question of offers of assistance. The other matters were neither numerous nor pressing and could be laid aside for the present so that Nabha was 'permitted to render to their suzerain what little service they can at the present juncture'. The Maharaja gave the assurance that he did not wish to bring forward any other question for the consideration of the government 'during the war'. The only thing he desired was to be allowed 'to fight in the service of the King-Emperor'.[33] In other words, the provincial government should neither make a political issue of his offers nor insist on a personal interview.

As in the past, O'Dwyer insisted that personal discussion between the rulers of states and the political authorities was a recognized form of procedure which had often been found more useful than lengthy correspondence in smoothing over difficulties and controversies.[34] The Maharaja eventually agreed to pay a visit to the Lieutenant Governor in the last week of April 1915.[35] However, before proceeding for this meeting, on 18 April Ripudaman Singh wrote to O'Dwyer:

> Your Honour has decided that the line is ruled black and firm across my offer of service to the Throne. I do not desire to re-open old wounds. I have no wish to incur new wounds. And when we meet I pray Your Honour will respect my desire, if unhappily you are not in sympathy with the reasons for silence.[36]

The implication was clear: the Maharaja was not inclined even to discuss the offers made.

The interview took place at Lahore on 28 April 1915. O'Dwyer told the Maharaja in no uncertain terms that friendly relations with Nabha were based on sanads which embodied not only the rights of the Darbar, but also its duties and responsibilities towards the

Supreme Government. The historical situations in which these sanads were granted clearly showed who was the suppliant and who was the protector. To a 'request' from Raja Jaswant Singh, the 'principles of attachment and obedience' were explicitly stated as the condition of 'protection' in the reply of the British Government. His son, Raja Devinder Singh, failed to show these qualities in the first Sikh war and he was deposed in 1846, and one-fourth of his territory was confiscated. His son, Raja Bharpur Singh, showed good behaviour during 'the Mutiny', and received territories and the sanad of 1860 as rewards. This sanad reiterated that 'the Chief and his successors will never fail in their faithful and devoted obedience to the Queen Empress and her successors'. The sanad also stipulated that the Raja would exert himself 'to promote the welfare of the people, and redress the grievances of the oppressed and the injured'. Thus, 'internal independence' was contingent upon loyalty and obedience and 'a decent standard of administration', maintained O'Dwyer. The Nabha Darbar, however, appeared to claim 'a position of complete independence from, and equality with, the Supreme Government', which was inconsistent with the status conferred by the sanads. There was no appreciable change in the Darbar even after the last interview of October 1913, and whatever 'acquiescence' was in witness was not voluntary but due to the threat of retaliatory measures.

With regard to the main points raised by the Maharaja in his letter of 18 April, the government had no desire to interfere with his rights but it expected him to fulfil his reciprocal obligations. The government had no difficulties with Patiala and Jind, which had the same kinds of sanads as Nabha. Therefore, 'the responsibility for the present unsatisfactory relations with Nabha rested not with Government but with the Darbar'. O'Dwyer repeated the advice given in 1913 that the Nabha Darbar should not persist in its obstructive, discourteous, and unfriendly attitude towards the government and its representatives. The offers made by the Darbar had already been refused and if the Darbar persisted in its attitude, especially in serious matters, it would lead to 'even more serious results'. The examples of 'serious matters' were the arrest of a respectable British subject and indifference towards 'revolutionary' activities in the state. Finally, the Lieutenant Governor held out the ultimate threat:

> The permanent interests of the State must take priority over the temporary interests of the Chiefs for the time being, and where the conduct of the

Chief adversely affected the interest of the State, Government would have no hesitation in deciding that the former must give way to the latter.[37]

In other words, rulers may come and go but a feudatory state must run in accordance with the wishes of the paramount power. The personal interview could not possibly improve the situation despite O'Dwyer's impression that the Maharaja had been shown his proper place.

In May 1915, the Maharaja of Nabha approached the Maharaja of Patiala 'to resume friendly relations'. O'Dwyer remarked that the Nabha Maharaja probably feared that the government 'may take strong measures', and that he wanted 'his brother Chief to extricate him by presenting a united front'. The Political Agent reported in August that P. C. Chatterjee, who was continually urged by the Maharaja to draft contentious letters to the Agency, had resigned. There was a general impression in Nabha that the Maharaja was at heart disloyal to the government. Significantly, his minister and confidante, Lala Tippar Chand, was openly jubilant over the capture of Warsaw by the Germans and said that eventually they would be victorious. The Maharaja himself gave out that the Imperial Service Infantry of Nabha did not go on active service because he did not want his men to fight battles outside India.[38]

Intent on chastising the Maharaja, and to build a case against him, O'Dwyer resorted to the standard weapons in the arsenal of the paramount power. The Political Agent was asked by the Chief Secretary, Punjab to get 'confirmation' of the 'alleged misgovernment' and 'unfriendliness' on the part of the Nabha Darbar 'so that if occasion arises we may have, as far as possible, facts to go upon'. O'Dwyer was keen to take 'drastic measures', including deprivation of powers. When the Political Agent reported that the well-known pro-Congress barrister Eardley Norton had visited the Maharaja at Mussoorie for preparing a memorial for submission to the Viceroy or the Secretary of State, O'Dwyer thought that it might be 'a good thing to give us a basis for action'.[39] On his part, the Maharaja did not appear to have been overawed by the threats held out by the Lieutenant Governor.

The Maharaja's Memorial to the Viceroy

On 4 October 1915, Ripudaman Singh addressed a memorial to the Viceroy for justice at his hands; it could naturally not be pleasant to those against whom he was appealing but there was no alternative.[40] Now the Maharaja and the local authorities were clearly ranged on opposite sides, invoking the practice of Paramountcy in their day from two ends. Gurdon forwarded this memorial to the Chief Secretary with the suggestive remark that a British officer could inspect various state offices and institutions and find 'grave irregularities'.[41]

In his memorial of about 40,000 words, in all probability drafted by Eardley Norton, Maharaja Ripudaman Singh clearly questioned the Lieutenant Governor's stance. Briefly stating the circumstances leading to the interview of 28 April 1915, of which a record was kept by his Foreign Minister, Lala Atma Ram, the Maharaja pointed out that no previous ruler of Nabha was called upon to discuss 'questions relating to matters connected with the daily administrative work of the State'. He was reluctant to go because these discussions assumed the character of 'disciplinary lectures', interspersed with threats, which were not in keeping with his self-respect and did not lead to better mutual goodwill. Only because he was unable to accept every advice that issued from the Political Agent, he and his Darbar were described as being 'unfriendly and disrespectful'. Sir Michael O'Dwyer had no justification in saying that the Nabha State 'did not regard itself subordinate to the Supreme Government but as their equal in power'. On several occasions the Maharaja had explicitly acknowledged and underlined his subordination to the paramount power. The offers of the Maharaja made directly to His Excellency, even if considered deviation from official routine, should not have been magnified into 'a charge of insult or disrespect'. Thanks to the wrath of His Honour, Nabha was perhaps the only state in India held unworthy of contributing to what was seen as 'the greatest and most righteous war that history shall ever have recorded'.[42]

This last remark was made apparently with reference to an enthusiastic statement Maharaja Bhupinder Singh of Patiala had made a few months earlier. Speaking on the eve of the first anniversary of the war, the Maharaja of Patiala had referred to it as 'unparalleled in the history of the World'. The government was making 'tremendous sacrifices in the cause of civilization, freedom and justice'. He asserted that the whole Sikh nation was ready 'with its body, mind and wealth to serve the Government'. Bhupinder Singh invited the Sikhs to join him in praying that 'Britain may for ever continue to rule over us and may gain in power and influence day by day and its enemies may for ever be destroyed'.[43]

Maharaja Ripudaman Singh then went over all the issues to present his side of the story in the light of his own understanding. Apart from the protest of the Maharaja against the innovations at his installation, what was held against him was his 'unfortunate inability to accept at sight every piece of advice' offered by the Political Agent. The essence of the argument presented by His Honour was crisply put:

> If I do not forthwith agree, I am disrespectful; if I forthwith agree, I am contemptible as a blind obeyer; if I ultimately agree I am a coward; if I refuse to agree I am disloyal.

Ripudaman Singh felt constrained to complain that O'Dwyer had disclosed 'too much of the iron hand' and exposed 'too little of the velvet glove'. In their meeting at Simla in 1913, the Lieutenant Governor had pointed to the map of India to say that 'Hyderabad and Mysore have their own colouring, where is Nabha?' The Maharaja maintained that grievances, if legitimate, should be adjusted irrespective of the stature or wealth of a state. Nabha was 'unshackling herself slowly from the fetters of the past in order to be fit to receive and enjoy the larger enlightenment of the future', but he was constantly warned that unless he placed his reason without question at the disposal of Your Excellency's political staff, he would find himself 'either ruling with restricted powers or not ruling at all'.

Maharaja Ripudaman Singh concluded his memorial with an appeal to the Viceroy 'to review the whole situation regarding me and my State and to do us justice'. Under his sanad his two obligations were 'loyalty' to his sovereign and 'justice' to his people. At the inception of his tenure in 1913, the Lieutenant Governor had assured the Maharaja that on both these points the Government of the Punjab and the Government of India were satisfied. 'In these circumstances, I would very respectfully ask with what justice His Honour spoke to me in the terms in which he did at the interview I had with him at Lahore in April last?' The Lieutenant Governor had characterized the reply of the Nabha Darbar as worthy only of a second-grade petition writer (*doim darje ka arzinavis*) in the presence of two British officials and the Foreign Minister of Nabha. The Lieutenant Governor was not entitled to address the Maharaja in a discourteous language and an insulting tone. 'I am unacclimatised to such departures from ordinary courtesy. Against it I claim Your Excellency's protection.' The Maharaja prayed to the Viceroy to relieve him of the imputations levelled against him by the Lieutenant

Governor, and to accept the practical evidence of his 'loyalty to and cooperation with your rule'.

Reacting strongly to the memorial, Michael O'Dwyer remarked that in controverting the various points raised in his interview of 28 April 1915, the Maharaja had allowed himself 'a license of language such as has probably rarely, if ever, been used by a feudatory State in India towards the Paramount Power'. The style of the memorial was perhaps the most significant index of the Maharaja's disposition towards the government and its representatives. The Lieutenant Governor maintained that the Maharaja had an 'obsession' that it was the object of the Punjab Government to bully him and to humiliate him and that he could expect no justice or consideration.

O'Dwyer conceded that there was no precedent for a Lieutenant Governor to invite the Nabha chief for discussing routine matters, but there was no parallel to the situation now created since the deposition of Raja Devinder Singh. The Maharaja's attitude was reflected in the coat of arms employed as the crest on the envelope in which the present memorial was submitted to the Viceroy in spite of the official advice that a crown should not be used on the state coat of arms. The Lieutenant Governor maintained that the essential point made by him in the interview of 28 April was that despite professions of loyalty and obedience, the Maharaja did not give any practical demonstration of 'obedient and loyal conduct'. Several chiefs (probably Patiala, Jind, and Bikaner) regarded his attitude as 'contumacious and even disloyal'. The attitude of the state was reprehensible in the case of 'seditious gatherings' (of the Ghadarites and their sympathisers) at Lohatbadi in Nabha territory. O'Dwyer insisted that it was necessary to ensure due observance on several important points in future.

The outstanding difficulties with the Maharaja, according to the Lieutenant Governor, had their origin in his 'fundamentally wrong conception' of the relations between his state and the British Government.

> He seems to be quite incapable of realising that his protestation of loyalty and devotion to the Sovereign Power are utterly inconsistent with his persistent disregard of the advice tendered and the requests made by the representatives of that Power in accordance with established practice and the usage that governs political relations with the sister States of Patiala and Jind.

Thus, O'Dwyer and the Maharaja seemed to be in perfect agreement that the essential point of contention was 'advice'. Whereas the paramount power and its representatives went on the assumption that it was obligatory for the princes to accept 'advice', the Maharaja insisted that he had the right to accept only such advice that did not encroach upon his internal autonomy. O'Dwyer believed that it seemed impossible to oblige the Maharaja to renounce his claims and, perhaps, equally impossible for the paramount power to admit his claims. The conflict was inevitable.

In the Lieutenant Governor's opinion, the only course that would completely meet the present difficulties, in theory, was to separate the Maharaja entirely from the administration of his state and to entrust the administration to a Diwan or Council until such time as Government became assured that he had adopted the attitude of a loyal feudatory. He had been guilty of persistent obstruction and disobedience. Coupled with insubordination and claims to independence, his attitude provided grounds for interference. Significantly, however, the evidence for imputing 'any gross course of oppression or any open acts of disloyalty' to the Nabha ruler was not sufficient. For the present, therefore, other means could be tried and, if found inefficacious, the extreme action could be taken.

One of the alternatives suggested by O'Dwyer in this situation was employment of the Imperial Service Troops of Nabha by the Government of India in the defence of the empire, especially at the front; their conduct was likely to do them credit. The Maharaja could then possibly adopt 'a more reasonable attitude'. But if he failed to do so, there would be no alternative to the drastic measures suggested. A draft memorandum for the Viceroy was enclosed with the letter of the Punjab Government.[44]

The Government of India viewed things somewhat differently. Concurring with the overall position taken by O'Dwyer, his draft memorandum for the Viceroy was considered harsh and provocative in tone. It could discourage the Maharaja to listen to reason and to comply with the wishes of the government. Therefore, a revised memorandum, worded in a more conciliatory language, was sent to the Punjab Government in December 1915. With the Lieutenant Governor's permission, it could be presented to the Maharaja by the Political Agent at a personal interview. The Political Agent could also convey verbally the possibility of the reconsideration of the decision of the government regarding the employment of the Imperial Service Troops of Nabha. He should make every endeavour to persuade His Highness to comply with the 'advice' now tendered to him.[45]

The Punjab Government sent a copy of the revised memorandum to the Political Agent on 23 December 1915 to be presented to the Maharaja at an early personal interview. To persuade the Maharaja to accept it, the Political Agent was authorized to inform His Highness verbally that he should give the formal assurance required within three months. There was a possibility that the Government of India would be prepared to take into consideration the employment of the Imperial Service Troops of Nabha.[46]

The Viceroy's Memorandum Delivered to the Maharaja

After four days, Lieutenant Colonel Gurdon visited Nabha and delivered the memorandum to the Maharaja, who was accompanied by Purushottam Das Tandon, officiating Foreign Minister, and Sardar Bakhshish Singh, Agency Vakīl. His Highness was reported to be unusually calm and his manner was most friendly. He expressed no surprise or vexation at the nature of the reply to his memorial. After reading it, he continued to converse with Gurdon on general topics with perfect equanimity. When Gurdon mentioned that he would like to visit Nabha in January, the Maharaja said that he would be more welcome in February. His Highness proposed to go to Benares on the occasion of the laying of the foundation stone of the Hindu University by the Viceroy.[47]

The memorandum refers to the advice offered to the Maharaja by the Lieutenant Governor on 28 April 1915 resulting in no improvement in his attitude. He took exception to the terms in which the Lieutenant Governor addressed him, and asked to be relieved of the imputation then levelled against him. However, his memorial of 4 October 1915 addressed to the Viceroy contained nothing to justify his view. Therefore, His Highness was asked once again to show some tangible proof of his obligations to the paramount power. He was asked to comply with eight requirements. One of these related specifically to excise, another to the Nabha Mutual Benefit Marriage Fund, and yet another to the claim of Sardar Bahadur Sardar Jawala Singh, a British subject. The remaining five requirements were general: every facility should be given to the Political Agent to satisfy himself that the case of a British subject arrested and imprisoned in Nabha was being disposed of with justice and reasonable dispatch; on application from the Political Agent, statistical information should be provided; reference should be made to the Political Agent before any change was made in the Agency Vakīl; the Political Agent should be allowed to discuss official matters with the Maharaja; and, when invited by the Lieutenant Governor, the Maharaja should discuss official matters personally with His Honour.

Taken separately and placed outside the framework of paramountcy, these 'requirements' appear to be petty, but the essential point to be hammered was the power which the Political Agent and the Lieutenant Governor were authorized to exercise in relation to a feudatory state. The bogey of disloyalty and misgovernment was handy to oblige the Maharaja to fall in line with the other well-tamed princes. He was assured that 'if he frankly and fully accepts the advice, the Government of India will not be slow to welcome his change of attitude and to re-admit to their confidence'. Otherwise, the Governor General in Council would be compelled 'to secure in the Nabha State a situation analogous to that prevailing in the other Native States of India of similar standing'.[48] The implication of this understatement despite its vagueness was clear: Nabha could not be allowed to step out of the line.

Exactly three months later, and apparently after consulting Eardley Norton, the Maharaja sent his reply to the memorandum. He had expected his memorial to meet with a better fate. Under the present circumstances, there was no point in discussing any of the matters set forth in the memorandum. Therefore, he acceded to the demand that had emanated in the shape of a decision from the Government of India, 'subject to the right of appeal'. The Maharaja hoped that the government would now be pleased to employ the Nabha troops and accept all other offers made in connection with the war.

The New Viceroy's Concern for Conciliation

The policy of conciliation initiated by Lord Minto reached its peak under Lord Chelmsford, who had replaced Lord Hardinge on 4 April 1916. On 17 May, the new Viceroy wrote to the Maharaja of Gwalior, who was friendly with the Maharaja of Nabha: 'I am most anxious that bygones should be bygones, and I should like the Maharaja to know that my relations with him will be entirely governed by his future actions.' The Viceroy would not interfere with his choice of ministers but the Maharaja of Nabha could change his advisers in his own interest. This conciliatory stance appears to have stemmed also from the impression that Maharaja Ripudaman Singh could appeal to the Secretary of State for India. Continuing, the Viceroy suggested that if the Maharaja wanted to start afresh, 'he might be well advised to drop this and put before the Lieutenant-Governor all grievances which he feels he still has. I can assure you that any such action on his part would be sympathetically received'.[49]

Nabha's legal adviser, Sir Syed Ali Imam, KCSI, Bar-at-Law (later Chief Justice of Bihar High Court), wrote to the Personal Secretary of the Viceroy on 24 May 1916 that the necessity of appeal could be obviated if the authorities in India were prepared to 'review' their decision. 'Perhaps a round-table conference with the advisers of His Highness might do more to help in such matters than lengthy correspondence.' Therefore, Sir Ali Imam asked the Personal Secretary to place his letter before His Excellency. Its copy had been sent to the Lieutenant Governor. A copy of the government's memorandum was enclosed for ready reference.[50]

The Political Secretary, J. B. Wood, wrote to Ali Imam on 26 May 1916 that 'it would be contrary to practice to discuss a matter of this kind with His Highness' legal adviser'. However, His Excellency would be glad to consider any representation which His Highness 'may have to make to him, through the regular channel, on the subject of his differences with the Government of India or their local representatives'.[51] On 7 June, Ali Imam saw Wood to find a modus vivendi short of representation to the Secretary of State. Wood told him that no satisfactory settlement was likely to be arrived at 'unless the Maharaja of Nabha placed himself in the hands of the Government without reservation'. This would not debar him from making representation to get any existing orders modified.[52]

Meanwhile, Lord Chelmsford had invited Maharaja Ripudaman Singh to the Princes' Conference. He wrote to O'Dwyer: 'The Maharaja of Nabha has been an assiduous attendant at this Conference and, I understand, has taken a lively part in its proceedings. I think on the whole we were right to invite him to attend, but I have been careful not to extend to him any personal hospitality and I believe that he has felt that considerably.'[53]

Responding to the Viceroy's letter, O'Dwyer was suitably glad to hear that the Maharaja of Nabha had taken active part in the Conference and added, 'if only he would mix more with his own class and less with pettifogging lawyers of doubtful perspective'. However, not wanting the Viceroy to form a good impression of the Maharaja, O'Dwyer again referred to his 'private life' and administration in uncomplimentary terms. O'Dwyer tried to interfere even in the Maharaja's domestic affairs.[54] The Maharaja's stance of independence had become particularly galling to O'Dwyer who appears to have developed a personal antipathy to Ripudaman Singh.

On 20 February 1917, the new Political Agent, Leslie M. Crump, wrote to the Maharaja that the Viceroy proposed to hold a Darbar in Lahore early in April, but the Lieutenant Governor was not prepared to invite the Maharaja to the Darbar because of the 'unsatisfactory' administration of his state and his unconciliatory attitude towards the government. However, if the Maharaja desired to make his peace, he could ask for a personal interview with His Honour who would perhaps be disposed to save His Highness and his state from the loss of prestige involved in exclusion from His Excellency's Darbar. Crump urged the Maharaja to seek an interview at once. Crump also offered to help the Maharaja to draft a brief representation of his modified views on the list of incidents given in an annexure.[55]

The long list of Nabha's 'discourtesies' given in the annexure harped mostly on the often repeated incidents, starting with the Maharaja's refusal to receive a farewell visit from the previous Lieutenant Governor, Sir Louis Dane. Among the new 'offences' was the Maharaja's similar discourtesy to Lieutenant Colonel Gurdon on the occasion of his departure. No farewell visit was arranged and, when Gurdon wrote to the Maharaja bidding him farewell, the reply was sent by his Secretary, Sardar Bachan Singh. A few other discourtesies related to Crump himself.[56] The Maharaja felt obliged to remark that none of the old complaints had been allowed to lapse, and simple matters of omission were set down as 'deliberate acts of discourtesy'. He was keen to have 'better mutual relations' but not a personal interview with O'Dwyer. However, if Crump thought it would be helpful, he was prepared to go to Lahore. He also assured the Political Agent that he was more devoted to His Majesty's cause than any other ruling prince in the whole of India. 'I shall be even ready, as I have always been, to place myself, my men and the resources of my State at the service of His Gracious Majesty.'[57]

Crump tried unsuccessfully to persuade the Maharaja to satisfy the government. He told him frankly that his action in investing himself as ruler of the Nabha state and publishing its full account had given the impression that he desired to claim for his state 'a peculiarly independent and exclusive position'. Crump suggested that the Maharaja could refer to the recent Conference of the Chiefs as a proof of the importance they attached to the principles (of internal sovereignty and sanad rights) he upheld. In any case, the Maharaja should remove the suspicion of his motives and intentions, which unfortunately still existed. Crump added at last that the Maharaja could accept his advice as 'a matter of political tactics'. He could take 'the first step to meeting Government half-way'. A sympathetic reception from the Lieutenant Governor and the Government of India was sure to come.[58]

On 30 March, the Maharaja wrote from Dehra Dun: 'Nothing is nearer to my heart than that my relations with the Government should be of the most cordial character.' He had already given in writing that he would conform in practice to the articles of the memorandum of 1915. 'But if you consider it necessary, I am willing to repeat the assurance.'[59] On 4 April, Crump advised the Maharaja to reach Lahore on the day following on a private and informal visit, provided he was prepared 'to accept such further advice as His Honour will tender to secure further cordial working'. Ripudaman Singh now wanted to be enlightened on 'such further advice as His Honour will tender'. It seems the Maharaja was not at all keen about an interview on the Lieutenant Governor's terms. On 5 April, the Political Agent telegraphed: 'Regret it is now too late for interview to take place. His Honour will consider whole case at leisure after Durbar.'[60]

Taking the Maharaja's attitude as a personal umbrage, and assuming that he was not alone, Michael O'Dwyer had written to the Viceroy already on 28 March that the Maharaja was being strongly advised not to give way, at least for another year 'by which time I shall have left the Province, and when it would be easier for him to come to terms with my successor'. Writing somewhat defensively, O'Dwyer added: 'Two successive Lieutenant-Governors and four successive Political Agents had not succeeded in bringing him to take a reasonable view of things, the fault is clearly not with them, but with him.' O'Dwyer harped on his favourite theme, insinuating that the suspicion and jealousy which strained the Maharaja's relations with the government had spread to his private relations. He could not relish his brother chief of Patiala 'rapidly becoming a power in the land'.[61]

Concern of the Secretary of State

In the Chelmsford Papers there is a letter of 2 March 1917 addressed by the Secretary of State for India, Austen Chamberlain, to the

Viceroy, expressing surprise that neither he nor his predecessor, Lord Hardinge, had sent relevant papers on such an important matter as the case of Nabha. It could come before the Secretary of State on appeal. In any case, the matter was of sufficient importance in its possible consequences and did call for attention.

Meanwhile, the Maharaja gave the impression of being somewhat responsive. He had met the Lieutenant Governor at Simla and discussed matters with him. As recorded by O'Dwyer, statistical information was furnished by the Nabha Darbar for the first time. Reference was made to the Political Agent when a new Vakīl was appointed. The pending case of Sardar Jawala Singh, a British subject, was disposed of. The Darbar agreed to cooperate with the excise policy of the government. Even when O'Dwyer admitted that there was no further complaint on any other 'requirement' of the memorandum of December 1915, he underlined that relations with the Maharaja would ever be anything but 'difficult and uncertain'. He went on in a similar vein, pointing out that when there was a bomb blast at Jaito (in Nabha territory) in August 1917 and the Punjab Government offered the services of an officer of the Criminal Intelligence Department, the offer was declined by the Darbar. Furthermore, the Maharaja addressed himself directly to the Lieutenant Governor of the United Provinces for the purchase of property in that province. To pre-empt improvement in the Supreme Government's view of the Maharaja, O'Dwyer insinuated that his 'perverse disposition towards Government was the result of aberration amounting to mental derangement'.[62]

The India Office viewed things differently. They observed that the Maharaja had spoken with ability and force on various issues at the Chiefs' Conference, and an amendment proposed by the Maharaja was adopted by the Conference. Averse to 'compulsion' and 'inconvenient political obligations',[63] the Maharaja left the impression that unlike most other princes he thought for himself.

Apparently, much to his chagrin, O'Dwyer felt constrained to recommend through his Chief Secretary that the following offers made by the Maharaja could be accepted by the Government of India: (*a*) a sum of 300,000 rupees towards the expenses of the Expeditionary Forces, (*b*) 100 horses from his stables for the use of the army in the war, and (*c*) the use of his houses in Simla, Ambala, and Lahore for accommodation of the wounded in the war. The decision regarding the employment of the Imperial Service Troops of Nabha could be reconsidered. For the present, at least, 'the relations between the Darbar and Government have been put on a footing more satisfactory than at any time since the Maharaja's installation'.[64] The Viceroy sent a telegram to the Secretary of State on 27 October, recommending that the offers of the Maharaja of Nabha should be accepted.[65] On 2 November, the Political Secretary wrote to the Punjab Government that the Maharaja could be informed that his last two offers had been accepted, and the offer of 300,000 rupees had been referred to His Majesty's Government.[66] On 8 January 1918, when the papers regarding the relations of the Government of India with the Maharaja of Nabha were placed before the King Emperor, 'His Majesty was glad to note that the relations between the Darbar and the Government had been placed upon a more satisfactory footing'.[67]

On 12 June 1918, the Military Minister of the Nabha state was informed that the Nabha Imperial Service Infantry was required to entrain on 20 June 1918 to join the unit under Captain G. B. Anderson.[68] By this time, however, the war was almost over.[69]

Nabha had the distinction of having no honours, titles, or rewards after the war.[70] This was a measure of the Maharaja's calculated indifference to the expectations of the bureaucracy. He refused to be overawed by one of the strongest Lieutenant Governors of the Punjab. In fact, his tactics kept Sir Michael O'Dwyer on tenterhooks. It may be relevant to point out that the most outstanding contribution to the war was made by Patiala in men, money, materials, and general support. The state received great honours in large numbers. Maharaja Bhupinder Singh was made a GBE and a GCSI and granted the honorary rank of Major General. To his existing salute of 19 guns, 2 more were added as a personal distinction.[71] All this was in glaring contrast to the lukewarm response of Ripudaman Singh to the war and the annoyance of the government with him.

Notes

1. Michael O'Dwyer's political ideology appears to have been inextricably linked to the 'Punjab School' of administration, founded on a philosophy of benevolent personal rule. Invoking the Defence of India Act, the Punjab regime under O'Dwyer was particularly harsh and unrelenting towards all manner of opposition, let alone the Ghadarite revolutionaries. He supported the Jallianwala Bagh massacre to put down the 'Punjab Rebellion of 1919'. See Thomas R. Metcalf, *Ideologies of the Raj*, The New

Cambridge History of India, III.4 (New Delhi: Cambridge University Press, 2010, reprint), p. 228.

Significantly, after his return to England, O'Dwyer became a central figure in the passionate mobilization of the extreme right wing of the Tory party in opposition to Indian political reform. It was he who founded the Indian Empire Society in 1930 to oppose the Montagu–Chelmsford and subsequent reforms. He also played a key role in similar organizations like the India Defence League. Incidentally, Winston Churchill later became the principal figurehead of this movement. For some detail, see Carl Bridge, *Holding India to the Empire* (London: Oriental University Press, 1986), p. 48–9, 93, 100–1.

2. The Jallianwala Bagh massacre at Amritsar in which hundreds of unarmed and unsuspecting villagers and local people were killed by General Reginald Dyer, called in and backed by Michael O'Dwyer, was the crowning act of the cast of mind represented by the duo. O'Dwyer spent much of his time afterwards, both in India and the UK, defending the unrepentant Dyer. O'Dwyer first tried to have him exonerated and reinstated, and after his death led another campaign to build a memorial to him (Metcalf, *Ideologies of the Raj*, pp. 228–30). For details, see Nigel Collet, *The Butcher of Amritsar: General Reginald Dyer* (London: Hambledon Continum, 2005).

3. Punjab State Archives (PSA), Patiala, *Nabha Affairs 1912–17*, M. F. O'Dwyer to Maharaja Ripudaman Singh, 28 July 1913; A. Elliott to Maharaja Ripudaman Singh, 29 July 1913.

4. PSA, *Nabha Affairs 1912–17*, Maharaja Ripudaman Singh to Major Elliott, 13 August 1913; Maharaja Ripudman Singh to Sir Michael O'Dwyer, 13 August 1913.

5. Punjab Government Records (PGR), Political Department–1914, Annual File no. 30, 'General Attitude of the Maharaja of Nabha and the Darbar towards Government and its officers', draft letter of the Lieutenant Governor to be sent to Maharaja Ripudaman Singh.

6. National Archives of India (NAI), *Hardinge Papers*, 1913, vol. VI, pp. 86, 353–4.

7. NAI, *Hardinge Papers*, 1913, vol. VI, pp. 150–7, no. 232.

8. PGR, Political Department-1914, Annual File no. 30, 'General Attitude', B. E. M. Gurdon, Political Agent, to Chief Secretary to Government, Punjab, 19 June 1914.

9. PGR, Political Department-1914, Chief Secretary to Government, Punjab to B. E. M. Gurdon, 7 August 1914. Also, *Nabha Affairs 1912–17*, B. E. M. Gurdon's note dated 4 August 1914.

10. *Nabha Affairs 1912–17*, Maharaja Ripudaman Singh to Lt Col Gurdon, 25 August 1914. Also, B. E. M. Gurdon to Maharaja Ripudaman Singh, 4 September 1914; Maharaja Ripudaman Singh to Colonel Gurdon, 17 September 1914.

11. *Nabha Affairs 1912–17*, Maharaja Ripudaman Singh to Colonel Gurdon, 14 October 1914.
12. *Nabha Affairs, 1912–17*, express telegram of Maharaja of Nabha to the Viceroy, dated 7 August 1914.
13. *Nabha Affairs, 1912–17*, telegram from the Viceroy to Maharaja of Nabha, dated 8 August 1914.
14. *Nabha Affairs, 1912–17*, telegram from the Political Agent to Maharaja of Nabha dated 13 August 1914.
15. *Nabha Affairs, 1912–17*, express telegram from Maharaja of Nabha to Colonel Watson, dated 19 August 1914.
16. *Nabha Affairs, 1912–17*, B. E. M. Gurdon to Maharaja Ripudaman Singh, 22 August 1914.
17. *Nabha Affairs, 1912–17*, Inspector General of Imperial Service Troops to the Political Agent, Phulkian States, 20 August 1914.
18. *Nabha Affairs, 1912–17*, Maharaja Ripudaman Singh to Colonel Gurdon, 28 August 1914; B. E. M. Gurdon to Maharaja Ripudaman Singh, 6 September 1914; Atma Ram to B. E. M. Gurdon, 12 September 1914.
19. PGR, Political Department–1914, Annual File no. 30, 'General Attitude', B. E. M. Gurdon to Chief Secretary to Government, Punjab, 27 October 1914.
20. PGR, Political Department–1914, Annual File no. 30, 'General Attitude', Nos 30, 31, 36.
21. PGR, Political Department–1914, Annual File no. 30, 'General Attitude', Chief Secretary to Government, Punjab, to Political Secretary to Government of India, 28 November 1914.
22. PGR, Political Department–1914, Annual File no. 30, 'General Attitude', Political Secretary to the Government of India, to Chief Secretary to Government, Punjab, 4 December 1914, para 2.
23. PGR, Political Department–1914, Annual File no. 30, 'General Attitude', para 3.
24. *Nabha Affairs 1912–17*, B. E. M. Gurdon to Maharaja Ripudaman Singh, 16 December 1914.
25. *Nabha Affairs, 1912–17*, Maharaja Ripudaman Singh to Colonel Gurdon, 24 December 1914.
26. *Nabha Affairs, 1912–17*, B. E. M. Gurdon to Maharaja Ripudaman Singh, 26 December 1914.
27. *Nabha Affairs, 1912–17*, Maharaja Ripudaman Singh to Colonel Gurdon, 30 December 1914.
28. PGR, Political Department–1915, 'General Attitude', note by B. E. M. Gurdon on his visit to Nabha from 11 to 18 January 1915; B. E. M. Gurdon to Chief Secretary to Government, Punjab, 15 January 1915.
29. PGR, Political Department–1915, Chief Secretary to Government, Punjab to the Political Agent, Phulkian States, 30 January 1915.

30. *Nabha Affairs, 1912–17*, M. F. O'Dwyer to Maharaja Ripudaman Singh, 30 January 1915.
31. *Nabha Affairs, 1912–17*, Maharaja Ripudaman Singh to Colonel Gurdon, 18 February 1915, 2 March 1915.
32. *Nabha Affairs, 1912–17*, B. E. M. Gurdon to Maharaja Ripudaman Singh, 2 March 1915.
33. *Nabha Affairs, 1912–17*, Maharaja Ripudaman Singh to Sir Michael Franscis O'Dwyer, 6 March 1915.
34. *Nabha Affairs, 1912–17*, M. F. O'Dwyer to Maharaja Ripudaman Singh, 17 March 1915.
35. *Nabha Affairs, 1912–17*, Maharaja Ripudaman Singh to Colonel Gurdon, 30 March 1915; B. E. M. Gurdon to Maharaja Ripudaman Singh, 15 April 1915.
36. *Nabha Affairs, 1912–17*, Maharaja Ripudaman Singh to Sir Michael Francis O'Dwyer, 18 April 1915.
37. *Nabha Affairs, 1912–17*, note by His Honour the Lieutenant Governor on his interview with the Maharaja of Nabha at Lahore, 28 April 1915.
38. PGR, Political Department–1916, Annual File no. 2, extracts from the confidential diary of the Political Agent from May to August 1915.
39. PGR, Political Department–1916, Annual File no. 2, extract from the confidential diary of the Political Agent, 31 August 1915, and remarks of E. D. Maclagan and M. F. O'Dwyer.
40. *Nabha Affairs, 1912–17*, Maharaja Ripudaman Singh to the Governor General of India, 4 October 1915.
41. PGR, Political Department–1916, Annual File 2, p. 26.
42. *Nabha Affairs 1912–17*, Maharaja Ripudaman Singh's Memorial to the Viceroy, pp. 47–71.
43. For Patiala's enthusiastic response to war effort, see K. Natwar-Singh, *The Magnificent Maharaja* (New Delhi: Harper Collins Publishers India, 1998), pp. 64–74.
44. PGR, Political Department–1916, Annual File no. 2, Chief Secretary to Government, Punjab, to Political Secretary, Government of India, 11 November 1915.
45. PGR, Political Department–1916, Political Secretary to Government of India to Chief Secretary to Government, Punjab, 9 December 1915, with the revised memorandum.
46. PGR, Political Department–1916, Chief Secretary to Government, Punjab to the Political Agent, 23 December 1915.
47. PGR, Political Department–1916, B. E. M. Gurdon to Chief Secretary to Government, Punjab, 30 December 1915.
48. PGR, Political Department–1916, Enclosure II, Draft Memorandum for Presentation to His Highness.

49. India Office Records (IOR) (microfilm), MSS Eur E 264/17, Chelmsford to the Maharaja Scindia of Gwalior, 17 May 1916; letter of the Maharaja of Gwalior, 31 May 1916; telegram dated 2 June 1916; letters of 5 June 1916 and 24 June 1916.
50. IOR (microfilm), MSS Eur E 264/17, Sir Syed Ali Imam to the Personal Secretary to the Viceroy.
51. IOR (microfilm), MSS Eur E 264/17, Political Secretary to Sir Ali Imam, 26 May 1916.
52. IOR (microfilm), MSS Eur E 264/17, Political Secretary to the Personal Secretary to the Viceroy, 7 June 1916, with a note on his meeting with Sir Ali Imam.
53. IOR (microfilm), MSS Eur E 264/17, Chelmsford to Sir Michael O'Dwyer, 3 November 1916.
54. IOR (microfilm), MSS Eur E 264/17, M. F. O'Dwyer to Lord Chelmsford, 5 November 1916.
55. *Nabha Affairs, 1912–17*, L. M. Crump to Maharaja Ripudaman Singh, 28 February 1917.
56. *Nabha Affairs, 1912–17*, note enclosed with the Political Agent's letter of 28 February 1917 on 'Nabha's Discourtesies'.
57. *Nabha Affairs, 1912–17*, Maharaja Ripudaman Singh to L. M. Crump, 7 March 1917.
58. *Nabha Affairs, 1912–17*, L. M. Crump to Maharaja Ripudaman Singh, 9 March 1917.
59. *Nabha Affairs, 1912–17*, Maharaja Ripudaman Singh to the Political Agent, 30 March 1917.
60. *Nabha Affairs, 1912–17*, telegrams from L. M. Crump to Maharaja of Nabha, dated 2, 4, and 5 April 1917; telegraphic reply of Maharaja Ripudaman Singh.
61. IOR (microfilm), R/1/19/602, Foreign and Political Department. Proceedings February 1918, Nos 1–18, extract from a letter from Sir Michael O'Dwyer to the Viceroy, 28 March 1917.
62. IOR (microfilm), L/P and S/10/217, Reel no. 22, 164 (Political), 28 November 1917 (confidential).
63. IOR (microfilm), L/P and S/10/217, Reel no. 33, 'Nabha State: Steps taken by the Maharaja to meet the requirements of Government of India'.
64. IOR (microfilm), L/P and S/10/217, J. P. Thompson, Chief Secretary, Punjab to the Political Secretary to the Government of India, 11 October 1917.
65. IOR (microfilm), L/P and S/10/217, telegram from the Viceroy to India Office, dated 27 October 1917.
66. IOR (microfilm), L/P and S/10/217, Political Secretary to Government of India to J. P. Thompson, Memorandum no. 20 D/C, 2 November 1917.

67. IOR (microfilm), L/P and S/10/217, Under Secretary of State for India to Government of India, 8 January 1918.
68. PSA, Patiala, Imperial Service Troops 8 Front, Vol. VI, Miscellaneous Papers, with File 90A.
69. PSA, Patiala, Administrator's Office, Nabha State Records, File no. 28. The First Akal Infantry of Nabha was employed on active service in the Third Afghan War in 1919.
70. For Indian response to World War I, see *India's Contribution to the Great War* (Calcutta: Government of India, 1923), and M. S. Leigh, *The Punjab and the War* (Lahore: Punjab Government, 1922).
71. Leigh, *The Punjab and the War*, Appendices A, D, pp. 83–5, 181–2.

5

GOVERNMENT AND POLITICS

The administration of Nabha under Maharaja Hira Singh was comparable with the well-administered districts in British Punjab. Maharaja Ripudaman Singh made some changes in the structure and functioning of administration in view of the changing situation in his time. His attitude towards the paramount power and his relations with the Phulkian chiefs were influenced by his stance of independent thinking and personal dignity. His belief in the internal sovereignty of Nabha influenced his interpretations of the treaties and sanads. His strong sense of patriotism was reflected in his general sympathy with the anti-British movements. His self-image was reflected in his identification with the radical Sikh reformers, culminating in the movement for the reform of Gurdwaras.

Administration under Maharaja Hira Singh

The administration of Nabha under Maharaja Hira Singh combined features of British administration with the traditional and was generally seen as effective and humane. Apart from cultivating good relations with the representatives of the paramount power, Hira Singh took personal interest in the army, justice, law and order, revenue, administration, *dharmarth* (charitable grants), education, and buildings. The diary (*roznāmcha*) he kept in Urdu of his daily transactions reveals the regularity with which he attended to the affairs of the state and the attention he gave to detail. As a record of precedents, these roznāmchas also served as the source of rules.[1] The administrative manual of the Nabha Darbar was published in 1893 in five volumes, dedicated to Tikka Ripudaman Singh.[2]

Effective administration in the state of Nabha was especially challenging because its territories, covering nearly 1,000 square kilometres, were widely scattered. Its three large pockets, called Phul, Amloh, and Bawal, constituted three units of administration called *nizāmats*. Around Phul and Amloh there were chunks of 250 square kilometres each. Around Bawal, there was a chunk of 200 square kilometres. The remaining territory, more than one-fourth, consisted of a dozen isolated pockets, interspersed with the British territories and those of the other Phulkian states (Map 5.1). The capital, which gave its name to the state, was located in the Nizāmat of Amloh. All the important offices of the state were in the capital town of Nabha.[3]

The administration of the nizāmat was under a Nāzim (governor), supported by two deputies called Naib Nāzims. Together with the Tahsīldārs (officers in charge of a *tahsīl*), they were responsible for law and order, and the collection of revenues. They performed some judicial functions as well. Each nizāmat was divided into a number of police circles (*thānas*). There were five police circles in Phul, and three each in Amloh and Bawal. An outpost (*chaukī*) at Badagaon or Deh Kalan had the village Pehdani alone under its jurisdiction with a small police post stationed there. The police department was under the Bakhshī, and below him was a superintendent. In each thāna there was a deputy inspector of police, with a sergeant, a *dafedār* (cavalry sergeant), a tracker, two mounted men, and eleven constables. The officers and men in the police stations worked under the instructions of the magistrates. There was an auxiliary (*imdādī*) force stationed at Nabha to replace casualties or fill vacancies in the thānas.[4]

There was a regular hierarchy in judicial administration, with clearly laid down jurisdiction and powers of the Nāzims, the Naib Nāzim, and the Tahsīldār. There was a Sadr Adālat at Nabha. Above the Sadr Adālat was the Ijlās-i Khās, which was presided over by the Maharaja and had the absolute power to impose any sentence: fine, confiscation of property, banishment from the state, imprisonment, or death. For civil cases, there was a Munsif in each nizāmat, with appeal to the Nazim's court. In Nabha, civil cases went to the Naib Adālatī, with appeal to the Sadr Adālat.

For revenue purposes, the nizāmats were divided into *parganas*. The term 'Tahsīldār' was used for one of the two Naib Nāzims of a nizāmat. The smallest unit of administration was the village, with

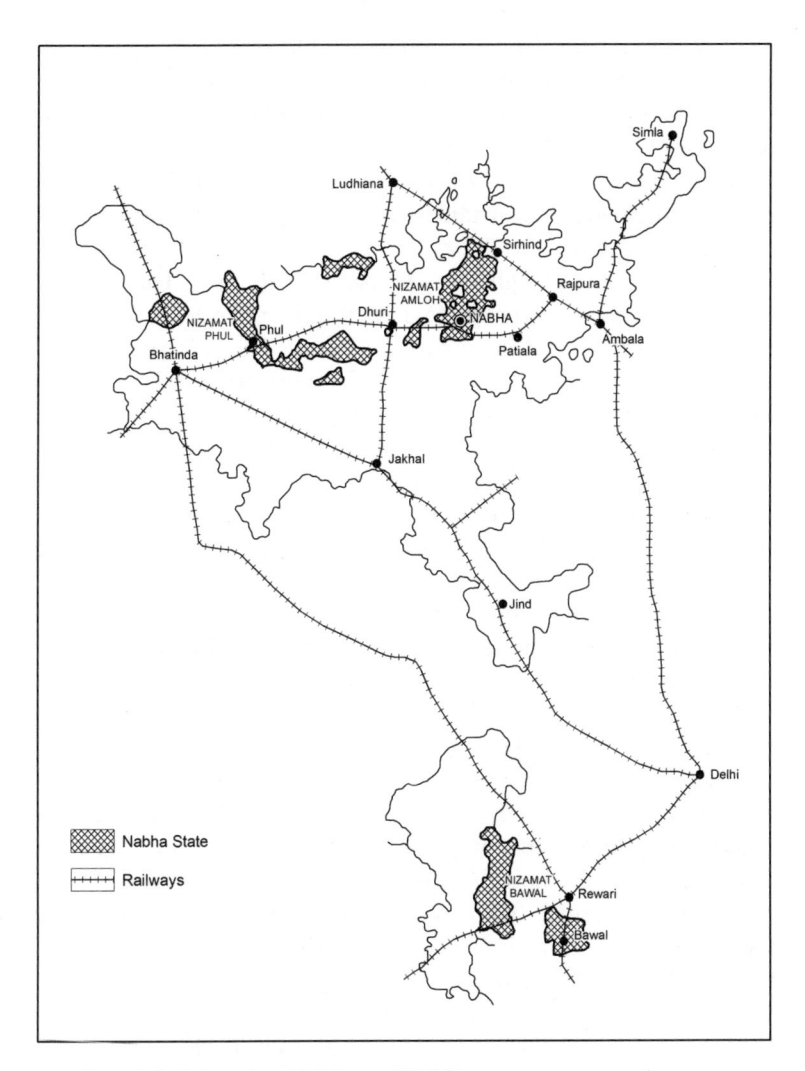

Map 5.1 Administrative Divisions of Nabha

Source: Adapted from Map 3, in Kuldeep, 'Modes of Colonial Control: A Case Study of Nabha under Maharaja Hira Singh, 1871–1911', MPhil dissertation, Panjab University, Chandigarh, 1999.

its headmen. The state had 12 Zaildārs (circle officers) appointed on the basis of local influence, personal ability, and service to the state. The Zaildār's duty was to assist the state officials in the prevention and detection of crime, to convey the orders of the government to the residents of his *zail* (circle), to protect public buildings and boundary pillars and to give notice when they needed repair, to look after indigent widows and orphans, and to act as the local commissioner in petty cases concerning land and wells.

Within a few years of his accession, Raja Hira Singh introduced regular settlement in the nizāmats for a fixed period on the pattern of the British Revenue Law. The entire land under cultivation was measured and a record of rights was prepared in all cases. The interests of traditional agriculturists were sought to be protected by the state through a measure that anticipated the Punjab Alienation of Land Act of 1900 by about a decade.[5] It forbade the mortgage or sale of land to Khatris, Brahmans, and the trading classes who were not cultivators themselves. This order was amended in 1892 to confine alienation of land within the caste of the cultivators.

Despite variations in fertility and natural resources, there was a substantial increase of revenue from land. Other sources of income included the sale of stamped sheets manufactured at Nabha itself, court fees, the sale of liquor prepared in the state distillery and, the sale of opium and imported drugs. The postal service yielded some income, and octroi was collected at places like Jaito, Phul, and Nabha.

The state capital came to have a municipal committee consisting of three nominated members from amongst the important traders and shopkeepers and a paid official member. They were under the control of a magistrate, and were assisted by a clerk and a number of *dāroghas* (superintendents). The octroi department was under the charge of an officer whose dāroghas examined all articles brought into the town. As in British India, collections from octroi were used to pay the municipal staff, the local police, and the conservancy and sanitation establishment of Nabha.

There was a popular impression that Maharaja Hira Singh believed that he would live as long as he went on building. Apart from his new residence, the 'Hira Mahal', the Lansdowne Hospital, and the *samādh* (structure over cremation spot of an important person) of Raja Bhagwan Singh in Nabha, he constructed a large number of buildings in the Nabha Estate at Simla. He strengthened the Public Works Department of the state with separate officers for buildings and roads, carrying out repairs, and superintendence of public works in the state. Maharaja Hira Singh purchased two residential buildings in Lahore that came to be known as 'Nabha House' and 'Lal Kothi'.

The Lansdowne Hospital in Nabha, built to commemorate the visit of Lord Lansdowne in 1890, had two wings, one each for male and female patients. Free food was given to in-patients. There was a military hospital in the cantonment at Nabha. In 1880, Yunānī dispensaries were established at Nabha, Amloh, Phul, and Bawal, each with a physician (*hakīm*), a surgeon (*jarrāh*), and a compounder. Allopathic dispensaries were established at these places in 1890. Still later, such dispensaries were established also at Dhanaula, Lohatbadi, Jaito, Kanti, and Kanina. All the medical institutions were under the control of the Chief Medical Officer (CMO) of Nabha. He was associated with jails too. The health of the prisoners was his chief concern. On the pattern of district jails in the British territory, prisoners were employed in carpet-weaving and paper-making.[6] The jail superintendent had strict orders to bathe them every day and to clothe them with clean garments.

Maharaja Hira Singh took great interest in education. A primary school in Nabha was raised to the middle standard in 1880, and a High School in 1888. It had fifteen teachers. Single-teacher schools were opened at Phul, Amloh, Dhanaula, Lohatbadi, and Bawal. The school at Bawal became a middle school. Two special schools were established by the state, one in the cantonment of Nabha and the other at the village Chotian. In the former, all the students received free board, clothing, and books. The school at Chotian was meant for the sons of agriculturists who received free education up to the middle standard. The Maharaja was interested in the education of girls. In a primary school at Nabha, a lady teacher taught Gurmukhi and Hindi to only girls.

Maharaja Hira Singh was keenly interested in the army of the state. The flower of the army was its trained infantry, created for imperial service in 1888 and much appreciated by the British for its smart turnout and effective service. The Imperial Service Troops of Nabha saw service in several theatres. In addition, the state maintained small units of cavalry, infantry, and artillery.

On the whole, the administration of Maharaja Hira Singh was a judicious mixture of the traditional and the modern. The Maharaja closely supervised every department of his administration. His initiatives were informed by his keenness to give a sound and caring administration to all his subjects. Hira Singh's administration was highly appreciated by the paramount power. In Lord Curzon's time the Political Agent was instructed not to interfere in the functioning of the state during the Maharaja's lifetime.

Changes Introduced by Maharaja Ripudaman Singh

At the end of the reign of Maharaja Hira Singh in 1911, there was an advisory council of three ministers—Khan Munawwar Ali Khan, Lala Nathu Ram, and Sardar Hazura Singh—representing a cross section of the state subjects. At the end of Maharaja Ripudaman Singh's rule in 1923, there was a Prime Minister (also called the Diwān) and six departments under separate ministers. The Home Department looked after the affairs of the police, jails, municipality, public works, and hospitals. The Foreign Department dealt with irrigation and post offices as well as foreign affairs. The Finance Department dealt with accounts, treasuries, *toshākhāna* (storehouse), state banks, revenue and settlement, education, and stamps. The Department of Commerce and Industries looked after the grain markets (*mandīs*), octroi, cattle fairs, excise and opium, cotton ginning, and other factories in the state. The Household Department (Khāngī Kārobārī) looked after the garages, stables, stores, gardens, forests, saloons, dairy farming, etc. The Military Department dealt only with military matters.

Among the important officials (ahlkārs), whom the Chief Secretary of the Punjab regarded as 'the old lot', were Lala Tippar Chand as the Chief Secretary in 1915, Lala Atma Ram as the Deputy Foreign Minister, and Sardar Bakhshish Singh as the state's Vakīl (representative) at the office of the Political Agent. The Foreign Minister, Lala Bishan Das, was the old tutor of the Maharaja. Sardar Gurdial Singh, who was Secretary of the Maharaja, was his old playmate. Sir P. C. Chatterjee, a retired Judge of the Punjab Chief Court, was appointed Prime Minister in 1914. A State Council was created with him as President, Khan Munawwar Ali Khan as its Senior Member, and Sardar Hazura Singh as its Junior Member. Among the other well-known persons brought from outside the state, and at the recommendation of Madan Mohan Malaviya, was Purushottam Das Tandon who later became President of the Indian National Congress. In 1917, D. M. Narasinga Rao was the Prime Minister, with Lala Nathu Ram, B. N. Sen, Lala Bishan Das, Lala Atma Ram, and Sardar Gurdial Singh as ministers.[7] On the whole, Maharaja Ripudaman Singh reorganized his administration with the help of Prime Ministers from outside but without displacing the individuals who had served the state. Some of their descendants were also employed in high offices.[8]

In 1918, Ripudaman Singh introduced a certain degree of democratic governance by establishing a Legislative Council in Nabha. This was the first example of its kind in north India. An Act was promulgated and eight members were taken in the Council. Its meetings were held regularly and a few important measures were passed. With the thickening of troubles for the Maharaja, however, this Council gradually became non-functional.[9]

Maharaja Ripudaman Singh made some important changes in the judicial system, the police department, and the revenue administration. The Maharaja appears to have been rather strict in granting permission for shooting birds and animals in his territory. The state banks, eight in all with a capital of 4,800,000 rupees, continued to lend money on easy terms to agriculturists and for other purposes.[10]

True to the position taken by him in the Imperial Legislative Council, Maharaja Ripudaman Singh introduced free primary education in the state in 1913, which proved to be a measure of lasting importance. The number of middle schools and qualified teachers also increased. The expenditure on hospitals and dispensaries increased from 16,000 rupees in 1910 to over 28,500 in his reign. For sanitation in Nabha, the Maharaja employed a well-qualified doctor, Baldev Singh, the son of Bhai Ditt Singh (the well-known 'outcaste' member of the Lahore Singh Sabha), who had been sent to England for education. In 1915, the Maharaja contacted an English firm to install electricity in Nabha.[11]

At the time of Maharaja Ripudaman Singh's deposition in 1923, the Nabha state was in debt. However, this was not due to any personal extravagance on his part. Rather, he adopted a style that was simpler and less ostentatious than that of even his father. The loans were actually invested in immovable properties in and outside the Punjab. A list of 28 properties in Mussoorie, Dehra Dun, Rajpura, Mashobra, Simla, Delhi, and Lahore was prepared in 1923 after his deposition. Several of these were *benāmī* (registered in the name of someone other than the real owner) transactions, but most of these purchases had been made with the sanction of the government. Possibly, the Maharaja hoped to use these properties in times of financial need. When his removal was under active consideration, he was told in December 1922 that the government would not allow any more purchases of property.[12]

The Dehra Dun Mussoorie Electric Tramway Company was a project in which Maharaja Ripudaman Singh invested a considerable amount of money. He held a preponderating influence on the Board of Directors and purchased 1,200,000 shares in the Company, but only

600,000 shares were paid up with 600,000 rupees. The Government of India decided in 1923 to allot the shares purchased by the Maharaja to the Darbar with the instruction that the Darbar should assume liability for the remainder of the shares.[13]

It is important to note that charges brought against Maharaja Ripudaman Singh later were not related to finances but to judicial matters. One of these related to Sardar Shivdev Singh, the elder son of Sardar Partap Singh who had served Nabha as a minister. At the time of Partap Singh's death, Shivdev was only six years old. He was adopted by Sardar Sewa Singh, who too had served Maharaja Hira Singh as a minister. Shivdev Singh was hoping to take the position of his father. He had to deal with Jang Singh, a rival claimant to family property. Jang Singh had been brought up by the wife of Sardar Sewa Singh. Hira Singh did not admit Jang Singh's claim on the argument that he was simply 'brought up' and not adopted. Jang Singh revived his claim in the time of Maharaja Ripudaman Singh. In 1917, Jang Singh fell ill suddenly and died within a few hours. Shivdev Singh was suspected of poisoning him and was put under house arrest. Kaur Sen, a compounder, was accused of actually administering the poison. He was arrested by the state police. Shivdev Singh managed to escape to Patiala first and then to Ambala in the British territory, where he claimed protection as a British subject. However, he was persuaded by Bhai Arjan Singh of Bagrian to return to Nabha. On his return, he was placed under house arrest. Eventually, he was tried along with his uncle Nidh Singh and Kaur Sen and all of them were found guilty and sentenced to imprisonment. This case was considered by the bureaucracy to be 'good' for use against Maharaja Ripudaman Singh.[14]

The other case of the supposed miscarriage of justice was that of Malik Muhammad Din. He had been brought to Nabha as a Judge of the High Court, and deputed to supervise investigation into the death of Jang Singh. Muhammad Din lifted two important statements from the police file and attributed their loss to Shivdev Singh. Later on, he suggested to the Maharaja that these documents could be purchased from the defence lawyer for 20,000 rupees. Narsinga Rao, the then Prime Minister of Nabha, however, reacted to Malik's obvious attempt to cheat the state and ordered him to discontinue his association with the case and resume his seat in the High Court, but he refused. Rao then ordered Malik's arrest and informed the Political Agent. Since Muhammad Din was a British subject, Rai Bahadur Pandit Pitambar Joshi, a retired District and Sessions Judge from the United Provinces, was selected to try the case. Muhammad Din was sentenced to three years' rigorous imprisonment. The letters he wrote from jail were intercepted and another case was started against him. He made a representation to the Government of India through Mian Muhammad Shafi of Lahore but the Law Minister of the Government of India found no substance in this representation. However, Sir John Thompson, the then Chief Secretary, Punjab, and subsequently also of Viceroy Reading, tried to secure his release on a personal basis. Maharaja Ripudaman Singh chose not to oblige. After serving his term of imprisonment, Malik Muhammad Din joined the Patiala Darbar as an adviser in its dispute with Nabha.[15]

Even when good governance and loyalty were emphasized as the twin obligations of a princely state under paramountcy, in reality absolute loyalty was far more important than a just and efficient administration. Good governance was appreciated if a prince was loyal, but doubtful loyalty could invite the charge of maladministration. Thus, what was commendable by all standards under Maharaja Hira Singh became 'maladministration' under his successor despite continuities in essential respects and modernization in some others. Indeed, the real reasons for annoyance of the paramount power with the Maharaja were political rather than administrative.

Attitude of 'Opposition and Resistance'

In 1915, the Political Agent told the Nabha Darbar that the coat of arms used by the Darbar was unauthorized and it should be replaced by the device exemplified on the banner presented to Raja Hira Singh at the Delhi assemblage of 1877. What was specially objected to was the use of the crown in the coat of arms. It appeared to carry the implication that sovereignty of the Nabha state was sanctioned by God. Maharaja Ripudaman Singh refused to change the coat of arms due to its historical and ideological significance. At its centre in a circle was placed the *Guru Granth Sahib*. The coat of arms also contained the words *Akāl Sahāi* (May God be our helper) in Gurmukhi, which was reminiscent of the seals of Maharaja Ranjit Singh and his Khalsa predecessors who did not acknowledge any earthly superior.[16]

In December 1916, the Nabha Darbar pointed out that it had been decided in 1899 that the Nabha state 'shall, as heretofore, exercise sovereignty over the lands occupied by railways in the State, and that the proceedings connected with extradition shall not apply to these lands on the grounds that these areas do not belong to British Government'. But this was omitted in the form revised in 1899 for the cession of criminal jurisdiction. When this omission was pointed out to the Government of India, it was ordered that the Nabha Darbar should cede jurisdiction over the two railways within one month by signing the prescribed form. The Joint Foreign Minister of Nabha signed the form under protest: 'No one can raise any objection to comply with the orders and no one can raise his voice (against orders). Hence, in the circumstances, the Darbar see no alternative but to sign and return the prescribed form of 1899.' The matter was not closed. The Darbar proposed to 'represent their case to seek redress for their rights' at some later stage. O'Dwyer was unhappy over this 'unwilling acceptance of the advice of Government'.[17]

The Government of India raised the still head duty on liquor distilled in the state and demanded a higher price for Bengal opium imported by the state. Maharaja Ripudaman Singh was not willing to accept these new demands. The controversy remained unresolved until his deposition. Soon after the deposition, the state was made to pay about 250,000 rupees as arrears to the Government of India on account of excise and import of opium.[18]

Maharaja Ripudaman Singh had no hesitation in expressing his views in the Chiefs' Conference, which was instituted to elicit maximum cooperation from the princely states during the war. As noted by Viceroy Chelmsford, Ripudaman Singh was one of the most articulate chiefs in the conference held in November 1917. On the subject of 'precedence of Ruling Chiefs *inter se* at social functions', he suggested that it should be dropped because only about one-twelfth of the ruling chiefs were present.

On the subject of horse breeding in the states, the Maharaja suggested that the first necessary step was to provide for a census of the local breeds and breeders. It was also necessary to create a separate fund for the encouragement and improvement of horse breeding, and to devise a system of liberal grants for the purpose.[19]

Regarding 'agricultural, cotton and other statistics in native states', Maharaja Ripudaman Singh underscored the importance of statistics in general and of agricultural statistics in particular. However, he insisted that 'each state should be left to decide for itself' about collecting agricultural statistics. He emphasized that the collection of statistics was 'purely a matter of internal administration'. To furnish such information 'should continue to be entirely voluntary not only in theory but also in practice'. The states not inclined to send information 'should be left alone'.[20]

Ripudaman Singh was equally forthright in expressing his views on 'agricultural development in native states'. He suggested the ways in which the government and its agriculture departments could help the Indian states. On 'rules for the conduct of the business of the conference', the Maharaja moved an amendment suggesting two changes with a bearing on the relative position of the princes. The Viceroy should preside over the conference throughout its deliberations, and not only on its 'opening and closing sessions'. When the Viceroy's absence was unavoidable, one of the ruling chiefs present should preside. By implication, the Political Secretary should not preside over the conference.[21]

To further his concern for the autonomy of the princely states, Maharaja Ripudaman Singh took keen interest in the first session of the Chamber of Princes which was inaugurated by the Duke of Connaught on 8 February 1921 in the Diwān-i Ām of the Red Fort in Delhi. The Maharaja moved a resolution and finally sought division over elevating the relative position of over 300 'lesser' or non-salute states so that they could have a larger say in the Chamber of Princes. The government did not approve of the motion and it was lost by 10 to 31 votes. The independent thinking and wide concerns of Maharaja Ripudaman Singh in the Chamber of Princes were in marked contrast with the pro-establishment role assumed by Bikaner and Patiala in particular.[22] The Maharaja of Bikaner remained the Chancellor of the Chamber till 1926 to be succeeded by the Maharaja of Patiala.[23] The very first session of the Chamber deepened Maharaja Ripudaman Singh's sense of disillusionment.

Worsening Relations with Maharaja Bhupinder Singh

The relations of Maharaja Ripudaman Singh with Maharaja Bhupinder Singh of Patiala were not cordial. Maharaja Hira Singh was the most important chief among the Phulkian rulers in 1911. On the other hand, Bhupinder Singh of Patiala had been invested by the government with full powers only a year earlier amidst misgivings about his personal conduct and companions. By then, however, the British had also begun to have misgivings about the politics of Tikka Ripudaman Singh for very different reasons—his rather too 'independent' politics.

The paramount power could overlook the questionable personal conduct of a ruler, but not the questioning of their decisions. Therefore, after Maharaja Hira Singh's death, the British were keen to project the enthusiastic and flamboyant Maharaja Bhupinder Singh of Patiala as the leader of the Phulkian chiefs. Ripudaman Singh, some years older than Bhupinder Singh, however, cherished the memory of Maharaja Hira Singh's well-acknowledged leadership of the Phulkians and the fact of the Nabha House belonging to their senior line. Moreover, Ripudaman Singh had a different kind of education compared to Bhupinder Singh. In fact, the two had diametrically opposite attitudes towards almost everything.

What distinguished Ripudaman Singh most from the ruler of Patiala was his marked stance of independence towards the paramount power and sympathy with the nationalist forces. In a communication to the Lieutenant Governor, Maharaja Bhupinder Singh wrote that both he and the Maharaja of Jind deplored the line of action taken by Nabha as a discredit to the Phulkian states, and looked to government 'to restore matters to a proper footing'. Bhupinder Singh asserted, quite erroneously, that one of the sublime teachings of the Gurus was 'unflinching loyalty to the ruler and implicit obedience to his orders'. He maintained that the Sikhs should not forget the words of the Gurus which, according to him, were: 'He who is impertinent to his master, is put to great shame. None should bear arms against his rulers!'[24]

The differences between Nabha and Patiala arose out of a multiplicity of situations. In the time of Raja Hira Singh, the services of Colonel Bakhshish Singh had been lent for a year to the young ruler of Patiala for training his Imperial Service Troops. Bakhshish Singh was not returned to Nabha. When Maharaja Ripudaman Singh asked for his return, Maharaja Bhupinder Singh brushed the request aside rather casually, showing a clear disregard for the new Maharaja of Nabha. The Political Agent and the Lieutenant Governor did not help Nabha because of their annoyance with Maharaja Ripudaman Singh. Bhai Kahn Singh Nabha, the erstwhile tutor of Tikka Ripudaman Singh, had left Nabha due to some misunderstanding and gone to Kashmir. He was persuaded to accept service in Patiala as the state's Vakīl to the Political Agent. This was a hard blow to Maharaja Ripudaman Singh because of his long personal association with Bhai Kahn Singh since childhood.[25]

In the rift between Nabha and Patiala, Jind tried directly or indirectly to poison the mind of the British authorities with fabricated reports against Nabha. The Foreign Minister of Nabha, Lala Bishan Das, made the request that 'should any person take into his head to tell a tale against the State, the authorities will kindly have the facts verified from us'. He also requested the Political Agent to convey the information to the Punjab Government, and through them to the Government of India.[26] When this letter was shown to Michael O'Dwyer, he remarked that, given Maharaja Ripudaman Singh's 'mistrust and sullenness' towards the paramount power, he need not fear any outside machinations. The Political Agent maintained that since the Nabha Darbar had not abandoned 'their unsatisfactory and unfriendly attitude', they had themselves to blame for 'rumours as to the probable results'.[27] These rumours hinted at the imminent removal of Maharaja Ripudaman Singh from the gaddī of Nabha.

A month later, the Foreign Minister of Nabha wrote to the Political Agent that while innocent things said in the course of correspondence were seen by His Honour as an 'unfriendly attitude', a real grievance of Nabha did not receive the consideration it deserved. 'It seems that the mind of His Honour the Lieutenant Governor has been prejudiced against the State.' The Darbar wanted to know whether or not the information given by the Foreign Minister had been conveyed to the Government of India.[28] The Darbar also wanted to know the nature of rumours referred to by the Lieutenant Governor. The rumour that the government would take strong action against the ruler of Nabha is mentioned in official records. Another rumour was that Maharaja Bhupinder Singh wanted to see his uncle on the gaddī of Nabha. Though married for over fifteen years, Maharaja Ripudaman Singh had no male child. This could lend plausibility to the rumour.

In 1917, reconciliation was effected between Maharaja Ripudaman Singh and Maharaja Bhupinder Singh through the mediacy of Bhai Arjan Singh of Bagrian, who was generally respected for the sanctity attached to his House especially by members of the ruling Phulkian families. Bhai Kahn Singh Nabha and Colonel Bakhshish Singh were returned to Nabha.[29] However, this rapprochement came to an end directly through an action of the Political Agent. Ishar Kaur, a subject of Nabha, had left the state and gone to Lahore. The Punjab Government refused the request of Nabha to extradite her. She then went to Patiala and, according to the long-standing rules of practice (*dastūr al-'amal*) adopted by the Phulkian states to govern their mutual relations, the Patiala Darbar ordered her extradition as a matter of routine, but the Political Agent intervened to stop the extradition. The

Nabha Darbar used its own resources to bring her back from Patiala. The intervention of the government's representative, thus, became the cause of renewed tension between Nabha and Patiala.[30]

A few years later, a dacoity took place in Patiala territory and a Nabha subject was suspected of the crime. Abdul Aziz, an Inspector of the Patiala police, entered Nabha territory to apprehend the accused. He was himself arrested in Nabha on 21 September 1921, tried for transgression, and sentenced. On Patiala's representation, the newly appointed Agent to the Governor General tried to intervene in its favour, but the Nabha Darbar again resisted this interference in its internal affairs.[31]

Like many large states, the Phulkian states were placed under the direct control of the Government of India in 1921. The 'Political Agent' now became Agent to the Governor General (AGG). Lieutenant Colonel A. B. Minchin was the first AGG for the Phulkian states. The Government of India drafted a programme of festivities to be observed on the official visit of the AGG to a state under his charge and sent it for comments by the ruling chiefs. Patiala and Jind were quite happy to accept the suggestion. Maharaja Ripudaman Singh rightly thought that the proposed programme lowered the status of the states in relation to the AGG. The argument of the government that the status of the Political Agent had been enhanced by his appointment and responsibility directly to the Government of India was used by the Maharaja for asserting that his own status too had been enhanced by direct link with the Government of India. In any case, he wanted the old procedures to be followed because these were based on equity so far as the rulers were concerned.[32] Minchin could not possibly have relished Ripudaman Singh's reluctance to organize a special reception for him.

Sympathy with Anti-British Movements

Maharaja Ripudaman Singh remained sympathetic to nearly all significant political movements and organizations in the country which resisted the colonial state in some way, or were seen as such by the paramount power.

Ripudaman Singh almost had a confrontation with the Punjab Government over his supportive stance towards the most important revolutionary movement in the Punjab during the war, the Ghadar movement. Named after its weekly paper, *Ghadar*, which denoted 'revolt' (after the Mutiny of 1857), the Ghadar Party was founded on the west coast of the United States of America to work for India's freedom by bringing about an armed insurrection against the British with help from the Indian soldiers in the British Army. In terms of its egalitarian, democratic, and internationalist outlook, the Ghadar movement has come to be regarded as the most progressive of all the political and revolutionary movements in India until the second decade of the twentieth century.[33]

At the time of his interview with Sir Michael O'Dwyer on 28 April 1915, the Maharaja was told that the Darbar had failed to discharge its elementary duty to the Supreme Government. Though warned in regard to the intentions of the Ghadarites, the Darbar had remained indifferent. Consequently, the village of Lohatbadi in Nabha territory was used for months by the Nabha subjects and others as a base for the revolutionary activity against British rule. Arms, ammunition, and materials for bombs were accumulated, and meetings of revolutionaries were held there. Dacoities in villages in the British territory and in the Malerkotla state were organized. In view of the generally obstructive attitude of the Nabha Darbar, the Punjab police had to take independent action by raiding the revolutionary headquarters, seizing arms, ammunition, and bomb materials concealed there, and arresting the chief promoters. 'One informer and at least two of the accused in the Conspiracy case now under trial are Nabha subjects.' Refusing to be bogged down by the accusation and the implied threat, the Maharaja retorted that 'plots and mutiny' were organized in the British territory too.[34]

Ripudaman Singh insisted that the Darbar had taken all reasonable measures against the returned emigrants and their adherents. Such measures were then listed. On 11 February 1915, when two sub-inspectors of Malerkotla came to search the houses of Achhra Singh and Narain Singh, suspected of sympathizing with the Ghadarites, the Nabha police assisted them. Four men and some goldsmith's instruments were handed over to the Malerkotla officers. 'In this operation the British police never had a hand.' Two days later, three officers of the British police accompanied the Malerkotla officers in connection with a dacoity in Ludhiana district. They received from the Nabha police the assistance they asked for. After search, some letters and clothing were handed over to the British police with the active help of the Nabha police. On 3 and 4 March another search was made with the aid of the Nabha police. When the Political Agent applied to the Nabha Darbar for extradition, the men were sent at once. This summary account 'exhibits no want of activity or sympathy with the Government on the part of the Nabha Police'. If Nabha was to be adjudged treacherous only because occasional offenders used its territories to escape British justice or to hatch offences, no portion of India would escape this charge. Questioning the Lieutenant Governor's stand, the Maharaja threw a challenge: 'I would request Your Excellency to invite His Honour to adduce proof in support of the charge or to withdraw it!'[35]

Much hardened in his antipathy to Nabha, Sir Michael O'Dwyer finally asked the Deputy Inspector General (DIG), CID, to prepare a special report on the attitude of the Nabha Darbar towards sedition at Lohatbadi in its territory. Submitted on 16 October 1915, this report points to the Maharaja's palpable sympathy with the Ghadarites. The information about Lohatbadi was first given by a subject of the Patiala state who was suspected of dacoity. This place had been the centre of activity of the tat Khalsa (the term used for radical Sikhs) for a long time, and meetings of the 'extremists' were held there frequently at which 'disloyal' speeches were delivered and 'objectionable' resolutions were passed. When the Ghadarite emigrants returned to India, they threw in their lot with the already disloyal tat Khalsa, 'carrying the latter altogether out of their depth'. Several emigrants, including Ganda Singh, who became a 'murderer' later, were harboured within the walls of Achhra Singh's Gurdwara 'within sight' of the Lohatbadi police station. The principal supporter of Achhra Singh was (Bhai) Randhir Singh; both of them were 'influential and respectable people'. That was why the local police cooperated only when ordered from above. On their own the officers and men of the Lohatbadi police station had shown no initiative or active cooperation. No officer of the Nabha state 'cooperated or helped in any way beyond suffering certain searches to take place and grudgingly handing over certain suspects and articles found by the British and Malerkotla Police'. The report also dwelt on Bhai Randhir Singh, who turned out to be 'a very active and prominent leader of the revolutionary movement'.[36]

Bhai Randhir Singh, a devout Sikh with university education, had refused to serve the corrupt and unfair government. When he was approached by the Ghadarites for help he agreed to join them. He was in touch with the well-known Ghadarite Kartar Singh Sarabha, among others. Randhir Singh's father, Natha Singh, was employed in Nabha as Assistant Legal Remembrancer. Randhir Singh used to live in his village Narangwal in Ludhiana district, but after the Lohatbadi exposure he moved to Nabha to live with his father. He was arrested in May 1915 and tried subsequently under the Supplementary Lahore Conspiracy Case and sentenced to life imprisonment for 'a war waged against the King'.[37]

The enquiry showed that the Nabha authorities were not 'willing and anxious to assist the British Police in rooting out the conspiracy'. An effort was made by Nabha to get Randhir Singh extradited from Ludhiana after his arrest. After the completion of the Lahore Conspiracy Case, the Maharaja ordered the arrest of all the witnesses who were subjects of the Nabha state: Sewa Singh, Kapura, Lalu, Fatta Chamar, and Harnam Singh. Three of them were related to the approvers Achhra Singh and Bhagat Singh. The DIG concluded his report with the remark:

> It is urged by the Maharaja that the attitude and actions of the Nabha Police in connection with the conspiracy exhibit no want of activity or sympathy with the Government, but I find it impossible to reconcile the facts given in this report with any desire or attempt by the Nabha Durbar to help or cooperate with Government.[38]

This deliberate understatement was meant to carry a serious indictment of the Nabha Darbar for its obvious sympathy not only for the Ghadarites but also for the radical Sikh reformers, the tat Khalsa.

In May 1913, about 400 feet of the outer wall of Gurdwara Rakabganj in Delhi were demolished by the engineers of the Public Works Department to construct a direct road to the Viceregal palace through the Gurdwara estate. It was seen as an attack on Sikh religion and culture. When the news spread to the Punjab, there was a spate of telegrams, petitions, and memoranda protesting against this sacrilege, addressed to the Chief Commissioner of Delhi, the Lieutenant Governor of the Punjab, and the Governor General. Public meetings (*diwāns*) were held at many places in the Punjab to protest against the action of the government. Bhai Randhir Singh was deeply upset over the demolition of the wall of Gurdwara Rakabganj by the government. To register the protest of the Sikhs against the demolition, he organized the largest-ever and most representative Panthic conference at Patti (Amritsar district) on Baisakhi day, 13 April 1914. Malcolm Hailey, then the Chief Commissioner of Delhi, asked Raja Sir Daljit Singh of Kapurthala to mobilize support for government action. He contacted the leaders of the Chief Khalsa Diwan and its Secretary,

Sir Sunder Singh Majithia, to defend the government. Opposition to the Chief Khalsa Diwan had begun to grow. In March 1914, the *Sikh Review*, with a pronounced reformist and nationalist slant, had been launched from Delhi under the ostensible patronage of Bhai Arjan Singh of Bagrian, a close personal friend of the Maharaja of Nabha. Sardul Singh Caveeshar, a close relative of Bhai Arjan Singh, was appointed as its editor. The *Sikh Review* was financed by Maharaja Ripudaman Singh, and Sardul Singh Caveeshar too was given financial support. It was believed that Maharaja Ripudaman Singh at some stage proposed even to finance a trip of Master Tara Singh to England to present the case of Bhai Randhir Singh before the British people and the Parliament. The movement for restoration of the wall subsided after the outbreak of World War I on 7 August 1914.[39]

After the war, the association of Maharaja Ripudaman Singh with the final phase of the Rakabganj agitation reinforced the impression that he was covertly supporting nationalist and Panthic causes. By this time, a new political party known as the Central Sikh League had been founded at Amritsar in 1919. It was closely aligned with the Indian National Congress and opposed to the pro-government Chief Khalsa Diwan. In the very first issue of the *Akali*, the organ of the Central Sikh League, rebuilding of the demolished wall of Gurdwara Rakabganj was proclaimed as one of its aims. The other aims of the Central Sikh League, declared in this issue of the *Akali*, were to bring the Khalsa College under the control of the Sikh community, to liberate Gurdwaras from the control of the Mahants in order to bring them under the control of the Panth, and to inspire the Sikhs to actively participate in the struggle for freedom.[40]

Sardul Singh Caveeshar, who had become a prominent leader of this organization, called for one hundred volunteers to proceed to Delhi to reconstruct the demolished wall. If the government tried to prevent them, they should lay down their lives in the attempt. Seven hundred persons responded to Caveeshar's call. The stage was set for confrontation. The government felt obliged to change its decision. Wide publicity was given to its plan for rebuilding the wall of Gurdwara Rakabganj. When the wall was reconstructed, its photographs were widely publicized. Open confrontation was obviated, but the Rakabganj agitation served as a prelude to the movement for the liberation of Gurdwaras from the control of the Mahants.[41]

The Central Sikh League demanded that management of the Golden Temple should be entrusted to a representative body of the

Sikhs. The League convened a general meeting in November 1920 in which 10,000 Sikhs elected a 175-member managing committee for all Sikh Gurdwaras. Called the Shiromani Gurdwara Prabandhak Committee (SGPC), it launched a movement to liberate all Gurdwaras and to coordinate the activities of local bands of volunteers. To assist in this self-assigned task, the Shiromani Akali Dal was formed at Amritsar in December 1920.[42] The admirers as well as detractors of the Maharaja attributed the Panthic developments of 1920 to him directly.[43] Appreciation for the role of Maharaja Ripudaman Singh in the Rakabganj affair was recorded by the SGPC on 24 January 1921. A special prayer (ardās) was offered to the effect that with God's grace he may serve the Panth in the true Sikh spirit, sincerity, confidence, and strength. Three active members of the SGPC were closely associated with the Maharaja: Bhai Teja Singh of Mastuana, S. S. Charan Singh 'Shahid', and Bhai Chanda Singh.[44]

It may be added that the Mahant of the Nankana Sahib Gurdwara had been encouraged by the local British authorities to make his own arrangements to deal with the Akalis. When more than a hundred Sikhs entered the Gurdwara on 20 February 1921, without any intention yet of taking it over, they were brutally attacked by over a score of the hired assassins of the Mahant. Most of the Sikhs were either killed or wounded or burnt on the spot. In protest, the Akalis reached the spot in thousands, and the authorities felt obliged to take action against the Mahant and his men. The Gurdwara was handed over to a committee.[45] A few months later, when 5 April was declared to be the day of mourning to commemorate the martyrdom of over one hundred Sikhs at Nankana Sahib, the Maharaja ordered that it should be observed as a mourning day (hartāl) in the Nabha state. He himself tied a black turban as a mark of mourning; all offices remained closed; no guns boomed; and no bells tolled.[46]

In July 1921, the SGPC members Mahtab Singh and Sardar Kharak Singh came to Nabha in connection with the formation of the Gurdwara Prabandhak Committee. Ripudaman Singh persuaded them to have three of his own men as members. The persons approved by the Maharaja were elected to the Gurdwara Prabandhak Committee at Nabha as well. By this time, Maharaja Ripudaman Singh had emerged as the most respected 'Sikh Prince'. It was seen as a threat to the pre-eminent position of Bhupinder Singh of Patiala. In August 1921, it was reported by his resourceful Prime Minister to the government that the Maharaja of Nabha was preaching disaffection to become popular among Sikh political workers and to have a voice in all Sikh political bodies.[47]

Furthermore, Maharaja Ripudaman Singh donated 200,000 rupees to the Benares Hindu University set up by Madan Mohan Malaviya, many-time President of the Congress, and attended its formal foundation-laying ceremony in 1916.[48] The Maharaja was also in touch with a revolutionary like Raja Mahendra Pratap, 'who was a declared rebel with price on his head'. As 'President' of the 'Provisional Government of India' he was 'at war with the Government of Great Britain'.[49] Mahendra Pratap exchanged messages with Ripudaman Singh, and believed that the Maharaja's 'co-operation with me was one factor in his removal'.[50] After his deposition, Mahendra Pratap organized a meeting in Kabul, attended by Afghan notables, and passed a resolution expressing 'great sympathies' for the Maharaja and the Akalis.[51] It may be interesting to note that Ripudaman Singh tried to have Michael O'Dwyer impeached for the Jallianwala Bagh tragedy and 'Martial Law' in the Punjab. For this, the Maharaja sought the help of Colonel Josiah Wedgewood, then a Labour Member of Parliament, who was staying at Lahore with Lala Harkishen Lal. Wedgewood is reported to have agreed to engage Sir John Simon, then a leading British lawyer, for this purpose.[52] During his two-month-long stay in Delhi at the time of the visit of the Duke of Connaught, the Maharaja was visited daily by Hakim Ajmal Khan, both as a physician and a Congress leader. He became President of the Indian National Congress in 1921.[53] Also, against the express advice of his Chief Minister, Maharaja Ripudaman Singh presided over a meeting of the Tilak School of Politics (established by Lala Lajpat Rai), held at Mussoorie in 1921 and spoke on the occasion.[54]

Significantly, in September 1921, Maharaja Ripudaman Singh celebrated the second birthday of Tikka Partap Singh, born to his second wife, Sarojini Devi, daughter of Sardar Prem Singh Grewal of Raipur, an officer of the Imperial Service Troops of Hyderabad. The birth of the Tikka was announced at Nabha by the booming of guns. Charity was distributed by the same officer who had performed this duty at the birth of Tikka Ripudaman Singh. Before the Maharaja came to Nabha, every evening there was a performance of dance and music. On his arrival, 'a reception unheard of in the history of Nabha' was held. The Maharaja drove in state. People showered flowers and coins. Festivities continued and promotions were announced in a public Darbar. The initiation (*pahul*) of the double-edged sword was administered to the Tikka at Dera Baba Ajaipal Singh by the now aged Bhai Narain Singh, who had administered pahul to Tikka Ripudaman Singh at the same place. Nabha now had a crown prince, setting at rest the speculations about a collateral replacing the Maharaja for want of an heir.

The birthday of Tikka Partap Singh was celebrated at Mussoorie in a special way. Maharaja Ripudaman Singh had asked several poets to compose poems on the Tikka in Urdu and Punjabi, and he had asked S. S. Charan Singh to write in verse a short but inspiring history of Nabha. All this material was printed from Amritsar as a book entitled *Partāp Ude* (the dawn of God's grace). The crown prince was expected to grow up as a protector of the Sikh Panth and a protagonist of freedom. His name symbolized great expectations. Among other things, the poem referred to Raja Devinder Singh's stance of independence and his sympathy with the Khalsa Panth, the stand taken by Tikka Ripudaman Singh in the Imperial Legislative Council, Keir Hardie taking up his case in Parliament and securing an unprecedented apology from the Secretary of State, and Maharaja Ripudaman Singh's support to the Khalsa Panth. Essentially, the poem emphasized Nahba's self-respecting and enlightened political stance and its service of the Panth as the obverse of Patiala's abject sycophancy towards the British and indifference towards its own people.[55]

In short, Maharaja Ripudaman Singh's insistence on the internal sovereignty of the princely states, his stance of independent thinking, and his sympathetic attitude towards individuals and movements opposed to the government further antagonized the bureaucracy.

Notes

1. The roznāmchas of Raja Hira Singh are available in the Punjab State Archives (PSA) at Patiala. S. Ranga Iyer made their selective use in his *Diary of the Late Maharaja of Nabha* (Lucknow: Indian Daily Telegraph, 1924).
2. These volumes provide detailed information on all aspects of state administration under the titles *Hidāyatnāma-i Mālguzārī, Hidāyatnāma-i Bandobast, Hidāyatnāma-i Diwānī, Majmua-i Ahkām-i Faujdārī*, and *Aīn-i Lashkarā wa Civil*. Their scope, therefore, is rather comprehensive.
3. *Punjab States Gazetteers*, Vol. XVII A, *Phulkian States: Patiala Jind and Nabha, 1904* (Lahore, 1909), pp. 339–85. All these pages relate to the Nabha State. Unless otherwise stated, the remaining paragraphs of this section are based on the *Gazetteer*.

4. PSA, Patiala, Office of the President, Council of Regency Nabha State (PCRNS), File no. 203/C, 'Constitutional and Administrative Reforms Introduced in the Nabha State', Statement 2, p. 1.
5. This Act, which became operative in the Punjab in 1901, aimed at checking alienation of land from the traditionally agriculturist castes to the traditionally non-agriculturist castes. For a discussion, see J. S. Grewal, 'Agrarian Production and Colonial Policy in Punjab', in *India's Colonial Encounter: Essays in Memory of Eric Stokes*, edited by Mushirul Hasan and Narayani Gupta (New Delhi: Manohar, 1993), pp. 293–308.
6. Iyer, *Diary of the Late Maharaja of Nabha*, pp. 103–4.
7. PSA, Patiala, 'Administrative Report of Nabha State', File no. 937E/1924.
8. For an insight into the changing character of the administrative personnel in the Nabha state after the reign of Maharaja Hira Singh, see J. S. Grewal and Veena Sachdeva, *Kinship and State Formation: The Gills of Nabha* (New Delhi: Manohar, 2007), pp. 25–7.
9. Munna Lal Syngal, *The Patriot Prince* (Ludhiana and Delhi: Doaba House, 1961), pp. 47–8.
10. PSA, PCRNS, File no. 203/C, Statement 2, pp. 1, 4; PSA, Patiala, File no. 937 E/1924.
11. PSA, Patiala, File no. 937 E/1924 and PSA, Patiala, PCRNS, File no. 203/C.
12. British Library, R/1/1/1526, File no. 64(27)-P (Secret) of 1924–5, Government of India, Foreign and Political Department, Serial Nos 1–2.
13. The Nabha Darbar paid 600,000 rupees in 18 months but the condition of the Company did not improve, and it was liquidated in 1926 (India Office Records (IOR) (microfilm), L/P and S/10/1027, 'The States Shares in the Dehra Dun-Mussoorie Electric Tramway Company'.
14. IOR (microfilm), R/1/29/53, File no. 838-P (Secret) 1923, View of H. V. B. Hare Scott, dated 9 January 1923.

    After the removal of the Maharaja from Nabha in July 1923, Shivdev Singh, along with Nidh Singh and Kaur Sen, was tried afresh by a special magistrate appointed by the Government of India and they were pronounced 'not guilty'. These efforts by the British to justify their position and the changed circumstances of the Maharaja lent plausibility to the impression spread by his detractors that the case against Shivdev Singh was 'false'. Syngal, *The Patriot Prince*, pp. 72–3, 77–9.
15. Syngal, *The Patriot Prince*, pp. 73–7.
16. PSA, Patiala, PCRNS Records, File no. 8702 E; see the photograph (of the coat of arms, which the available space will not permit).
17. Punjab Government Political Department Proceedings, January 1917, nos 62 A and 62 E.
18. PSA, Patiala, File no. 937 E/1924; PCRNS Records, File no. 203/C.
19. *Proceedings of the Chiefs Conference* (Delhi, 1917), pp. 46, 81.
20. *Proceedings of the Chiefs Conference*, pp. 64–5.

21. Proceedings of the Chiefs Conference, pp. 70, 88.
22. Proceedings of the Third Day of the Chamber of Princes, held at Delhi on 11 February 1921, Chamber of Princes Archive, PSA, Patiala, pp. 1–4, 15 in particular.
23. Maharaja Bhupinder Singh was the Chancellor for nine years, from 1926 to 1930 and from 1933 to 1938. The Chancellor was elected for one year only, but he could be re-elected (S. M. Verma, *Chamber of Princes (1921–1947)* [New Delhi: National Book Organisation, 1990], p. 47).
24. K. Natwar-Singh, *The Magnificent Maharaja* (New Delhi: Harper Collins Publishers, 1998), p. 111. Obviously, Bhupinder Singh was giving his own and patently erroneous interpretation of *Gurbāṇī*.
25. Syngal, *The Patriot Prince*, pp. 49–50.
26. Punjab Government Records (PGR), Political Department—1916, Annual File no. 2, 'Relations with Maharaja of Nabha', Enclosure V, 'Correspondence regarding the attitude of Patiala and Jind towards Nabha', Lala Bishan Das to Political Agent, 10 September 1915.
27. PGR, 'Correspondence regarding the attitude of Patiala and Jind towards Nabha', Political Agent to Lala Bishan Das, 18 September 1915.
28. PGR, 'Correspondence regarding the attitude of Patiala and Jind towards Nabha', Lala Bishan Das to Political Agent, 20 October 1915.
29. Reconciliation between Nabha and Patiala was hailed as a great event by the *Khalsa Advocate* of 8 September 1917. Bhai Arjan Singh of Bagrian was praised for his persistent efforts, which were crowned with success on 28 August 1917. He could not bear to see 'the state of dissatisfaction that prevailed between two great representatives of the Phulkian House'. By bringing about their reconciliation, Bhai Arjan Singh had earned 'gratitude of the entire Sikh community', wrote the *Khalsa Advocate*.
30. IOR (microfilm) R/1/29/32, File no. 628-P (Secret), Fortnightly report by the AGG [A. B. Minchin], dated 8 November 1921. Apparently, AGG is referring to the past here.
31. IOR, R/1/29/32, no. 628-P(S), note by J. P. Thompson, dated 24 November 1921.
32. Syngal, *The Patriot Prince*, pp. 83–4.
33. For detail, see J. S. Grewal, Harish K. Puri, and Indu Banga (eds), *The Ghadar Movement: Background, Ideology, Action and Legacies* (Patiala: Punjabi University, 2013).
34. PGR, Political Department-1916, Annual File no. 2, note by His Honour the Lieutenant Governor on his interview with the Maharaja of Nabha at Lahore, dated 28 April 1915.
35. IOR (microfilm) R/1/1/1024, Simla Records, Foreign and Political Department, nos 78–80 of 1915.
36. PGR, Political Department-1916, Annual File no.2, note by Deputy Inspector General, Criminal Intelligence Department, Punjab, on the

attitude of the Nabha Darbar towards sedition at Lohatbadi, dated 16 October 1915.
37. Bhai Sahib Randhir Singh, *Jail Chitthian* (Ludhiana: Bhai Randhir Singh Trust, 2010, 14th impression), pp. 88–102. See also, Indu Banga, 'Ideology and Revolution: A Case Study of Bhai Randhir Singh', paper presented at the National Seminar on Revolutionary Nationalism in India, University of Calcutta, 7–9 February 2014.
38. PGR, Political Department-1916, Annual File no. 2, note by Deputy Inspector General.
39. Harjot Singh [Oberoi], 'From Gurdwara Rikabganj to the Viceregal Palace—A Study of Religious Protest', *The Panjab Past and Present*, vol. XIV, part I (1980): 182–98.
40. J. S. Grewal, *The Sikhs of the Punjab*, The New Cambridge History of India, II.3 (Cambridge: Cambridge University Press, 2014, reprint), p. 157.
41. Harjot Singh [Oberoi], 'From Gurdwara Rikabganj to the Viceregal Palace': 182–98.
42. Grewal, *The Sikhs of the Punjab*, p. 158.
43. IOR (microfilm) R/1/29/53, File no. 838-Pol (Secret)/1923.
44. IOR, R/1/29/53, no. 838-P(S)/1923, Enclosure A: 'Maharaja Nabha's Political Activities', Report submitted by Daya Kishan Kaul, Prime Minister of Patiala State, dated 7 December 1921. 'Maharaja of Nabha and Sardul Singh Cavessur', CID Report, dated 31 October 1922.
45. Grewal, *The Sikhs of the Punjab*, p. 159.
46. IOR, R/1/29/53, no. 838-P(S)/1923.
47. IOR, R/1/29/53, no. 838-P(S)/1923. Important among the proofs cited by the Prime Minister of Patiala were the publication of the *Partāp Ude*, the Bagrian Diary, a letter of Sardul Singh Caveeshar, and copies of orders issued by Maharaja Ripudaman Singh.
48. Syngal, *The Patriot Prince*, pp. 14, 64.
   Ripudaman Singh was said to be close to Pandit Madan Mohan Malaviya, and at his invitation in 1914, the Maharaja had gone to Benares at the time of the foundation of the Sanskrit College. At Malaviya's request, the Maharaja took along Sant Attar Singh of Mastuana, who combined spirituality with radical Sikh reform, to perform a series of *akhand pāṭhs* (uninterrupted readings of the *Guru Granth Sahib*) on the occasion (Harjeet Singh, *Faith and Philosophy of Sikhism* [New Delhi: Gyan Publishing House, 2009], p. 71).
49. National Archives of India, New Delhi (NAI), Home/Pol. 1924 & KW File 320 K, p. 2.
50. Syngal, *The Patriot Prince*, 'A Word'.
51. NAI, Home/Pol. 1923, 5/II, '"Raja" Mahendra Pratap's Seditious Activities', p. 108.

52. Syngal, *The Patriot Prince*, pp. 81–2. Significantly, the Maharaja had sent his Chief Minister and Munna Lal Syngal to Lahore to discuss the details with Wedgewood, who was a guest of Harkishen Lal. Incidentally, Harkishen Lal himself had been jailed for his politics, particularly his role in the agitation against the Rowlatt Act (K. L. Gauba, *The Rebel Minister: The Story of the Rise and Fall of Lala Harkishen Lal* [Lahore: Premier Publishing House, 1938], pp. 65–95).
53. Syngal, *The Patriot Prince*, p. 61. S. P. Sen, ed., *Dictionary of National Biography* (Calcutta: Institute of Historical Studies, 1972), vol. I, pp. 33–5.
54. Syngal, *The Patriot Prince*, pp. 14, 71.
55. IOR, R/1/29/53, no. 838-P(S)/1923. After S. S. Charan Singh was won over by Daya Kishan Kaul, he procured the manuscript copy of the poem *Partāp Ude* and passed it on to the enquiry officer from the CID appointed by the Government of India. It was translated into English for official use and regarded by the Political Department as a reliable evidence of the Maharaja's 'disloyalty'. Though no formal proceedings were instituted on its basis, it was high on the list of the so-called cases against the Maharaja.

6

GOVERNMENT PREPARES GROUNDS FOR DEPOSITION

On 27 October 1921, the Secretary of State for India, Lord Montagu, sent a telegram to the new Viceroy, Lord Reading, that Maharaja Bhupinder Singh of Patiala, who was in England, had just paid him a farewell visit. In the course of their conversation, the Maharaja mentioned that he had received the news from India that Nabha had arrested two of his police officers, who 'in accordance with an extradition treaty between the two states' were seeking a miscreant, who was a subject of Patiala, in Nabha. The Secretary of State added that this story showed how the Nabha ruler was becoming 'terribly difficult'. He was 'a bad neighbour to his fellow Princes', and 'cruel to people in his power'. Moreover, he was 'suspected of complicity with the Sikh agitation in Punjab'. Montagu knew that the words of Patiala against Nabha could not be taken as literally true, but Patiala was an eager collaborator. Montagu hinted that the Viceroy could place 'implicit confidence' in him and have a 'frank talk with him'. The telegram ended with the suggestion that there was 'every reason to weigh carefully the condition of affairs in the Nabha State'.[1] This marked the beginning of a process that led ultimately to the deposition of the Maharaja of Nabha. Possibly Montagu remembered that nearly a decade earlier, as the Under Secretary of State, he had to offer Maharaja Ripudaman Singh an apology in Parliament.

The Government of India Decide to Make a Secret Enquiry against Nabha

In his reply of 8 November, Reading talked of 'the difficulties we are likely to have with Nabha'. Already 'a certain amount of information with regard to his suspected complicity with Sikh agitators' had been collected. The Maharaja had 'long aimed at the position of religious leader of the Sikhs and [was] said to be behind a good deal of the Akali agitation'. Reading assured Montagu that A. B. Minchin, AGG, was 'fully alive to the situation'.[2] In fact, Minchin, turned out to be the key player in this conspiracy at the highest level; he nursed a personal grouse against Maharaja Ripudaman Singh who had shown no interest in welcoming him when he joined as the AGG, and ignored him as far as possible. Minchin's relations with Maharaja Bhupinder Singh were rather cordial. Minchin took active interest in the situation to the disadvantage of Nabha.

Thus, the three key representatives of the paramount power joined in a planned offensive against Maharaja Ripudaman Singh, whose nationalist and Akali sympathies were a threat alike to Patiala's aspirations to be the acknowledged leader of the Sikhs and to the loyalties of the Sikh soldiers in the British Indian Army.

Minchin's report of 8 November refers to relations between Nabha and Patiala as generally friendly 'until the present Maharaja of Nabha's accession'. Since then there had been 'trouble'. The Maharaja of Nabha was embittered by the refusal of Patiala, 'on the advice of the Political Agent', to extradite certain persons to Nabha. Minchin hinted that Nabha had concocted all these cases 'for his private purposes'. With reference to the dacoity committed in Patiala territory in July 1921, Minchin supported the demand of the Patiala Darbar to hand over the culprits 'so that the cases against them could be enquired into by an independent tribunal'. Minchin justified the request of Patiala in view of 'a reign of terror' in Nabha that made fair trial 'impossible'.[3]

The Maharaja's close connection with the leaders of the Central Sikh League figures in a report of the CID on his political activities. As noted earlier, his sympathy with the Akalis was reflected in the state mourning he ordered after the Nankana Sahib tragedy in February 1921. The Maharaja was supporting the publication of Chanda Singh's *Panth Sewak*, which was regarded as a radical paper. The editor of the *Shahid*, S. S. Charan Singh, was employed by the Maharaja for the publication of *Partāp Ude*, a poem that highlighted Raja Devinder Singh's stance of independence during the Sikh War (1845-6) and his sympathy with the Khalsa Panth. The Nabha ruler was associated with Harchand Singh of Lyallpur, a radical Sikh leader. Moreover, Ripudaman Singh gave a lecture at Mussoorie under the aegis of the Tilak School of Politics, instituted by Lala Lajpat Rai. The Maharaja was reported to have practically taken 'all Sikh religious and political workers into his own hands'. His influence in his own territory, in the other princely states, and in the British Punjab had increased greatly. There was a plan to project him as 'the Jathedar of the Sikh Panth' after his intended participation in *kār sewā* (lit. service or physical labour for cleansing the sacred tank) at the Golden Temple. As 'Jathedar' of the Panth, he was expected to 'give trouble to Government'.[4]

The Home Member in the Governor General's Council, Sir W. H. Vincent, found this report 'disquieting', and added on his own that the Maharaja of Nabha had 'a passion for intrigue' and had 'long been coquetting with Sikhs hostile to the Government'. Nabha's association with the Kuka movement, which was essentially anti-government, was considered 'reprehensible'. The Punjab was 'one of the most dangerous provinces in India at the moment and very little encouragement to the Sikhs may have serious effects'. Sir Vincent suggested that the Governor General may send for the Maharaja to tell him of the danger involved in the course he was pursuing.[5] Not inclined just to warn him, the Governor General preferred to collect more information about his political activities. Reading was keen to know whether the Kukas were linked with 'the extreme elements in Sikh politics'. The Additional Political Secretary, J. P. Thompson, asked Minchin to send his report by the middle of December.[6] It is not without significance that as the Chief Secretary to O'Dwyer, Thompson had shared his staunch imperialist inclinations as well as disquiet over Nabha's stance of independence.

Daya Kishan Kaul, Prime Minister of Patiala, had apparently been entrusted by his master with the job of furnishing or even fabricating incriminating evidence against Maharaja Ripudaman Singh. On 12 December 1921, Minchin sent to Thompson a note by Kaul stating that the Maharaja of Nabha had shown favours to both the Akalis and the Kukas. It was alleged at the same time that attempts were being made to create unrest in Patiala with the help of Harchand Singh, 'one of Nabha's right-hand men', and that paid 'agents' were probably employed by Nabha to keep the Akali agitation alive.[7]

Within a week, Thompson forwarded Minchin's report to the Home Department, saying that there were definite statements in the papers sent by Minchin. It was for the Home Department to determine whether or not any of these allegations were serious enough to justify further action in relation to the Maharaja of Nabha. If they thought that these allegations were prima facie of sufficient gravity, 'the best thing to do would be to put a police officer on special duty to go into the case'.[8] The Home Department drew the general conclusion that the Maharaja of Nabha had been trying to become the recognized head of the Sikh community. Therefore, even when there was no clear evidence to establish that he had been 'directly promoting anti-Government activities on the part of the Akalis', his connection with such a body was considered 'very objectionable and unfair'.[9]

On 9 January 1922, Thompson wrote to the Chief Secretary of the Punjab that the Government of India were thinking of making a secret enquiry about the political activities of the Maharaja of Nabha by an officer specially deputed for the purpose. They liked to have a report from the Punjab Government, showing precisely the relations of the Maharaja with the Akalis, the Gurdwara Prabandhak Committee, and the Kukas, with evidence in regard to these relations, and its nature. The Government of India wanted also to know whether further enquiries by a specially deputed officer were likely to lead to any 'useful result'.[10]

In his telegram to the Viceroy on 11 January 1922, the Secretary of State wanted to have further reports of Nabha's activities and to know whether or not any action was contemplated with regard to him.[11] He was informed by the Viceroy that further report had been called for from the Punjab Government.[12] The provincial government supported the idea of a secret enquiry by a special officer.[13] The Chief Secretary of the Punjab was informed on 2 March 1922 that the Viceroy had agreed to an enquiry. The Director, Intelligence Bureau, would depute one of his officers for this purpose. They should give all assistance to the special officer, and they could have direct communication with the Director on any matter connected with the enquiry.[14]

On 21 April 1922, Minchin informed Thompson that Patiala had secured 'very important documentary evidence implicating Nabha in Akali sedition'. He wanted to know if the Director, Intelligence Bureau, could immediately depute an officer to Patiala to conduct secret enquiries.[15] Thompson replied promptly that the deputed officer had 'instructions to report to Minchin on his arrival in Patiala'.[16] A secret enquiry was started by Rai Sahib Bhagwan Das.

The Grounds for a Parallel Political Enquiry

Tension between Nabha and Patiala had begun to mount in March and April 1922. Patiala adopted an aggressive attitude, largely with encouragement from Minchin. In the last week of March, a police officer of Nabha, Arjan Singh, was arrested by the Patiala police from the railway precincts at Dhuri, to be tried and sentenced. Ten days later, a police Head Constable of Patiala, Muhammad Yakub, was arrested by the Nabha police, to be tried and sentenced. On 24 April, Patiala tried to rescue Yakub by force. In the last week of April, Patiala blockaded Nabha, with the idea of forcing Nabha to approach the British authorities for intervention.

The Nabha Diwan (Prime Minister), Narasinga Rao, met Thompson personally to inform him that Patiala had blocked the road between Barnala and Dhanaula and picketed the road in the north of Nabha. Rao told Thompson that reprisals had been going on between the two states but a new situation had arisen now with 'the stopping of the high ways'. The sanad of 1860 entitled Nabha to 'a right of way though Patiala territory from one portion of Nabha to another'. This situation called for intervention by the Government of India. Thompson told Narasinga Rao that he would look into the matter.[17]

Immediately, Thompson asked Minchin if there was any ground now for intervention.[18] Minchin took the position that Patiala was not at fault. The Patiala Darbar had abrogated the dastūr al-'amal (rules of practice) but refrained from any form of reprisal inspite of strong provocation. Minchin gave his own version of the incidents, which presented Patiala in a better light. When the Diwan of Nabha complained to the AGG against the action of Patiala troops and suggested a conference to sort matters out, Minchin discouraged such negotiations as very difficult because the Patiala Maharaja was highly incensed against Nabha. He was said to be 'bitter' because he had lost 'so much prestige with his own subjects'.[19]

To prejudice the Diwan against the Darbar, Minchin told Narasinga Rao on 2 May 1922 that the Maharaja of Nabha was trying to replace him. Undeterred, Rao gave a list of the 'acts of lawlessness' committed by Patiala, and Minchin retorted that Patiala could quote five such instances for each instance given by Nabha. Therefore, Patiala would not agree to any conference until all the arrested persons of Patiala were released. Minchin highlighted the contention of Patiala that Nabha was 'disloyal to the British Government'. After this browbeating, he came to the real point: the Government of India wanted to appoint 'a committee of their own officers to enquire into every complaint which Patiala had against Nabha and which Nabha had against Patiala'. This proposal was 'acceptable' to the Maharaja of Patiala.

Rao opposed this proposition on grounds of political principles. He argued that this procedure would suspend 'the sovereignty of His Highness in regard to the administration of justice in his own State', and create a precedent for British interference in matters of 'internal administration of the state'. Consistent with the position upheld so far, Nabha could not go against 'settled political principles and political rights of the Darbar'. Rao insisted that the government should advise Patiala to desist from obstructing the highway and from making 'warlike preparations' by mobilizing police and troops. Minchin unhesitatingly maintained that he had no objection 'to any kind of disposition of troops by the Maharaja of Patiala within his own State'. When this was reported to the Maharaja of Nabha, he remarked that Minchin was 'a party to the whole affair'.[20]

On 3 May, Minchin informed Narasinga Rao that the Government of India would 'appoint a special officer to enquire into and report upon only such cases as involve, according to the statement of each party, a breach or violation of territorial sovereignty', and Rao was asked to give a list of such cases to Minchin.[21] Rao was not enthusiastic about sending such a list. He was certain that all the disputes would not be settled and the atmosphere of tension would not improve. Therefore, he considered reconciliation with Patiala as the most suitable approach.[22] Maharaja Ripudaman Singh was inclined to agree with him.[23]

The Government of India had already decided to hold a formal enquiry. Minchin wrote to the Prime Minister of Patiala and the Diwan of Nabha that they should submit full details of the acts instigated or connived at by the Darbar complained against, amounting to 'a violation of territorial sovereignty'. Subsequently, he asked, 'whether the Darbar would prefer in this matter to adhere to the usual rule under which the intervention of Counsel is not permitted in political cases'.[24] Minchin knew that the counsels would be kept out as the enquiry would be political.

Ripudaman Singh had an inkling that the AGG, Patiala, and Thompson, the Additional Political Secretary to the Governor General were working in tandem. The Maharaja, therefore, approved of Rao's suggestion that Nabha should work for an amicable settlement with Patiala.[25] Narasinga Rao happened to meet the Maharaja of Patiala in Simla on 10 May and suggested that some amicable settlement should be arrived at. Bhupinder Singh responded indifferently, saying that Rao should meet him on 16 May when Sir Daya Kishan Kaul would also be in Simla.[26]

Meanwhile, Rao wrote to Minchin on 13 May that the Nabha Darbar would be prepared to release Muhammad Yakub, who had been arrested by Nabha, as an act of grace, provided Patiala released Sardar Arjan Singh, the Naib Kotwal of Nabha, who had been forcibly taken away from the Dhuri (in Patiala territory) railway station by the Patiala police and later sentenced to imprisonment on some fabricated charges.[27] In his reply to Rao on 19 May, Minchin maintained that Arjan Singh was arrested in Patiala territory. Therefore, the two cases were not alike. He added on his own that the Patiala Darbar were not at all likely to agree to mutual surrender. He then asked Rao to send the Nabha allegations against Patiala without waiting for the Patiala allegations against Nabha.[28]

Narasinga Rao had personally informed Thompson of Minchin's concurrence with the posting of troops by Patiala to rescue Muhammad Yakub by force. Rao pointed out that the consent of the AGG in this illegal venture was deviation from neutrality. It was absolutely desirable that the British representative should keep himself above suspicion. Thompson promised to consider the suggestion that Patiala might be advised to see that no such breaches were allowed to occur in the future. He told Rao that H. A. Casson, President of the Punjab Legislative Council, was likely to conduct the enquiry proposed to be started at Ambala early in June. Narasinga Rao could see that the Political Secretary too was strongly in favour of an enquiry.[29] When Rao again met the Maharaja of Patiala he invoked 'prestige and honour' in support of his 'grim determination to fight Nabha to the bitter end'.[30]

The attitudes of Thompson and Bhupinder Singh convinced Narasinga Rao that both of them wanted an enquiry. Rao also felt that the Government of India would be glad to interfere in the disputes between the two states 'to push the proposed enquiry to its conclusion'. Therefore, Rao suggested once again to Maharaja Ripudaman Singh to go in for a direct settlement with the Maharaja of Patiala, who seemed to hold the key to a settlement as well as an enquiry whose outcome would most certainly be prejudicial to Nabha.[31]

Meanwhile, it was pointed out to Maharaja Ripudaman Singh by Syed Hasan Imam, who had been appointed recently as Remembrancer of Legal Affairs of Nabha State, that all along since 3 May 1922, it had been assumed that the only course open to the two states was the appointment of a special officer to look into their complaints. The provision existing for the appointment of a Court of Arbitration in case of a dispute between a state and the paramount power, or between two and more Indian states, was completely ignored. The Resolution of 29 October 1920 for a Court of Arbitration had laid down the following constitution: (*a*) one Judicial Officer not lower in rank than a Judge of Chartered High Court of Judicature in British India, and (*b*) one nominee of each of the parties concerned. The Resolution further laid down that each party 'will be entitled to represent its case to the Court by the Counsel or otherwise'. Nabha's charges against Patiala were ready but Maharaja Ripudaman Singh desired the settlement of the issue of Court of Arbitration first. He took the position that on hearing that a Court of Arbitration had been ordered by the Governor General, charges would be forwarded to the AGG.[32]

While forwarding Daya Kishan Kaul's confidential letter against the appointment of a Court of Arbitration, Minchin argued that the appointment of a Court of Arbitration was not mandatory under the terms of the Resolution of October 1920. The matter was 'at the discretion of the Viceroy' and neither of the Darbars had the right to contest his decision; 'nor does any appeal lie to the Secretary of State'.[33] The Political Department maintained that it was impossible for His Excellency to entertain any request to the appointment of a Court of Arbitration until he was acquainted with the charges which the two Darbars wished to bring against each other. The AGG should, therefore, ask Nabha to send their fresh charges against Patiala within a week, or to authorize him to open the sealed letter already sent with the stipulation that it should be opened after the Viceroy's decision regarding the Court of Arbitration. That the Court of Arbitration had been ruled out is evident from the instructions to Minchin to forward the charges received from both the Darbars with his recommendations 'as to the terms of reference to the enquiring officer'.[34]

In his communication of 28 November 1922 to the new Secretary of State (Montagu had resigned in March 1922), the Viceroy explained that he refused to appoint a Court of Arbitration on the ground that the Patiala Darbar had alleged a course of conduct on the part of Nabha which would, if proved, constitute an offence against 'the King's peace'. It was emphasized that the British Government was solely responsible for 'the King's peace', a feature of the British domestic law but a novel concept for India. It was contended that the proper course in an inter-state dispute affecting the 'King's peace' was 'to appoint an officer to investigate charges and to submit a report to the Government of India to enable it to take appropriate action'. The case, thus, was not yet one for action under Resolution no. 426-R of 1920 meant to resolve disputes between princes. The Viceroy added that by insisting on its application the Maharaja of Nabha had shown a tendency to adopt an 'obstructive' attitude and he might try to delay the proceedings by appealing to the Secretary of State against the orders of the Viceroy on the Court of Arbitration. The Viceroy, therefore, wanted the concurrence of the Secretary of State to go ahead with the enquiry even if Nabha appealed to the Secretary of State.[35]

The second issue on which the Viceroy wanted to have clearance from the Secretary of State was essentially that of sending a force to Nabha if it refused removal of the Patiala state subjects, allegedly arrested and jailed at Nabha, and cited by the Patiala Darbar as necessary witnesses. The Viceroy proposed to demand their surrender, and if Nabha refused compliance, a difficult situation would arise.

> If necessary, therefore, as a last resort, I propose, after solemn warning, to bring strong pressure to bear upon him including, if necessary, visit to Nabha of Agent to the Governor-General, Punjab States, with escort of troops.[36]

In fact, the countdown had begun with Montagu's telegram of 21 October 1921 to the Viceroy. After the rejection of the Court of Arbitration and the decision to go ahead with the political enquiry with the active cooperation of Patiala, the possibility of any reconciliation was virtually ruled out.

Attempts at Reconciliation Foiled

Minchin was strongly opposed to the idea of reconciliation. He informed Thompson on 15 January 1922 that Nabha had sent a deputation to Patiala in December 1921 asking for reconciliation. While ensuring Patiala's irreconcilability, Minchin assured Thompson that there was no chance of Nabha accepting the four difficult conditions laid down by the Maharaja of Patiala, failing which Patiala intended 'to break off all direct communications with Nabha'.[37]

In April 1922, Narasinga Rao asked Minchin whether a conference between the two rulers was feasible and Minchin showed him the terms on which Patiala insisted. As a pre-condition for this conference, the Maharaja of Patiala wanted the unconditional release of Abdul Aziz, Muhammad Yakub, and other Patiala men and women allegedly under custody in Nabha. Narasinga Rao could see that the Maharaja of Nabha could not accept these terms, which compromised his internal sovereignty and cast a negative reflection on his administration and justice. Again, in May 1922, when the Maharaja of Jind tried to bring about a reconciliation between Nabha and Patiala, Minchin did not think that there was any chance of success.[38]

The most serious attempt at reconciliation was made by the Nawab of Malerkotla, who met Thompson on 12 September 1922 with the idea of 'arbitration' between the Maharajas of Nabha and Patiala. What the Nawab had in mind was a commission composed of two ruling princes and a British official in order to enquire into 'the allegations of violation of territory' and to effect a complete reconciliation on all outstanding points. Thompson informed the Nawab that it was no longer a question of the offences alleged by the two Darbars against each other, 'but offences against the King's peace'. If proved, it would 'necessitate punitive action' by the government. Moreover, the government would require some sort of guarantee to prevent a repetition of 'such acts' against the 'King's peace'.[39]

However, when Thompson mentioned the proposal to the Viceroy on 29 September, he said that 'he would be prepared not to press the point that any territorial violation which might be proved against Patiala or Nabha would be an offence against the King's peace'. Apparently, with his legal training, he knew that application of such a concept could not be defended in Parliament. He insisted, however, that the settlement must cover the whole ground and there must be guarantees against recurrence of bickering in future. The Nawab called on Thompson on 30 September, and he was told that the Viceroy would be glad if a settlement could be arrived at and all the conditions stipulated were fulfilled. The first step was to get letters from both the parties and to submit them to Colonel Minchin before 15 October.

On a question from the Nawab, Thompson clarified that the British Government might find it necessary to take further action if the findings were unfavourable in regard to the kidnapping and ill treatment of women. On 4 October 1922, Thompson gave a copy of his note to the Nawab, requiring that the point about the 'ill-treatment' of women should be mentioned to 'the parties'.[40]

In this backdrop, Nabha looked upon arbitration on the whole as an honourable way out. On 2 December, the Nawab informed Patiala that the Maharaja of Nabha had accepted private arbitration unconditionally and without any reservation. He had also agreed that the decision of the arbitrators would be final. The Viceroy was prepared to agree to the proposal of arbitration on certain conditions which, probably, had been communicated to the Maharaja of Patiala by Colonel Minchin. Sincerely wishing that the Maharaja should also agree to arbitration, the Nawab wanted to know Patiala's views about this matter at his earliest convenience.[41]

Minchin appears to have pre-empted reconciliation by giving a different slant in his report of the Nawab's visits to Nabha and Patiala. The Nawab had gone to Nabha ahead of Minchin and obtained a letter signed by the Maharaja in which he agreed to accept the arbitration of Malerkotla and Jind for the settlement of all matters in dispute between him and the Maharaja of Patiala. But, short of flatly refusing arbitration, the Maharaja of Patiala said that he would accept arbitration only if the Viceroy advised him to do so. Patiala went on to add that the government could not give the guarantees required without abrogating clauses VI and VIII of the sanads of 1860. Minchin maintained that the Maharaja of Patiala was right in refusing arbitration because a final settlement of the matters in dispute was impossible without the intervention of the Government of India.[42] On the same day, Minchin wrote again to the Government of India that the Nawab of Malerkotla was still hopeful of settlement by arbitration, but it was very 'doubtful' if Patiala would agree to that. Minchin underlined that the Maharaja of Nabha would never cease from 'insidious attacks' on Patiala. The Maharaja of Nabha, in his view, was of such an 'abnormal mentality' that he was 'a danger to the whole of India'. It would be wrong not to utilize the present opportunity of 'bringing him fully to book', pleaded Minchin.[43]

On 6 December 1922, the Viceroy sent a telegram to the Secretary of State, referring to the belated proposals of amicable arbitration between Patiala and Nabha by a brother prince. Nabha was willing, and the Viceroy had tentatively consented to overtures being made to the parties on specified conditions, even though he did not think it likely that Patiala would agree. The latest reports indicated, indeed, that the chances of reconciliation were very small. This was meant simply for the information of the Secretary of State and not because much was likely to come of it.[44] The Secretary of State replied that he was prepared to support the Viceroy in any action that he might take to secure a satisfactory investigation of charges on the conditions laid down by the Viceroy.[45]

Minchin reported with satisfaction to the Political Secretary that his discussion with Patiala reconfirmed that he would not willingly agree to reconciliation. Minchin had no doubt that the Maharaja of Nabha would be keen on a private settlement but the Maharaja of Patiala would not accept any terms unless the Viceroy especially asked him to do so. In his communication to Thompson on 13 December 1922, Minchin emphasized that the enquiry should proceed.[46] On the following day, Sir Daya Kishan Kaul wrote to Minchin that the Maharaja of Patiala continued to think that the method of settlement proposed by the Nawab could not secure due redress for Patiala and assurance for the future. Kaul added that the violation of territory was a rankling sting to the Patiala Darbar. Therefore, no satisfactory result could come out of the arbitration advocated by the Nawab Sahib. Next day Kaul informed Minchin that the Maharaja was sending a reply to the Nawab of Malerkotla that private arbitration was out of the question.[47]

Though the matter of arbitration was closed all the time for the Government of India and Patiala, Sir Ali Imam continued to pursue his negotiations with Sir Daya Kishan Kaul on behalf of Nabha and he continued to apprise Minchin of the developments. Minchin had a design of his own. A complete surrender on Nabha's part could be regarded as a full justification by Patiala and secure him indemnity. In Minchin's view, it could be proved that the Maharaja of Nabha was responsible for a breach of the 'King's peace', and acts of 'injustice' and 'maladministration'. This might justify the suspension of the Maharaja's powers, as already suggested by Minchin. He was confident that it would then be easy to prepare indictment against him. If the proposed settlement was approved, it should not be difficult to 'generate' sufficient evidence to justify the step suggested by Minchin. He would go to Patiala to 'assist' the Darbar in working out the final arrangements.[48]

As a lawyer by training, Reading wanted to be sure about the procedures and technicalities involved. The Government of India sent a telegram to Minchin on 2 January 1923, to clarify the position on a few points. At the same time, Minchin was informed that Justice Louis Stuart, a Judge of the Allahabad High Court, had been recommended by the UP Governor as 'a suitable officer for the proposed enquiry'. Stuart was known to be inimical to the nationalist forces.[49] On the following day, Minchin telegraphed his reply to the questions raised by the Government of India, suggesting, among other things, that the enquiry by Justice Stuart be delayed.[50] But Justice Stuart had already started his enquiry at Ambala in the forenoon of 3 January 1923.

It is quite obvious that Minchin and the Patiala Darbar were working in tandem and under the overall direction of Thompson in the Political Department and the Viceroy in conjunction with the Secretary of State. Even more than the Maharaja of Patiala, Minchin and his bosses were keen to see the fall of Maharaja Ripudaman Singh. It is not surprising that as their man on the spot, Minchin was far from being impartial in the performance of his official duties. He succeeded in keeping two important cases against Patiala out of the enquiry. One of these related to the unjustified blockade of Nabha and the other to the illegal arrest of Sardar Arjan Singh, the Naib Kotwal of Nabha, by two Patiala policemen, both of which were the clearest examples of Patiala's violation of the so-called 'King's Peace'. In his argument against their trial, Minchin maintained that 'to do so would be to nullify in part the object with which the Government of India' had instituted the enquiry. Integral to this conspiracy was the brushing aside of Patiala's known high-handedness and the overlooking of his notoriety in regard to women, which ironically were being held against Nabha.[51]

The Enquiry Tilted against Nabha

In the enquiry conducted by Justice Stuart the first decision taken was about restricting the role of counsels on the ground that it was a political enquiry. The charges were so framed as to give crucial importance to 'territorial sovereignty' and its violation, which was treated as violation of the 'King's peace'. The proceedings also indicate how witnesses were manipulated to the disadvantage of Nabha. On Patiala's plea with the Government of India that Nabha was influencing public opinion through the press, Patiala was allowed to indulge in vicious propaganda in the press in its favour and buy or browbeat the key witnesses. The use of high-handed tactics by the Patiala police was ignored by the British authorities. Ostensibly on ground of 'neutrality', Minchin declined to appear in the court as a witness to be cross-examined by Nabha. The findings were leaked by Justice Stuart before the enquiry was over, and people were encouraged to speculate about the results of the enquiry, which affected the loyalties of the Nabha officials in particular and popular sympathy for the Maharaja in general.

Patiala regarded the engaging of Legal Remembrancer by Nabha as 'nothing but a device to defeat the Government of India's decision restricting appearance of counsels'. After the very first day, Patiala contended that counsels could not be allowed to prompt or pass on slips of paper to the state representative examining witnesses or conducting other proceedings. This contention was based on a letter of the Political Department, dated 5 July 1922, addressed to Minchin, which allowed the Darbars to employ counsels to advise them 'privately both before and during the enquiry', but counsels could not 'undertake the examination of witnesses in such cases'. This was then modified by a letter of 10 October 1922, written in continuation of the letter of 5 July, stating that no practising lawyer would be allowed to appear as the state representative before the Enquiry Officer but such persons were allowed to watch the case and to advise the Darbar representative 'out of court'.[52]

To reinforce matters, Minchin telephoned Thompson on 5 January 1923 to know his view and he affirmed that all consultations should take place outside the court of the Enquiry Officer, otherwise the previous orders of the Government of India would be stultified.[53] On 6 January, Patiala sent a telegram to the Political Department to say that 'either the counsel should be allowed to represent straight away, or even the passing of slips and prompting or taking any part whatever by them in the Court Room disallowed'.[54] The Political Department wrote to Justice Stuart on the same day that the instructions contained in their letter of 10 October 1922, addressed to the AGG, were approved by the Governor General and, therefore, counsels were 'precluded from advising the Darbar representative' in the court.[55]

How elaborately the charges of Patiala were framed may be illustrated with reference to the case of Head Constable Muhammad Yakub. Six principles of international law were set out in a 'preamble' before coming to the 'statement of the case' in the second section and, finally, to the 'legal exposition of the case' in the third. All kinds of authorities and documents were cited to establish and define 'full sovereignty' of Patiala (and Nabha) as 'international persons'. The point sought to be made was that Nabha and Patiala, though subject to the paramount power, were sovereign states for the purposes of international law. The authority of three legal luminaries of Europe was invoked to underline that 'In unequal alliances, the inferior power remains a *sovereign state*'. Five principles of international law were stated, and authorities on international law were cited for each principle.[56]

Simultaneously, several steps were taken to influence the proceedings in favour of Patiala. Given the dispersed nature of the Nabha territory, most of its officials had landed property in the Patiala state. To put pressure on them a circular notice was issued, requiring them to appear in person at Patiala on a given date. The objective was to win over or intimidate the Nabha officials in general and to get hold of Suchet Singh, the Sub-Inspector under whom Muhammad Yakub, the Head Constable of Patiala, had spent his days in Dhanaula jail. Suchet Singh did not go 'even on the pain of his landed property being confiscated', observes Syngal. But such loyalty remained an exception.[57]

There was an effort also to browbeat some Akalis arrested by the Government of India on the suspicion of having conspired to throw a bomb on the Prince of Wales during his visit to India. The principal suspects, Bijla Singh and his wife, Prem Kaur, were arrested by Patiala. Every effort was made to extort from them the confession that the Maharaja of Nabha was involved in this conspiracy. A Punjab police officer was deputed to record their statements, but they refused to implicate Maharaja Ripudaman Singh.[58]

Through the good offices of the Maharaja of Patiala, however, the government was eventually able to extort 'evidence' from Prem Kaur against Nabha in the case of Muhammad Yakub. Minchin's Secretary informed the Foreign and Political Department on 25 January: 'Today Prem Kaur has made statements of most important nature at Ambala about Akali and other revolutionary propaganda in Nabha.'[59] On 9 February, the Maharaja of Nabha met Thompson, and mentioned 'awful things' being said against him by some of the witnesses, in particular by Prem Kaur. On 5 March, Justice Stuart informed the Political Secretary that he did not require Prem Kaur's attendance anymore and recommended her application for removal to Patiala's custody. The approval came within a fortnight. Prem Kaur was hoping to be released on the Baisakhi day for having given evidence in favour of Patiala.[60]

Bijla Singh's statement too was now 'satisfactory' from the official viewpoint. Minchin had sent a telegram to Thompson on 22 January 1923 to say that Bijla Singh was getting suspicious of the delay, and that if 'the plan' was not carried out at once it might miscarry. Bijla Singh was not prepared to make any statement or to surrender except to the Maharaja of Patiala. The Viceroy was not prepared to grant pardon unless Bijla Singh made 'full and true statement'. Bijla Singh's statement was expected to provide strong corroboration of the statements made by his wife, Prem Kaur. The matter had become even more urgent in view of the possibility of evidence being destroyed after Prem Kaur's statements. The Punjab Government agreed to surrender Bijla Singh to the Patiala state on certain conditions. Bijla Singh was apprehended by Patiala on 27 January. The Maharaja personally explained the terms to him in the presence of Minchin's Secretary. Everything went well from their viewpoint, and Bijla Singh was taken to Lahore by the Punjab official who had come for the meeting.[61] This case is a telling example of how the Governor General, his Political Secretary, the Punjab Governor, the AGG, and the Maharaja of Patiala were directly involved in turning Bijla Singh into an approver.

In this context, it is not surprising that Justice Stuart, an arch imperialist himself,[62] was expected to further the cause of the government and its collaborator. By the middle of February 1923, Justice Stuart completed all the evidence connected with the case of firing at Jiundan and the case of Muhammad Yakub, and the papers were handed over on 17 February. Justice Stuart also informed the Foreign and Political Department that Patiala was willing to drop Ishar Kaur's case, which had been a contentious issue between the two states. Patiala could not proceed without her and did not hope to obtain her attendance.[63]

Meanwhile, the Maharaja of Patiala met the Governor General on 9 February 1923 to make a formal complaint against Nabha's propaganda mainly through the Sikh newspapers to influence the highly placed government officials, respectable members of the Indian public, including the legislators, and the Sikhs in general. The Maharaja of Patiala was alleged to be high-handed and immoral, using his position to kidnap girls, and to commit other acts of tyranny. He was held responsible for the continuance of the enquiry against Nabha to ruin the smaller Sikh state and his own 'cousin'. He was untrue to the Sikh faith, and opposed to those elements who were desirous of purifying and reforming the Sikh religion. The complaint of the Maharaja of Patiala to the Governor General was placed on record. His Prime Minister, Sir Daya Kishan Kaul, met the Political Secretary on the same day to complain of the propaganda being conducted in support of the Maharaja of Nabha. Kaul then asked Thompson if starting counter-propaganda would be justified. The Political Secretary told him that 'the Patiala Darbar would no doubt take such steps as they thought fit'.[64] The ground was thus cleared for supporting the enquiry through a vicious propaganda by Patiala.

Munna Lal Syngal observes that the case of another Patiala official, Abdul Aziz, who was charged with rape, took a considerable time and several officers of the Nabha police and other officials of Nabha connected with the enquiry decamped with important papers to join the Patiala state for pecuniary rewards. Particularly helpful to Patiala was Bishan Singh, a former Kotwal of Nabha, who had been suspended on a charge of trading in women but eventually acquitted and reinstated. Because of his grudge against Nabha, he was easily induced to change sides.[65]

Justice Stuart initially thought that Minchin's evidence was 'essential' in the case of Abdul Aziz. Minchin was averse to appearing personally for his obvious lack of neutrality, but maintained that 'it would necessarily involve a departure from the attitude of strict neutrality'. It would also have 'a prejudicial effect' on his work as a political officer. He could send a certified copy of the report of his visit to Nabha in October 1921, if necessary. He added significantly that Justice Stuart was not bound by 'the strict rules of evidence'. On 24 February 1923, Justice Stuart sounded both Patiala and Nabha. The Nabha Darbar stated on the same day that the presence of Minchin was necessary on points relevant to the proper presentation of their case. 'The Darbar are prepared to cross-examine Colonel Minchin but not to call him as their own witness.' As expected, Patiala Darbar did not insist on Minchin appearing as a witness in the case.[66] Justice Stuart then wrote to Minchin that it would not be fair to call him. However, it was necessary for Stuart to write to the Government of India for a formal decision. In reply to his letter, Thompson wrote to Justice Stuart on 28 February that the Governor General agreed with him that Nabha should not be allowed to summon Minchin merely for cross-examination. Justice Stuart used his discretion to drop Minchin, allowing him to have his way again.[67]

Patiala was getting desperate and aggressive about the case of Abdul Aziz. According to Syngal, when Rahmat un-Nisa, who had allegedly been raped by Abdul Aziz, was under cross-examination before Justice Stuart, the Patiala police made a daring attempt to carry her away from the court precincts. In the row that followed, some of the Nabha men received injuries. There was sufficient ground to register a criminal case. Therefore, Eardley Norton, who had been the backroom adviser of Nabha in the enquiry, was happy that Justice Stuart and the government would not be able to stop him from cross-examination in this case. But the case was intentionally delayed and never came up for hearing.[68] However, Justice Stuart was unhappy over the incident violating the dignity of his court.[69]

The case of Pehdani firing was the most important from the viewpoint of Nabha. On 28 April and 13 May 1922, according to the complaint of Nabha, the village Pehdani, which was surrounded on all sides by Patiala territory, was invaded by the residents of a neighbouring village, supported by rowdy elements of other places and led by a Patiala Sub-Inspector, Bakhshish Singh. A large number of buffaloes and the headman (Lambardār) of Pehdani were carried away. It was a clear breach of the territorial sovereign rights of Nabha. Eardley Norton could not handle this case because he had to leave for Kodaikanal. But even from there he wrote to Syngal twice to the effect that 'whatever may be the outcome of the enquiry he was convinced that the Patiala Maharaja was clearly guilty in that case and that was a big thing'.[70]

However, the genuine grievances of Nabha were either ignored or turned upside down in the name of 'King's peace', holding Nabha responsible for its violation. Before the enquiry was over, and as expected, people had begun to speculate about its outcome. Syngal rued that 'it is difficult to control the flow of circumstances and destiny'. A general impression was created that Maharaja Ripudaman Singh would be deposed. A deep sense of insecurity prevailed among services in Nabha and nobody was putting his heart and soul into work. The police officers were fighting among themselves.[71] The sense of responsibility in services and love for the Maharaja amply evident until a few months earlier eroded under the cumulative pressures of the disapproval and disfavour of the government and the propaganda and purse of its collaborator. A part of this 'destiny' came through the leakage of Stuart's findings.

Notes

1. India Office Records (IOR) (microfilm), R/1/29/32, File no. 628-P (Secret)/1923 (cited hereafter as IOR, 628-P(S), 1923). This thick file on 'Patiala–Nabha Disputes' opens with the telegram of the Secretary of State for India to the Viceroy, dated 27 October 1921, as 'very confidential, private and personal'. There is hardly any doubt that this telegram started a new phase in the attitude of the paramount power towards Maharaja Ripudaman Singh.
2. IOR, 628-P(S), 1923, telegram from Viceroy to the Secretary of State for India, dated 8 November 1921.
3. IOR, 628-P(S), 1923, A. B. Minchin's report, dated 8 November 1921.
4. IOR (microfilm), R/1/29/53, File no. 838-Pol (Secret) of 1923 (cited hereafter as IOR, 838-P(S), 1923), Punjab CID report to the Intelligence Bureau, dated 1 November 1921.
5. IOR, 838-P(S), 1923, note by W. H. Vincent, dated 8 November 1921.
6. IOR, 838-P(S), 1923, J. P. Thompson to A. B. Minchin, 15 November 1921.
7. IOR, 838-P(S), 1923, A. B. Minchin to J. P. Thompson, 12 December 1921, with enclosure.
8. IOR, 838-P(S), 1923, note by J. P. Thompson, dated 18 December 1921. O'Donell's note dated 19 December 1921.
9. IOR, 838-P(S), 1923, O'Donell's note dated 22 December 1921.
10. IOR, 838-P(S), 1923, J. P. Thompson to E. Joseph (Chief Secretary to Punjab Government), 9 January 1922.
11. IOR, 838-P(S), 1923, telegram from the Secretary of State to the Viceroy, dated 11 January 1922.
12. IOR, 838-P(S), 1923, telegram from the Viceroy to the Secretary of State, dated 23 January 1922.
13. IOR, 838-P(S), 1923, E. Joseph to J. P. Thompson, 31 January 1922.
14. IOR, 838-P(S), 1923, J. P. Thompson to A. B. Minchin, 2 March 1922.
15. IOR, 838-P(S), 1923, telegram from the AGG to the Political Secretary, dated 21 April 1922.
16. IOR, 838-P(S), 1923, telegram from the Political Secretary to the AGG, dated 21 April 1922.
17. IOR, 628-P(S), 1923, note by J. P. Thompson, dated 26 April 1922.
18. IOR, 628-P(S), 1923, J. P. Thompson to A. B. Minchin, 26 April 1922.
19. IOR, 628-P(S), 1923, A. B. Minchin's fortnightly report for the second half of April 1922.
20. Punjab State Archives (PSA), Patiala, Diwan and Chief Secretary Nabha State Office Records (DCNS), note of interview with Col. Minchin, dated 2 May 1922.
21. PCA, DCNS, a note of interview with Col. Minchin, dated 3 May 1922.

22. PCA, DCNS, a note of D. M. Narasinga Rao's interview with Col. Minchin, submitted to His Highness the Maharaja of Nabha on 3 May 1922.
23. PCA, DCNS, a note of D. M. Narasinga Rao's interview with Col. Minchin, submitted to His Highness the Maharaja of Nabha on 4 May 1922.
24. PCA, DCNS, A. B. Minchin to D. M. Narasinga Rao, 10 May 1922.
25. PCA, DCNS, note by D. M. Narasinga Rao, submitted to His Highness the Maharaja of Nabha on 10 May 1922.
26. PCA, DCNS, Narasinga Rao to His Highness the Maharaja of Nabha, 11 May 1922.
27. PCA, DCNS, Narasinga Rao to Minchin, 13 May 1922.
28. PCA, DCNS, A. B. Minchin to D. M. Narasinga Rao, 19 May 1922. Also, note submitted by D. M. Narasinga Rao to His Highness on 13 May 1922.
29. PCA, DCNS, note of interview with Mr J. P. Thompson, dated 17 May 1922.
30. PCA, DCNS, note of interview with His Highness the Maharaja of Patiala, dated 17 and 18 May 1922.
31. PCA, DCNS, D. M. Narasinga Rao to His Highness the Maharaja of Nabha, 19 May 1922.
32. IOR, 628-P(S), 1923, copy of letter no. 1-AGG-P.L., dated 5 October 1922.
    The Resolution of the Foreign and Political Department providing for a Court of Arbitration was included in the recommendations of the Report of Indian Constitutional Reforms.
33. IOR, 628-P(S), 1923, AGG to the Government of India, 5 October 1922 and 7 November 1922.
34. IOR, 628-P(S), 1923, Confidential letter to A.B. Minchin from the Viceroy's Camp, 31 October 1922.
35. IOR, 628-P(S), 1923, Governor General to the Secretary of State, 28 November 1922. Significantly, the Political Secretary had already informed the AGG about the Governor General's decision and instructed the AGG to notify Nabha and open the sealed packet containing Nabha's charges and frame the terms of reference accordingly. Thompson to Minchin, 23 November 1922.
36. IOR, 628-P(S), 1923, Governor General to the Secretary of State, 28 November 1922. The Governor General was obviously clearing the deck for a determined course of action by making the new Secretary of State a party.
37. IOR, 838-P(S), 1923, extract from a letter of A. B. Minchin to J. P. Thompson, dated 15 January 1922.
38. IOR, 628-P(S), 1923, A. B. Minchin to the Government of India, 20/22 May 1922.
39. IOR, 628-P(S), 1923, note by J. P. Thompson, dated 12 September 1922.
40. IOR, 628-P(S), 1923, notes by J. P. Thompson, dated 30 September and 4 October 1922.

41. IOR, 628-P(S), 1923, Nawab of Malerkotla to the Maharaja of Patiala, 2 December 1922.
42. IOR, 628-P(S), 1923, A. B. Minchin to the Government of India, 1/2 December 1922.
43. IOR, 628-P(S), 1923, 2 December 1922.
44. IOR, 628-P(S), 1923, telegram from the Viceroy to the Secretary of State for India, dated 6 December 1922.
45. IOR, 628-P(S), 1923, telegram from the Secretary of State for India to the Viceroy, dated 11 December 1922.
46. IOR, 628-P(S), 1923, AGG to Political Secretary, 13 December 1922.
47. IOR, 628-P(S), 1923, Prime Minister of Patiala to AGG, 14 December 1922; letter of the Maharaja of Patiala to the Nawab of Malerkotla, 15 December 1922.
48. IOR, 628-P(S), 1923, AGG to Government of India, 31 December 1922.
49. IOR, 628-P(S), 1923, telegram from Government of India to AGG, dated 2 January 1923. Also see note 62.
50. IOR, 628-P(S), 1923, telegram from AGG to Government of India, dated 3 January 1923.
51. Ian Copland, *The Princes of India in the Endgame of Empire 1917–1947* (Cambridge: Cambridge University Press, 1997), p. 51. It is not unlikely that like his successor Fitzpatrick, Minchin was a beneficiary of Patiala's well-known hospitality and generosity. Significantly, Minchin was shunted out of the Political Department soon afterwards because he was 'too close to Patiala'.
52. IOR, 838-P(S), 1923, representation made by S. M. Bapna to Justice Stuart on 4 January 1923.
53. IOR, 838-P(S), 1923, note by J. P. Thompson, dated 5 January 1923.
54. IOR, 838-P(S), 1923, telegram from Prime Minister of Patiala to Government of India, dated 6 January 1923.
55. IOR, 838-P(S), 1923, Government of India to Justice Stuart, 6 January 1923. Interestingly, as early as May 1922, Minchin had written to Thompson that if counsel was allowed to cross-examine witnesses it would 'obscure' rather than elucidate the cases, because 'the points of international law' were involved. IOR, 838-P(S), 1923, A. B. Minchin to J. P. Thompson, 20/22 and 26 May 1922.
56. For all the cases submitted by Patiala against Nabha, see Punjab State Archives (PSA), Patiala, Patiala Government, Ijlas-i-Khas Office, 'Patiala's Complaints against Nabha of Violation of Sovereignty'.
57. Munna Lal Syngal, *The Patriot Prince* (Ludhiana and Delhi: Doaba House, 1961), p. 122.
58. Syngal, *The Patriot Prince*, p. 104.
59. IOR, 838-P(S), 1923, telegram from Secretary to AGG to Government of India, dated 25 January 1923.

60. IOR, 838-P(S), 1923, note by J. P. Thompson, dated 9 February 1923; Justice Stuart to Government of India, 5 March 1923; Government of India to Justice Stuart, 19 March 1923.
61. IOR, 838-P(S), 1923, Deputy Secretary, Government of India to Political Secretary to Government of India, 27 January 1923; Secretary to AGG to Government of India, 28 January 1923.
62. Significantly and like O'Dwyer (p. 88n1), Louis Stuart later became a founder member of the Indian Empire Society, a London-based lobbying organization formed in 1930 to promote the cause of the British Empire in India. He soon became its Secretary, and also edited its organ. As a member of the India Defence League founded in 1933 as a British pressure group he consistently opposed constitutional reforms in India. See, for example, *The Times*, London (3 November 1933), p. 17; (1 February 1934), p. 8; (29 December 1949), p. 7.
63. IOR, 838-P(S), 1923, note by G. D. Ogilvie, dated 21 February 1923.
64. IOR, 838-P(S), 1923, note by G. F. de Montmorency, dated 10 February 1923; note by J. P. Thompson, dated 9 February 1923.
65. Syngal, *The Patriot Prince*, pp. 116–17.
66. IOR, 628-P(S), 1923, Justice Stuart to Government of India, 20 February 1923; A. B. Minchin to Justice Stuart, 22 February 1923; application from Patiala, dated 25 February 1923.
67. IOR, 628-P(S), 1923, A. B. Minchin to Justice Stuart, 25 February 1923; Government of India to Justice Stuart, 27/28 February 1923.
68. Syngal, *The Patriot Prince*, p. 121.
69. IOR, 628-P(S), 1923, Justice Stuart to Government of India, 16 March 1923.
70. Syngal, *The Patriot Prince*, p. 121.
71. Syngal, *The Patriot Prince*, p. 122.

7

REMOVAL FROM NABHA UNDER DURESS

Contrary to the general impression among historians, neither the official enquiry by Stuart nor the secret enquiry by Bhagwan Das was used formally by the Government of India to remove Maharaja Ripudaman Singh from Nabha. The 'findings' of these enquiries, which were never made public, were used to put pressure on the Maharaja to accept an 'agreement' that was actually imposed on him by the government with the approval and active connivance of the Secretary of State for India. There is hardly any doubt that Maharaja Ripudaman Singh was removed from Nabha under duress.

Proposals for Voluntary Dissociation

Justice Stuart submitted his report to the Viceroy on each case under dispute even before the enquiry was over. Therefore, rumours about his findings began to spread while the enquiry was in progress. The outcome could also be leaked through what the bureaucrats called 'the natural channels'. The refusal of the Maharaja of Patiala to come to any compromise with the Maharaja of Nabha, which was virtually ensured by the Government of India, confirmed the impression that Nabha's day of reckoning had come. In this situation, Maharaja Ripudaman Singh was persuaded to think in terms of his temporary dissociation from the administration of Nabha. This idea eventually became the basis of his permanent dissociation.

On 21 April 1923, Narasinga Rao, the Diwan of Nabha, submitted a proposal to Major G. D. Ogilvie of the Political Department that in view of His Highness' failing health since 1921, he was pleased to sanction administrative arrangements with the concurrence of the Government of India. The Diwan was vested with full powers to devise, introduce, and carry out salutary reforms in the administration as soon as possible, and to consult and take the advice of the Agent to the Governor General in all important matters. His Highness would retain the power of appointing the Diwan and other Ministers. Besides state guards and servants, the Civil List of His Highness would be fixed at 300,000 rupees a year. The proposal was shown to the Viceroy by the Political Secretary J. P. Thompson on 24 April 1923.[1]

A fortnight later, Narasinga Rao submitted an alternative scheme to AGG Minchin, addressed by the Maharaja of Nabha to the Viceroy for his approval. In the new proposal, the administration of the state was to be entrusted to the senior Maharani (Jagdish Kaur) who was to be assisted by a Council, with Narasinga Rao as its President. Rao informed Minchin that the Maharaja proposed to reserve 300,000 rupees for his private purposes and another 200,000 for the Maharanis, Tikka Sahib, and other domestic purposes. Even so, 2,500,000 rupees would be at the disposal of the Council. The arrangement could remain in force for two years. The powers and functions of the senior Maharani, the composition of the Council and the powers and functions of its President and members were detailed in 10 clauses. Minchin, however, did not see how the Council could effect any great improvement in the existing conditions as there was no mention of any reforms to be effected and no specified period for the operation of the scheme.[2]

On 7 May 1923, Maharaja Ripudaman Singh wrote to Minchin with reference to Narasinga Rao's meeting with him two days earlier that 'the Council will be free to introduce such administrative reforms as it deems necessary'. The Council was to have two years' time to complete the work.[3] Since the Government of India had a different plan for Nabha, Minchin found none of the proposals under consideration of 'any practical importance'. He asserted that they could not make for better government as the Council would be dependent entirely on the goodwill of the Maharaja, and there was nothing to prevent him from resuming control at any time.[4]

Thompson, however, thought that the new proposal could be examined. The Diwan as head of the administration was replaced by the senior

Maharani as the Regent. It was clearly understood that the Government of India could not assume any responsibility for the administration of the state. It was also clear that the hands of the government could not be tied for the future by agreeing to the arrangements proposed. In any case, there was no need to take a decision immediately in view of the completion of Stuart's enquiry in about three weeks.[5] An *ad interim* reply saying that His Excellency was considering the matter was conveyed to the Maharaja on 25 May.[6] The reply of the Government of India was as disconcerting to the Maharaja as to his 'interested and corrupt officials'. They persistently urged him to make his 'settlement' with the government, or be prepared to face reprisals. Outwitted by the government's agents and intimidated by its general stance, the Maharaja emphasized that in his interview with the AGG he did not 'offer to abdicate'; it was the AGG 'who demanded abdication from me'.[7]

Imposition of a Counter-Proposal

On 5 June 1923, Minchin wrote to Thompson that the Maharaja of Nabha had come to see him at Kasauli and he would accept his advice in all matters related to his own and to the Patiala Darbar. Old friendly relations with Patiala could be re-established and the old practice of extradition between the two states could be re-introduced. However, Minchin did not see any possibility of eradicating hostility between the two rulers even if the cases covered by Stuart's enquiry were settled. Minchin's own solution to the whole problem was resignation of His Highness from the gaddī of Nabha. He insisted on a reply 'within two days'.[8]

Minchin went to Simla to discuss the case of Nabha personally with Thompson, and informed him on 7 June that Maharaja Ripudaman Singh was now prepared to sever his connection with the administration of his state on the following terms:

1. The Maharaja to retain salute and title of Highness, but to hand over the administration of the state to the Government of India to be conducted as they think fit in the interests of his son, if possible by an officer of the ICS or the Political Department.
2. The Maharaja would live outside the state, probably at Mussoorie and Dehra Dun but would visit the state at intervals for the purpose of religious ceremonies, with the permission of Government of India.

3. The Maharaja would formally abdicate when his son came of age.
4. The heir would remain in charge of Regency Government.
5. The Maharaja would be prepared to pay up to 5,000,000 rupees as compensation to Patiala.
6. The Maharaja would like to retain certain houses for his own use. He mentioned Stirling Castle and Kenilworth and three or four houses elsewhere.

As regards (5), Thompson said that expenses plus 1,000,000 rupees would be a reasonable compensation to Patiala; to this would be added compensation to others who had suffered. As regards (6), he said that Stirling Castle was out of the question; a house at Dehra Dun and another at Mussoorie would suffice.[9] It was a considered view of the government that Maharaja Ripudaman Singh should never be allowed to live in Simla.

Thompson suggested that Minchin could go over to the Maharaja of Patiala to talk about the compensation and 'find out whether the terms proposed would be acceptable to Patiala'. The Viceroy ordered that Minchin should not discuss the matter of compensation with the Maharaja of Patiala. 'The case was now before the Government of India and it was for them to say what compensation was proper.' He should tell the Maharaja of Nabha that the Viceroy would be willing to receive and consider a written application to abdicate on the lines proposed. Minchin was asked to add on his own that this 'might have the effect of softening the attitude which the Government of India might have to adopt towards him as a result of the enquiry'. The threat of the possible result of the enquiry was to be held out to induce the Maharaja to agree to abdication as the better option for him.

Thompson sent a telegram to Minchin on the same day that the Maharaja should be informed that the Government of India would be bound 'to take most serious view of his position as case against Nabha found to be substantially correct'. But the Government of India would not ask for greater penalties and would accept 'voluntary submission' on terms he had suggested with 'slight amendments'.[10] Minchin reported that the Maharaja met him again at Kasauli on 9 June with two letters (actually both drafted by Minchin himself). In one of these letters, Maharaja wrote: 'Under the circumstances which have arisen I have decided to adopt the following arrangements which are, I understand, acceptable to the Government of India:

1. I should retain my salute and customary titles but would hand over to Government of India the administration of my state.
2. I shall reside in future outside the state, which I will visit only with the permission of the Government of India for religious ceremonies; and I request that a State bunglow be allotted to me at Mussoorie and Dehra Dun for my residence.
3. When my son comes of age I shall abdicate in his favour. The Government of India will undertake the responsibility of his education.'

The Maharaja went on to say that he had no objection to the payment of indemnity to the Maharaja of Patiala, not exceeding 5,000,000 rupees out of the revenues of the Nabha state. An allowance of 300,000 rupees a year was to be paid to the Maharaja for his lifetime. He undertook not to interfere with the affairs of the Nabha state. The Maharaja was 'persuaded' to sign this letter at Kasauli in the presence of Minchin.[11]

In the other letter, dated 10 June, the Maharaja wrote that it would be possible for him 'to assist' towards the payment of compensation that might be awarded to Patiala. It committed the Maharaja to cooperate with the Nabha administration after his departure from Nabha in recovering over 5,000,000 rupees for compensation and other purposes. The forced character of the letter is evident from its language. It was actually obtained by Minchin after a good deal of persuasion in which he was joined by the Prime Minister and the Foreign Minister of Nabha. This letter too was signed in Minchin's presence.[12]

On 10 June Minchin responded to Thompson's telegram of the 7th by sending copies of these two letters of the Maharaja of Nabha. The AGG hoped that these letters met the conditions laid down in Thompson's telegram. He requested that the Viceroy's approval of the arrangements might be conveyed to him telegraphically as His Highness was waiting at Kasauli to know the result. If the Maharaja's submission was accepted, an officer might be deputed for taking over the administration of Nabha and sent to Kasauli for appropriate instructions from the AGG. The reason for Minchin's urgent request was that it had 'not been at all easy to induce His Highness to write the letters'. It was only with the assistance of Narasinga Rao and Sen that 'His Highness was at last prevailed upon to act reasonably'.

Referring to their role Minchin added that these two officials had requested that 'in order to save them from disgrace, His Excellency may be pleased to write to the Maharaja ...that it was only after very careful consideration that he had decided to agree to the concessions which have been granted under the arrangement sanctioned by him'. Minchin believed that the Maharaja was under the impression that 'his officials may have exaggerated the gravity of the situation, and it would save their faces if some communication of the kind I have suggested could be sent to His Highness in accordance with their prayer'. Obtained by intimidation and with the orchestrated connivance of the Nabha officials, the letters signed by the Maharaja were too precious to be sent by post. Therefore, only copies were sent by Minchin; the originals of the two letters were retained by him to be sent later through a special messenger.[13]

Minchin went on to say that the Maharaja was much concerned with 'whether his movements are to be restricted in any way'. He was anxious to have the freedom to travel in India and in Europe. Minchin expressed the view that, having regard to the past connections of the Maharaja with the Akalis and the Kukas, it was very desirable that 'he should not be allowed to enter the Punjab in future without special permission'. The Maharaja also desired keenly that during the minority of his son the state should be administered by an officer of the Indian Civil Service, either British or Indian. Minchin was strongly opposed to the appointment of an Indian, at present at any rate, and suggested that special care might be exercised in the selection for the post of Superintendent in Nabha.

On the 10th itself Minchin had three conversations with Thompson. He rang up in the morning to say that the Maharaja of Nabha 'had signed the first letter after five hours discussion'. The Maharaja was not willing to give up the money he had but he had no objection to the sale of residential properties. Thompson told Minchin to 'press the Maharaja further, saying that the Government of India had calculated on getting the 50 lakhs down'. He should give up 600,000, and accept 200,000 as his allowance instead of 300,000. The houses in any case belonged to the state and could be sold without his consent. Minchin told Thompson that his long discussion with the Maharaja on these lines left the impression that he was 'giving in merely because he was at the end of his resources'. Shortly before 1 p.m. Minchin rang up again to say that according to Narasinga Rao and Sen the Maharaja had 900,000 rupees worth of securities and 100,000 in cash. Minchin had, therefore, persuaded the Maharaja to part with his 1,000,000 and to agree to the sale of houses in Mussoorie and Simla, including the sprawling Nabha Estate in Simla. All this would bring in 4,000,000, the amount originally thought of by the Viceroy. Thompson told Minchin that if the Maharaja agreed to this, he would recommend it to the Viceroy.

Minchin now wanted to know if he could say to the Maharaja 'that if the case was allowed to take its course, Nabha would fare worse'. Using the typically bureaucratic understatement, Thompson said that the Viceroy 'had felt some doubt whether Nabha was not getting off too lightly, though he had in the end come to the conclusion that a speedy settlement would be best'. Therefore, it would be safe to tell the Maharaja that 'if he went further with the case, he might fare worse'. Minchin finally rang up at 8 p.m. to inform Thompson that the Maharaja had 'accepted the position'. He also reminded Thompson of the request made by Narasinga Rao and Sen. In other words, coercion alone would not have had the desired result without the cooperation of the Nabha officials, which enabled Minchin to get the Maharaja's signatures on the second letter. About Minchin's idea regarding the Maharaja's visit to the Punjab, Thompson now felt that there might be practical difficulties because the Maharaja could always make excuses that he wanted to visit Amritsar for religious purposes. It would, therefore, be necessary to discuss the matter with the Punjab Government. In any case, Thompson told Minchin that he would speak to the Viceroy on the following day about the whole case.[14]

New Conditions Imposed by the Secretary of State

On 12 June the Viceroy sent a cable to the Secretary of State for India to explain the situation at some length. Justice Stuart had completed his report. His findings were in favour of Patiala in most of the cases, and 'in no case in favour of Nabha'. The Maharaja was prepared to sever his connection with the state on an annual allowance of 300,000 rupees with his salute and title. He was prepared to give compensation to Patiala up to 5,000,000 rupees. He would formally abdicate when his son came of age, but make over the administration to the government at once. It was requested by the Maharaja that this act of virtual abdication might be regarded 'as wiping the slate clean'. 'Though we have one or two other matters against him and there is a possibility of further revelations later, I have agreed to accept his submission and have caused him to be told that we will exact no further penalties.' The Viceroy gave this promise because the 'only practical difference between the formal deposition which would be the maximum penalty we could inflict and Nabha's voluntary abdication are that he gets more freedom and a larger allowance than he would as a deposed prince, and retains his salute and title'. There was of course something to be said 'for making an example of him' and there might be some criticism for not having done so if the report was made public, 'but the Princes as a body will probably be grateful that he has been saved from disgrace'. Moreover, it was likely that he would 'fight to the last if we refuse to allow him to retain title and salute'—and that could be 'a very long business'. Reading admitted that without being offered a commission of enquiry (which would include two ruling Princes, a High Court Judge, and two other persons of high status), the Maharaja could not be deprived of his powers or deposed. This would mean 'another long and very expensive enquiry'. If the settlement was delayed he would come to be regarded as the victim of oppression gallantly struggling to secure his rights.

The Viceroy underscored the political connection of Maharaja Ripudaman Singh with the Akalis. It was very generally believed that 'he has given more than his sympathy to the Akali movement and in the small but turbulent community of the Sikhs he is a big enough man to cause us a good deal of trouble'. To remove him from the sphere of Sikh politics, suddenly, by his own act in the hour of his unpopularity was largely to avert the risk. A minor advantage was to get compensation for Patiala from the 'private hoards' of the Maharaja of Nabha. Furthermore, the Maharaja might change his mind as he had done in the past. Therefore, it was necessary for the Viceroy to take a decision immediately after the delivery of Stuart's judgment in its final form.[15]

In his telegram of 14 June, Lord Peel, the Secretary of State for India, generally approved of what had been done, but questioned the propriety of taking over the administration of Nabha and also of allowing the Maharaja to abdicate in the face of Justice Stuart's findings.[16]

Meanwhile, Minchin had rung up Ogilvie from Kasauli twice on 13 and 14 June, begging for early orders. The Maharaja was in 'an excitable and vascillating condition'. Delay in conveying the orders of the government 'may have a prejudicial effect on the Maharaja who may be induced by interested persons to resile from the position he has taken up'. It was necessary to 'strike while the iron is hot'. If the orders were to take some time, Minchin could be authorized 'to tell the Maharaja at once that the Government of India have accepted the Maharaja's proposals generally, but that certain details are under consideration with regard to which His Highness will receive the decision later'. Minchin should be able to induce the Maharaja to leave Nabha as soon as possible. He was authorized to communicate the following message to the Maharaja of Nabha: 'His Excellency has received His Highness' two letters dated 9th and 10th June. His Excellency approves of the general lines of His Highness' proposals, subject to arrangements regarding certain minor details which will be communicated early next week.'[17]

On 19 June, the Secretary of State for India sent a private telegram to the Viceroy (at the same time as his official telegram) which contained some new conditions. With regard to the Maharaja of Nabha he observed: 'If he is to resign I attach great importance to the conditions outlined in my official telegram and especially the last' that 'without permission of the Government of India he should not be allowed to visit Europe or America and he should understand that grant of permission will be conditional on abstention from all kinds of political activity and on good and loyal behaviour'. The Secretary of State feared that 'Nabha in Europe or America might be a most dangerous focus of anti-British intrigue'. He also wanted to know if the Viceroy contemplated publishing any statement in India: 'If questions be asked in Parliament as for reasons of his resignation, it will be impossible to conceal facts.'[18]

It took the Political Department a week more to inform Minchin of the 'full conditions' on which the Maharaja would be permitted to sever his connection with the state. The Viceroy had studied the case more closely, with the result that 'his first impression as to the gravity of the situation' had been confirmed. He now thought it was desirable to add three new conditions to the seven already conveyed. Therefore, the 'full conditions' were as follows:

1. The administration will be made over to the Government of India and His Highness will refrain from all interference in State affairs.
2. His Highness will formally abdicate when his son comes of age.
3. His Highness will in future reside outside the State, and one State bunaglow at Dehra Dun and another at Mussoorie will be placed at his disposal for his residence.

4. His Highness will not visit the Nabha State except for the purpose of religious ceremonies and then only with the previous permission of the Government of India.
5. His Highness will not visit the Punjab, Europe, or America except with the previous permission of the Government of India.
6. The Government of India will be responsible for the education of the heir apparent.
7. The Patiala Darbar will be paid as compensation such sum not exceeding 5,000,000 rupees as the Government of India may fix, and with the object of enabling the necessary sum to be raised, His Highness the Maharaja agrees to place immediately at the disposal of the Government of India securities of the value of approximately 900,000, and to give any of such properties in Simla or elsewhere (including as it may be decided to sell); whether such properties shall have been acquired benami or otherwise.
8. His Highness will remain subject to the obligations of loyalty and obedience to the British Crown and the Government of India, which are imposed on the Rulers of Nabha by the Sanad of 1860.
9. His Highness will retain his salute and customary titles and will be paid an allowance of 300,000 rupees annually for life from the revenues of the State.
10. Should His Highness the Maharaja fail to fulfil any of the obligations hereby imposed on him, the Government of India will hold itself free to annul or to modify any of the above conditions.

Minchin was asked to insist on the transfer to himself, or to the Administrator, of securities and title deeds of all properties before the Maharaja left the state. He was to acquaint the Maharaja immediately with the procedure proposed to be adopted by the Government of India: (a) for recording the conclusions at which they have arrived and the conditions on which the Maharaja was to be allowed to sever his connection with the state; and (b) for making public the tenor of those conclusions and conditions. The first was to take the form of a formal resolution of the Government of India to be communicated to the Nabha and Patiala Darbars but not to be published. The second was to be issued as an official communiqué.[19]

Minchin conveyed the orders of the Viceroy to the Maharaja on 29 June through Narasinga Rao, who was at Kasauli. He asked Minchin whether he might be authorized to inform the Maharaja that these terms were 'a full and final settlement' and that 'no further penalties will be exacted'. Minchin rang up Ogilvie for advice, saying that he himself thought it desirable that the Maharaja 'should be assured that when he signs the final conditions further penalties will not be exacted from him'. Ogilvie knew that this was the intention of the Viceroy as he had conveyed it already to the Secretary of State for India on 12 June. Therefore, Ogilvie prepared a draft telegram to be sent to Minchin. The Viceroy approved of the draft with a slight addition. The telegram was sent to Minchin, and he wrote to the Maharaja that he had been authorized by the Viceroy to inform His Highness that, on his undertaking in writing to abide by the 10 conditions specified in his confidential letter of 28 June 1923, 'the Government of India agree to exact no further penalties beyond those explained in that letter so long as Your Highness observes on your part the obligations imposed upon you by those conditions'.[20] If Rao and Minchin were keen to soften the Maharaja, the Viceroy was keen to bind him to the conditions added by the Secretary of State for India.

Threats Held Out by the AGG

As Minchin wrote to A. J. Macnabb of the Political Department, the three extra conditions imposed by the Secretary of State seemed to have upset the 'compromise with Nabha'. Narasinga Rao had secretly informed Minchin that two Akalis from the Central Sikh League had got hold of the Maharaja and told him that they would send *jathās* (groups) to fight for him. The Maharaja had thrown over all his trusted counsellors 'who were urging him to accept Government's terms'. On 1 July he had 'practically made up his mind to refuse them'. He was inclined to go to Amritsar to take part in the kār sewā (collective cleansing of the holy tank).[21] While the Nabha officials were working on the Maharaja in support of the Government of India, the Akali leaders were encouraging him to take a stand against the government.

Minchin appeared to be keen on an early action. He suggested that if the Maharaja refused the terms offered to him now, he should be held to the agreement contained in his letters of 9 and 10 June. Minchin could be authorized to take an adequate force from Ambala and proceed to Nabha to enforce the terms. Ogilvie suggested that since the Maharaja had received the final terms only a day before he could be given a day or two for consideration. Minchin could inform the Maharaja that the Government of India would give him time till the coming Thursday, that is, 5 July, to accept the terms. If his reply did not come by then, the Government of India 'will consider themselves free to take such steps as they may consider necessary'. The military authorities at Ambala could be asked meanwhile to hold troops in readiness to proceed to Nabha. 'If His Highness comes to his senses before Thursday evening, well and good; if not, it will be necessary for us to send the A.G.G. into Nabha with troops.' He could be armed also with a proclamation, suspending the Maharaja from ruling powers. Removed from Nabha and placed under surveillance, the Maharaja would be given a Court of Enquiry 'should he demand to be given one'. The agreement contained in his letters of 9 and 10 June was too lenient. 'We could clearly not allow him his rank and titles and a liberal allowance. It would be a case of suspension from Ruling Powers, and eventual deposition, with severe restrictions on his movements.' The Viceroy favoured the idea that the Maharaja should be given a full opportunity of 'thinking over the consequences of recalcitrancy'. Minchin was asked to inform the Maharaja that the Government of India awaited a reply to the letter of 28 June, hoping that the Maharaja would reply by 5 July. If His Highness did not reply by then, it should be reported at once to the Government of India. 'His Excellency will then consider what further steps are necessary.'[22]

An intelligence report sent by the Chief Secretary, Punjab, to the Political Department contained the information that Sant Teja Singh, who had left the Akal College at Mastuana and joined Guru Nanak College at Gujranwala as its Principal, had met the Maharaja of Nabha secretly on 25 and 26 June. The Maharaja told him that Minchin had put pressure on him and he had given in writing to the Government of India that he was prepared to abdicate and live at Dehra Dun and Mussoorie on certain conditions. He was now repenting and thinking of retracting the written undertaking given under pressure 'as he was told there will be a public trial'. As desired by the Maharaja, Teja Singh had gone to Amritsar to win over the SGPC leaders for passing a resolution of sympathy with the Maharaja. If any action was taken against him, efforts would be made to stir up the Akalis.[23]

On 4 July, the Viceroy sent a telegram to the Secretary of State to say that the conditions were communicated to the Chief Minister of Nabha who took them to the Maharaja immediately on Sunday last.

The Chief Minister had reported that the Maharaja was reluctant to give assent on the grounds that new conditions were added to the ones he had voluntarily offered to abide by. An intimation was sent to him that the Government of India desired to receive his reply by the day following. The Viceroy had received secret information through Rao that the Maharaja was packing heirlooms and valuables, trying to raise money from state revenues and by disposal of state lands, and cash, and destroying documents which could be used against him. Two Akalis had approached him to urge him to abandon voluntary retirement from the state administration and to resist punitive measures, promising help of Akali jathās from the Punjab. The Maharaja was reported to have made advances to the SGPC at Amritsar. To enlist support, he had been advised to send to Amritsar the *saropā* (robe of honour) of the Tenth Master, Guru Gobind Singh, a sacred heirloom of the Phulkian family preserved in the Gurdwara of the Nabha fort-palace. Meanwhile, the Central Sikh League had passed a resolution in support of the Maharaja on the basis of a rumour that he contemplated resigning due to pressure from the government or in the alternative he would be deposed.

Having made the case, the Viceroy informed the Secretary of State that if he did not receive the Maharaja's reply till the morning of Friday the 6th he would ask for a telegraphic reply. If there was no response, the proper course would be to suspend the Maharaja of Nabha and to send an officer to take over the administration accompanied by sufficient military force to make an impression and prevent any demonstrations or local rioting. There was a precedent for the action proposed: administration of Panna in central India was taken over this way before the deposition of its Maharaja. The matter being urgent, the Viceroy asked for an early response from the Secretary of State.[24] The reply on 5 July simply said: 'I agree.' With the Secretary of State's approval received on the 6th, the Viceroy was finally ready for action.[25]

Already, on receiving the secret telegram from the Political Department on 3 July, Minchin had sent the following telegram to the Maharaja: 'Viceroy has requested me to inform Your Highness that he will await your acceptance of terms communicated in my letter of 28th June up to Thursday night fifth July. I strongly advise Your Highness to come to immediate decision.' The Maharaja replied to this telegram on 5 July, stating that his letter of acceptance would be delivered on the day following, but nothing transpired till the evening of the 6th. However, Minchin received a telegram from O'Grady, a Nabha employee who had been in contact with the Political Department, stating that he was delayed at Nabha but he would hand over the Maharaja's letter on the 7th. O'Grady turned up on the 7th morning with a letter signed by the Maharaja dated 5 July.

O'Grady told Minchin that he had reached Nabha on the 6th morning 'in order to help the Maharaja to come to a decision'. He had to talk to His Highness for 10 hours to induce the Maharaja to sign the letter. He was under the influence of some Akalis from Amritsar. Soon after he had signed the letter, he asked O'Grady to return it to him. He told the Maharaja that 'to refuse the terms offered to him was pure madness'. O'Grady left Nabha at 4 p.m. on the 6th. He was overtaken at Ambala by a car sent by the Maharaja, and Sardar Gurdial Singh told him that he should either return to Nabha or hand over the letter to him. O'Grady refused both these requests on the grounds that he had been commissioned by the Maharaja to carry the letter to the AGG and he could deviate from this course only on written orders of the Maharaja. O'Grady then boarded the train at Ambala and reached Kasauli on the 7th morning.[26]

The helplessness with which Maharaja Ripudaman Singh signed the letter of acceptance is reflected in the letter itself: 'I recognise that nothing is left to me but to make the submission demanded of me and I have accordingly sent you a telegram. I now write this letter in confirmation of that telegram accepting all the terms imposed by His Excellency the Viceroy.'[27]

The resolution of the Government of India on the report of the Special Commissioner on disputes between Patiala and Nabha states, which was meant to be conveyed to both the parties, was adopted on 7 July 1923. However, its core consisted of the conclusions drawn already by the Viceroy on 1 July that the common features of all the cases showed 'a deliberate perversion, by highly placed officials in the state, of the whole machinery for the administration of justice, for the purpose of damaging Patiala'.[28]

It is significant to note that the purpose of the enquiry now shifted from 'violation of territorial rights' to 'maladministration', a deliberately undefined term to cloak British disapproval of the political conduct of a ruler. The ruler of Nabha was bound to 'exert himself by every possible means in promoting the welfare of his people and the happiness of his subjects and redressing the grievances of the oppressed and injured in the proper way'. The resolution goes on to add that the sanad of 1860 bound the ruler of Nabha to loyalty and obedience to the British Crown and the Government of India, but this obligation too was broken.[29] However, it is evident from the resolution itself that only in one case violation of Patiala's territorial rights was established. Therefore, the strong condemnation of the Nabha Darbar by the government was more rhetorical and for public consumption. In the ultimate analysis, it had been inspired by the Political Department's antipathy towards the Maharaja's 'independent attitude towards Government' as well as his sympathies with its opponents, especially the Akalis.

Indeed, the Viceroy appears to have been aware of the weakness of the case made against Maharaja Ripudaman Singh. He was keen that the Maharaja should not insist on a proper Commission of Enquiry which was intended to foster transparency in the Political Department's actions vis-à-vis a prince.[30] The best course for the paramount power was to use duress in a number of ways to ensure that the Maharaja appeared to have 'suddenly, by his own act' retired from the administration of his state. The resolution refers to this situation in words which conceal the truth: While measures against the Maharaja were under consideration, 'the Maharaja of Nabha on his own initiative visited the Agent to the Governor General, Punjab States at Kasauli and voluntarily expressed his desire to sever his connection with the administration of the State upon certain conditions'. Not only is this statement factually incorrect, the resolution says that the Viceroy accepted this offer because 'the advantages of a speedy settlement' outweighed other considerations.[31] This speedy settlement was actually imposed on Maharaja Ripudaman Singh.

Removal from Nabha under a Military Escort

Minchin had begun to think of an officer for Nabha early in June 1923. The officer selected had to receive instructions from him. The Government of India thought of Colonel S. B. Patterson, Resident at Jaipur, but he requested to be allowed to decline the offer. Ogilvie suggested that Minchin's Secretary, Mackenzie, could take over the administration, pending the arrival of a permanent incumbent. By 23 June the Viceroy had approved of Wilson-Johnston as Administrator of the Nabha state. The Punjab Governor was asked to finalize terms with him and to ask whether he was prepared to return to India latest by the end of August. The Punjab Government had agreed also to allow Ogilvie to go to Nabha as a temporary measure. On 26 June, Thompson wrote to Minchin to think out carefully the arrangements to be made for the actual transfer of the administration. The balances in the state treasuries should of course be secured and steps must be taken to see that the state jewels were not removed. The state records should be taken over intact as far as possible. No ceremony should be observed on the occasion of the Maharaja's departure. However, there was no objection to a salute being fired. There should be no military demonstration but a detachment of British or Indian troops could be sent to Nabha for a short period, if necessary. It would be necessary to get rid of a number of state officials as soon as possible, including the Chief Minister, Narasinga Rao, the Sessions Judge, Sardar Harbakhsh Singh, the Chief of Police, Sardar Kahla Singh, and the Foreign Minister, Sardar Bakhshish Singh.[32]

Thompson finalized the plan of action. As soon as the Maharaja signified his readiness to abide by the terms, Minchin was to get hold of Ogilvie and make preliminary arrangements for taking over Nabha. As soon as Minchin informed that the Maharaja had accepted the terms, the Resolution of the Government of India should be sent to the press; the communiqué should be issued; orders should be issued to the AGG to take over charge; and orders should be issued for the release of the Patiala men, Abdul Aziz, Muhammad Yakub, Ali Sher, and Abdul Latif. Copies of the resolution should be sent to the Secretary of State as well as to the Nabha and Patiala Darbars. The communiqué should be telegraphed to the Secretary of State, with a formal report of the handing over of the administration.[33]

Minchin received the orders on 7 July that he should proceed to Nabha with Major Ogilvie as soon as possible. There was no objection to his taking armoured cars as escort, and such other force that he might consider necessary for the custody of treasure and other valuables that he would take over. On his arrival at Nabha he should inform the Maharaja that the government had directed him to take over the administration of the state immediately. The accepted conditions would become operative from the moment the administration was taken over by him. The Maharaja should leave Nabha and the Punjab. Minchin was to inform the government of the date of the Maharaja's departure from Nabha and the place of his residence outside Nabha. With regard to the rumours about the Maharaja's disposal of state property, Minchin was to take necessary steps for safeguarding it but he was instructed not to be 'too drastic as we shall hereafter be able to bring pressure upon him if he has wrongfully removed State valuables'.

> The important action is to get Maharaja out of Nabha and Punjab and this should not be delayed for any enquiry into or controversy respecting Maharaja's recent actions.

The orders were unambiguous and final. There was nothing but to execute them. Major Ogilvie, who was to take over administration, was to be left with a military escort at Nabha, including the armoured cars, if necessary. Minchin started for Nabha very early on the 8th with three armoured cars and a company of the 28th Punjab Infantry. On 9 July, Maharaja Ripudaman Singh left Nabha with Maharani Sarojini Devi and Tikka Partap Singh.

Minchin held an informal Darbar at Nabha on the 9th morning to inform the Sardars and the officials and subjects of Nabha that its administration had been taken over by the government. The Maharaja had finally severed his connection with the state and the loyalty of the courtiers henceforth was due to the Administrator appointed by the government to manage the state on behalf of the Tikka Sahib. The officials were warned against sedition or intrigue. The state subjects were asked to refrain from correspondence with Maharaja Ripudaman Singh.

Minchin found the state jewels intact in the hands of the Senior Mother of Maharaja Ripudaman Singh. The minor state jewels in the toshākhāna were checked with the list supplied by the Darbar. Minchin personally checked the saropā to ensure that all its jewels were in place and that one of the keys was with the hereditary guardian of the saropā. The other key that was with the Maharaja was now entrusted to his Senior Mother. According to Minchin, Maharaja Ripudaman Singh had confessed that the three Maharanis, like the hereditary custodian of the saropā, had frustrated his intention of offering this saropā of the Tenth Master to the Golden Temple at Amritsar.

Minchin now made keen enquiries about the individuals believed to have suffered at the hands of Maharaja Ripudaman Singh. The idea was to get confirmation of the charges informally brought against the Maharaja from time to time by Minchin—the great revelations which he had promised after the Maharaja was removed from the gaddī. Minchin impressed upon Ogilvie the necessity of retaining the administration in its existing form.

C. M. G. Ogilvie took control of the various departments and started functioning as the temporary Administrator of Nabha. J. Wilson-Johnston assumed charge of administration on 3 September 1923. The high officials who had aligned themselves closely with Maharaja Ripudaman Singh were removed and those who had aligned themselves with the AGG and the Government of India were not only retained but also rewarded. Those who took the place of the removed ones came from the Punjab. Their induction ensured loyalty to the new regime, and their functioning made for assimilation of Nabha administrative practices to the prevalent system in the Punjab. All that the new regime could do was to introduce a certain degree of efficiency, particularly in financial matters, and maintain law and order. There was no possibility of introducing any constitutional changes involving democratic or representative measures. This limitation suited the paramount power. They needed an autocratic Administrator responsible to them alone. As the instrument of higher authorities, he could handle the political situation with a strong arm.

A. B. Minchin's rather unusual personal interest in the case against Nabha was not lost on the higher authorities. Despite his use as an instrument in the bigger political game, Viceroy Reading concluded in August 1923 that 'Col. Minchin was unbalanced in his judgement and apt to embarrass Govt. by indiscreet and unauthorized actions'. The Viceroy had 'grave doubts' regarding his 'fitness for further promotion in the Political Deptt'. This understatement probably alludes to Minchin's unabashed partiality for Patiala and possible acceptance of gratification from its Maharaja.[34]

Notes

1. Based on India Office Records (IOR), R/1/1/1375(1), File no. 628(3) Political [hereinafter IOR, 628(3)P]: letter signed by D. M. Narasinga Rao, dated 21 April 1923; note by D. G. Ogilvie, dated 21 April 1923; note by J. P. Thompson, dated 24 April 1923.
2. IOR, 628(3)P, A. B. Minchin to Political Department, 5/7 May 1923.
3. IOR, 628(3)P, Maharaja of Nabha to Agent to Governor General, 7 May 1923.
4. IOR, 628(3)P, A. B. Minchin to Political Department, 5/7 May 1923.
5. IOR, 628(3)P, note by Thompson, dated 9 May 1923; note by G. D. Ogilvie, dated 10 May.
6. IOR, 628(3)P, Political Department to A. B. Minchin, 25 May 1925.

7. IOR MSS Eur E 238/25, Reading Collection, Letters and Telegrams to and from Persons in India, no. 432a, From His Highness the Maharaja of Nabha to Viceroy, dated 14 December 1923, Dehra Dun.
8. IOR, 628(3)P, A. B. Minchin to Political Department, 5/6 June 1923.
9. IOR, 628(3)P, note by J. P. Thompson, dated 7 June 1923.
10. IOR, 628(3)P, telegram from Political Department to AGG, dated 7 June 1923.
11. IOR, 628(3)P, Maharaja Ripudaman Singh to A. B. Minchin, 9 June 1923; note by A. B. Minchin.
12. IOR, 628(3)P, Maharaja Ripudaman Singh to A. B. Minchin, 10 June 1923.
13. IOR, 628(3)P, A. B. Minchin to Political Department, 10 June 1923.
14. IOR, 628(3)P, note by J. P. Thompson, dated 11 June 1923.
15. IOR, 628(3)P, telegram from Viceroy to Secretary of State, dated 12 June 1923.
16. IOR, 628(3)P, telegram from Secretary of State to the Viceroy, dated 14 June 1923.
17. IOR, 628(3)P, note by G. D. Ogilvie, date 15 June 1923.
18. IOR, 628(3)P, Sir Geoffrey de Montmorency to Private Secretary to Viceroy, 19 June 1923.
19. IOR, 628(3)P, Political Department to A. B. Minchin, 26 June 1923.
20. IOR, 628(3)P, Agent to Governor General to Maharaja Ripudaman Singh, 28 June 1923.
21. IOR, 628(3)P, note by A. J. Macnabb, date 2 July 1923.
22. IOR, 628(3)P, note by G. D. Ogilvie, dated 2 July 1923; Political Department to A. B. Minchin, 3 July 1923.
23. IOR, 628(3)P, Chief Secretary to Government of Punjab to Political Department, 3 July 1923.
24. IOR, 628(3)P, telegram from Viceroy to Secretary of State, dated 4 July 1923.
25. IOR, 628(3)P, telegram from Secretary of State to Viceroy, dated 5 July 1923.
26. IOR, 628(3)P, A. B. Minchin to Political Department, 7 July 1923.
27. IOR, 628(3)P, note by G. D. Ogilvie, dated 7 July 1923.
28. IOR, 628(3)P, note by Lord Reading, dated 1 July 1923. This note appears in the Government of India's resolution of 7 July 1923 with only a few modifications in its wording.
29. National Archives of India, New Delhi (NAI), Home Department, Political Branch (1924), File no. 401, pp. 279–90. The printed resolution of the Government of India, dated 7 July 1923 on the report of Justice Stuart has its own consecutive pagination. The quotation given here is on page 10.
30. NAI, H-P, 1924, no. 401, pp. 10–11.

31. NAI, H-P, 1924, no. 401, Political Department to A. B. Minchin, 26 June 1923.
32. NAI, H-P, 1924, no. 401, note by J. P. Thompson, date 26 June 1923.
33. Punjab State Archives, Patiala, no. 937-P, 'Administration Report of the Nabha State' (1924): 7–23.
34. G. D. Oglivie's note recording the Viceroy's views expressed on 11 August 1923 was placed in Colonel Minchin's personal file.

8

ISSUE OF RESTORATION AND THE JAITO MORCHA

Reaction to the removal of Maharaja Ripudaman Singh from Nabha was immediate among the Akalis of the Nabha state and the SGPC, as well as the Shiromani Akali Dal. Meetings began to be held and resolutions passed in support of the Maharaja, culminating in the demand for his restoration. Quite early in the movement for restoration, an akhand pāṭh in Gurdwara Gangsar at Jaito in the Nabha territory was interrupted by the State Administration set up by the bureaucracy. The issue of interference in a religious matter got added to the demand for restoration of the Maharaja. The long-standing Akali demand for suitable legislation for the Panthic control and management of historic Gurdwaras was never forgotten by them. The Jaito Morcha ended in the Sikh Gurdwaras Act in July 1925. This legislation was essentially a compromise. The Act was passed by setting aside the demand for the restoration of Maharaja Ripudaman Singh to the gaddī of Nabha.

Reactions in Nabha

A reliable and more or less detailed report of the way in which Maharaja Ripudaman Singh was removed from his capital was published in *The Tribune*, throwing 'a flood of light on the real attitude of Government officials'. Early on the morning of 8 July, a number of cars, lorries, and machine guns suddenly appeared in Nabha with the AGG, A. B. Minchin, along with other British officials and British and Dogra troops. After posting machine guns around the palace, the British officials entered the Maharaja's residence and asked him to prepare for leaving the next morning. A Darbar was held in the Diwān Khāna to announce the circumstances in which the Maharaja of Nabha had become separated from the state administration. It was declared that

> His Highness had made his submission to the Government of India that in future he would have nothing to do with the State. He would formally abdicate when the Tikka Sahib attained his majority, and in the meanwhile the State would be administered by the Government of India.

Then the official communiqué, dated Simla, 7 July, was read out, after which it was proclaimed that anybody daring to correspond with the Maharaja would be severely dealt with.

A little before 9 o'clock, Major C. M. G. Ogilvie, now the British Administrator, went to the Maharaja and required him to be ready to depart. His Highness heaved a long sigh and exclaimed, 'Thy will be done.' Exactly at nine, the Maharaja with his wife and son got ready to pass out of his state like a stranger. The Maharaja sat in the car with a British military officer to escort him. The Maharani and the Tikka Sahib were in the second car. A number of cars with British and Dogra soldiers followed them. Only one attendant, Bhai Indar Singh, was allowed to accompany the royal family. He was later dismissed from the state service for his faithfulness to the ruler of the state.

The party reached Ambala Cantonment at noon and the members of the escort took their food there, but the Maharaja had to go without it, as no arrangements had been made for him. At 11 p.m. they reached Dehra Dun, and there too no food or other arrangements had been made. Bhai Indar Singh improvised some comforts. Next morning the motor drivers came to take leave of the Maharaja who shook hands with them and touchingly bade adieu to them as a fellow subject of the Nabha state.[1]

The people of Nabha held public meetings at Nabha on 20, 21, and 22 July to protest against the deposition of the Maharaja. Speeches were made fearlessly, exposing the falsity of the statement that the 'abdication' of the Maharaja was 'voluntary'. The non-Sikh subjects of the state were wholeheartedly working with the Sikhs. In the *diwān* (public meeting) of 22 July, the following resolutions were passed:

1. This great diwān of the Nabha public unreservedly condemns the action of the British Government in deposing H.H. the

Maharaja Sahib of Nabha and removing him from the state, which has given a severe shock to hearts of his loving subjects.
2. This diwān humbly requests the Shiromani Gurdwara Prabandhak Committee to quickly devise measures for the reinstatement of the Maharaja Sahib and thus redeem the 'Panthic' honour. We assure the Committee that we are ready to make every sacrifice to carry out the Committee's behests.
3. This diwān fully hopes that the Maharajas of Patiala and Jind, as scions of the Phul dynasty, will join the Panth in maintaining the honour of the community and the integrity of the House of Phul.
4. This diwān severely condemns the behaviour of those people who while eating the salt of the state have betrayed the Maharaja and heartily sympathizes with those who for their loyalty to their master are being harassed.

The Tribune referred deliberately to 'the other side', reporting on the formation of a Praja Rakshak Committee of Nabha, orchestrated by its new administration.[2] The Nabha Administration had begun to divide the people who were one in support of the Maharaja's return. It prepared the lists of Akalis at all the thānās of Nabha, with the idea of persecuting them. Cavalry reinforcements were called in to deal with the 'extremist elements' among the Akalis in the state.[3]

Sikh Organizations Raise the Issue of Restoration

On 9 July 1923, the SGPC passed a resolution to the effect that the hereditary ruler of Nabha was unjustly and forcibly detached from the administration of his state by the Government of India, and forced to leave his state under humiliating circumstances with an unnecessary and insolent show of military force. Propaganda in favour of Maharaja Ripudaman Singh gained an almost immediate momentum. The SGPC fixed 29 July as the day of prayer for the restoration of the Maharaja. A barefoot march and singing of hymns (kīrtan) in the streets in protest against his removal was to be held on 9 September. A special prayer (ardās) for his restoration was to be made in local Gurdwaras.[4]

The Patiala Darbar began to organize counter-propaganda in support of the government. Maharaja Bhupinder Singh issued a press communiqué to assert that 'voluntary' abdication by Maharaja Ripudaman

Singh was a wise step on his part as it obviated more drastic consequences. His Prime Minister, Daya Kishan Kaul, began to coordinate an extensive propaganda campaign. The SGPC members amenable to Patiala's influence were persuaded to work against the supporters of Nabha at the Committee's meetings. Some of the Sikh subjects of Nabha were encouraged to hold public meetings to protest against 'state oppression' under Maharaja Ripudaman Singh. Articles were supplied to the press in support of Patiala and the British Government.[5]

In anticipation of agitation against Maharaja Ripudaman Singh's ouster, the Government of India began to plan the strategy to be adopted by the Administrator of Nabha. Two meetings were held on 25 and 26 July 1923. Present in the first meeting were the Home Member, Political Secretary, Agent to Governor General, Punjab Governor, and a few Punjab officials. Present in the second meeting were also the Maharaja of Patiala, Sir Daya Kishan Kaul, Dr Bihari Lal Dhingra (Chief Minister of Jind), and Major Ogilvie. It was decided not to stop the jathās in the Punjab since it would be easier to handle them in the Nabha territory without the restraining laws and procedures of British India. If the jathās remained passive, they would not be disturbed but if they turned violent their leaders would be arrested and others merely expelled from the state. In case of active resistance, firing after warning could be resorted to. The Government of India would support the Administrator fully in any 'reasonable action' he decided to take.[6] In order to have a say in the affairs of Nabha, the Maharaja of Patiala suggested that a Council of Regency be established in Nabha, which would take the wind out of the sails of the Akalis. The Government of India issued a communiqué at the beginning of August to say that a Council of Regency would replace the Administrator at Nabha as soon as possible.[7]

In view of the mounting agitation, it was suggested in the meeting of 26 July that Maharaja Ripudaman Singh should be persuaded to disown the agitation. Minchin went to Dehra Dun on 31 July to get signatures of the Maharaja to the following statement:

I wish to state that my action in severing myself from the administration of the Nabha State was entirely voluntary and was taken by me after full consideration, that the agitation in favour of my restoration to ruling powers is not supported by me and that I deprecate strongly any action taken with this object.

To overcome the Maharaja's resistance, Minchin asserted that it was an order of the government. On Maharaja's insistence, Minchin felt obliged to add: 'The Government of India have asked me to request Your Highness kindly to sign the above statement as signifying your views on the subject.' The Maharaja finally wrote: 'I am not responsible for the present agitation about Nabha affairs.' On Minchin's insistence Ripudaman Singh added as postscript 'and have no sympathy with it', but added on his own, 'As ordered and desired by the Government of India I sign it.'[8]

The Associated Press of India was then authorized by the government to state that the Maharaja of Nabha had sent the following telegram to the SGPC from Dehra Dun: 'I desire to have it known that, while thanking the sympathizers who are showing interest in my present difficulties, I disapprove any action on their part which may embarrass the Government. I also desire to dissociate myself with any movement disloyal to the British Government which must lead to misery.'[9] Knowing that Maharaja Ripudaman Singh had been forced to sign the statement, the SGPC sent a telegram to Viceroy Reading on 2 August to the effect that threats had been used to oblige the Maharaja to relinquish his gaddī, and that an independent enquiry into his abdication should be instituted. Not to give any legitimacy to the SGPC in a matter between the Government of India and a princely state, the government chose to adopt silence.[10]

The resolutions passed by the SGPC on 5 and 6 August recorded that the Government of India had 'deliberately taken advantage of the Patiala–Nabha dispute to wrest the administration of Nabha state from His Highness Maharaja Ripduaman Singh'; 'threats and intimidation' had been used to force His Highness to sever his connection with the administration of the state on humiliating terms; the decision of the government was 'vindictive, unjustified and absolutely uncalled for'. The action taken by the government against 'a Sikh State of great historical and religious traditions and an orthodox, self-respecting Sikh Prince' was calculated 'to give a severe blow to the Panthic orthodoxy, organization and well-being'. Therefore, the SGPC strongly condemned this move 'as a side-attack on the Reform Movement of which the Shiromani Committee is the custodian', and sent 'its full and affectionate sympathy to His Highness, his family, and their subjects in their present affliction'. The Akalis were convinced and rightly so, that the removal of the Maharaja was meant, among other things, to weaken the Akali movement.

The SGPC expressed its sympathy with those who were being persecuted in Nabha on account of their loyalty to the Maharaja, and its disgust with those who had acted treacherously towards him during the enquiry. The SGPC condemned the activities of those who were carrying on a false and malicious propaganda to defame and discredit Maharaja Ripudaman Singh. The Executive Committee of the SGPC was authorized 'to get the wrong done to Nabha and the Panth righted by all peaceful and legitimate means'.[11]

Meetings began to be held to condemn the action of the government and to support Maharaja Ripudaman Singh's restoration. On 24 August, Ogilvie issued orders prohibiting political meetings (diwāns) in the Nabha state. On 27 August, the organizers of a diwān in Gurdwara Gangsar at Jaito were arrested on the charge of delivering 'political speeches'. The local administrator (Nāzim) of Phul, who had witnessed the proceedings, reported:

> The diwan might have dispersed had not Inder Singh been arrested. Now they have determined to remain here until the departure of state forces. I have also come to know that they have got some promises of help from the SGPC. If it is so, the agitation will not be put down easily.[12]

Indeed, more and more Akalis started coming to Jaito, including some members of the SGPC.

The Executive Committee of the SGPC took charge of the agitation at Jaito on 4 September. Nabha Day was observed on 9 September, with prayers, processions, and protest meetings against the forced abdication of Maharaja Ripudaman Singh. The new Administrator of Nabha, Wilson-Johnston, a former Chief Secretary of the Punjab, and the states of Patiala, Jind, and Faridkot began to take more stringent measures against all expressions of support for the restoration of Maharaja Ripudaman Singh. Back in the Political Department, Major Ogilvie argued in favour of a strong stand against the Akalis to maintain the prestige of the government.[13]

The SGPC published the *Truth about Nabha* on 9 September to convince all lovers of truth that the government wanted to get rid of a 'self-respecting Sikh Prince' and to undermine the Sikh organization for religious reforms. The Sikh community was compelled to get 'the grievous wrong done to Nabha and the Panth' redressed by all peaceful and legitimate means. Starting with the origins of the Nabha state, the book dwelt on its relations with the British Government, especially its 'treaties' with Nabha, and the rule of Maharaja Ripudaman Singh as the background and the context for his removal from the state. Coming to the conclusion that the government 'had not got even the shred of a case for severe punitive measure, much less the drastic step of deposition', the book ended with justification for the agitation in favour of the Maharaja's restoration.[14]

The Morcha at Jaito

On 11 September 1923 a jathā of 110 Akali volunteers reached Jaito. In the eyes of the British Administrator of Nabha, a reference to the Maharaja's restoration in the prayer (ardās) offered at the Gurdwara was a political act that justified stern action. Another jathā of 102 Akalis arrived at Jaito on 14 September. They held a protest meeting outside the precincts of Gurdwara Gangsar, made several speeches in favour of the Maharaja's restoration, and initiated continuous recitation of the holy Granth (akhand pāṭh). The Assistant Administrator of Nabha, Sardar Gurdial Singh, forcibly removed and arrested the reader (paṭhī) along with the people inside the Gurdwara.[15] This was regarded as a violation of a well-established practice of the Sikhs. Gurdial Singh felt obliged to defend his action and to argue that the pāṭh was completed, parshād (sacred food) was offered, and the bhog ceremony (conclusion of the reading of the Guru Granth Sahib) had been performed. But all this was done under his orders and at the expense of the state.[16] The SGPC started sending jathās of 25 barefoot volunteers to perform akhand pāṭh at Jaito. The jathās sent by the SGPC were allowed to enter the state's territories but not to reach the Gurdwara at Jaito. They were arrested, severely beaten, and removed to the most distant parts of the Nabha state some 300 to 500 kilometres away, to be left there without any means to return.[17]

The SGPC resolved to send a large jathā of 500 Akalis. The leaders of the SGPC and the Akali Dal were arrested on 12 October 1923 on charges of sedition and conspiracy, and both the organizations were declared to be unlawful. Simultaneously, the Viceroy made it clear in a speech at Shimla on 17 October that the decision of the Government of India in the case of Maharaja Ripudaman Singh was unalterable.[18]

The Akali leaders began to think that the charges of sedition and conspiracy could be brought against them only because the abdication of Maharaja Ripudaman Singh was given out to be 'voluntary'. On their behalf, Sant Didar Singh approached the Maharaja to deliver the message of Sardar Bahadur Mehtab Singh and his colleagues in the SGPC that the Maharaja should make the circumstances of his abdication clear to all through a representation to the Viceroy.[19]

Maharaja Ripudaman Singh wrote to Lord Reading on 14 December 1923 that he owed it to the supreme head of the Government of India and representative of the British Crown to place before him the 'true facts' of his 'abdication'. The self-seeking officials of Nabha, whether under the influence of Patiala or the officials of the Political Department, overwhelmed him with the suggestion that he should leave his state in their hands and placate the Government of India by allowing them intervention in the affairs of Nabha. The schemes of temporary dissociation from the administration of Nabha were sent to the government in these circumstances. As these schemes were not approved by the Viceroy, the corrupt officials of Nabha then urged the Maharaja to approach the AGG to make his 'settlement' with the government. Realizing that the threats originated from government circles, he was compelled to see Minchin who demanded abdication, threatening 'worse and dire consequences' in case of his non-compliance. Even a compromise with Patiala became secondary; the primary objective became abdication. He was threatened that if he did not abdicate 'a trial on serious charges and something like imprisonment' would follow. Minchin insinuated and acted all along as if there was some serious and grave complaint of the Government 'which needed settlement before tackling the Nabha–Patiala issue'. He presented the document of abdication for his signatures as orders from the Viceroy.

The words added by the Maharaja, 'I recognise that nothing is left to me but make the submission demanded of me', showed clearly that his acceptance of the terms imposed by the Viceroy was 'anything but voluntary'. Later on, soldiers surrounded his palace and Minchin barged into his rooms unannounced. 'In my capital and in my own palace I was insulted, treated like a rebel and a prisoner and practically deported out of the State within a few hours.' This shows that his severance from Nabha was not voluntary. If any further proof was needed it was provided by Minchin during his surprise visit to Dehra Dun on 31 July 1923, demanding the Maharaja's signatures on an already typed document. The Maharaja expected an early redressal of his grievances from Lord Reading, the former Chief Justice of England.[20]

On 7 January 1924, about 200 policemen and a Gurkha guard, armed with rifles and *lāthīs* (long sticks), tried to enter the Akal Takht where a general meeting of the SGPC was being held. But they could not break through the Akalis crowding the entrance. The SGPC endorsed the actions of the previous Executive Committee, confirmed the proceedings of the present, and congratulated the Akalis who had suffered in their attempt to restart the akhand pāṭh at Jaito where they were subjected to brutal assaults, merciless beatings, and fatal starvation, besides being exposed to freezing cold at night. The SGPC condemned the autocratic action of the government in declaring the SGPC and the Shiromani Akali Dal as unlawful associations. The SGPC empowered the Executive Committee to take all possible steps 'to effectually deal with the situation' and save the honour of the Sikh faith. The SGPC also resolved to record its firm determination that 'Khalsa shall avenge by all non-violent methods' the insult offered to their holy places.[21] The leading members of the SGPC were arrested. This did not deter the Akali leaders from sending a jathā to Jaito.

On 6 February 1924, Wilson-Johnston and Minchin held a conference with the Punjab Governor, the Finance Member, and other officers. The measures proposed were discussed at another meeting held in Delhi on 8 February. It was decided that 50 men could be allowed to perform akhand pāṭh and the remaining 450 would be ordered to leave the state forthwith. If they refused to accept the terms but remained 'non-violent' they were to be deported. If, however, they showed a disposition to break the vow of non-violence and to resist arrest or to employ forcible methods of entry into the Gurdwara, the Administrator was to declare the jathā to be an illegal assembly. In the last resort, force was to be used to restore order, employing gunfire, if necessary. The offer of support from the Patiala Darbar was to be accepted in the form of 'a small body of troops' to bring home to the Akalis that all the states were united in opposition to them.[22]

On 9 February 1924, the Jathedār of the Akal Takht addressed a congregation of over 30,000 persons when a jathā of 500 'martyrs' was to start for Jaito in accordance with the decision of the Executive Committee of the SGPC. The sanctity of the *Sri Guru Granth Sahib* as 'the personified life and living light of the Satguru' had been violated at Jaito. The time was ripe now for the Sikh nation to make all kinds of sacrifices to re-establish the right of the freedom of worship. The examples of non-violent martyrdom of Guru Arjan and Guru Tegh Bahadur and of the well-known Sikhs Bhai Mati Das and Bhai Mani Singh were there to be followed.[23] They were to remain non-violent under all circumstances: 'Do not cherish the slightest ill-will against any person in thought, word, or deed.'[24]

Great enthusiasm was reported as the *shahīdi jathā* (group of martyrs) marched through the British territory. When the jathā was close to Jaito on 21 February, it was accompanied by a large crowd on its right and left. The Congress leaders A. T. Gidwani and Saifuddin Kitchlew (and also Zimand, a reporter of the *New York Times*) were with the jathā as observers. At about 150 yards from Gurdwara Tibbi Sahib in Jaito, Wilson-Johnston ordered the jathā to stop. The jathā continued to move and turned towards the Gurdwara. The Administrator gave the signal to open fire. The first round of firing lasted for two minutes from 2.45 to 2.47 p.m. A second round of firing at 2.55 lasted for three minutes. Many members of the jathā fell dead or wounded but the others went on to Tibbi Sahib. The members of the jathā were beaten to senselessness, tied with ropes, huddled into bullock carts, and taken to the barbed wire enclosures prepared for the purpose. Subsequently, they were taken to the fort.[25]

The official communiqué stated that the Akalis not only refused to halt but also used firearms, which obliged the authorities to open fire. The jathā itself was not fired upon and none of its members was injured. Great care was taken to deposit the *Guru Granth Sahib* with due respect in the Gurdwara. A special enquiry by a magistrate was ordered.[26]

The Pioneer reported that the members of the jathā were told that only 50 of them could go to the Gurdwara on giving an undertaking that they would return forthwith after they had paid their respects. They replied that they had come to resume akhand pāṭh at Gangsar Gurdwara. The jathā advanced singing *shabads* (hymns from the *Guru Granth Sahib*), and the crowds eagerly followed. The state officers ordered the jathā to retire, but the Akalis were determined to advance. The authorities opened fire and there were some casualties. When the firing ceased the jathā lifted up their dead and wounded, and advanced again. The firing was resumed a second time. The crowd stopped but the jathā continued to advance and there were more casualties.[27]

There is little doubt about the peaceful conduct of the jathā. Bhai Niranjan Singh, who had received bullet injuries on 21 February at Jatio, stated later that both the jathā and the crowd (*sangat*) were unarmed and remained peaceful. Sodhi Jagat Singh, a policeman who was on duty at Jaito on that day, stated later that there was a plan to fire on the shahīdī jathā even if it remained peaceful, and that firearms had been collected to be blamed on the jathā. Kishan Singh of the Akal Infantry, who had been selected to fire on the jathā, stated later that the jathā was unarmed and peaceful and that no gun was fired by the jathā either before or after the firing by the Nabha authorities. This was supported by two other participants in the firing: Bhai Sewa Singh and Hardit Singh of the Akal Infantry of Nabha.[28]

The 'disturbances at Jaito' figured in the House of Commons. George Lansbery, a Member of Parliament from the Labour Party and later its Chairman, wanted to know why no one was injured on 'our side' when 21 people were killed and 33 wounded on the other side, which was said to be carrying arms. He read out an extract from a letter of Diwan Chaman Lal, President of the Punjab Labour Party and a supporter of the Congress programme, which said that not a single individual carried any firearms. The government had never alleged that any firearm was captured from the jathā or the crowd. The Member asked the Secretary of State to tell the Viceroy to order 'a full and impartial inquiry' to remove the impression that the life of an Indian was 'very cheap'. It was necessary to establish that 'at least the British Parliament do value the life even of the poorest Indian'. Two other Members wanted to know what steps had been taken to prevent the repetition of the disastrous results of 21 February in connection with the jathā of 500 which had started subsequently from Amritsar on 28 February.[29]

Reading replied to the representation of Maharaja Ripudaman Singh on 3 March 1924, saying that he had 'carefully re-examined' the matter in the light of the 'allegations' of His Highness but could find 'no ground for revision of the decision arrived at after much anxious thought and full consideration of every point'. He recounted the familiar stages selectively from the offer of dissociation from administration in April 1923 to the signing of the letter of abdication on 5 July to give the impression that the initiative and the major terms had come from the Maharaja himself. The conditions added later (on the advice of the Secretary of State) were referred to as 'minor'. The whole statement was patently false. Reading referred to his speech of 17 October saying clearly that His Highness had ceased for all times to rule in Nabha. 'To that pronouncement I and my Government adhere and Your Highness must definitely understand that the decision is irrevocable.'[30]

Towards Legislation

The Legislative Assembly had unanimously recommended to the Governor General in Council on 26 February 1924 to appoint a committee to inquire into 'the causes of discontent' among the Sikh community and to suggest measures for its removal. Sir Malcolm Hailey, then the Home Member, was not in favour of such an initiative, but the Government of India agreed in principle to appoint a committee, with General Sir William Birdwood as its President.[31]

Early in March 1924, an informal and private suggestion was conveyed to certain Sikh leaders that if the Sikhs relaxed their demands regarding Nabha, the government would be ready to bring a law about the Gurdwaras and the *kirpān* (curved sword) to their entire satisfaction and to release all prisoners.[32] Several drafts of the proposed agreement were prepared by both sides, which were exchanged and discussed in meetings that took place in April and May 1924. The Sikh members of the Legislative Council, Professor Bhai Jodh Singh and Narain Singh, Pleader, mediated between the government and the negotiating committee of the SGPC. The conditions imposed by the Government of India steadily became more stringent, and the Punjab Government successively diluted the terms offered to the SGPC. It also became clear that the Sikh members of the Council had no sympathy with the cause of Nabha and were practically working on behalf of the Government.

When the negotiations started on 17 April, the Nabha issue was included in the proposals for settlement. The government was keen to secure Maharaja Ripudaman Singh's written admission that he had voluntarily abdicated his right to rule, and that he did not want the agitation for his restoration to continue. A draft letter to be sent by the Maharaja to the SGPC had also been prepared. On 24 April, the government brought in an attested copy of the Maharaja's statement of 31 July 1923, which had been extorted from him by Minchin. Since the SGPC had passed the resolution on Nabha in August 1923, a fresh document was now needed. But no such document was forthcoming, and the negotiating committee was persuaded to 'leave the Nabha affair open'. On 28 April, certain amendments were suggested by the SGPC leaders for incorporation in the draft for confidential agreement, and on 30 April Bhai Jodh Singh and Sardar Narain Singh were authorized to sign the agreement on behalf of the SGPC.

On 1 May, the SGPC leaders were told that the government did not want to make a confidential agreement and gave a draft resolution which was to be published by agreement and was subject to the approval of the Government of India. When the SGPC leaders said that they could consider something in a final shape and not tentative proposals, another draft of proposed resolution by the Punjab Government, revised by the Government of India, was brought to them on 17 May. In this draft, the undertaking to release prisoners was changed into 'intention'. The number of days for performing akhand pāṭhs was to be fixed 'to again pin us down to the same undertaking in a round about way'. The revised resolution wanted the Akali leaders to abandon all propaganda against the government instead of 'suspending' it as originally proposed. On 18 May 1924, Daulat Singh, Secretary, negotiations sub-committee of the SGPC, wrote to Bhai Jodh Singh and Sardar Narain Singh to make it absolutely clear that[33] they could not see their way to agree to the settlement proposed in the revised draft resolution.

The SGPC issued a communiqué on 27 May 1924 which accommodated some of the new terms proposed by the government. There were two points, however, on which the SGPC leaders were not willing to compromise. They could not make any commitment on behalf of the Shiromani Akali Dal because the two organizations were quite different. This point was important because it was on the insistence of the Jathedar of the Shiromani Akali Dal that the Nabha Morcha was initially launched. Second, the SGPC made it clear that the Nabha question was still open. Should the necessity arise, the SGPC would be free to make an announcement to this effect.[34]

Sir Malcolm Hailey replaced Sir Edward Maclagan as the Punjab Governor on 31 May 1924. The first thing he did was to give one month to the SGPC and the Akali leaders to accept the terms offered by the provincial government. Exactly a month later, a communiqué was issued by the government that the idea of the Birdwood Committee had been abandoned.

As he wrote to Lord Reading on 19 June 1924, Hailey was doubtful about 'the ability of the British Government to continue repressive measures of an extraordinary nature for any great length of time'. The best possible course open to the government was to reduce 'the authority of the extremist section' by 'encouraging moderate and reasonable Sikhs to combat the extremists'. To isolate Maharaja Ripudaman Singh from his supporters, it was necessary to elicit the sympathy and support of other Phulkian states, strengthening the British Administrator of Nabha, to penalize the government functionaries and pensioners who had marked Akali sympathies, and to encourage formation of anti-Akali organizations among the Sikhs.[35]

By then, a cross-section of the Sikhs had been feeling that the Jaito affair had deflected the Akali movement from its main goal of securing a law for the management of Gurdwaras. Bhai Jodh Singh and the other Sikh Members of Legislative Council, Punjab, at any rate, subscribed to the idea of separating the religious from the political issues, and were in favour of arriving at an understanding with the government. The SGPC leadership was in a quandary because, while the majority wanted to end the stalemate, there was a hard core opposed to dropping the Nabha issue altogether.[36]

Arjan Singh and Raja Singh, members of the SGPC Working Committee, met Maharaja Ripudaman Singh at Dehra Dun in July 1924 to come to a clear understanding with him. After some discussion they thought of a way in which the Maharaja would state that he was not satisfied with the decision of the Government of India with regard to Nabha. A reporter of the Associated Press could ask him that whereas Lord Peel, the Secretary of State for India, had said in the House of Lords that Birdwood negotiations failed because the SGPC insisted on the restoration of the Maharaja of Nabha, the speeches of Lord Reading and others gave the impression that His Highness was satisfied with the decision of the Government of India. The Maharaja could say in reply that he was not satisfied with the decision of his case which was entirely the result of 'intrigues and bribery, not without the hand of the officials of the Political Department'.[37]

On this point, the talks between the Maharaja and his supporters began to drag. The emissaries of the SGPC were thinking of demanding an enquiry for which the proposed statement could be helpful, but the Maharaja did not favour the idea of an enquiry that did not include the issue of his restoration. The SGPC representatives suggested that an attested copy of the representation that the Maharaja had made to the Viceroy in December 1923 could serve the same purpose. The Maharaja wanted to know if the SGPC would drop the Nabha issue if they did not get any of the documents. The two representatives assured him that the SGPC would not like to drop it. 'The Panth' as a whole had given the mandate to the SGPC.[38] Raja Singh went to see the Maharaja again on 25 July 1924. The Maharaja indicated that he had not been treated fairly by the Sikh leaders. The attitude of the government towards him hardened due to his trust in them. He did not want to provide a handle to the government for further action against him.[39]

On the following day, Raja Singh took another draft to the Maharaja. It was a letter addressed to the SGPC by him, saying that it was rumoured that Birdwood negotiations failed mainly because of the SGPC insisting on the restoration of the Maharaja, which was confirmed by Lord Peel's statement in the House of Lords. The Maharaja was thankful to the Panth for their goodwill, but he considered it to be in the interest of all concerned that the Panth should set aside his case. On seeing this draft, the Maharaja remarked that the SGPC wanted a pretext to give up the Nabha question. The Maharaja added that he had made his representation to the Viceroy against his own judgement only because the suggestion was presented to him as a wish of the Panth, and he was 'left with no alternative but to sign the representation'. Raja Singh again explained the position of the SGPC with regard to the Nabha question, and the Maharaja agreed finally to give a statement to Mahatma Gandhi if there was a letter from him. Then Mahatma Gandhi could make it public that the Maharaja had suffered great wrong and grave injustice, without a proper judicial enquiry.[40] Though the negotiations ended on a somewhat positive note, no action appears to have followed the agreement arrived at.

Hailey had expressed the view even before taking over the governorship of the province that no reasonable settlement could be expected 'until we have hit the present leadership of the movement much harder than we have done so far; in fact, until they feel themselves that the game is up'. The only way to ensure a settlement on his own terms was to bring the Akalis to their knees. This was precisely what Hailey set out to do.[41] Apart from harsh measures to clear the ground for Gurdwara legislation without the Nabha issue, his strategy was to actively promote legislation through the Sikh Sudhar Committee as an alternative to the SGPC.[42]

As the provincial governor, Hailey thought of associating the Sikh princely states with his programme. In September 1924, he held a conference with several senior officials of the central and provincial governments and the Sikh states. Hailey stated that the Sikh Sudhar Committee was trying to formulate 'a constructive policy for the reformation of the Gurdwaras'. The SGPC was not 'the only body representing the Sikhs'. The objective of the conference was to have officially inspired committees in the Sikh states as well to strengthen the movement orchestrated in the British Punjab.[43]

Early in October 1924, H. D. Craik, the Chief Secretary, Punjab, told Ogilvie of the Foreign and Political Department that the Sikh Sudhar Committee proposed to send a jathā to Jaito in which all Sikh districts would be represented. The visit of the jathā might not do any good, but it could do no harm. In any case, Wilson-Johnston thought that permission could not be refused. The Viceroy approved of the project. It was understood that the jathā would accept the usual conditions. The body of pilgrims was to be styled 'a sangat and not a jathā' to avoid political undertones.[44]

This sangat was duly informed through a notice by the Nabha Administrator that no more than 50 Sikhs could be allowed to enter the Gurdwara at Gangsar, which had always been open to Sikhs purely for religious purposes. The sangat had to give written guarantees that they would leave the Gurdwara after performing an akhand pāṭh, would not indulge in political speeches, and would leave the state territory after the conclusion of the religious ceremony.[45] As expected, the Sikh Sudhar Sangat readily accepted these conditions.

The sangat was taken to Gurdwara Gangsar in a big procession. The 'pilgrims', consisted of 'honourable members of Imperial Assembly, Raises, big jagirdars and landlords, and all arrangements were made for their comfort'. The akhand pāṭh was started on 21 October 1924, and finished on 22 October. The sangat left Jaito by the afternoon train amidst 'great rejoicings', leaving what was thought by the Nabha Administration to be 'a very wholesome effect on the public mind'.[46] The success of the akhand pāṭh ceremony was telegraphically intimated to the Viceroy, and the Secretary of State for India. Obviously, the akhand pāṭh by the sangat was important in the eyes of the government. It made the Central Sudhar Committee of Amritsar a rival in authority to the SGPC.

Legislation without Restoration

On 24 March 1925, 50 members of the Imperial Legislative Assembly gave a representation to Sir Alexander Muddiman, the Home Member, about Sikh grievances. Referring to the resolution of 26 February 1924, which had remained unimplemented, they requested the Governor General in Council to take up the matter at an early date. Among other things, they recommended the desirability of publishing such correspondence or reports 'as the Government may have in its possession or power to satisfy the public that H.H. the Maharaja of Nabha *voluntarily* abdicated his *gaddi*'. They also recommended an independent enquiry into the occurrences at Jaito and the complaints relating to Jaito prisoners. They wanted the government 'to establish a Council of Administration at Nabha'. In their view, it was desirable to withdraw the declaration made against the SGPC and the prosecutions of its office bearers and members, to release all Sikh political prisoners, and to expedite the passing of a satisfactory Gurdwara Bill.[47]

The Government of India wrote to the Punjab Government for its views on 'measures to expedite the passing of a satisfactory Gurdwara Bill'. In Hailey's view, to withdraw the declaration that the SGPC was an unlawful body would be 'the height of unwisdom' when the extreme section of the SGPC was beginning to lose its influence among the Sikhs at large. The real solution to the Sikh problem was to isolate the religious issue, and this had been done. A Gurdwara Bill was about to be introduced in the Punjab Legislative Council. The atmosphere created by the new Governor should not be disturbed at this juncture by 'any talk of concessions or conciliation'.

Hailey went on to explain that the Bill was now being introduced by the Sikh Members of the Legislative Council, after consultation with the government, purely on its own merits. No extraneous consideration had been demanded by them and none had been accepted by the government. The situation was now radically different from what it had been a year ago. 'If the Bill is passed and if an honest attempt is made to put it into operation, Government can then proceed to consider its next step.'[48]

Out of the 34 members of the SGPC detained in the Lahore Fort Jail, 24 authorized the members outside to take any decision in the 'interest of the Panth'. The majority of these members were now in favour of legislation without any reference to the Nabha issue.[49] The Gurdwaras Bill was passed on 7 July 1925.

Maharaja Ripudaman Singh was the most unhappy person about the Sikh Gurdwaras Act: it left him in the lurch. Had not the SGPC taken up his cause, he could have thought of other means to come out of his predicament. He had argued with the SGPC leaders, Teja Singh Samundari, Bawa Harkishan Singh, and Master Tara Singh, who had come to see him, that they should not take up his cause because they would not be able to take it to its logical conclusion. But in his enthusiasm, Bawa Harkishan Singh went to the extent of saying that either the Maharaja would be restored to his gaddī or the entire nation would perish in the struggle. The Maharaja had warned the other representatives of the SGPC, who met him later at Dehra Dun, of the politico-legal consequences of their suggestions for him. By coming to an understanding with the government, the SGPC had now left him to the wolves. He could foresee that before long, the

British bureaucrats would grind him, take him to Burma or some such place to imprison him for the rest of his life.[50]

Notes

1. The Tribune, 1 August 1923, p. 4, columns 1, 2. Also, Akālī te Pardesī, 29 July 1923, p. 1.
2. The Tribune, 1 August 1923, p. 4, column 3.
3. The Tribune, 2 August 1923, p. 4, column 3.
4. For the exact wording of the ardās, see Akālī te Pardesī, 20 July 1923, p. 3. See also, Sohan Singh Josh, Akali Morchon Ka Itihas (Hindi) (New Delhi: Peoples Publishing House, 1974), pp. 290–1. Josh was an eyewitness to these events. See also, Mohinder Singh, 'Akali Involvement in the Nabha Affair', The Panjab Past and Present, vol. VII, no. 2 (October 1971): 372.
5. The booklet entitled The Morcha of Nabha, published in the name of G. B. Singh of Nabha, contains some of the material orchestrated by the Patiala Darbar in connection with their propaganda against Maharaja Ripudaman Singh.
6. This authorization made it easy for Wilson-Johnston to resort to firing. Indirectly, he was encouraged to do it.
7. It may be pointed out that Maharaja Ripudaman Singh was opposed to the idea of a Council of Regency in order not to give an opportunity to the Maharaja of Patiala to intervene in the affairs of Nabha through a protégé.
8. India Office Records (IOR), (microfilm) L/P and S/10/1022, Register no. 3607, pp. 5–10. The statement actually signed by the Maharaja is given in Ganda Singh, ed., Some Confidential Papers of the Akali Movement (Amritsar: Shiromani Gurdwara Prabandhak Committee, 1965), p. 74. To overcome the Maharaja's resistance, Minchin asserted that it was an order of the government (The Tribune, 3 August, 1923).
9. The Tribune, 3 August 1923.
10. IOR, L/P and S/10/1022, Shiromani Gurdwara Prabandhak Committee to Viceroy, 2 August 1923.
11. Quoted in Mohinder Singh, 'Akali Involvement in the Nabha Affair': 372–3.
12. Mohinder Singh, 'Akali Involvement in the Nabha Affair': 373–4.
13. IOR (microfilm), R/1/29/26, File no. 583-P II-(S)/1923, correspondence between AGG and G. D. Oglivie (Officiating Secretary to the Government of India), 17 July, 2 and 16 August, 2, 15 and 28 September, and 14 and 30 October 1923.
14. Truth about Nabha (Amritsar: Shiromani Gurdwara Prabandhak Committee, 1923), p. 110.
15. Josh, Akālī Morchon kā Itihās, p. 297.

16. Ganda Singh, *Confidential Papers*, p. xvi. See IOR, L/P and S/10/1022, for Sardar Gurdial Singh's explanation of the akhand pāṭh at Jaito and denial of interruption, 4 October 1923.
17. IOR, MSS Eur E 236/26, no. 286, Sir Malcolm Hailey, Governor, Punjab to Viscount Reading, dated 19 June 1924.
18. IOR (microfilm), R/1/29/26, File no. 583-P II-(S)/1923, AGG to G. D. Oglivie, 30 October 1923. The Viceroy had given a speech at the Lady Chelmsford Club, which was reported in the *Pioneer* of 24 October, stating that there was no chance of the Maharaja of Nabha returning to his gaddī. Minchin thought that its effect on the people of the Nabha state was good.
19. Ganda Singh, *Confidential Papers*, pp. 115–16.
20. Ganda Singh, *Confidential Papers*, pp. 18–24.
21. Ganda Singh, *Confidential Papers*, pp. 28–34.
22. IOR (microfilm), Reel no. 32 R/1/1/1518(1), J. Wilson-Johnston, Administrator Nabha State, dated 7 February 1924; meeting held at the Imperial Secretariat, Delhi, 8 February 1924; telegram to Agent to Governor General, dated 13 February 1924.
23. For the importance of martyrdom in Sikh ideology and literature, see J. S. Grewal, *Recent Debates in Sikh Studies: An Assessment* (New Delhi: Manohar, 2011) pp. 195–216.
24. Ganda Singh, *Confidential Papers*, pp. 35–7.
25. IOR, R/1/1/1518(1), Report on action taken regarding shahīdī jathā and other Akalis at Jaito, 21 February 1924. See also Ganda Singh, *Confidential Papers*, pp. 37–45.
26. IOR, R/1/1/1518(1), Press-Communiqué, dated 22 February 1921.
27. Extract from *The Pioneer*, dated 24 February 1924.
28. Ganda Singh, *Confidential Papers*, pp. 37–45.
29. IOR (microfilm), R/1/1/1518(I), debate in the House of Commons, 1 March 1924, questions 2 and 7. The answer given by the Under Secretary of State for India, however, insinuated that firing was in response to violation of the government order: 'The Akalis themselves have issued an appeal to the public that crowd should not accompany the Jatha, and I trust violence will not be used on their side on this occasion and that the question of using force against the Jatha will not arise.'

It is interesting to note that K. M. Panikkar, who enquired into the firing at Jaito on behalf of the Indian National Congress, reported that the Administrator of Nabha had become 'panicky and ordered fire as a result of fear'. He had made ample preparations for such a contingency. But there was no justification whatsoever for his action (M. L. Ahluwalia, ed., *Select Documents of Gurdwara Reform Movement 1919–1925* [New Delhi: Ashoka International Publishers 1985], pp. 406–11).

30. IOR, MSS Eur E 238/26, *Reading Collection*, vol. IV, 1924, Reading to Nabha, no. 76b.
31. IOR (microfilm), R/1/1/1727, Resolution of the Assembly, dated 25 February 1925.
32. Ganda Singh, *Confidential Papers*, p. 101.
33. Ganda Singh, *Confidential Papers*, pp. 91–4.
34. Ganda Singh, *Confidential Papers*, pp. 94, 98–100.
35. IOR, MSS Eur E 238/26, *Reading Collection*, vol. IV, 1924, no. 286, Hailey to Reading, dated 19 June 1924.
36. Ganda Singh, *Confidential Papers*, pp. 124–7, 129–39, 142, 143, 180, for example.
37. Ganda Singh, *Confidential Papers*, p. 118.
38. Ganda Singh, *Confidential Papers*, p. 113.
39. Ganda Singh, *Confidential Papers*, p. 114–17.
40. Ganda Singh, *Confidential Papers*, pp. 117, 119–20.
41. Described as 'a virile dominating personality' by Reading, Hailey was deeply committed to the Empire (IOR, MSS E 238/7, *Reading Collection*, Reading to Ramsden, 5 June 1924, no. 22).

    In his disdainful attitude towards Indian nationalism Hailey was like Michael O'Dwyer, and very much in tune with the imperialistic ideology and authoritarian approach of the Punjab School.
42. IOR (microfilm), R/1/1/1520, File no. 64 (17) P/1924. In a note on 'Sikh Publicity in the Punjab States', J. P. Thompson clearly states that the Sikh Sudhar Committees that had been established in the British districts owed their origin to official inspiration. The Viceroy's thinking on the subject is given in 'notes' dated 15 November 1924. This was conveyed to Sir Malcolm Hailey by the Political Secretary in his letter of 17 November 1924.
43. IOR, R/1/1/1520, File no. 64 (17) P/1924. Minutes of a Conference held at Barnes Court, Simla, at 5.30 p.m. in September 1924.
44. IOR (microfilm), R/1/1/1520, File no. 64 (17) P/1924, note by G. D. Ogilvie, dated 4 October 1924.
45. Punjab State Archives, Patiala, Office of the Administrator, Nabha State, File no. 225, copy of the notice.
46. IOR (microfilm), R/1/29/77, File no. 14-P (Secret) of 1924, 'Visit of Sikh Sudhar Sangat to Jaito', note by Gurdial Singh (Assistant Administrator), dated 25 October 1924.
47. IOR, R/1/1/1727, File no. 155-P (Secret)/1928, 'Memorial from Certain members of the Legislative Assembly in regard to the grievances of the Sikh community'.
48. IOR, 1/1/1727, File no. 155P(S) 1928, H. D. Craik to Home Secretary, J. Crerar, 28 April, 1925.
49. Ganda Singh, *Confidential Papers*, pp. 138–44.

It may be mentioned that two communications from the Lahore Fort Jail expressing the minority views did not want the SGPC to forget the Nabha issue (Ganda Singh, *Confidential Papers*, pp. 172–4). The Maharaja added that while he had been without financial support for the last two years, his powerful enemy (Patiala?) and his men were resolutely after his life.

9

ATTITUDE OF THE CONGRESS AND ITS LEADERS

The Jaito Morcha for Maharaja Ripudaman Singh's restoration was the culmination of the Akali movement. However, the Congress was not yet interested in princely India so far as its political programme was concerned. The close identification of the Akalis with the Maharaja and his marked sympathies for Indian nationalism made his position somewhat different. Therefore, the Congress deviated from its policy to pass resolutions in his support. The 'Swarajist interlude', meanwhile, had resulted in reorientation in the strategy of the Congress Party under some senior leaders, notably Pandit Motilal Nehru. He and his son, Jawaharlal, got involved in the Nabha issue. But the Congress–Akali dialogue for active collaboration did not make much headway even after the release of Mahatma Gandhi from jail. Looking upon the Akali demand for Maharaja Ripudaman Singh's reinstatement to be a political one, the Mahatma wanted the Akalis to separate the political from the religious demands. His attitude towards the Jaito Morcha was in marked contrast to his attitude of unqualified appreciation for the earlier phase of the Akali movement. He appeared to be keen to harness the Akali fervour for his own political programme.

The Nehrus and the Jaito Morcha

In his *Autobiography*, Jawaharlal Nehru talks of 'An Interlude at Nabha' to narrate his experience during the Jaito Morcha. The Akalis had displayed an amazing tenacity and courage at Guru ka Bagh, referred to later in this chapter. Jawaharlal had been reading accounts of how Akali jathās were stopped, beaten, arrested, and carried to an out-of-the way place in the jungle and left there. Immediately after the special session of the Congress at Delhi, he went to Jaito with two of his Congress colleagues, A. T. Gidwani and K. Santanam. They joined the Akali jathā as 'spectators', but they were arrested on entering Nabha territory and tried for breach of orders not to enter Nabha along with a fourth man who had absolutely nothing to do with them. The trial ended about a fortnight later. The whole procedure was 'farcical'. The police under the British Administrator did what they pleased and often ignored the magistrate. 'If this was the state of affairs when more or less prominent politicians like us were concerned, what, I wonder, would be the fate of others less known?'[1]

Desperate to secure his son's release, Pandit Motilal had sent telegrams to a number of persons, including the Viceroy, Punjab Governor, Nabha Administrator, other highly placed Nabha officials, and members of the central and provincial legislatures.[2] His telegram of 22 September to Harkishen Lal, who was a Minister in the Punjab Government at that time, had been forwarded to the Nabha Administrator, J. Wilson-Johnston, who informed Pandit Motilal on the 24th that his son had arrived at Jaito on the 21st afternoon in the company of K. Santanam and Gidwani. They came with a large Akali jathā from Muktsar. Their presence under the circumstances was most inadvisable in Jaito, and notice was served on them under Section 144 of the Criminal Procedure Code by the Administrator's orders. They received the notice and signed a copy. But they entered the state with the jathā. They were arrested under Section 188 of the Indian Penal Code and they were being tried under Section 145 as well.[3]

Pandit Motilal sent a telegram to the Viceroy on 24 September stating that he was proceeding to Nabha to interview his son who had taken no part in the Akali agitation but was reported to have been arrested; the sole object of his own visit was to see his son. This telegram was 'repeated' in a telegraphic message to the Administrator of Nabha with the remark that it was 'evidently intended to establish *bonafides* of Pandit Motilal Nehru's visit to Nabha'. Wilson-Johnston telegraphed in reply that he had given instructions that Motilal should not enter the state. 'In view of his recent utterances in the Congress I considered his presence in the State most undesirable.' Unless he received orders to the contrary, the Administrator would not change his instructions. The Government of India, however, advised him to allow Pandit Motilal to enter Nabha on the condition that he undertook not to say anything on the political situation in the state and to leave it immediately after his interview with Jawaharlal.[4]

The Chief Police Officer of Nabha met Pandit Motilal at the Nabha railway station, and told him that the Administrator could not permit him to interview his son 'at the present stage'; he could apply 'to have an interview later on'.[5] A verbal message was communicated to him that he could see his son on the condition that he guaranteed 'not to engage in any political activities in the State', and to leave 'immediately after the interview'. Pandit Motilal contended that it was his right to have an interview and not a matter to bargain about. Therefore, he was unable to give any undertaking whatever in consideration of being allowed to see his son.[6] The Administrator repeated the conditions and insisted on a written undertaking, but Pandit Motilal insisted on his rights.[7] On 25 September, a telegram from the Government of India informed Motilal that the Administrator had been told that 'you should be allowed to give all necessary legal assistance to your son', subject to giving 'guarantee' to the Administrator.[8] Wilson-Johnston sent a notice to be served upon Motilal under Section 144, asking him 'to leave the State territory by the first train' in view of his presence 'tending to disturb the public tranquility', and not to enter the state territory 'for a period of two months'. Finally, on 27 September 1923, Pandit Motilal felt obliged to send 'the guarantee in the exact form and words' stipulated by the Nabha Administration. He was allowed to see Jawaharlal and the record of proceedings against him.[9]

On 28 September 1923, Kapil Deva Malaviya was allowed to represent Pandit Motilal because of his indisposition and to conduct the case in his absence.[10] The written statements of the accused had been filed already on the 25th. The statement by Jawaharlal opened with the sentence that he did not wish to defend himself by producing any witness or offering any defence against the proceedings: 'As a non-cooperator I merely wish to inform the court of the facts as I know them and to correct any wrong statements that have been made.' He pointed out 'a number of illegalities and irregularities' which had occurred in the case. In the third paragraph, Jawaharlal questioned the validity of the appointment of the Administrator, also referring to the dispossession of Maharaja Ripudaman Singh, 'the Rightful ruler of Nabha state'. Jawaharlal ended by saying that if the action of the

Government of India was bona fide and in the interest of the state, 'I would imagine that they would welcome enquiry and outsiders' investigation'. He and his colleagues had come with open minds but their liberty of movement was restricted. Their intention was to leave Jaito by the next train but they could not be a party to 'an illegal and immoral order'. He maintained that the restrictions imposed by the present administration in Nabha 'on our undoubted rights are indefensible and raise a wider issue. On that issue my duty is clear. If that results in a conviction and sentence I shall gladly welcome it'. He had come to know of what happened on 24 September and how his father had to return from Nabha without seeing him. Therefore, he saw no point in adjourning the case; his colleagues gave their written assent at 4.40 p.m. on 25 September 1923.[11]

The trial ended on 3 October 1923, with the sentence of two and a half years' imprisonment—two years under Section 145 and six months under Section 188. One year of the former and all the six months of the latter were of 'rigorous imprisonment'. The case had been tried by a special magistrate. The evidence of the 'witnesses' was seen as more credible than the statements made by Jawaharlal and his two colleagues. Whatever their original intention, they did join the Akali jathā and they did refuse to disperse. Their refusal to obey the orders under Section 144 made them liable for trial and punishment under Section 145. This travesty of justice, thought Jawaharlal, had resulted from an unexceptionable combination—the autocratic state administration under a British officer invoking the repressive laws of British India at will.[12]

On the same evening, however, Johnston asked the Superintendent of the Central Jail to personally announce to the three accused first the suspension of the sentences passed on them, and then the executive order calling upon them to leave the state territory forthwith, and to refrain from returning thereto. No copy of the order was to be given to them. The Administrator's order stated that they were forbidden to return to Nabha territory 'without my express permission'.[13] They left Nabha on 3 October itself. Jawaharlal went to Allahabad, where he was to contest the Mayoral election, and wrote to the Administrator of Nabha to send copies of both the orders, together with copies of the two judgments. But Nabha authorities refused to supply any copy. 'For aught I know, these sentences may still be hanging over me, and may take effect whenever the Nabha authorities or the British Government so choose.'[14]

By now it was clear that the Viceroy took personal interest at all stages, and that the sentence was suspended because of his intervention.[15] His positive response to Pandit Motilal's telegrams as an anxious parent whose son was soon to start his public career, in all probability, sprang from the government's keenness to implement the Reform Act. Thus, Reading's concerns converged with those of the Nehrus.

About a week later, Pandit Motilal sent a letter to the *Pioneer* which, in Wilson-Johnston's view, did not present the correct position. He sought advice from the Government of India. He was advised by C. M. G. Ogilvie of the Political Department that it would be a mistake to start a press controversy in this matter. 'There is no doubt that Nehru and his son were substantially defeated over the Nabha affair and they know this full well.' Motilal Nehru had given in writing the guarantee 'he had vowed he would never give and his wrigglings will deceive no one'. He could be ignored. If he returns to the attack, 'we can then if necessary give a damaging reply'.[16]

On 31 October 1923, Jawaharlal wrote to the Administrator of Nabha that the Registrar, Chief Judicial Court, Nabha, had refused to supply copies of judgments on the plea that the laws or procedures of the state did not allow copies to be given to 'outsiders'. Nehru enclosed with this letter a copy of his letter to the Registrar, requesting the Administrator to direct that copies of judgments be supplied to him forthwith. Johnston wrote to AGG Minchin that it would be unwise to give copies to Jawaharlal who obviously wanted them for political purposes. Already, *The Tribune* and *The Nation* had commented upon the matter. Minchin advised Johnston that if Jawaharlal wrote again, the matter could be referred for orders to the Government of India.[17] The case was filed.

The *Autobiography* mentions 'yet another sequel' to the Nabha episode. Gidwani was acting as the Congress representative in Amritsar in February 1924, keeping in touch with the Sikh Gurdwara Committee. He decided to accompany the shahīdī jathā of 500 as an observer. He had no intention of entering Nabha territory. The jathā was fired upon by the police near the border, and many persons were killed and wounded. 'Gidwani went to the help of the wounded when he was pounced upon by the police and taken away. No proceedings in court were taken against him. He was simply kept in prison for the best part of a year when, terribly broken in health, he was discharged.'[18] He was released from jail on 22 February 1925.[19]

Gidwani's arrest seemed to Jawaharlal to be a monstrous abuse of executive authority. He wrote to the Administrator asking why Gidwani had been treated in this way. The Administrator replied that Gidwani was imprisoned because he had broken the order not to enter Nabha territory without permission. Jawaharlal challenged the legality of this order and of arresting a man who was giving succour to the wounded. He asked the Administrator to send or publish a copy of the order in question but he refused to do so. Jawaharlal felt inclined to go to Nabha and allow the Administrator to treat him as he had treated Gidwani. He would probably have been treated the same way, he was told. He did not go.

> Loyalty to a colleague seemed to demand it. But many friends thought otherwise and dissuaded me. I took shelter behind the advice of friends, and made of it a pretext to cover my own weakness. For, after all, it was my weakness and disinclination to go to Nabha Gaol again that kept me away, and I have always felt a little ashamed of thus deserting a colleague. As often with us all, discretion was preferred to valour.[20]

With this candid confession aptly ended his 'interlude'.

Jawaharlal Nehru continued to express appreciation for the Akalis. On 13 October 1923, he wrote in his presidential address for the Varanasi Conference: 'Today all our eyes are turned to the North where the gallant Akalis are challenging the might of the Government. They have taken up the proud position of the vanguard in our army of freedom and they are worthy of it.' On 27 October, in a statement addressed to the students of the Allahabad University, from the Nainital Jail, he reminded them of the agony of the Sikh people: 'Little news is allowed to come but we know that the Government is trying its utmost to crush the brave and gallant people, who with their backs to the wall are fighting for their very existence. They ask for your sympathy for a gesture of encouragement.' Jawaharlal asked them to express their sympathy with the Akalis.[21]

At the annual session of the Indian National Congress in December 1923, Jawaharlal referred to the Akali *satyāgraha* (non-violent resistance) at Jaito in which the whole Sikh community was involved. In terms of training and organization, they presented an example for others, including the Congress. Though small in numbers, the community was able to oppose the British Government. There were people among Hindus and Muslims who were capable of as much suffering. But the Sikhs had got the necessary training. They were well organized whereas the Congressmen were not.[22] On this argument the Congress could learn from the Akalis and also help them in their struggle. With reference to the nonviolent activities of the Shiromani Akali Dal and the SGPC, and the government's decision in October 1923 to treat them as unlawful associations, the Congress resolved to stand by the Sikhs in their 'present' struggle and to render all possible assistance, including men and money.[23]

The Akali Sahayak Bureau

A conference of members of the All India Congress Committee (AICC) was held at Amritsar on 14 November 1923. In his lecture at the Jallianwala Bagh on the same day, Maulana Azad announced that all leaders were agreed that 'the present Sikh situation and the Nabha question' were not the affairs of any one province or community but were all-India affairs concerning all communities. He added that the 'leaders conference' had also arrived at a decision to give all the help required by the SGPC and the Shiromani Akali Dal. The Akalis, however, had made it clear that they would have their campaign independently of the Congress Civil Disobedience campaign. The Akali leaders were not keen about a joint movement, but they wanted the Congress to help them with funds and propaganda work. The AICC decided to issue an all-India appeal for funds for the SGPC and to form 'Akali Aid Committees' in all the provinces. The announcement was issued to the press by Pandit Motilal as President of the AICC. A. T. Gidwani was chosen for organizing propaganda work.[24]

On 23 January 1924, Gidwani wrote to Jawaharlal Nehru as Secretary of the AICC that an embassy (Sahayak Bureau) had been established at Amritsar to keep in touch with the Akali movement, watch its interests in the press, and present to its leaders and workers the point of view and programme of the Congress. He suggested to Jawaharlal that he could strengthen 'the hold of the Congress on the Sikh community' by taking action on the resolutions regarding the funds. 'A definite sum should be fixed', Gidwani said, 'and announced even if it has to be collected.' Jawaharlal wrote back on 25 January that he would try to send more money. But the Congress at the moment had no funds. Therefore, it was decided to make every effort to get money for the Sahayak Fund and then make a grant out of it to the Akalis, who were in the thick of the Jaito Morcha. Nehru, however, maintained that 'the greatest help that the Congress can give to the

Sikhs is to perfect its own organisation and throw in its whole weight at the moment of crisis'. Meanwhile, publicity could be promoted.[25] The Working Committee of the Congress sanctioned 25,000 rupees for helping the families of the Akalis going to jail for offering civil disobedience at Jaito.

In his letter of 10 February Jawaharlal says: 'Now that Mahatma Ji is out we can no longer afford to let matters drift.'[26] This appears to carry the implication that Mahatma Gandhi was more seriously interested in the Akali movement than the other Congress leaders.

When the first shahīdī jathā of 500 started from Amritsar on 9 February, the Akali Sahayak Bureau issued a press telegram to the dailies like the *Chronicle, Forward, Servant, Swarajya, Voice of India, Bande Matram, Partap, Zamindar,* and *The Tribune* about its march. On the initiative of the Congress members of the Legislative Assembly, a resolution was moved in favour of an early solution to the problems of the Sikhs.[27] On 23 April 1924, K. M. Panikkar wrote to Jawaharlal from Amritsar that he expected the Working Committee to discuss the Akali situation and the probable role of the Congress. In Panikkar's opinion, it was difficult for the Congress to interfere directly in a matter that was claimed to be essentially religious. The Congress had done wisely to limit its help to financial grants. However, it was his conviction that 'the time may come when greater support would be required'. That time, he emphasized, was 'very near'.[28]

The situation in April 1924 showed no sign of easing. The government showed no sign of yielding and the Sikhs on their part were determined not to yield. 'The situation may slightly be easier', said Panikkar, 'when the SGPC issues its promised statement that the Morcha at Jaito has nothing whatever to do with the agitation for the restoration of the Maharaja of Nabha.' Panikkar had been pressing Sardar Mangal Singh, 'President of the Central Sikh League and a member of the Working Committee of the Indian National Congress', for such a declaration. Like the Punjab Governor, Malcolm Hailey, the Congress leadership also was trying to separate the religious and political issues. Taking his cue from the position held by the Congress leadership, Mangal Singh made a not quite correct statement to the Akali Sahayak Bureau that the Jaito satyāgraha 'as such was quite apart from the agitation about the deposition of the Maharaja of Nabha'. Mangal Singh asserted that the Akali movement though essentially religious in spirit, was 'a powerful auxiliary to the national cause'.[29]

Mahatma Gandhi and the Nabha Issue

Interested in the Akali movement from the beginning, Mahatma Gandhi had visited Nankana Sahib with Maulana Shaukat Ali on 3 March 1921 to assure the Sikhs: 'Your grief is mine.' If the brave men who died at Nankana Sahib did not use their kirpāns and battle-axes in self-defence, the event 'must electrify the whole world'. It should be regarded as 'an act of national bravery'. Mahatma Gandhi exhorted the Sikhs to dedicate this martyrdom to Bharat Mata (Mother India) and to remember that 'the Khalsa can remain free only in a free India'. All the national associations had recognized the necessity of non-violence: 'Your *kirpans* must therefore remain scrupulously sheathed and hatchets buried.' All the matchless bravery of the Khalsa should be dedicated 'to the service of the country and her redemption'. The movement for freeing the Gurdwaras could thus become a part of the national struggle for freedom.[30]

Mahatma Gandhi had made his view quite clear in his message to the Sikhs of Lahore on 4 March 1921. What happened at Nankana Sahib was 'a second edition of Dyerism more barbarous, more calculated and more fiendish than the Dyerism of Jallianwala'. India wept over 'the awful tragedy'. He advised his 'Sikh friends to shape their future conduct in accordance with the need of the nation'. The whole of India wanted to sweep the British Government out of existence 'unless the system under which it is being carried on is radically altered'. In this situation, it would be wrong 'to divert the attention of any section of the nation from the main or the only issue which is before the country'. Mahatma Gandhi at this time had promised swarāj in a year. His advice to the Akalis, therefore, was to suspend their movement.[31]

On 9 March 1921, Mahatma Gandhi thanked the members of the SGPC for appointing him Chairman of an unofficial Committee of Enquiry into the Nankana tragedy. If the idea of this enquiry was merely to counteract any mischievous effects of the official enquiry, he would not be able to render any useful service. He then urged the SGPC members to reconsider their resolution and come to 'a decision in terms of non-cooperation', like the Central Sikh League and the other national organizations. If they could not join the non-cooperation movement, they should relieve the Mahatma from the responsibility imposed on him. *The Tribune* of 13 March carried Mahatma Gandhi's article on 'Sikh Awakening' in which he outlined the events of the Akali movement, underscoring the importance of the Nankana tragedy as 'a perfect example of non-violent non-cooperation'. He firmly believed that 'its impact on the freedom movement will be tremendous'.[32] Eventually, in May 1921, the SGPC passed a resolution in support of joining non-cooperation.[33]

In October, the Executive Committee of the SGPC asked its Secretary, Sardar Sunder Singh Ramgarhia, the officially appointed Manager of the Golden Temple, to hand over the bunch of its 53 keys to Sardar Kharak Singh, President of the SGPC. On advice from the government, the Deputy Commissioner of Amritsar deposited the keys in the government treasury for 'safe' custody. The SGPC decided to hold protest meetings against this interference. A large number of protesters were arrested and imprisoned. Eventually, all the Akali workers were released unconditionally on 17 January 1922, and the keys of the Golden Temple were handed over to Sardar Kharak Singh in a public meeting. Mahatma Gandhi sent a telegraphic message to him: 'First decisive battle for India's freedom won. Congratulations.'[34]

In August 1922, the SGPC had launched the famous Guru ka Bagh Morcha, which came to be regarded as the supreme example of passive resistance. The police brutalities and the perseverance of the Akalis attracted the attention of national leaders. C. F. Andrews, the British missionary who sympathized with the Indian people and their struggle for freedom, visited the Guru ka Bagh in September. He was shocked by the brutality and inhumanity of the British administrators and their henchmen. He admired the Akalis for their patient suffering without any sign of fear. In his eyes, the Guru ka Bagh Morcha was a 'new lesson in moral warfare'. In a specially convened meeting of the Congress Working Committee on 17 September 1922, two resolutions were passed to condemn the brutalities of the police, and to appoint a subcommittee to enquire into their excesses. Its report was extremely critical of the police. Unnerved by the widespread criticism of its actions and their possibly adverse effect on the Sikh soldiers, the government finally found a way out. The Gurdwara and its adjacent land were handed over to the SGPC on 17 November 1922, and more than five thousand Akalis who had been jailed on account of the Morcha were released in March 1923.[35]

By this time, the non-cooperation movement had been suspended by Mahatma Gandhi, because the agitators had turned violent at Chauri Chaura in February 1922. He was arrested in March on a charge of sedition, and sentenced to six years' imprisonment. Among the top leaders of the Congress there was no unanimity about the form of non-cooperation. Pandit Motilal Nehru, V. J. Patel, and Hakim Ajmal Khan were in favour of contesting elections to offer opposition from within the central and provincial legislatures and to check repression of political movements. In the winter of 1922 it was no longer possible to conceal the rift within the Congress.[36] The idea of fighting 'the battle for swaraj' in the legislatures did not gain majority support in the Gaya Session of the Congress in December 1922. A new organization was created on 1 January 1923 called the 'Congress Khilafat Swaraj Party', with C. R. Das as President and Motilal Nehru as General Secretary. Popularly known as the Swaraj Party, it decided to take part in elections to be held in November 1923.[37]

A special session of the Congress held at Delhi in September 1923 marked a stage in the Swarajist advance. In deference to the views of the pro-Council party, it was declared that 'such Congressmen as have no religious or other conscientious objections against entering the legislatures are at liberty to stand as candidates and to exercise their right of voting at the forthcoming election'. Thus, a split within the Congress was averted. By now, the Akalis with their turbans, the slogan of 'Sat Sri Akal', and their unfailing langar, had become a familiar feature of the Congress sessions. A suitable resolution was passed at the special session in sympathy with Maharaja Ripudaman Singh:

> This Congress strongly condemns the action of the Government of India in bringing about the forced abdication of H.H. Maharaja Ripudaman Singh Malvendra Bahadur of Nabha as being unjust and unconstitutional and establishing a very dangerous precedent for the Indian States.
>
> The Congress conveyed its heartfelt sympathy to the Maharaja in the grave wrong that had befallen him.[38]

Motilal Nehru was quite articulate on the subject.[39] How far could he, or his fellow Swarajists, go in support of this resolution was yet to be seen.

As noted earlier, the Jaito Morcha was the apex of the Akali struggle. Mahatma Gandhi was released from jail about a fortnight before the firing on the first shahīdī jathā on 21 February 1924. He expressed his sympathy with the Akalis in the loss of so many brave men, and many more being wounded. But he was not sure whether or not the march of a large number of men to pay devotion at the Gangsar Gurdwara at Jaito was justified. Therefore, his advice to the Akalis was that another jathā 'should not be sent before perfect stock-taking and review of the whole situation'. Mahatma Gandhi had been informed that the jathā had remained strictly nonviolent throughout, and from the very beginning the Akalis had claimed that their movement was nonviolent. But he was not in agreement with their kind of nonviolence.[40]

Owing to Mahatma Gandhi's message, no Congress or Khilafat leaders were noticed at the time of the second shahīdī jathā. The local Congress leaders were disappointed to find that the Akalis had ignored the Mahatma's advice. It was believed that the Congressmen were already getting suspicious and, perhaps, jealous of the Akalis. However, Gandhi's message brought about no change in the attitude of the general public, and the shahīdī jathā received a tremendous ovation.

Evidently, there was considerable lack of clarity, bordering even on confusion, about the objectives and methods of the Akalis among the top Congress leaders. Early in March 1924, Mahatma Gandhi again sought clarification from the representatives of the Akalis and other political leaders who met him in connection with the Jaito Morcha in particular and the Gurdwara movement in general. Reiterating his ideal of nonviolence based on truth, he thought it was necessary for the SGPC to state the scope of this movement, the implications of the akhand pāṭh in the Gangsar Gurdwara, and the position of the SGPC with regard to the forced abdication or deposition of the Maharaja of Nabha.[41]

Mahatma Gandhi was given to understand that every member of the jathā would sit at his post and die there with calm resignation without any retaliation. This, however, was not true nonviolence or civil disobedience, maintained the Mahatma. 'The natural course would be to obey the order of deportation when it is accompanied by physical force, be it ever so light.' He desired the SGPC to make a declaration in the clearest possible terms that the object of the jathā was purely to assert the right to perform akhand pāṭh, and that the SGPC had no desire to carry on under cover of akhand pāṭh any prohibited propaganda in the Nabha state. Thus, the issue of the Maharaja of Nabha could be pursued by the SGPC on its own merit and not linked with the akhand pāṭh affair. Mahatma Gandhi then suggested that if the sending of a jathā of 500 was suspended for the time being and a declaration made on the lines suggested by him, the way for a 'third party' (presumably, the Mahatma himself) to negotiate would be opened with a view to removing the deadlock.[42]

The restoration of Maharaja Ripudaman Singh was one of the two main demands of the Akalis. The position of the SGPC with regard to the Maharaja, as explained to Mahatma Gandhi by the Akalis on behalf of the SGPC, was that the Maharaja had been forced to abdicate essentially for his public spirit and his active sympathy for the Akali cause. This, maintained the Mahatma, called for 'an open and impartial enquiry' to enable the SGPC to present the evidence in its possession. In another letter, Mahatma Gandhi expressed his view that whatever the facts, the Maharaja had made it practically impossible for his well-wishers to carry on an effective agitation for his restoration. Yet, the Mahatma left the door open under certain, albeit demanding, conditions. If the Maharaja made a public statement that the writings were practically extorted from him and that he was quite willing and anxious that all the facts against him should be published, and if he was prepared to face all the consequences of the agitation, such as deprivation of titles, annuity, and so on, and if all his allegations regarding duress could be proved, it was possible to carry on an effective and even successful agitation. In that case, the agitation should be an 'all-India agitation', and the Akalis should 'merely assist in the elucidation of facts'.[43]

Mahatma Gandhi required satisfaction on several points. One of these was that a clear manifesto should publicly state that the performance of akhand pāṭh in Gangsar Gurdwara had no political end, that the Akalis did not desire to use it for carrying on an agitation directly or indirectly for the restoration of the Maharaja of Nabha, and that the Akali agitation for his restoration would be on an independent footing and would be a separate movement. The Secretary of the SGPC replied to all the communications of Mahatma Gandhi on 20 April 1924. He assured the Mahatma that the Gurdwara movement, though religious in spirit and objectives, was 'thoroughly national in outlook'. The SGPC was clear that its resolution to get the wrong done to the Maharaja of Nabha 'righted by all peaceful and legitimate means stood in full force', and it would 'leave no stone unturned to carry out that resolution in consonance with its wording'. However, the Secretary skirted the suggestion about making Nabha deposition an 'all-India' question under the Mahatma's leadership. The SGPC thought that it required much consideration and there was no pressing need of coming to a decision on the matter.[44]

There seemed to be an improvement in Mahatma Gandhi's understanding about 'the Akali Struggle' as was evident from his article in the *Young India* of 25 June 1924. 'No community has shown so much bravery, sacrifice and skill in the prosecution of its object as the Akalis.

No community has maintained the passive spirit so admirably as they.' It was the duty of Hindus and Muslims, and other sister communities, to help the Akalis with their moral support so that the government should know clearly that the Akalis have the moral support of the whole of India. To everyone's satisfaction, added the Mahatma, the Akalis had refuted the charge that their intention was to establish Sikh Raj. He could now advise the people to judge every 'communal movement' on its own merit and give it support when it is sound in itself and the means employed are 'honourable, open and peaceful'.[45] On 5 December 1924, Mahatma Gandhi visited the Golden Temple. He was given a saropā (robe of honour). Within the precincts of the Golden Temple he exhorted the Sikhs to free their motherland, which was a 'bigger Gurdwara'; he warned the Akalis against Malcolm Hailey's intention of dividing them.[46] Like the government, he too wanted the Akalis to drop the demand for restoration of the Maharaja.

Finally, the Sikh Gurdwaras Act was passed in July 1925, and restoration of Maharaja Ripudaman Singh was allowed to remain in suspended animation. The annual session of the Indian National Congress was held at Gauhati (Guwahati) in 1926 under the Presidentship of S. Srinivasa Iyengar. When some members from the Punjab, including Gurdit Singh *Komagata Maru*,[47] wanted the Maharaja's case to be taken up, Motilal Nehru made a statement that he had been 'briefed' by the Maharaja and could not commit himself to a speech at a public meeting on a matter in which he had been briefed. The subject of the Nabha 'abdication' was, therefore, dropped. It was raised again in 1927 by B. G. Horniman, a well-known pro-Congress British journalist and editor of the *Bombay Chronicle*, who had been penalized by the British Government for his active sympathies for Indian nationalism.[48] On 28 October, he moved a resolution on the forced abdication of Maharaja Ripudaman Singh at a requisitioned meeting of the All India Congress Committee:

> This meeting of the AICC reaffirms the resolution passed at the Delhi special session of the Congress in 1923, strongly condemning the action of the Government in bringing about the enforced abdication of His Highness the Maharaja of Nabha as being unjust and unconstitutional, and in reaffirming the heartfelt sympathy of the nation with the Maharaja Saheb in the grave wrong that has befallen him, demands that justice be done to the Nabha cause by the restoration of the Maharaja to the *gaddi* and in all other respects.[49]

However, by itself, a resolution could hardly cut any ice with the authorities. Despite their mutual appreciation, the Akalis and the Congress could not put up a joint front in support of Maharaja Ripudaman Singh. Both Malcolm Hailey and Mahatma Gandhi had ensured, albeit for different reasons, that the political demand of the Maharaja's restoration was separated from the religious demand of Gurdwara legislation, substantially diffusing the former in the process. Furthermore, though a significant departure from the existing policy of the Congress, the Mahatma had laid down almost impossible conditions for taking up the Maharaja's case. Ironically, at that time, Gandhi's own position within the Congress was rather weak. It is not clear whether he refused collaboration with the Akalis because of his scepticism about their total commitment to nonviolent passive resistance or to conceal his own inability at that time to take the movement further. Whatever his reasons, after the withdrawal of non-cooperation, the Mahatma did not appear to be keen on the success of the Akali programme, which presented a somewhat different model of passive resistance, coming as it did from a people who cherished their martial tradition.

When the Maharaja was taken to Kodaikanal as a state prisoner in February 1928, the Congress, this time under the Presidentship of Pandit Motilal Nehru, passed a resolution at its Calcutta session in 1928 expressing sympathy with the ex-Maharaja of Nabha and referring to his internment as 'unjust, unconstitutional and vindictive'.[50] The restoration of Maharaja Ripudaman Singh had become almost impossible now, though individual Congressmen continued to visit him at Kodaikanal and make efforts for his release.

Notes

1. Jawaharlal Nehru, *An Autobiography* (New Delhi: Oxford University Press, 1982, reprint), pp. 109–13.
2. Among the Indian notables contacted by Pandit Motilal Nehru were Lala Harkishen Lal, Sardar Sunder Singh Majithia, Mian Fazl-i Husain, Mian Muhammad Shafi, Pandit Madan Mohan Malaviya, and B. N. Sarma. Nehru Memorial Museum and Library, New Delhi (NMML), All India Congress Committee (AICC) (Supplementary), F. no. 56, items 240, 247. Among others, Shafi, Sarma, and Malaviya informed Motilal that the Viceroy had been apprised of his situation. Items 253, 254, 262.

3. Punjab State Archives (PSA), Patiala, Office of the President, Council of Regency the Nabha State (PCRNS) Records, File no. 60, J. Wilson-Johnston to Pandit Motilal Nehru, 24 September 1923.
4. PSA, PCRNS Records, no. 60, telegrams from Motilal Nehru to Political Department, the Administrator of Nabha, and 'Polindia'. Also, NMML, AICC (Supp), no. 56, items 241, 248.
5. PSA, PCRNS, no. 60, Motilal Nehru to the Administrator (from the waiting room of the Nabha Railway Station), 24 September 1923.
6. PSA, PCRNS Records, no. 60, Postscript.
7. PSA, PCRNS Records, no. 60, Correspondence between Wilson-Johnston and Motilal Nehru, 24 September 1923.
8. NMML, AICC (Supp), No. 56, item 249 (Home D/2505 Poll).
9. PSA, PCRNS Records, no. 60, Wilson-Johnston to Motilal Nehru, 24 September 1923, with the order of section 144 of the Criminal Procedure Code; Motilal Nehru to Wilson-Johnston, 27 September 1923; notes by Wilson-Johnston, dated 27 September 1923.
10. PSA, PCRNS Records, no. 60, Correspondence between Moti Lal Nehru, Kapil Deva Malaviya and Wilston-Johnston.
11. PSA, PCRNS Records, File no. 381, written statement by Jawaharlal Nehru, dated 25 September 1923, signed also by K. Santanam and A. T. Gidwani. Also NMML, AICC (Supp), no. 56, item 268.
12. PSA, PCRNS Records, File no. 14, 'Warrant of Conviction'.
13. PSA, PCRNS Records, File no. 168, Wilson-Johnston to Superintendent Central Jail, Nabha, dated 3 October 1923, with his order dated 3 October 1923.
14. Nehru, *An Autobiography*, pp. 113–15.
15. Several files in the PSA, Patiala, relate to this trial and provide much detail, including the Governor General's intervention. See J. S. Grewal, *Master Tara Singh in Indian History: Colonialism, Nationalism, and Politics of Sikh Identity* (New Delhi: Oxford University Press, 2017), pp. 131–2.
16. PSA, Patiala, PCRNS Records, File no. 60, G. D. Ogilvie to J. Wilson-Johnston, 9 October 1923.
17. PSA, PCRNS Records, File no. 1 C, 'Correspondence with Pandit Jawaharlal Nehru regarding a copy of judgement in the case against him'.
18. J. Nehru, *An Autobiography*, p. 115.
19. PSA, Patiala, PCRNS Records, File no. 168, 'Sentence Passed against A. T. Gidwani'.
20. J. Nehru, *An Autobiography*, p. 116.
21. M. L. Ahluwalia, ed., *Select Documents: Gurdwara Reform Movement 1919–1925: An Era of Congress–Akali Collaboration* (New Delhi: International Publishers, 1985), pp. 415–16.
22. Ahluwalia, *Select Documents*, p. 416.

23. B. Pattabhi Sitaramayya, *The History of the Indian National Congress*, vol. I (1885–1935) (Bombay: Padma Publications, n.d.), p. 262.
24. Ahluwalia, *Select Documents*, pp. 373–6. Present among the thirty participants were Pandit Motilal Nehru, Maulana Muhammad Ali, Maulana Shaukat Ali, Sarojini Naidu, Maulana Abul Kalam Azad, Dr M. A. Ansari, Dr Saifuddin Kitchlew, Dr Satya Pal, and Pandit Achint Ram.
25. Ahluwalia, *Select Documents*, pp. 377–80.
26. Ahluwalia, *Select Documents*, pp. 380–1.
27. Ahluwalia, *Select Documents*, pp. 381–5.
28. Ahluwalia, *Select Documents*, pp. 396–7.
29. Ahluwalia, *Select Documents*, pp. 401–5.
30. Ahluwalia, *Select Documents*, pp. 100–1. For a brief account of the Nankana tragedy, refer to chapter 5 in the present work.
31. Ahluwalia, *Select Documents*, pp. 102–5.
32. Ahluwalia, *Select Documents*, pp. 368–72.
33. The programme of non-cooperation given by Mahatma Gandhi essentially entailed boycott of schools, courts, councils, and British goods. These were to be replaced by 'national' institutions and indigenous goods, with stress laid on the spinning wheel and *khādī* (home-spun cloth). For detail, S. L. Malhotra, *Gandhi and the Punjab* (Chandigarh: Panjab University, 2010, reprint), pp. 104–28; Ganeshi Mahajan, *Congress Politics in the Punjab (1885–1947)* (Shimla: K.K. Publishers, 2002), pp. 61–77.
34. Ganda Singh, ed., *Some Confidential Papers of the Akali Movement* (Amritsar: SGPC, 1965), p. 11.
35. Ruchi Ram Sahni, *Struggle for Freedom in Sikh Shrines* (Amritsar: SGPC, n.d.), pp. 176–83.
36. Sitaramayya, *History of the Indian National Congress*, vol. I, pp. 237, 241, 242, 245, 247.
37. Bipan Chandra, Mridula Mukherjee, Aditya Mukherjee, K. N. Panikkar, and Sucheta Mahajan, *India's Struggle for Independence 1857–1947* (New Delhi: Penguin Books, 1989 [1988]), pp. 235–6. Also Ravinder Kumar, ed., *A Centenary History of Indian National Congress (1885–1985)* (New Delhi: AICC (I)/Vikas, 1985), vol. II, pp. 20–2.
38. NMML, AICC-G-19, F. No. 19/1927, p. 1.
39. Sitaramayya, *History of the Indian National Congress*, vol. I, pp. 260–6.
40. Ganda Singh, *Confidential Papers*, pp. 48–50.
41. Ganda Singh, *Confidential Papers*, pp. 45–6.
42. Ganda Singh, *Confidential Papers*, p. 51.
43. Ganda Singh, *Confidential Papers*, p. 55.
44. Ganda Singh, *Confidential Papers*, pp. 59–60.
45. Ahluwalia, *Select Documents*, pp. 419–21.
46. Ahluwalia, *Select Documents*, pp. 417–18.

47. Gurdit Singh had chartered the Japanese ship *Komagata Maru* in 1914 in an attempt of the Canadian government before to defeat the 'continuous journey' requirement (to exclude Indian immigrants who did not come straight from India or on through-tickets from Indian ports), and emerged as a hero in the eyes of Sikhs. For detail, see Hugh J. M. Johnston, *The Voyage of the Komagata Maru: The Sikh Challenge to Canada's Colour Bar* (Vancouver: UBC Press, 2014, rev. edn.), pp. 53–188. He remained aligned with the Congress. In December 1921, the Congress passed a resolution in praise of Baba Gurdit Singh (H. N. Mitra and N. N. Mitra, eds, *The Indian Annual Register, 1919–1947* [New Delhi: Gyan Publishing House, 2000, reprint], vol. VII, p. 62).
48. B. G. Horniman had been closely aligned with the Congress since 1915. He upheld the principle of liberty and supported Home Rule and self-government for Indians. He edited the *Bombay Chronicle* with a marked anti-government stance. He actively supported Mahatma Gandhi in the satyāgraha against the Rowlatt Act. Horniman was deported to Britain in April 1919 'for public safety and the defence of British India', with no specific charges preferred against him. His passport was impounded by the Home Government. On 19 February 1924, the Imperial Legislative Assembly passed a resolution for removal of restrictions on his return to India. His case was supported also by the Liberal and Labour Members of Parliament (*Debate of Imperial Legislative Assembly*, vol. IV, no. 14, resolution moved by V. G. Patel; also NAI, telegram from Viceroy to Secretary of State, Home/Political, no. D 395–Pol, dated 22 February 1922).
49. S. H. Patil, *The Congress Party and Princely States* (Bombay: Himalaya Publishing House, 1981), p. 19.
50. H. N. Mitra, *The Indian Annual Register*, 1928 (New Delhi: Gyan Publishing House, 1990, reprint), vol. 20, part II, p. 57.

10

DEFIANCE AND DEPOSITION

Maharaja Ripudaman Singh continued to offer resistance to the paramount power even after his removal from Nabha. Notwithstanding the clause in the Agreement of 1923 that made the paramount power responsible for the welfare and upbringing of the future ruler of the state, the Maharaja was not willing to entrust the education of Tikka Partap Singh to the bureaucracy. Nor was he willing to abstain from politics, which was seen by the bureaucracy as an attack on the Government of India and its arch collaborator, the Maharaja of Patiala. The idea of removal of Maharaja Ripudaman Singh from Dehra Dun to a remote place and curtailment of his allowance was never far from the minds of the bureaucrats. They took the decision in 1927 and removed the Maharaja to Kodaikanal as a political prisoner early in 1928.

The Issue of the Tikka's Custody and Education

In July 1923, Sardar Balbir Singh, the Tikka's maternal uncle, was appointed by the government as his guardian on the monthly pay of 800 rupees and a free house at Dehra Dun or Mussoorie, wherever the Tikka might be. Sardar Balbir Singh died in October and Sodhi Hira Singh, Inspector of Schools, was appointed on a much lower monthly pay as 'Officer in Attendance on the Tikka Sahib'. The Maharaja wrote to Nabha Administrator Wilson-Johnston that Sodhi Hira Singh was a stranger to the family which was bound to create unnecessary inconvenience and trouble. Therefore, 'some body else', in whose case the 'difficulties pointed out' did not exist, could be appointed.

When Sodhi Hira Singh reached Dehra Dun, he was denied access to Tikka Partap Singh. Even Wilson-Johnston was not allowed to see the Tikka. The government decided to withdraw Sodhi Hira Singh and to appoint no one else in his place.

In July 1926, the new Secretary of State for India, the Earl of Birkenhead, wrote privately to the new Viceroy, Lord Irwin, that the future of the Tikka Sahib was an important issue:

> The well-being of Nabha State, the smoothness of its relations with the Government of India, and possibly the tranquility of the Punjab, depend very largely on the way in which this boy is brought up. I appreciate that it may be difficult to take him away from his father, and still more from his mother, and agitators will no doubt make capital out of such ruthlessness. But I am sure you will not be deterred by that consideration if you are satisfied that it is the right thing to do, and you may rely on my support.[1]

In view of the concern of the Secretary of State 'to save the next generation', early in August the Political Secretary and the new AGG, Lieutenant Colonel H. B. St. John, discussed the matter with Wilson-Johnston. One possible line of action was to declare that the Maharaja's refusal constituted a breach of Agreement, which entitled the government to depose him and to place the Tikka on the gaddī of Nabha. Another was to threaten the Maharaja with formal deposition or 'further disgrace'. The Maharani, who was devoted to her children, would then use her influence to make the Maharaja accede to the government's proposals.[2]

The Viceroy wrote to the Secretary of State for India that in the event of the Maharaja being really obstructive in the matter of the Tikka's education, 'we shall have to decide in what form pressure can best be put on him'. Irwin was inclined to think that 'deposition, with or without a revision of his allowance', could make him more reasonable. However, there was not much to be gained 'by showing our hand to the Maharaja at present' as the Tikka's education was not to start immediately.[3]

Maharaja Ripudaman Singh was not prepared to entrust the Tikka's education to the paramount power. *The Himalayan Times* reflected his well-considered views early in 1927. The idea of sending young Indian princes to foreign countries for being trained was reprehensible, and so was the system of education provided in the Chiefs' Colleges and other similar institutions. No person could be as responsible for the education and training of children as the parents themselves. Therefore, the proposal to remove the Tikka from the custody of the Maharaja and Maharani of Nabha was fraught with danger of several kinds.[4]

The AGG wrote to the Maharaja in March 1927 about the education of Tikka Partap Singh. The Maharaja referred to his letters of 30 July 1925, 4 January 1926, 25 February 1926, and 29 January 1927, and said that he had nothing more to add.[5] Essentially, Maharaja Ripudaman Singh was keen that the Tikka should remain away from alien influences. The government, on the other hand, insisted on its general responsibility for the education of a minor prince as well as the specific clause of its Agreement with the Maharaja of Nabha.

Writing in the *Punjab* of Amritsar, Sardul Singh Caveeshar presented the Tikka's education as a national concern. The Aitchison College, Lahore, in his view, had not produced a single student of outstanding ability and character, and produced 'some of the world's greatest rakes'. Educated at the Aitchison College, the Maharajas of Kapurthala, Jind, and Patiala had 'almost left the Sikh fold'. The Sikhs would not tolerate any interference with the education of Tikka Partap Singh. Indian politicians and nation builders should feel concerned about how the rulers of the native states brought up and educated their sons. The Indian princes could be a source of national strength, if they were properly educated. 'We could have hundreds of Nabhas in our midst capable of courage of conviction and ready to work shoulder to shoulder with the other patriotically minded Indians.'[6] The education of Tikka Partap Singh had a political dimension for the government as well as the Maharaja.

Public Expression of Political Views

Early in 1926, the Maharaja of Nabha sent signed letters to newspapers for publication. One of these letters referred to the Indore Enquiry ordered by Viceroy Reading into the murder of a rich merchant of Bombay and forcible abduction of a dancing girl to bring her back to Tukoji Rao Holkar. Unwilling to face a Commission of Enquiry, Holkar abdicated in favour of his son. However, the government's concern for justice was selective. Another chief who had got one of his relatives murdered and married his wife was left free to play with 'the personal honour and lives of his servants and subjects, all these years, since coming to power'.[7] The chief in question was clearly Maharaja

Bhupinder Singh. The sympathizers of the Maharaja of Nabha in Delhi had begun to say that the Viceroy was going to call Maharaja Bhupinder Singh for explanation in connection with the charges of murder openly levelled against him.[8]

In the first week of April 1926 the Central Sikh League held its annual session in Bradlaugh Hall at Lahore. Resolutions were passed to express sympathy with the executed and imprisoned Babbar Akalis and with the Ghadar revolutionaries. However, the Nabha question loomed larger than any other. It received attention in the addresses of the Chairman of the Reception Committee and the President of the session. It was the subject of five resolutions and a good many speeches. A large photograph of the Maharaja was placed conspicuously as the only decoration on the dais. One of the resolutions passed by the Central Sikh League called upon the government to ascertain from the people of Nabha whether they wanted British rule or the rule of their Maharaja. Referring to the amount of attention devoted to the Nabha question, the CID reports suggested that the Maharaja must have been in close communication with the promoters of the Sikh League session, and that one of the main, if not the sole, objects of the session was to bring this question again prominently before the Sikh public.[9]

A letter of Maharaja Ripudaman Singh, published in the *Forward* and the *Leader* early in May 1926, was regarded by the bureaucracy as an adverse comment on the working of the paramount power. It was written with reference to a long letter by Reading to the Nizam of Hyderabad only three days before the end of his term on 30 March 1926. The Nizam had been pressing for the restoration of Berar to the state of Hyderabad. Touching upon several aspects of basic importance to his idea of paramountcy, the Viceroy maintained that an already decided issue could not be reopened, or taken up by a Commission of Enquiry. He upheld the 'supremacy of the British Crown', which existed 'independently' of 'Treaties and Engagements'. Published in the government's *Gazette* as a 'classic statement of the doctrine of unfettered paramountcy', it was meant for all the princely states, irrespective of their size and status.[10]

The Berar question reminded Maharaja Ripudaman Singh of a long-pending issue between the paramount power and the state of Nabha. The Political Agent, Major James Dunlop-Smith, had assured Maharaja Hira Singh of sympathetic consideration with regard to the Nabha territories seized from Raja Devinder Singh. However, a day before he went on leave he sent a long letter giving reasons for rejecting the claims of Maharaja Hira Singh. Major Dunlop-Smith was promoted as Private Secretary to Lord Minto, which saved him from an awkward meeting with the Maharaja. Lord Reading too would be saved of a reply from the Nizam if he chose to send one. Ripudaman Singh emphasized that everything was done 'according to certain diplomatic policy and plan carefully laid down'.[11]

A letter to the *Hindustan Times* referred to the news that Mahatma Gandhi was in search of a guru. Maharaja Ripudaman Singh suggested that all his doubts and difficulties would vanish by following Guru Nanak. When the Bairagi Madho Das became 'Banda' of the Guru and became a Singh, he served his country with the sword (to liberate it). By becoming a follower of Guru Nanak, the Mahatma might 'serve his mother-land by peaceful means and achieve an equal glory and success through Guru's Grace and Favour'. The political import of this letter hinting at the liberation of India from the British was not missed by the CID officers keeping an eye on the Maharaja.[12]

On instruction from the Government of India, the AGG conveyed a warning to Maharaja Ripudaman Singh on 1 June 1926 against attacks in the press on government officers and the Maharaja of Patiala. An article in the *Akali* of 6 March 1926, regarded as 'a malicious attack' on Patiala, had not been repudiated by the Maharaja of Nabha and was, therefore, presumed to be genuine. The AGG drew the attention of the Maharaja to clause (8) of the Agreement under which the Maharaja was subject to 'the obligation of loyalty and obedience to the British Crown and the Government of India'. In view of its binding nature, the Maharaja was directed 'to abstain from further attacks on the Maharaja of Patiala'. A breach of condition (8) would entitle the government to take action under clause (10), by which the government could 'annul' or 'modify any of the conditions' agreed upon. The AGG went on to add that 'secret propaganda' instigated or subsidized by the Maharaja 'would be regarded as coming within the scope of this warning'. On 9 June 1926, the AGG again issued a stern warning that the publication of any further letters of the kind written with reference to Lord Reading's letter to the Nizam of Hyderabad would lead to action under clause (10).[13]

Maharaja Ripudaman Singh replied to the letters of warning on 28 August 1926, saying that he did not know how far the said conditions curtailed his 'ordinary rights as a human being'. He had never denied or disputed the obligation of 'loyalty' and 'obedience' in the well-understood constitutional sense of these terms. In his case, constitutional obedience was cheerfully rendered, but unconstitutional obedience was respectfully declined. The Maharaja differed with the government's interpretation and reserved to himself the right to protect his friends and denounce his enemies 'within the limits of the law of the land'. Referring to the article regarded as a 'malicious attack', he maintained that specific facts had been stated with due sense of responsibility. The facts called for a thorough enquiry, but anything emanating from him was not subject to 'the usual rules of administrative procedure'. The Maharaja enclosed a cutting from the *Riyasat* of 22 May 1926 in order to show that though propaganda against him was instigated or subsidized by the Maharaja of Patiala, no action appeared to have been taken against him. The Maharaja concluded by claiming that when every member of the public had the right to use the press for public purposes, he did not see why he alone should be treated as an exception.[14]

The AGG regarded the Maharaja's attitude as 'defiant and insolent', but hoped that he would not publish letters under his own name in future. He should be told that the Government of India were unable to accept his view and in the event of his disregarding the warning conveyed to him action would be taken against him under clause (10) of the Agreement. The Viceroy approved of the proposed reply, and added that a copy of paragraph 11 of the Foreign and Political Department Resolution of 7 July 1923 should be sent to the Maharaja so that he could not plead ignorance of the conditions on which he was allowed to sever his connection with the Nabha state.[15]

The Secretary of State advised the Government of India through his telegram of 8 July 1926 to think seriously about drastic action. The Maharaja of Nabha had disregarded the warning and laid himself open to penalty, but his action was not so serious as to justify his removal from Dehra Dun, 'a step which would be for many reasons highly desirable'. Bhagwan Das, who had been rewarded with the title of 'Rai Bahadur', was now made to dig up additional information on the activities of the Maharaja.[16] He reported that a statement of various acts of misconduct and maladministration attributed to the Maharaja of Patiala had been printed in a booklet in the form of questions to be raised in the House of Commons. Diwan Chaman Lal, the well-known leader of the trade union movement in India and a Congressman, was to place this material in the hands of some Labour Members of Parliament, and to induce them to ask the questions given in this book marked 'Private and Confidential'.[17] On Thompson's suggestion, the Viceroy saw 'the red volume said to have been prepared under the orders of the Maharaja of Nabha'.[18]

Thompson informed the India Office on 30 September 1926 that the Government of India had received a printed pamphlet containing a number of questions intended to be asked in Parliament regarding the Maharaja of Patiala. The questions were highly offensive and related to the alleged immoral character of Maharaja Bhupinder Singh, his extravagance, and certain scandals of his administration. There was no proof as yet of the authorship of this pamphlet but there were reasons to believe that it had been inspired by the Maharaja of Nabha. Diwan Chaman Lal had been engaged to place this material in the hands of some Labour Members. This was for the information of the Secretary of State because an attempt might be made to raise these questions in Parliament.[19]

The Tribune of 21 September 1926 had reproduced a telegram sent by Maharaja Ripudaman Singh to Sardul Singh Caveeshar in response to an invitation to attend a garden party at Lahore in honour of Sardar Ranbir Singh on the occasion of his marriage. The Maharaja and the Maharani of Nabha had expressed their regret for their inability to be present at the party due to 'extraordinary conditions':

> Owing to continuous intrigues and treachery, we are still rotting in exile, and we believe it to be our fate to perish as such.

This was regarded by H. D. Craik as 'objectionably worded' and he forwarded its extract from *The Tribune* to Sir J. P. Thompson.[20]

The Tribune of 30 September 1926 published a message from Maharaja Ripudaman Singh, offering his 'homage of great esteem and regard' to Akali prisoners as 'great heroes'. This congratulatory telegram was regarded by David Petric as essentially political. The 'great heroes' of the telegram had been arrested for supporting the Jaito Morcha and charged with 'conspiracy to wage war against the King'. Now the termination of legal proceedings against them was referred to as the 'triumph of truth'. All this amounted to something 'not very unlike participation in politics'.[21]

On 15 September 1926, Maharaja Ripudaman Singh had expressed his doubts about the reported suicide of Tikka Raghunath Singh of Patiala in the Ripon Hospital at Simla. The Tikka had been arrested, released, and allowed to have an interview with the Maharaja of Patiala. Two hours before the appointed time, it was said, he had cut his throat. But he had also entreated the doctor to save his life.[22] This information was contradictory. The real cause and facts of this incident were still obscure. A letter of Maharaja Ripudaman Singh, published in *The Tribune* and the *Akali*, was regarded as a veiled attempt at implicating the Maharaja of Patiala in the alleged murder of Tikka Raghunath Singh, and to bring His Highness and his administration into hatred and contempt.[23] The Viceroy accepted the view that this letter was propaganda against Patiala. The Punjab Government could be consulted by the AGG before he responded to the punishments proposed: (*a*) docking allowances or (*b*) removal from Dehra Dun.[24]

Meanwhile, it was reported that Maharaja Ripudaman Singh had prepared a revised version of the pamphlet against Patiala. A copy of the revised edition was sent to the Political Department with the information that in all 5,000 copies had been sent to England. This information was sent to the India Office with the remark that the revised edition was intended to prove the licentious conduct of the Maharaja and to show that the Government of India had been shielding him, or at least treating him with undeserved leniency. Early in November 1926, Thompson brought to the notice of the Viceroy further news about Nabha propaganda against Patiala.[25]

On 12 November 1926, Maharaja Ripudaman Singh replied to the AGG's communication about the death of Tikka Raghunath Singh of Patiala. The Maharaja wrote that he had sent to the press a letter in English regarding Tikka Raghunath Singh's death published in the *Civil and Military Gazette* of 12 September 1926. The translation enclosed by the AGG was not what the Maharaja had written. Unless the Maharaja was informed of the reasons that prompted the Government of India to make this enquiry, he did not consider himself called upon to answer such questions.[26]

Early in December 1926, the AGG wrote to Thompson that he had received a report regarding the political activities of Maharaja Ripudaman Singh sent to him by a reliable gentleman. According to this report the Central Sikh League and the Executive Committee of the Central Board (that is, the SGPC) were thinking of giving 'another battle to the Government' to bring the Maharaja of Nabha back to his gaddī.[27] According to D. Petric, a deputation of Nabha deportees reached Gauhati (presently Guwahati) at the time of the annual session of the Indian National Congress to apprise its leaders that the government had forcibly removed the Maharaja of Nabha, and the British Administrator was practising great oppression on the Nabha subjects. The deputation appealed to the Congress leaders to do something for them. B. G. Horniman, the pro-Congress British journalist, assured the deputation that he would support the resolution about the Maharaja of Nabha in the Subjects Committee. He also informed them that the Government of India intended to send the Maharaja to a more distant place and to separate the Tikka from His Highness. The deputation met several other leaders, and distributed Nabha-related literature at the Congress. David Petrie drew the obvious inference that the Maharaja was making a bid for Congress support.[28]

Early in 1927, the AGG wrote to Thompson that a letter of Maharaja Ripudaman Singh published in *The Tribune*, though cautiously worded, could reasonably be regarded as propaganda against the Maharaja of Patiala. The Maharaja of Nabha had wilfully disregarded the warning conveyed to him on 1 June 1926. In order to bring him to his senses, his annual allowance should be reduced and he should be removed from Dehra Dun. He could be sent to some station in the Nilgiri Hills so that he could not complain of unhealthy climate. The adoption of both the measures would not give rise to more agitation than the adoption of one.

Malcolm Hailey favoured the idea of a 'sufficiently drastic' action to prevent the Maharaja from his present activities. Hailey felt confident that a certain amount of excitement would be there for some time but no serious results would follow. It was important to ensure secrecy. The manner of the Maharaja's removal from Dehra Dun should be discussed verbally with the authorities concerned. With reference to the draft letter of the AGG, Hailey said:

> The more I see the way in which the allowances of the Maharaja are being used, the more confident am I that the step you propose is necessary. I do not think that if carefully carried out it would have any political reactions of any importance. The ultimate benefit would certainly outweigh any little trouble it might cause.[29]

At the behest of the Viceroy all the reports throwing light on the general political activities of the Maharaja, with particular reference to his propaganda against Patiala and the Government of India, were examined. The Viceroy then discussed with the Punjab Governor on 18 February 1927 the question of action to be taken in regard to Maharaja Ripudaman Singh. The government had a case against him and Hailey was in favour of cutting his allowance and removing him from Dehra Dun. The Political Secretary favoured the idea that for the present only the allowance should be reduced: 'Banishment to Ooty would be an appropriate punishment if we could prove a seditious connection with Punjab agitators.' The Viceroy was inclined to accept Hailey's view that 'the double punishment' would create no more outcry than curtailment of the allowance alone. Another possible form of punishment was suggested by the Political Secretary: to deprive the Maharaja of his title. This, said the Viceroy, could be imposed in addition to the other punishments.[30] The details of the action to be taken were to be worked out and implemented at an opportune time.

A public notice appeared at Dehra Dun on 11 February 1927 that the Maharaja of Nabha was given the new name of Gurucharan Singh by the 'High Authority' of the Sikh Gurdwara at Nander (Hyderabad) on 6 February 1927.[31] This was done at the time of his fresh initiation into the order of the Khalsa.

On his return from Nander, Maharaja Gurucharan Singh (henceforth referred to as Ripudaman Singh) married Gurucharan Kaur, daughter of Dr Ganga Singh of Rawalpindi. Her mother's sister was married to Babu Teja Singh, the well-known radical Sikh reformer of Panch Khalsa Diwan, Bhasaur, in the Patiala state. Among many other things, he had instituted a school for girls where they were given good education in the Sikh way of life. Gurucharan Kaur had received her education at Bhasaur before obtaining a Master's degree from the well-known Isabella Thobin College, Lucknow. Maharaja Ripudaman Singh knew Babu Teja Singh whose close relationship with Dr Ganga Singh explains the marriage of Gurucharan Kaur to the Maharaja. There are indications that the Government of India disapproved of this alliance. In any case, Babu Teja Singh as well as the father and mother of Gurucharan Kaur were present at the time of marriage. Among the other witnesses to the Anand marriage were the Principal and the Superintendent of the Girls' College at Bhasaur as well as the *rāgīs* (singers) who performed kīrtan, the granthī who recited the *lāvān* (composed by Guru Ramdas), and the poet who recited a composition appropriate for the occasion.[32] This marriage would acquire political significance later in the life of Maharaja Ripudaman Singh.

In April 1927, Maharaja Ripudaman Singh headed a procession at Hardwar. He arrived at Kankhal with some important persons, like Sewa Singh of the *Kirpan Bahadur*, Sardar Mangal Singh of the Sikh League, and Hazura Singh of the Chief Khalsa Diwan. The procession started from the Gurdwara of Guru Amar Das at Kankhal, with the Maharaja seated on the leading elephant. The processionists included

Nirmala, Akali, and Nihang Sikhs. Gopal Singh Kaumi, 'a well known firebrand', joined the other leaders in the procession. The procession reached the camp of the Nirmalas near the railway station and a diwān was held there. Mangal Singh welcomed the Maharaja on behalf of the SGPC and the Shiromani Akali Dal, and said that they would be pleased when they got justice done to the Maharaja and got him reinstated. The Maharaja then attended the Akali diwān at which Baba Gurdit Singh of the *Komagata Maru* fame spoke about what the Sikhs had suffered for the sake of the Maharaja, and assured him that 'the Sikh nation would not rest as long as it did not reinstate him'.[33] When the report reached the Viceroy, he remarked: 'This also must be regarded as propaganda against Government.'[34]

Maharaja Ripudaman Singh wrote to the Home Member of the Government of India on 2 April 1927 that he had received no reply to his request for a passport to leave the country. If the Government were unwilling to grant him a passport, at least general passports could be granted to the Maharani and the children to go to foreign lands, not only for health, travel, and change but also for the 'safety of their lives and personal honour', which was in very grave danger in this country at the hands of the Maharaja of Patiala.[35]

The Viceroy sent a telegram to the Secretary of State that the Maharaja of Nabha had again made an informal request for passports. His principal objective was to go to Germany and Austria, though he had expressed a wish to visit England. He had been trying 'to engineer agitation on a larger scale than before'. On this account, and also on account of Ripudaman Singh's attacks on Patiala, the Viceroy was in consultation with the Punjab Governor about the advisability of taking action against the Maharaja of Nabha. They were of the view that, if considered desirable, passports could be issued to the Maharaja. 'Nabha can do no harm in England, and Hailey would be glad to have him at a distance from the Sikhs. Things in Punjab are, we hope, settling down, but the Maharaja is still a potential danger among the extremist Sikhs.' If he wanted to visit Europe, he could be warned of immediate recall in case he associated with 'undesirables'. The Viceroy expected the Secretary of State to approve of his proposal with regard to the Maharaja 'as it might be a very great convenience to us here and to the Punjab to get rid of him for a while'.[36]

The Secretary of State, however, looked upon the presence of the Maharaja of Nabha in Europe as 'most undesirable'. He would almost certainly attract extremist Sikhs and others, particularly if he was in a position to spend money freely, and his activities might cause embarrassment to authorities in England. 'It might not be easy to control his movements or compel his return to India.' The Secretary of State favoured the reduction of allowance and removal of the Maharaja 'to some place remote from Sikh centres'.[37]

David Petrie surmised that the Secretary of State had based his apprehensions on what was known regarding the Comintern's efforts to exploit the revolutionary and terrorist elements among the Sikhs. Giving an outline of the activities of the Ghadar Party since 1911, particularly after its contacts with Moscow in 1922, and the role of the Marxist Ghadarites such as Teja Singh Swatantar, Santokh Singh, Rattan Singh, and Raja Mahendra Pratap,[38] Petrie remarked that the Maharaja of Nabha had been in touch with 'the worst elements of Sikh extremism' and knew their value for securing popular sympathy. The Sikh extremists had been equally alive to the advantage of allying themselves with 'a reputed sufferer in the cause of Sikh nationalism', who was also an unfailing source of financial support.

David Petrie liked to believe that possibly the Maharaja of Nabha was 'already in touch with the Indian end of the undesirable activities he may be expected to aid and abet in Europe'. His presence in India kept alive among certain section of the Sikhs 'the very kind of spirit which disposes them to meet the advances of Moscow more than half way'. His removal from India could improve the situation in this respect. If the Punjab Government thought that the province would gain appreciably by his absence, Petrie would advise that he be allowed to go. His considered opinion was that

> ... as between keeping the ex-Maharaja in India under present conditions and allowing him to go abroad, the latter course holds out the prospect of certain definite advantages. If, however, the third course of 'reduction of allowances and his removal to some place remote from Sikh centres' is equally open to Government, it is far preferable to either of the other two alternatives.[39]

It was decided not to take any action unless the Maharaja made a formal application for passports.[40]

Preparations for Removal to Kodaikanal

The question of the status of Maharaja Ripudaman Singh was raised in connection with the case of Maharani Jagdish Kaur's death on 4 August 1927, in which the UP Government ordered a formal enquiry.[41] Initially, it was thought that the Maharaja was still the de jure ruler of Nabha, entitled to claim the privileges of ruling chiefs. But his legal position appeared to be anomalous. He had not been 'deposed' and he had not 'abdicated'. At the same time, the use of the term 'de jure ruler' for him was considered improper by the Political Department because the Maharaja was not entitled to resume active governance of his state at his own pleasure. His position could not be distinguished from abdication, 'temporary perhaps but none the less effective'. The use of the phrase 'formally abdicate' in the Agreement implied 'an informal abdication'. And there was nothing about the full privileges of a sovereign ruler in the Agreement.[42]

For other reasons too it was thought necessary to be clear about the 'legal status' of the Maharaja of Nabha. Thompson held the view that when the Maharaja was permitted to sever his connection with the state he ceased to enjoy all privileges for the retention of which he had not expressly stipulated. Furthermore, when the terms were settled, it was never contemplated that the government would have to appoint a commission before taking action under clause (10) of the terms. When the name of Maharaja Ripudaman Singh was proposed for nomination on the UP Council, the Returning Officer had rejected his nomination on the ground that he was not a British subject.[43] Thus, the status of the Maharaja was sought to be defined in terms of what he was not: he was not a ruler; he was not a subject of Nabha; and he was not a British subject. He appeared to have lost all his rights except the ones conceded to him by the government.

The case against the Maharaja was made out on the basis of clause (8) regarding the mandatory obligations of 'loyalty and obedience' to the British Crown and the Government of India. The Maharaja could legitimately make a representation to the Crown but he could not carry on agitation through the press, or from the platform against the orders of the government. An infringement of clause (8) was clear enough on count of 'obedience'. As regards 'loyalty', it was possible to produce evidence that the Maharaja had supported and financed persons who were well known for their hostility to the government, such as Baba Gurdit Singh and Lala Lajpat Rai. On 8 June 1927, the Maharaja had sent a telegram to Sardar Kharak Singh, President of the Akali Dal, on his release from jail: 'I send you these few words of my respectful homage and sincere admiration of your triumphant victory over forces of darkness and tyranny.'

The foregoing evidence of the Maharaja's activities convinced the authorities that he had tried 'to create general unrest and agitation as a means of forcing Government to give way to him'. And this he tried to do through Johnston's connection with 'the worst type of newspapers and with extremists and dissatisfied Sikhs'. The Maharaja also tried to vilify the Maharaja of Patiala. 'These activities cannot be said to be compatible with his obligations of loyalty and obedience.'[44]

In August 1927, the Nabha Administrator, Wilson-Johnston, raised the issue of Tikka Partap Singh once again. Wilson-Johnston was feeling disturbed to hear that doubts had been felt about the desirability of separating the Tikka from the Maharaja. His argument was that the Tikka was being brought up to hate all the prominent men of Nabha serving under the Administration as 'traitors'; they were in a state of growing apprehension as to what would happen to them if the Tikka remained under the influence of the Maharaja until the former's accession; probably after succeeding to the gaddī, he would take action against the Sardars 'disloyal' to his father. Furthermore, the Tikka was being brought up under the influence of his mother, who was said to be a Kuka. The Kukas were fanatical Sikhs and regarded the Tikka as a reincarnation of Guru Ram Singh who had died in Burma in exile; their headquarters, Bhaini Maharaj, was only a little over 20 kilometres from the Nabha border. These facts had a bearing on the question of action to be taken in regard to the Maharaja of Nabha.[45]

The Viceroy saw a good deal of force in Wilson-Johnston's argument about the close bearing of a decision regarding the Tikka on the proposed removal of the Maharaja from Dehra Dun. At a meeting called by the Viceroy on 5 September 1927, there were two issues to be discussed: (a) the problem of the Maharaja himself and (b) the future of the Tikka. There was a general consensus that the Maharaja should take up his residence in the Nilgiris, his allowance should be reduced, and no detailed charges against him should be published. The Punjab Governor was of the view that the Maharaja's deposition should take place at the same time as his removal and that the succession of the Tikka to the gaddī should be formally recognized. This was generally agreed to.

As regards the Tikka, Wilson-Johnston suggested that the Tikka's mother should be given the choice of going to Nabha with him, or to accompany the Maharaja. There were reasons to believe that the Maharaja and the Maharani by then were not on good terms. Hailey was strongly against the Tikka's removal without his mother's consent. If the Maharani chose to go with the Maharaja, the question of the Tikka's removal without the consent of his parents would become difficult. It was suggested that the Maharani's father, Sardar Prem Singh, who was reported to be residing at Hyderabad, might be invited to come to Dehra Dun to advise his daughter over whom he was believed to exercise a good influence.[46]

Another meeting was held at the Viceregal Lodge at Simla about a month later in which Scott O'Conner, DIG UP, was also present. The proceedings of the last meeting were read out by the Viceroy, and various questions were discussed to arrive at the following conclusions:

1. The resolution of 29 October 1920 did not apply to the case of the Maharaja of Nabha. He could not claim a Commission as he was not a ruler.
2. Though deposition was not referred to in the conditions of Agreement, it was evident that a breach of the conditions might involve deposition. But if the Maharaja was not a ruler he could not be deposed. Therefore, the best solution was to deprive the Maharaja of all his rights and dignities while not formally deposing him; his son could then be installed on the gaddī in his place.
3. A warrant should be issued under Bengal Regulation III of 1818. It should be addressed to the officer in whose custody the Maharaja was to be detained. In consultation with the Madras Government, a suitable residence for the Maharaja might be selected at Ootacamand or some other place.
4. The police should be allowed reasonable latitude in deciding the place at which the Maharaja should be apprehended. His arrest should be neatly effected. A special train should be in waiting at Saharanpur without undue obtrusiveness. At a convenient station, the AGG would meet the Maharaja to explain the position fully to him, and depute his Secretary to accompany the Maharaja to his destination.
5. It would be necessary to search the Maharaja's person as he was believed to be in the habit of carrying arms, but no search of his premises was advisable.
6. The AGG should proceed as soon as possible to Mussoorie and interview the Maharani. Her father was understood to be there already. Wilson-Johnston should also reach there. The Maharani

should then be left to decide whether she would go to Nabha with the Tikka or accompany the Maharaja to his destination.
7. The Secretary of State should be informed forthwith of the proposed action. The actual action should be deferred to about the middle of November when the Viceroy would be in Delhi. In deciding the exact time for action, due consideration should be given to the Sikh situation.
8. A communiqué prepared for the occasion should be issued after the Maharaja had left Saharanpur.[47]

Thus, the removal of the Maharaja was thoroughly discussed and meticulously worked out. The stage was finally set for his internment.

On 10 October 1927, the Viceroy sent a long cable to the Secretary of State to the effect that there was satisfactory evidence to show that the Maharaja of Nabha had been continually and flagrantly violating clause (8) of the conditions under which he was permitted to sever his connection with his state. He had actively engaged in seditious propaganda, associated with notorious agitators, and spent lakhs of rupees in a press campaign extending to Delhi, Punjab, United Provinces, Bombay, and Bengal. He had personally taken part in demonstrations and meetings in various places, such as Bombay, Hardwar, and Delhi, and tried to arouse public sympathy in his favour by a visit to the Sikh shrine at Nander. His object was to effect his return to Nabha but he had not hesitated to attack the Maharaja of Patiala and the Government of India. He had done much to keep the Akali agitation alive and to create difficulties for the Nabha administration. He had tried to stir up trouble in Nepal and was believed to have subsidized disaffection in Bengal and elsewhere. As if not to miss out on any charge that could be levelled against the Maharaja, the Viceroy disapprovingly commented on his private life as well.

The Viceroy went on to add that, in view of the Maharaja's attacks on the government and Patiala despite clear warnings, it was considered to be unsafe to allow his dangerous activities to remain unchecked. It was accordingly proposed that he should be deprived of his rights and dignities and that his son should be placed on the gaddī; Ripudaman Singh should be removed to Ootacamand, or some other suitable locality in the Madras Presidency, and his allowance should be reduced from 25,000 rupees to 10,000 rupees per month. The Maharani was intended to be given the choice of proceeding with the Tikka to Nabha, or accompanying the Maharaja to his new destination. It was hoped that she would prefer the former alternative, but if not, it would be inadvisable at present to separate the Tikka from both his parents against their wishes. As Ripudaman Singh was no longer in any sense the ruler of Nabha, it would not be necessary to offer him a Commission of Enquiry. A breach of any of the conditions entitled the government to modify the Agreement. There was no need to order deposition. It was enough to deprive him of his remaining dignities and privileges in order to formally recognize the accession of the Tikka. Hailey did not anticipate any serious trouble to the proposed action. A warrant under Bengal Regulation III of 1818 was to be issued. The Viceroy concluded: 'We would issue a very brief communiqué announcing our decision and explaining that we are satisfied that the action contemplated was necessary.'[48]

The Secretary of State wanted to know if the Maharaja would be an ordinary prisoner under Bengal Regulation III of 1818, and if the arrangements in Nabha would follow the ordinary lines of a minority administration. He also wanted to know if the conditions of detention in Madras would be suitable to be shared by the Tikka after his accession to the gaddī, and if this arrangement would find favour in Nabha. Could the Tikka be sent to the Queen Mary's College at once? In what terms would the decision be conveyed to the Maharaja, and how would the communiqué be worded? How would the ruling princes take this decision?[49] On 25 October 1927, the Viceroy sent his replies to the questions raised by the Secretary of State who approved of his proposals with the following suggestions about the wording of the communiqué: The word 'annulment' could be used in place of 'modification', which was likely to provoke criticism. There was no need to refer to attacks on the Maharaja of Patiala because it was 'doubtful whether such attacks constitute a breach of the conditions except that they are breach of the conditions of loyalty'. There was no need to refer to the choice to be given to the Maharani. 'She should be invited, in whatever manner you consider most persuasive, to take an immediate decision before any communiqué issues.'[50]

The Viceroy held what was called the 'Nabha Conference' on 21 January 1928. He explained that action was deliberately delayed to avoid complicating the position in regard to the Simon Commission with special reference to the Sikh situation. The points now to be considered were: (a) whether there was any reason for further delay and (b) whether the procedures proposed required any modification.

The Punjab Governor was confident that no action against the Maharaja of Nabha would materially affect the situation. The Punjab Government had no objection to the action contemplated. The Political Secretary argued that further delay might result in leakage. It was clearly desirable to avoid any unnecessary delay. It was finally decided that the situation remaining unaltered, the 'zero day' should be 17 February 1928.[51]

David Petrie had already visited Madras and worked out arrangements for 'the detenu' to reside in 'The Observatory' at Kodaikanal.[52] On 23 January 1928, the Chief Secretary to Madras Government was informed that the ex-Maharaja would probably arrive at Kodaikanal Road arout 20 February under police escort. A suitable officer should conduct the party to Kodaikanal. The Observatory House should be made ready. It was important that 'arrangements should be made for observing the ex-Maharaja's movements so that any attempt at absconding may be reported and frustrated without delay'. The warrant under Bengal Regulation III of 1818, Section 2, would be addressed to the Revenue Divisional Officer to obviate the necessity of inspection by Judges.[53] On 16 February 1928, the Political Secretary was informed that 'European Revenue Divisional Officer' had arrived at Kodaikanal and reported that arrangements there were complete.[54]

Arrangements were made for two special trains: one, from Saharanpur to Kodaikanal Road to take the Maharaja to Kodaikanal, and the other, to Nabha to take the Tikka and the Maharani to the state for installation. The communiqué was finalized to be issued simultaneously from Delhi, Lahore, and London, immediately after the Maharaja's arrest. The new AGG, James Fitzpatrick, was to read out a letter to the Maharaja in the special train at a suitable place, containing more or less the same information as the communiqué. A kharīta (official communication) for the Tikka and a letter from the Viceroy to the Maharani were prepared. Fitzpatrick told Wilson-Johnston on the 18th: 'We hope Maharaja will be arrested at Allahabad this evening. I am leaving Delhi by car at noon today for Saharanpur.' The Maharaja had left Delhi for Allahabad on 17 February, followed by the UP police 'with instructions to effect arrest if no difficulties occurred this evening or later'. The special train to convey the Maharaja to Kodaikanal Road had left Delhi for Allahabad. At 11.00 p.m. on the 18th, David Petrie received the message: 'Action has been taken.'[55]

Notes

1. India Office Records (IOR), R/1/1/1525, extract from a private letter from Secretary of State for India (Earl of Birkenhead) to Viceroy, dated 8 July 1926.
2. IOR, R/1/1/1525, AGG to Sir John P. Thompson (Political Secretary to the Government of India), 20/21 August 1926; also 29/30 August 1926.
3. IOR, R/1/1/1525, extract from a private letter from Viceroy to Secretary of State, dated 23 September 1926.
4. IOR, R/1/1/1525, extract from *The Himalayan Times*, dated 16 December 1926, entitled 'The Nabha Tragedy'.
5. IOR, R/1/1/1525, AGG to J. P. Thompson, 1 July 1927; Maharaja Gurucharan Singh and Maharani Sarojni Gurucharan Singh to AGG, dated 15 June 1927.
6. IOR, R/1/1/1525, cuttings from *The Punjab* of Amritsar, 25 July 1927; 15 August 1927.
7. IOR (microfilm), R/1/1/1707 B, File no. 752-P (Secret) of 1927, CID Delhi to Deputy Director Intelligence Bureau, dated 13 March 1926, with enclosures giving details about happenings in the Patiala state.
8. IOR, R/1/1/1707 B, no. 752-P(S)/1927, notes by David Petrie, dated 18 March 1926; notes by Bhagwan Das, dated 3 and 19 March 1926, with enclosures. In his note of 31 March, Petrie agreed with the Foreign and Political Department that the evidence in question was 'interesting and instructive', but it 'could not' serve as the basis of any action.
9. IOR, R/1/1/1707 B, no. 752-P(S)/1927, note by Bhagwan Das, dated 31 March 1926 with enclosures; note by D. Petrie, dated 7 May 1926.
10. Ian Copland, *The Princes of India in the Endgame of Empire, 1917–1947* (Cambridge: Cambridge University Press, 1997), pp. 54–5.
11. IOR, R/1/1/1707 B, no. 752-P(S)/1927, CID Delhi, extract from the *Forward* of 7 May 1926.
12. IOR, R/1/1/1707 B, no. 752-P(S)/1927, letter of Maharaja of Nabha to editor of *The Hindustan Times*, dated 18 May 1926; note by D. Petrie, dated 1 June 1926.
13. IOR (microfilm), R/1/1/1635, File no. 404-P (Secret)/1927, AGG to Maharaja Ripudaman Singh, dated 1 and 9 June 1926.
14. IOR, R/1/1/1635, no. 404-P(S)/1927, Ripudaman Singh to AGG, dated 28 August 1926.
15. IOR, R/1/1/1635, no. 404-P(S)/1927, note by H. R. Lynch Blosse, dated 9 September 1926; note by J. P. Thompson, dated 9 September 1926; Government of India to AGG.
16. IOR, R/1/1/1635, no. 404-P(S)/1927, note by Bhagwan Das, dated 16 September 1926.
17. IOR, R/1/1/1635, no. 404-P(S)/1927, note by Bhagwan Das, dated 18 September 1926.

18. IOR, R/1/1/1635, no. 404-P(S)/1927, note by D. Petrie, dated 21 September 1926; note by H. R. Lynch Blosse, dated 22 September; note by J. P. Thompson, dated 22 September; note by G. Cunningham, dated 23 September.
19. IOR, R/1/1/1635, no. 404-P(S)/1927, J. P. Thompson to Political Secretary, India Office, dated 30 September 1926.
20. IOR, R/1/1/1635, no. 404-P(S)/1927, extract from *The Tribune*, dated 21 September 1926.
21. IOR, R/1/1/1635, no. 404-P(S)/1927, H. D. Craik to J. P. Thompson, dated 5 October 1926; cutting from *The Tribune*, dated 30 September 1926.
22. IOR, R/1/1/1635, no. 404-P(S)/1927, cuttings from the *Akali* of Amritsar, dated 9 October 1926; *The Tribune*, dated 21 September 1926.
23. IOR, R/1/1/1635, no. 404-P(S)/1927, note by D. Petrie, dated 6 October 1926; note by H.R. Lynch Blosse, dated 9 October 1926.
24. IOR, R/1/1/1635, no. 404-P(S)/1927, note by J. P. Thompson, 12 October 1926; H. R. Lynch Blosse to the AGG, 18 October 1926; H. R. Lynch Blosse to H. D. Craik, dated 18 October 1926.
25. IOR, R/1/1/1635, no. 404-P(S)/1927, report by Bhagwan Das, dated 23 October 1926; note by J. P. Thompson, dated 3 November 1926.
26. IOR, R/1/1/1635, no. 404-P(S)/1927, copy of a letter from Maharaja Ripudaman Singh to AGG, dated 12 November 1926.
27. IOR, R/1/1/1635, no. 404-P(S)/1927, AGG to J. P. Thompson, 7 December 1926, with extract from a report on the ex-Maharaja of Nabha's activities, dated 28 October 1926.
28. IOR, R/1/1/1635, no. 404-P(S)/1927, H. R. Lynch Blosse to AGG, 30 December 1926, with a list of Nabha deportees and their activity; note by D. Petrie, dated 31 December 1926.
29. IOR, R/1/1/1635, no. 404-P(S)/1927, H. B. St. John to J. P. Thompson, 27 January 1927.
30. IOR, R/1/1/1635, no. 404-P(S)/1927, G. Cunningham to J. P. Thompson, dated 11 February 1927; note by H. R. Lynch Blosse, 15 February 1927; note of the meeting by Private Secretary to Viceroy, dated 19 February 1927.
31. IOR, R/1/1/1635, no. 404-P(S)/1927, copy of the notice, dated 11 February 1927.
32. We have seen a copy of the marriage certificate in the possession of the Maharaja's daughter. Even if prepared later, this certificate refers to the actual event for which there is also the statement of Niranjan Singh Talib, the well-known Sikh leader and later a member of Indian Parliament, who was in Dehra Dun at that time.
33. As noted in Ch. 9, Gurdit Singh was well respected in the Sikh and Congress circles for organizing the voyage of the *Komagata Maru*.

34. IOR, R/1/1/1635, no. 404-P(S)/1927, report by Sub-Inspector Dhian Singh, dated 12/13 April 1927; note by J. P. Thompson, dated 22 April 1927.
35. IOR, R/1/1/1635, no. 404-P(S)/1927, Maharaja Gurucharan henceforth [Ripudaman] Singh to the Home Member (Sir Alexander Muddiman), dated 2 April 1927.
36. IOR, R/1/1/1635, no. 404-P(S)/1927, telegram from Viceroy to Secretary of State, dated 17 May 1927.
37. IOR, R/1/1/1635, no. 404-P(S)/1927, telegram from Secretary of State to Viceroy, dated 12 June 1927.
38. In the second and third decades of the twentieth century, Raja Mahendra Pratap was well known to his contemporaries in India and outside as a revolutionary. As noted in Ch. 5, he was reported to be 'President of the Provisional Government of India' which was 'at war' with the Government of Great Britain (National Archives of India, New Delhi. [NAI], Home/Political 1224 and KW F320).
39. IOR (microfilm), R/1/1/1635, File no. 404-P (S)/1927, note by D. Petrie, dated 21 June 1927.
40. IOR, R/1/1/1635, no. 404-P(S)/1927, note by B. J. Glancy, dated 23 July 1927.
41. IOR (microfilm), R/1/1/1696, File no. 694-P (Secret)/1927, Chief Secretary, UP to Political Department, 27 July 1927.
42. IOR, R/1/1/1696, no. 694-P(S)/1927, note by Legislative Department; telegram from 'Polindia' to 'Upao', Nainital, dated 2 August 1927; 'Polindia', Simla, to 'Polindia Camp', dated 4 August 1927.
43. IOR, R/1/1/1696, no. 694-P(S)/1927, note by J. P. Thompson, dated 5 October 1927.
44. IOR, R/1/1/1635, no. 404-P (S)/1927, 'Nabha Case'.
45. IOR (microfilm), R/1/1/1729, J. P. Thompson to G. Cunningham, 20 August 1927.
46. IOR, R/1/1/1729, minutes of the Conference on Nabha, dated 5 September 1927. See also, G. Cunningham to J. P. Thompson, 24 August 1927; J. P. Thompson to James Crerar of the Home Department, 29 August 1927.
47. IOR, R/1/1/1729, minutes of the Conference on Nabha, dated 7 October 1927.
48. IOR, R/1/1/1729, telegram from Viceroy to Secretary of State, dated 10 October 1927.
    For resort to Bengal Regulation III of 1818, the Government of India satisfied itself essentially that (*a*) 'danger' from a situation was 'so serious as to demand the adoption of extraordinary measures'; and (*b*) that there was 'no direct evidence' to ensure 'a practical certainty of a conviction' (NAI, Home/Pol 1923, no. 103 (Pt. I); Home/Pol 1924, File no. 262 II; Home/Pol, 1924, File no. IX, serial nos. 1–11).

49. IOR, R/1/1/1729, telegram from Secretary of State to Viceroy,, dated 15 October 1927.
50. IOR, R/1/1/1729, telegram from Secretary of State to Viceroy, dated 4 November 1927.
51. IOR, R/1/1/1729, Watson to Hailey, 5 November 1927; Hailey to Watson, 13 November 1927; telegram from 'Polindia', New Delhi to 'Polindia Camp', dated 17 November 1927; telegram from Viceroy to Secretary of State, dated 28 November 1927.
52. IOR, R/1/1/1729, note by Watson, dated 29 November 1927; telegram from Madras to 'Polindia', dated 26 November 1927; telegram from Madras to 'Polindia', dated 2 December 1927.
53. This old Act was used generally for detaining the revolutionaries in British India. However, it was used also for other important leaders who were seen as a threat due to their immediate activities in a critical situation. It is interesting to note that this Regulation was used to detain Master Tara Singh in 1949.
55. IOR (microfilm), R/1/1/1729, telegram from 'Polindia' to Chief Secretary Madras, dated 23 January 1928; telegram from Political Secretary to Chief Secretary Madras, dated 28 January 1928; telegram from Chief Secretary Madras to Political Secretary, dated 16 February, 1928. IOR, R/1/1/1729, telegram from Political Secretary to AGG, 2 February 1928; telegram from AGG to the Political Secretary, dated 15 February 1928; telegram from Political Secretary to AGG, dated 16 February 1928; telegram from AGG to Wilson-Johnston, dated 18 February 1928; B. J. Glancy to AGG, dated 18 February 1928.

11

THE *INDICTMENT OF PATIALA* TURNED INTO AN INDICTMENT OF NABHA

Ten subjects of the Patiala state submitted a memorial to the Viceroy against the Maharaja of Patiala in May 1929. They sent a copy of this memorial to the All India States' People's Conference. The Working Committee of the Conference constituted a committee to investigate the allegations against the Maharaja. The Patiala Enquiry Committee completed its work and prepared its report, called *The Indictment of Patiala*. The Conference submitted this report to the Viceroy, demanding a formal enquiry. After a careful consideration of the whole situation the Viceroy decided to entrust the enquiry to the AGG, Sir James Fitzpatrick, who conducted the enquiry in June–July 1930. Not only did he exonerate the Maharaja of Patiala, he also held Maharaja Ripudaman Singh mainly responsible for orchestrating the indictment, and proposed action against him. Thus, the indictment of Patiala was turned into an indictment of Nabha. The way in which this was manipulated shows at all levels that paramountcy could not function without partisanship. A soft attitude towards collaborators and harshness towards the enemies of the empire were the obverse and reverse of the same political coin.

Political Awakening in the Punjab States and Formulation of Charges against the Maharaja of Patiala

The Akali movement did not leave the people of the Punjab princely states unaffected. They began to form associations of their own, meant primarily for political activity within the states. The peasant proprietors of the Malerkotla state formed Zamindara Association on 10 January 1927 for the protection of their rights, and decided to present a memorial to the Viceroy. The Nawab of Malerkotla ordered the state forces to stop a meeting of the Association on 18 July 1927. Their action resulted in the death of 14 men, women, and children. On a charge of conspiracy against the state, hundreds of peasants were arrested, including many of those who had gone to Simla in deputation. Some of those who were sentenced in the conspiracy case became active political workers after their release.[1]

The Punjab States Shiromani Darbar was formed at Mastuana in the Jind state in September 1927. Its workers welcomed the veteran Akali leader Baba Kharak Singh on his political tour in Patiala and Jind. He advised them to keep up their spirit of independence. The Nabha police reported to the Administrator that the objectives of the Shiromani Darbar were (a) to redress the grievances of the people of the states and (b) to work for the re-instatement of the Maharaja of Nabha.[2]

The printed matter in honour of Baba Kharak Singh emphasized that the British bureaucracy had increased its hold over the states to the disadvantage of local interests; the rulers were spending revenues on themselves rather than public welfare; there were no hospitals or educational institutions worth the name, and trade and agriculture were on the decline. The Maharaja of Patiala had spent 2,100,000 rupees on his European tour in 1921, and the state was under heavy debt. The Punjab States Shiromani Darbar desired to work for progress and peace by finding solutions to the problems of the states, their people, and their rulers.[3]

Baba Kharak Singh's political activity came to its climax with the formation of the Punjab Riyasati Praja Mandal at Mansa in the Patiala state on 17 July 1928 in the presence of a representative of the All India States' People's Conference, which had been formulated in December 1927. Sewa Singh Thikriwala was elected its President and Bhagwan Singh Longowalia its General Secretary, both of them in absentia. An official reporter remarked that the Akalis were trying 'to give a secular character to their movement'.[4] The aims and objectives of the Punjab Riyasati Praja Mandal were similar to those of the All India States' People's Conference.[5]

The Patiala Darbar tried to label all the leaders and workers of the Praja Mandal as hirelings of Maharaja Ripudaman Singh. Bhagwan Singh Longowalia, 'a pucca anti-Patiala propagandist', who was regarded as 'one of the most dangerous' political agitators in the Patiala state, made it very clear in October 1928 that the Praja Mandal had not been founded to oppose or support any particular Raja or Maharaja. Rather, its objective was to reform the administration of all states and get the grievances of the states' people redressed. From his viewpoint, Patiala under Maharaja Bhupinder Singh and Nabha under Wilson-Johnston were equally autocratic. Maharaja Bhupinder Singh reacted strongly to the political activity of the Praja Mandalists. He told his cabinet that in 'Personal Rule' like Patiala, it was necessary to deal with extremist agitators with a firm hand from the very beginning.[6]

In May 1929, Bhagwan Singh Longowalia and nine other 'citizens' of the Patiala state submitted a memorial to the Viceroy, requesting him 'to rescue the people of the state from the ruthless oppression, to which they have been subjected ever since the present Maharaja became the ruler'. Since the Maharaja was indifferent or hostile to complaints and the Legislative Assembly could not take up matters related to the native states, the Viceroy was the only authority to whom grievances could be addressed.

The memorialists referred to the principle enunciated by Lord Reading in his letter of 27 March 1926 to the Nizam of Hyderabad, that where the general welfare of the people of a state was seriously and grievously affected by the action of its government, the ultimate responsibility of taking remedial action, if necessary, lay with the paramount power. The subjects of the Patiala state had 'a long and terrible tale of woe'. The Maharaja had no scruples when it came to sexual gratification. Regular and irregular wives, women abducted by force or fraud, wives and daughters procured by money, close female relatives and wives of officials, dancing girls and actresses, hill girls and European women—all served the Maharaja's carnal purposes. The honour of no beautiful woman was safe in Patiala. Sardar Lal Singh, the younger brother of the Maharaja's father-in-law, Sardar Gurnam Singh of Sangrur, was murdered at the Maharaja's instance because he refused to divorce his wife whom the Maharaja eventually married. There was inefficiency and corruption in the departments of education, public works, religious endowments, revenue, and taxation. The extravagance of the Maharaja had brought the state to the verge of bankruptcy. The Maharaja openly boasted that the British Government would not touch him because of his lavish hospitality to British officials and his war services.[7]

A copy of the memorial was submitted also to the All India States' People's Conference at Bombay in May 1929. The Working Committee of the Conference took a serious view of the matter and appointed a committee, known as the Patiala Enquiry Committee, to investigate the allegations contained in the memorial. Sardul Singh Caveeshar was a member of the committee but he expressed his inability to serve on it, and he was replaced by Amritlal V. Thakker. While the Committee was doing its own work, a regular session of the Punjab Riyasati Praja Mandal was held at Lahore on 27 December 1929. Activists from the Punjab states came for this session. They were addressed by leaders of the All India States' People's Conference, and leaders of the Punjab Congress came for this session, and a number of resolutions were passed in this session against the Maharaja of Patiala. He was presented as guilty of gross maladministration and personal misconduct and misdeeds. The Conference demanded enquiry into all these charges against the Maharaja and, if proved, they desired his removal from the gaddī of Patiala. If the Government of India failed in their duty, the people of the state would launch a campaign for deposing the Maharaja.[8]

The Patiala Enquiry Committee visited the Punjab in December 1929, and, finalized its report by February 1930. In all, over a thousand persons appeared before the Committee. It examined 46 witnesses and took 35 oral statements. All the 12 charges in the memorandum of the 10 citizens referred to earlier were examined in the light of the evidence thus collected. A prima facie case for an official enquiry was strongly made. The Committee had reasons to believe that Sardar Lal Singh had been murdered by Gamdur Singh, under instructions received directly or indirectly from the Maharaja, to secure the Maharaja's favour. The Maharaja maintained for some time a bomb factory in the fort of Bahadurgarh in his territories, probably to implicate Maharaja Ripudaman Singh. The Patiala Darbar was accountable for the disappearance of Bachittar Kaur, the wife of Dr Bakhshish Singh, and her daughter; the Maharaja was personally liable for the disappearance of Dr Bakhshish Singh's son. The Maharaja kept with him the wife of Sardar Amar Singh against his appeals for her restoration to him. Sardar Harchand Singh Jeji, an important leader of the Praja Mandal, was illegally arrested and confined without any trial; and his property worth lakhs of rupees was confiscated. False cases were deliberately instituted to harass a number of individuals. In all, there were 12 counts of high-handedness in the indictment.[9]

The Indictment of Patiala

In view of the gravity of charges the Government of India could not help but take the *Indictment of Patiala* seriously. A preliminary report tabulated information in three columns: (*a*) detail of charges, (*b*) whether the complaint was mentioned in any petition sent to the Government of India, and (*c*) remarks of the AGG and action taken. Some of these complaints had been received earlier and disposed of: (*a*) the murder of Lal Singh, (*b*) a bomb factory in the fort of Bahadurgarh, (*c*) the disappearance of Bachittar Kaur (wife of Dr Bakshish Singh) and her daughter and son, (*d*) forcible confinement of the wife of Amar Singh, (*e*) false cases against Amar Singh, Santa Singh, Bakhshish Singh, and Diwan Singh Maftun, and (*f*) hardships arising from *begār* (unpaid forced labour) and *shikār* (hunting). James Fitzpatrick, the AGG, had exonerated the Maharaja from the first and the most serious charge, and no action had been taken by the Maharaja on the rest.

Half of the charges were new: (*a*) the arrest and confinement of Sardar Harchand Singh Jeji without any trial, and the confiscation of his large properties; (*b*) the inhuman torture, illegal arrests and imprisonment, and confiscation of the properties of persons cooperating with Baba Kharak Singh; (*c*) forced labour on a large scale; (*d*) increase in land revenue; (*e*) no return of war loans amounting to more than 1,150,000 rupees; and (*f*) misappropriation of funds raised by the state for public purposes. Despite the sympathy of the British officials with the Maharaja, they could not deny that some of the allegations made in the report appeared to be genuine.

The Government of India committed itself to redress the grievances of the Patiala state subjects 'if they were well founded'. The Maharaja would resent an open enquiry 'but we cannot perhaps close our eyes to the agitation'. The matter could be discussed with the Maharaja who had already agreed to have a European Finance Minister; he could be advised to take a European in charge also of his police, judiciary, and revenue administration, which might stop the agitation against the state. Any case of oppression could then be redressed by the state.[10]

H. Wilberforce-Bell, the Deputy Political Secretary, appreciated this detailed examination of charges. However, in his view, it was necessary to refer to two aspects of the whole matter. One was the role of the Maharaja of Patiala in connection with the Akali movement, which made him the target of attack. Second, Nabha was said to be instigating and financing the agitation as a bitter enemy of the Maharaja of Patiala. He went on to add that in several cases, the complaints made by the Patiala subjects had been looked into. To conduct an enquiry, it would be necessary 'to intervene in the affairs of Patiala to restrict His Highness' sovereignty temporarily at first and afterwards, if necessary, permanently'.

After these general observations, Wilberforce-Bell took up the main items of the *Indictment*. Referring to the cases of obvious judicial nature, it was reluctantly conceded that it was not impossible that the Maharaja was aware of the plan to murder Lal Singh, which was instigated either by Sir Daya Kishan Kaul or Nanak Singh. The allegation about the bomb factory in the Bahadurgarh Fort could neither be proved nor disproved. The story told by Dr Bakhshish Singh about the disappearance of his wife and children appeared to contain 'at least a certain amount of truth'. The accusation made by Amar Singh was true. He was arrested and sentenced to imprisonment in 1914 on a false charge of theft, and his wife had already been abducted. The Maharaja had admitted his fault. But nothing could be done about it now. The case of Sardar Harchand Singh Jeji 'also could suitably be made a subject of enquiry'. It was conceded that the case against Diwan Singh Maftun was concocted by the state, like the case against Amar Singh.

The charges of general ill treatment of people could be ignored more easily. Wilberforce-Bell dismissed stories of inhuman tortures and illegal arrests by saying: 'Strong measures were taken to put down a situation full of potential danger, but we have no information as to whether those measures were inhuman or unnecessarily harsh.' The available evidence at any rate did not warrant any special enquiry on the point. About the hardships caused to the people by shikār, the game rules were revised recently by the Maharaja and there was no other information on this subject. The issue of begār was not important enough for instituting an enquiry. Much of the war loan had not been repaid. But this matter could be looked into by the Finance Minister, Sir Frederick Gauntlet, on assuming charge. The matter of increase in the revenue demand could also be examined by him. About the misappropriation of funds, it was grudgingly conceded that there was some truth in the allegation. 'If an enquiry is to be conducted this item might suitably form one of the subjects of it.'

Finally, the principal charges were undoubtedly related to the Maharaja's 'predilection for women' and 'high handedness' with respect to those who opposed him in his desires, or whose presence was inconvenient. His tendency towards the wives and daughters of his subjects in the plains was the same as he had exhibited towards hill girls. If enquiries on more serious cases were to be held, the Maharaja 'must be prepared to afford facilities in connection with them or to stand aside while they are conducted'. Wilberforce-Bell went on to add that the serious financial situation in the state afforded 'an additional reason for proceeding to extremes, if necessary'.[11] On the whole, thus, he was inclined towards an enquiry on certain items, and to take strict action, if necessary.

The comments of the Political Secretary, C. C. Watson, reflect greater awareness of the objectives of the government and also provide an insight into its character and priorities. He began by agreeing that 'an impartial enquiry' would *not* be justified in relation to begār, shikār, revenue rates, and ill-treatment of the Akali agitators by the police. But the *Indictment of Patiala* went beyond those items and supported allegations by proofs. Watson went over the charges which added some more facts and arguments. On the whole, he thought there would be justification to enquire into several of the charges brought against the Maharaja. However, in view of his past services in the war and Akali troubles, 'a private enquiry' could perhaps be recommended, and the Maharaja could be advised to reform the police and the judiciary of the state as much as its finances.

> But I fear things have got beyond the stage where this will suffice. Either His Highness must take action publicly by prosecuting the paper—with the attendant risks of comment by the Court or the High Court in appeal, or we must make some statement, either in reply to the Patiala People's memorial or otherwise, saying that after an enquiry we are satisfied that there is no case for proceeding further in the matter.

The Maharaja should be given the option to prosecute the writers of the *Indictment*, or to face an enquiry by the AGG. Otherwise, the

Government of India and His Excellency would be charged with suppressing enquiry into allegations of 'gross injustice and serious mal-administration'.[12]

James Fitzpatrick, AGG, tried to minimize the seriousness of the charges against the Maharaja of Patiala by playing upon the Nabha angle. A diehard Tory, Fitzpatrick distrusted the Indian nationalists and hated Maharaja Ripudaman Singh in particular. He wrote to Watson on 23 March 1930 that, according to the Home Minister of Patiala, the original petition drafted by 'the notorious Akali-Congress agitator Sardul Singh Caveeshar' on behalf of the Patiala subjects had been secured by the Patiala Darbar who further informed Fitzpatrick that Sardul Singh had received 50,000 rupees from the ex-Maharaja of Nabha to finance the present propaganda against the Maharaja of Patiala. All this convinced Fitzpatrick that the present agitation was not based on the existence of genuine grievances of the Patiala subjects; it was being engineered from outside by anti-government agents and financed by an enemy 'who has learnt nothing and forgotten nothing from his enforced residence in Kodaikanal and appears still to have money for anti-Patiala propaganda'.[13]

Even the Viceroy and the Political Secretary were keen on salvaging the reputation of the Maharaja of Patiala. The Viceroy saw him on 25 March 1930 in the presence of Watson. A day earlier the Maharaja had been told by Watson that tentatively only two courses were open: either the Maharaja should prosecute under the Princes Protection Act, or he should ask the Government of India to hold an enquiry to clear his honour from the charges. The Maharaja asked if an enquiry by Fitzpatrick, who was a qualified barrister, would suffice. Watson argued that it was desirable to have a judicial rather than a political enquiry. But from the Maharaja's viewpoint a judicial enquiry had its 'drawbacks'. The Viceroy was more accommodating and suggested a middle course: a judicial officer and a political officer associated together. The Maharaja did not like this either. Keeping up the appearance before his subordinates, the Viceroy said that between the vindication of the honour of His Highness and the vindication of the truth he would have to choose the truth. The Maharaja replied in the same vein that he had nothing to fear. But, when he was alone with the Viceroy, he made a personal appeal against an enquiry on the allegations of men who were of no account and who were admittedly the enemies of both the Maharaja and the British Government.[14]

Fitzpatrick Made the Enquiry Officer

On the following day, the Viceroy wrote to the Secretary of State that the problem of the Maharaja of Patiala was causing him great concern. The *Indictment of Patiala* was not something that one could 'quietly smother'. Neither could the government easily refuse to enquire into the charges. 'The best course was that Patiala should himself prosecute', but he would not dare. 'This is tantamount to an admission that the charges are not altogether ill founded, and if this is the deduction I am back at my difficulty that we cannot afford to sponsor an administration which has thus laid itself open to attack that it dare not meet.' The Viceroy proposed to ask the Maharaja to come for 'a very frank talk' in a day or two.[15]

Maharaja Bhupinder Singh saw Fitzpatrick on 30 March and spoke strongly about the ingratitude of the government in sacrificing him after all his loyal services in order to conciliate 'extremist politicians'. The Maharaja complained that the 'revolutionaries' and Akalis were opposed to him 'partly on political grounds and partly to earn their wages from the ex-Maharaja of Nabha'. The Maharaja of Patiala was a loyal prince and those who attacked him were enemies of the government. They both agreed that the object of action should be to satisfy the Viceroy and the British politicians and public, but not the politicians of British India. The Maharaja, therefore, wanted Fitzpatrick to conduct the enquiry as a senior political officer with local knowledge, legal qualifications, judicial experience, and inside acquaintance with the administration of a Punjab state. Fitzpatrick himself thought that 'the considered finding of a Political Officer should suffice to satisfy the Viceroy and through him the British Parliament and public, however, vehemently British India might repudiate it'. Alternatively, Fitzpatrick suggested to the Political Secretary that he could be associated with a High Court Judge in a joint enquiry so that the weight could be given to considerations other than purely legal. Fitzpatrick emphasized that a judgment based on purely legal principles and couched in legal phraseology would make 'no allowance for such political considerations and might complicate the position of Government'. He went on to add that it was his duty as the AGG to ensure 'a fair trial' for the Maharaja of Patiala who had earned consideration from the government by his loyalty and services.[16]

Feeling confident that loyalty was the highest virtue in the eyes of the paramount power, Maharaja Bhupinder Singh himself saw the

Political Secretary Watson on the following day to assure him that he would welcome 'the fullest enquiry' by a political officer, or a political officer combined with a judicial officer, provided the political officer was Fitzpatrick or B. J. Glancy (later Governor, Punjab). He also assured Watson that he would accept any advice given by the government on the basis of such an enquiry. He wanted to be assured that this enquiry would not be a preliminary one. He was told that the question of further enquiry would arise only in the event of his refusing to accept the government's advice, or if he himself asked for a regular Commission of Enquiry.[17]

The Viceroy sent a telegram to the Secretary of State on 2 April to apprise him of the situation and the course of action contemplated to extricate Bhupinder Singh and silence the critics of the government. Minimizing the import of the *Indictment of Patiala*, the Viceroy maintained that it was the result of an unofficial enquiry held by five politicians of British India claiming to represent Indian States' People's Conference, into alleged grievances of the Patiala state subjects against the Maharaja and his administration. The book was the outcome of extensive propaganda against the Maharaja financed by his enemies: the Maharaja of Nabha, the editor of the *Riyasat*, the Akalis, and the 'extremists' who were angry at his declaration against the Congress Resolution for Independence. The Viceroy conceded that the *Indictment* was 'at first sight very damaging to Patiala'. But, mercifully, many of the charges had already been enquired into and some judicial decisions had also been taken. Nevertheless, some action was now required in view of the statements of alleged witnesses recorded in the *Indictment*. At a personal meeting with the Viceroy, the Maharaja was advised to consider whether his best course would not be to prosecute the authors of the *Indictment* under the Princes Protection Act, but he was averse to this course for fear of exposure, adverse publicity, delays, and, possibly, huge legal costs.

Therefore, the alternative of an enquiry seemed more acceptable. The Viceroy then dwelt at some length on its mode as well as safeguards from the government's viewpoint. For that it was necessary to ensure that (a) there was no publicity (in other words, the hearing should be in camera); (b) the proceedings should not be greatly protracted and there should be no chance of an appeal to a High Court (in other words, the enquiry should not be judicial); and (c) it should be final so that the necessity of appointing a Commission after the enquiry should not arise (that is, no risk should be taken about the outcome). In these circumstances, it was preferable to order Fitzpatrick to make a 'full enquiry' into the charges without delay and report the result in a couple of months. The Viceroy conceded that an enquiry by Fitzpatrick would not satisfy the enemies of the Maharaja, but it would have the advantage of 'being the usual form of preliminary enquiry into allegations of maladministration'. Moreover, the appointment of a special officer or a Commission at this stage would carry the implication of the Maharaja's guilt. In the (unlikely) event of serious charges of murder or abetment of murder being proved, it might become necessary to ask the Maharaja to abdicate, or to accept a formal Commission of Enquiry set up by the Viceroy.[18] But, the Viceroy added, 'I don't think this result is at all likely.'

Fitzpatrick was unusually keen to handle the enquiry. On 2 April itself he wrote to Watson that he was sorry 'it was considered undesirable to adhere to the usual practice of directing an enquiry by the local political officer before taking the extreme step of offering the alternative of a prosecution by the Maharaja under the Princes' Protection Act or of a judicial enquiry which in practice amounts to a commission'. If the Maharaja was eventually exonerated through a judicial enquiry his role in the Chamber of Princes and in Sikh politics would not remain the same as now. Fitzpatrick informed Watson that the Maharaja felt strongly that despite his loyalty he was being made 'a scapegoat in the game of British Indian politics'. It was Fitzpatrick's duty to draw Watson's attention to 'the probable reactions of the case and the need of caution'. He admitted that he had 'some personal influence' with Patiala which he could employ 'to good purpose'.[19]

The Secretary of State had two comments to make on the Viceroy's telegram. One was simply to remind the Viceroy that the paramount power had the right to demand and enforce measures for improvements; the exercise of this prerogative should not appear to depend on the ruler's consent. Secondly, if the Government of India were satisfied after the enquiry that the charges were not sustainable they should proscribe the *Indictment* even if the Maharaja did not prosecute its authors.[20] The Viceroy readily agreed with the Secretary of State.[21] The Viceroy told the Maharaja in the presence of the Political Secretary on 20 April that he had decided to have an enquiry conducted by Fitzpatrick. He would enquire into all the allegations made in the *Indictment*. Counsel would be allowed on both sides. The press would be excluded. No copies of the enquiry report would be given to any party. As far as the government were concerned, this would be the only enquiry. The Maharaja would have to accept any advice given by the government as a result of the enquiry. Alternatively, the Maharaja himself could ask for a Commission of Enquiry under the Resolution of 1920. A further enquiry, therefore, could take place only on the initiative of the Maharaja. Finally, it was suggested to the Maharaja that he should himself ask for an enquiry by the AGG.

For record, Maharaja Bhupinder Singh wrote to Viceroy Irwin on 5 May 1930 that the *Indictment of Patiala* had been widely circulated both in India and England by his 'powerful and unscrupulous enemies'. He owed it to himself that he 'must voluntarily ask for a thorough searching and independent enquiry'. He added nonchalantly: 'Should Your Excellency, in view of all the circumstances of the case decide to entrust the enquiry to the Honourable Agent to the G.G., Punjab States, I shall agree to such a course if I am allowed to be represented by counsel of my choice.' He reminded the Viceroy that neither as a ruler of his state nor as the official representative of the princely order could he afford any longer to sit silent against the campaign of calumny that had been gathering in volume and virulence of late. Therefore, the Viceroy could draw up the terms of reference and give the necessary directions to the enquiring officer for the method and procedure to be adopted so that the parties concerned were apprised of the conduct of enquiry at an early date.[22]

Lord Irwin wrote to the Maharaja on 10 May that after reading his letter of 5 May he had decided to order his Agent to hold a 'full enquiry' into the charges made against him in the *Indictment of Patiala*. The Viceroy's letter laid down the manner in which the enquiry was to be conducted. The only difference he saw between this and Justice Stuart's enquiry was that the parties concerned were entitled to have counsels (against the usual practice). Lord Irwin appreciated 'very fully the motives, so cogently stated in Your Highness' letter, which have inspired you to demand a full and independent enquiry'.[23]

Fitzpatrick's Farce

Fitzpatrick fixed 9 June for the opening of enquiry at Dalhousie, and notified the concerned parties.[24] The Secretary of the Punjab Riyasati Praja Mandal, Bhagwan Singh Longowalia, wrote to the Political Secretary that the Executive Committee of the Praja Mandal was grateful to the Viceroy for ordering an enquiry, making its terms of reference as wide as possible. At the same time, the Committee protested most strongly against the appointment of Fitzpatrick as the Commissioner of Enquiry. Even if the government did not have the courage at the present critical juncture to appoint public men of reputation and integrity as commissioners, it could at least select commissioners having an independent and judicial mind. Fitzpatrick was a choice of the Maharaja; it would have been only fair to associate with him a nominee of the All India States' People's Conference. Apart from being closely associated with the Maharaja and strongly biased in his favour, Fitzpatrick had set views on many cases, and he was not likely to change them. The Committee requested the Viceroy to appoint commissioners who should command the confidence of the public and who could look afresh into the cases to be taken up. The Committee also requested that prisoners connected with the enquiry should be transferred from Patiala to British jails. Together with a list of such prisoners, Bhagwan Singh enclosed another list of persons who had been imprisoned after they gave evidence before the Enquiry Committee of the All India States' People's Conference, and requested their release. Furthermore, in view of the resolution of the Punjab Riyasati Praja Mandal sent to the Viceroy on 22 April 1930, the Maharaja should not be allowed to remain in control of the state and its finances during the time of the enquiry. A deputation of the Patiala state subjects should be given a proper hearing by the Viceroy.[25] The Private Secretary to the Viceroy wrote to Bhagwan Singh that His Excellency had no reason to believe that the apprehensions expressed by him had any real basis.[26]

On 20 May 1930, the Executive Committee of the All India States' People's Conference resolved to not participate in the enquiry, and to not accept it.[27] A number of representations were made to the Punjab Government that the enquiry should be dropped because the opponents of the Maharaja had refused to bring any proof in support of their allegations.[28] 'Engineered' apparently by Patiala, these representations came from jāgīrdārs, zaildārs, and presidents of Gurdwara committees of the districts of Ludhiana, Firozpur, and Hissar. But the government had its own reasons to continue with the enquiry, and Fitzpatrick's ex parte enquiry began as scheduled, on 9 June 1930.

Patiala was represented by a galaxy of lawyers, including Sir Tej Bahadur Sapru and Sir C. P. Ramaswamy Iyer, the liberal nationalists well regarded by the government.[29] Amritlal Sheth, who was a member of the Patiala Enquiry Committee, and had appeared at the Patiala session of the enquiry on 26 June, published a statement in the *Hindu Herald* to underline that the whole enquiry was actually 'a Patiala show'. It was strongly resented by the Patiala Darbar as a public attack on the honour of their counsels as well as the 'impartiality' of the tribunal appointed by the government for the enquiry. Fitzpatrick allowed the Patiala Darbar to issue a rejoinder.[30] It was published in *The Times of India* of 8 July, and Sheth responded by arguing that the allegations made by him were virtually accepted by the Patiala authorities in their rejoinder.[31]

In the House of Commons, on 25 and 30 June 1930, the Secretary of State deftly handled all the questions related to Fitzpatrick's appointment. He had the simple answer that it was made in accordance with 'the usual and natural procedure'. To some other questions he responded by saying that he required 'notice'. To several other questions, he had one answer: 'The enquiry decided upon was with the object of testing the allegations, and it was considered to be generally desirable that such an enquiry should be held in camera. As I have previously stated, I am in entire agreement with the course of action which the Government of India adopted.'[32] Fitzpatrick was jubilant over the defence of his appointment in the British Parliament.

Fitzpatrick was quick with the job; it was finished in four weeks. He submitted his report to the Political Secretary on 11 July 1930. After dwelling on the terms of reference and the procedure followed by him, he went on to state that the boycott of the enquiry by the Indian States' People's Conference and the Punjab Riyasati Praja Mandal was a reflection of their weakness; it deprived Patiala of the opportunity of cross-examination. Justifying his appointment as a matter of routine, he dismissed all the objections as baseless.[33]

Outlining the 'genesis' of the *Indictment of Patiala*, Fitzpatrick underscored its connection with the Maharaja of Nabha: 500 copies of the memorial had been printed at the expense of Sardar Sardul Singh Caveeshar, who was said to be a paid agent of the Maharaja. Far from being the spontaneous outpourings of the wrongs of the oppressed and downtrodden subjects of Patiala, the *Indictment* was said to be the work of the enemies of the Maharaja of Patiala and the princely order. It was emphasized that the charges had been collected and published by an outside body unconnected with Patiala and the publication had been inspired, edited, and financed by the former Maharaja of Nabha. Fitzpatrick asserted that the anti-Patiala agitation could be traced to Stuart's enquiry. Since 1926, a systematic campaign had been conducted by the Maharaja of Nabha to purchase support from public men, associations, and the press to malign the Maharaja of Patiala as an integral part of his efforts to secure his own reinstatement. Every effort was made to poison the atmosphere not only of the Punjab or India but also of England. The non-government Patiala Enquiry Committee had played into the hands of the Maharaja of Nabha who was motivated by a personal vendetta. The SGPC was against the Maharaja of Patiala because of his loyalty to the British and his consistent refusal to patronize the Akalis, who actually plotted to overthrow him. Fitzpatrick's general tenor was thus at odds with the assurance that he would 'examine the evidence on both sides in each count critically and fully in order to come to a finding on the merits'.[34]

The Fitzpatrick Enquiry was virtually 'operation crisis management', and its report 'a master-piece of disingenuousness', says a recent biographer of Maharaja Bhupinder Singh.[35] Fitzpatrick exonerated the Maharaja from the murder of Lal Singh. His wife Dalip Kaur had lived in the Maharaja's palace since 1910, given birth to their children, and acquired a dominating influence in the palace. This was resented by the Maharani and her father Sardar Gurnam Singh. They induced Lal Singh to ask for Dalip Kaur's return. The Maharaja mentioned the matter to Sardar Nanak Singh, the Superintendent of CID in Patiala. Nanak Singh was under a cloud in 1918. In order to recover the lost ground he got Lal Singh murdered. The Maharaja was in England at that time. In other words, there was no evidence connecting the Maharaja with the murder of Lal Singh.[36] By exonerating the Maharaja from the most serious charge against him, Fitzpatrick had done more than half of his work. The remaining charges could be dismissed more easily.

For Fitzpatrick, the bomb factory charge collapsed like a house of cards with the repudiation of statements by the witnesses and the exposure of Dr Bakhshish Singh's 'diary' as a fabricated piece of evidence. Fitzpatrick asserted that no such factory ever existed. Regarding the disappearance of Bakhshish Singh's wife, Bachittar Kaur, and the alleged death of their daughter and the disappearance of their son, there was little evidence to support the charges. With regard to the wife of Sardar Amar Singh, the Maharaja could not be defended on moral grounds but there was nothing in the case to justify drastic action by the paramount power. The Maharaja was still offering ample amends, and he could not possibly do anything more. Patiala's action against Sardar Harchand Singh Jeji, who had identified himself with revolutionary agitation, was justified; in fact, it was salutary and successful. Now that a settlement had been arrived at, Jeji having 'apologized' to the Maharaja, there was no need to discuss the case further.[37] No other count was really important for Fitzpatrick. His personal role in bringing about compromise between Harchand Singh and the Maharaja was a masterstroke.

In summing up his report, Fitzpatrick again dwelt on the conspiracy between the Maharaja of Nabha, the SGPC, and the Punjab Riyasati Praja Mandal. It was underlined that the crucial role in this conspiracy could safely be attributed to the Maharaja of Nabha. In fact, his role in the conspiracy initiated the whole proceedings of the Committee and 'deprived their opinions and conclusions of any real value'.[38] Fitzpatrick deliberately magnified the role of Maharaja Ripudaman Singh who was a political prisoner at this time.

Fitzpatrick sought to minimize the gravity of charges against the Maharaja of Patiala through a highly selective mode of presenting evidence and a strongly rhetorical mode of argumentation. His defence of the Maharaja of Patiala was essentially political. The British empire had its own raison d'être, and its supporters must be defended against those revolutionaries and extremists who aspired to see the end of imperial rule. Fitzpatrick approached the issue not as a judge but as an advocate, an advocate on behalf of the Maharaja of Patiala against the Maharaja of Nabha, who was seen as an enemy of the empire.

The response of the Political Department to Fitzpatrick's much laboured insinuation against Nabha was somewhat different. While accepting Patiala's exoneration, Wilberforce-Bell, who had no personal liking for the Maharaja of Patiala, did not agree with Fitzpatrick that action should be taken against Maharaja Ripudaman Singh. Watson did not agree with his Deputy that the Maharaja of Nabha's connection with 'the conspiracy was justified by the revelation of shortcomings in the Patiala Judiciary or the state's financial position'. Instead, Watson drew attention to two other relevant questions to be decided upon: proscription of the *Indictment of Patiala* and publication of a communiqué.[39]

The Viceroy sent a telegram to the Secretary of State on 28 July 1930 to apprise him of Fitzpatrick's report. Before stating the findings briefly in each count, the Viceroy underlined the drift of the report, which happily was in line with the government's thinking. He referred to the 'two societies of a revolutionary nature supported financially by the ex-Maharaja of Nabha with the object of accomplishing Patiala's downfall and disgrace'. It was in marked contrast to the loyalty of the

Maharaja of Patiala to the Government of India and his refusal to show sympathy for the Akali agitation and disloyal activities both in British India and the Patiala state. Therefore, the draft communiqué stated, among other things, that the Government of India had satisfied themselves that the evidence failed to substantiate any of the charges made against the Maharaja in the *Indictment of Patiala*. Those charges were the outcome of a deliberate 'conspiracy' between certain individuals and public bodies with the object of vilifying the Maharaja and disgracing him in the eyes of his subjects and the Government of India. The Viceroy dealt with the issue of maladministration by proposing to take immediate steps for improvement of the state's judiciary and fulfilment of the state's financial obligations to its subjects. In addition, he was thinking of taking cognizance of the Maharaja of Nabha's association with the 'conspiracy' and of addressing the Secretary of State later on this point. The legal advisers of the Viceroy, however, were against the proscription of the *Indictment of Patiala*, for this would unduly draw attention towards the Maharaja of Patiala.[40]

The Secretary of State was glad to learn that the enquiry was favourable to Patiala. However, he was of the view that the word 'unproved' for the charges against the Maharaja in the draft communiqué was hardly appropriate. It was well understood that the *Indictment* was the outcome of a conspiracy, and that the character of the Maharaja of Patiala was sufficiently cleared to permit of his going to England as a delegate to the Round Table Conference. No room should, therefore, be left for implying that the Government of India entertained some doubt about his 'innocence'; the Maharaja could regard it as an unsatisfactory outcome of his request for 'a thorough searching and independent enquiry'. Furthermore, the Secretary of State wanted to know whether the Viceroy's view was (*a*) that charges made against Patiala in the *Indictment* were without foundation or (*b*) that the authors had failed to substantiate their charges. If (*a*), the word 'unproved' seemed to be unfair to Patiala; if (*b*), it would still be open to the Viceroy to make a further enquiry on additional evidence being furnished. Therefore, the communiqué could be issued with suitable alterations. The Secretary of State agreed with the Viceroy about dropping the idea of proscribing the *Indictment*.[41]

The Viceroy lost no time to write to the Maharaja of Patiala on 4 August to congratulate him. Now that the enquiry had exonerated him from the charges made against him, the Maharaja could make arrangements for going to the Conference in London.[42] Watson congratulated the Maharaja in his letter on the following day.[43] The responsibility for the recorded instances of the Maharaja's alleged high-handedness was transferred completely on to his judicial and police officers. On advice from Fitzpatrick, Hazura Singh Dhillon, Judge, High Court, was dismissed. The Puisne Judge, Arjan Singh, was removed from the High Court. Diwan Bahadur Pindi Das was made Chief Justice. In the Police Department, Bharpur Singh, an Assistant Superintendent, was dismissed and Gurdial Singh Dhillon, the Senior Superintendent of CID, was demoted.[44] It is interesting to recall that at the time of the Stuart Enquiry the government had held Maharaja Ripudaman Singh responsible for the lapses of his functionaries.

In fact, the adverse comment on the administration of Patiala was part of the intended outcome of the Fitzpatrick Enquiry. All cogs in the giant wheel of the government had acted in unison to achieve the objective of exonerating its princely favourite. Even King George V had indicated that he would want the charges against Patiala to be 'disproved'. Unlike the Stuart Enquiry, which disallowed counsels or arbitration to Nabha, the legal luminaries engaged by Patiala had a field day in the ex-parte Fitzpatrick Enquiry, picking holes in the preliminary evidence provided by the *Indictment*. In short, if the Stuart Enquiry was designed from the very beginning to trap Nabha, the Fitzpatrick Enquiry was structured to extricate Patiala from a really bad situation. It is termed as 'a close shave' by his biographer.[45] In the process, serious issues of personal and public morality were glossed over, and maladministration par excellence was sidetracked. For the paramount power there was no virtue beyond loyalty and no morality beyond holding on to the empire.

Fitzpatrick Proposes Action against Maharaja Ripudaman Singh

The exoneration of Maharaja Bhupinder Singh and the deprecation of Maharaja Ripudaman Singh were the obverse and reverse of the same political coin. Acting almost as an agent of Patiala who still feared Ripudaman Singh's reinstatement, Fitzpatrick made a strong case for further action against him. On the basis of all the reports received in the Agency since his removal to Kodaikanal, Fitzpatrick concluded that the ex-Maharaja had continued to instigate and subsidize propaganda against Maharaja Bhupinder Singh. All the bits and pieces of information coming to Fitzpatrick had convinced him that Ripudaman Singh was working against Patiala as much himself as through some of the national and Akali leaders who were in contact with the leaders of the Punjab Riyasati Praja Mandal and the All India States' People's Conference. With reference to this 'conspiracy', Fitzpatrick recommended that the allowance of the Maharaja of Nabha should be reduced from 10,000 rupees to 2,000 rupees. He suggested further that his liberty should be restricted in future either by a definite order of internment or by restricting his visitors and censoring his correspondence. If the Government of India accepted the proposal, Fitzpatrick would ask the Council of Regency, Nabha, to send only 2,000 rupees a month to the Maharaja in future.[46] Like Minchin, Fitzpatrick appears to have been more vindictive than the Maharaja of Patiala towards Maharaja Ripudaman Singh.

Fitzpatrick's proposal was discussed at length in the Political Department. One opinion was to cut the allowance to 5,000 rupees: 'If such a reduction is made, the ex-Maharaja will realize that the Government of India are determined to put an end to intrigue and the financing of the propaganda work.' Watson was in favour of 'no action at present'. Another view was to inform the Secretary of State of the intention to reduce the allowance. The question of current negotiations with Maharani Sarojini Devi influenced this line of thinking: 'A reduction in her husband's allowance will further embitter her and will destroy or at least minimize the chances of our getting her to agree to our proposals in regard to the young Maharaja's education.'[47] Fitzpatrick had meanwhile been working on her.

On 28 August 1930, the Viceroy sent a telegram to the Secretary of State, stating that the ex-Maharaja of Nabha had been in close association with the Akali agitation since his deposition in 1928, both in the Patiala state and British India. A considerable portion of his allowance was utilized by him in these 'subversive interests'. He had financed the Riyasati Praja Mandal, which was recognized as 'a revolutionary body' in the Punjab. The Punjab Government was now considering the question of declaring it 'an unlawful association'. In these circumstances it was necessary to take appropriate notice of the activities of the Maharaja. The Viceroy proposed to place a censorship at Kodaikanal upon his correspondence and to reduce his monthly allowance to 5,000 rupees. The proposals could be upheld legally, he assured the Secretary of State. Before giving effect to his intentions, the Viceroy wanted to ascertain that the Secretary of State had 'no objection'. The Viceroy sent another telegram on 1 October for an early reply to his telegram of 28 August.[48]

Wedgewood Benn, the Secretary of State for India, took some time to respond. In his telegram of 29 October, he informed the Viceroy that the whole issue had been discussed in the India Office.[49] The Secretary of State had no objection to the proposed action. He only wanted the Viceroy to ensure that it would be based on specific evidence cited in Fitzpatrick's report and not on clause (8) of the Agreement of 1923 regarding the 'obligation of loyalty and obedience'. 'But in replying to possible parliamentary enquiries it would be helpful to know what action if any has been taken or it is decided to take against individuals or public bodies whose disloyal activities Maharaja has financed.'[50] On an enquiry from the India Office in March 1931, Political Secretary Watson informed them that the Maharaja of Nabha was still receiving an allowance of 10,000 rupees per month. No action could be taken against the Maharaja since no action had been taken against individuals or public bodies whose 'disloyal' activities he had financed.[51]

According to Copland, Fitzpatrick 'saw Patiala privately several times during and after the inquiry'.[52] Though there is no record, Fitzpatrick was widely believed to have been heavily bribed by the Maharaja of Patiala. It is on record, however, that when Sir James Fitzpatrick retired as AGG, the Maharaja sought permission to appoint him as his Prime Minister, but was curtly informed by the then Viceroy Willingdon that the employment of ex-political officers was 'not in accordance with the policy of the government'.[53] In 1935, when Fitzpatrick was in England, Maharaja Bhupinder Singh offered him a house in London for residence as the informal guardian of two sons of the Maharaja who were going to Cambridge. The proposal was dropped because the Secretary of State considered it inappropriate for an officer of Fitzpatrick's rank to accept such an assignment. The Punjab Governor, Sir Bertrand Glancy, who was in the Political Department earlier, minced no words about its implications:

> No Indian will believe that a retired officer is giving his services for nothing under such an arrangement. Princes will be encouraged to think they can square their Residents by promises of employment after retirement. The prestige of the Department will suffer with the public all over India.
>
> In the case of Sir James, these objections have special force, as more scandals have attached to his name in connection with easements than to any other officer of his rank in recent times.[54]

Notes

1. Ramesh Walia, *Praja Mandal Movement in East Punjab States* (Patiala: Punjabi University, 1972), pp. 48–9.
2. Administrator of Nabha State (AONS) Records, File no. 3530-E, Report of the Chief Police Officer, Nabha State to Assistant Administrator Nabha, dated 19 September 1927.
3. AONS Records, File no. 3530-E, copy of the printed leaflet distributed by the Punjab States Shiromani Darbar.
4. Quoted in Walia, *Praja Mandal Movement*, pp. 53–6.
5. Walia, *Praja Mandal Movement*, pp. 56–8.
6. Walia, *Praja Mandal Movement*, p. 61.
7. *Indictment of Patiala* (Being a report of the Patiala Enquiry Committee Appointed by the Indian States' People's Conference), 1930, Appendix-C: 'Memorial to the Viceroy by 10 citizens of the Patiala State'.
8. Walia, *Praja Mandal Movement*, pp. 77–80, 90–4. Crown Representative Records (CRR), Punjab States, Accession no. 13, File no. 115-P (Secret), 1930, Part I, pp. 3–4.
9. CRR, no. 115-P(S), 1930, Part I. Proceedings of the Patiala Enquiry Committee.
10. CRR, no. 115-P(S), 1930, Part I, pp. 31, 40.
11. CRR, no. 115-P(S), 1930, Part I, pp. 41, 44–53.
12. CRR, no. 115-P(S), 1930, Part I, pp. 54–62.
13. CRR, no. 115-P(S), 1930, Part I, pp. 75–7.
14. CRR, no. 115-P(S), 1930, Part I, pp. 77–81.
15. National Archives of India, New Delhi (NAI), Halifax Collection, no. 3885, Viceroy to Secretary of State, 26 March 1930.
16. CRR, no. 115-P(S), 1930, Part I, Fitzpatrick to Watson, 31 March 1930, pp. 82–7.
17. CRR, no. 115-P(S), 1930, Part I, Watson's note dated 7 April 1930, pp. 98–9.
18. NAI, Halifax Collection, no. 3895, Viceroy to Secretary of State, 2 April 1930.
19. CRR, no. 115-P(S), 1930, Part I, Fitzpatrick to Watson, 2 April 1930.
20. NAI, Halifax Collection, no. 3890, telegram from Secretary of State to Viceroy, dated 10 April 1930.
21. NAI, Halifax Collection, no. 3890, telegram from Viceroy to Secretary of State, dated 24 April 1930.
22. The Maharaja's letter is quoted in full as 'one of the most important letters of his life' by K. Natwar-Singh in *The Magnificent Maharaja: The Life and Times of Maharaja Bhupinder Singh of Patiala 1891–1938* (New Delhi: Harper Collins Publishers India, 1998), pp. 178–80.
23. NAI, Halifax Collection, Accession no. 3940, Lord Irwin to Maharaja Bhupinder Singh, 10 May 1930.

24. CRR, no. 115-P(S), 1930, Part I, Fitzpatrick to Watson, 10 May 1930, p. 154.
25. CRR, no. 115-P(S), 1930, Part I, pp. 157–60.
26. CRR, no. 115-P(S), 1930, Part I, p. 172: G. Cunningham to Punjab Riyasati Praja Mandal, Lahore.
27. CRR, no. 115-P(S), 1930, Part I, pp. 175–80.
28. CRR, no. 115-P(S), 1930, Part I, Punjab Government to Watson, 10 June 1930, p. 190; note by Wilberforce-Bell, dated 13 June 1930, p. 192.
29. CRR, no. 115-P(S), 1930, Part I, Fitzpatrick to Watson, 15 June 1930, p. 210.
30. CRR, no. 115-P(S), 1930, Part I, Fitzpatrick to Watson, 3 July 1930, p. 232.
31. CRR, no. 115-P(S), 1930, Part I, pp. 43–4.
32. CRR, no. 115-P(S), 1930, Part I, pp. 151–5.
33. CRR, Punjab States (microfilm), Accession no. 7, Reel no. 2, File no. 115-(2), Political (Secret), 1930, Foreign and Political Department, pp. 1–5.
34. CRR, Punjab States (microfilm), Accession no. 7, Reel no. 2, File no. 115-(2), Political (S), 1930, pp. 5–14.
35. Natwar-Singh, *The Magnificent Maharaja*, p. 183.
36. CRR, Punjab States (microfilm), Accession no. 7, Reel no. 2 File no. 115-(2), Political (S), 1930, Foreign and Political Department, pp. 14–23.
37. CRR, Punjab States (microfilm), Accession no. 7, Reel no. 2 File no. 115-(2), Political (S), 1930, paras 33–67.
38. CRR, Punjab States (microfilm), Accession no. 7, Reel no. 2 File no. 115-(2), Political (S), 1930, paras 68–112.
39. CRR, Punjab States (microfilm), Accession no. 7, Reel no. 2 File no. 115-(2), Political (S), 1930, comment on Fitzpatrick's report by H. Wilberforce-Bell, dated 19 July 1930, paras 1–31; Watson's note, dated 21 July 1930, pp. 7–8; and dated 22 July 1930, p. 8.
40. NAI, Halifax Collection, no. 3890, telegram of Viceroy to Secretary of State, dated 28 July 1930.
41. NAI, Halifax Collection, no. 3890, telegram from Secretary of State for India to Viceroy, dated 2 August 1930.
42. CRR, Punjab States (microfilm), Accession no. 7, Reel no. 2, File no. 115-(2), Political (S), 1930, p. 10: letter from Viceroy to Maharaja of Patiala, 4 August 1930.
43. CRR, Punjab States (microfilm), Accession no. 7, Reel no. 2, File no. 115-(2), Political (S), 1930, p. 11.
44. Delhi Record-4, File no. 115-(2) Political (S), 1930, Government of India, Foreign and Political Department, letter from Political Department to AGG, 4 August 1930; letter from Maharaja of Patiala to AGG, 22 August 1930; letter from AGG to Political Department, 29 August 1930.
45. Natwar-Singh, *The Magnificent Maharaja*, pp. 172–93. The chapter dealing with the *Indictment* is titled as 'The Indictment: A Close Shave'.

46. NAI, CRR (microfilm), Accession no. 8, Reel no. 3, File no. 390-P (Secret)/1930, Fitzpatrick to Political Secretary, 8 August 1930. Fitzpatrick gave a summary of the reports of November 1928, March 1929, April 1929, September 1929, October 1929, and April 1930.
47. NAI, CRR (microfilm), Accession no. 8, Reel no. 3, File no. 390-P (S)/1930, note of discussion.
48. IOR (microfilm), R/1/1/1981, no. 390-P (S), 1930, telegrams from Viceroy to Secretary of State, 28 August 1930 and 1 October 1930.
49. IOR (microfilm), L/P and S/10/100028, Reel no. 37, Register no. 6832/30, 'Nabha: Association of ex-Maharaja with Conspiracy against Patiala. Proposed reduction of allowance and censorship of correspondence'.
50. IOR, R/1/1/1981, no. 390-P(S), 1930, telegram from Secretary of State to Viceroy, dated 29 October 1930.
51. IOR, R/1/1/1981, no. 390-P(S), 1930, C. C. Watson to P. J. Patrick, India Office, 24 April 1931.
52. Ian Copland, *Princes of India in the Endgame of Empire, 1917–1947* (Cambridge: Cambridge University Press, 1997), p. 82.
53. Copland, *Princes of India in the Endgame*, p. 128.
54. Quoted in Natwar-Singh, *The Magnificent Maharaja*, p. 271.

12

THE MAHARAJA LOSES CUSTODY OF THE TIKKA

A crucial factor in the Maharaja Ripudaman Singh's unequal contest with the paramount power was the custody and education of the heir apparent, Tikka Partap Singh. The Maharaja had been totally opposed to the idea of entrusting his education to the paramount power, which looked upon the education of a minor prince as its exclusive prerogative and an opportunity to mould him. After the removal of the Maharaja to Kodaikanal, the Tikka's mother, Maharani Sarojini Devi, could play a crucial role, and the bureaucrats were obviously aware of her importance. From the very beginning, therefore, their idea was to detach her from the Maharaja. They finally succeeded in their design after the failure of the *Indictment* of Patiala in 1930.

The Issue of Custody

On 19 February 1928, Fitzpatrick went to Dehra Dun to inform Maharani Sarojini Devi of the formal deposition of the Maharaja, and to deliver Lord Irwin's letter to her, expressing his 'sincere sympathy' with Her Highness, and hoping that the 'future will atone for the sorrows of the past'. Her son was to be installed on the gaddī of Nabha in the best interests of the state, the Maharani herself, and her son.

> It is my earnest hope therefore that Your Highness will not hesitate to accompany your son to Nabha with the least possible delay and that you will remain there by his side, so that he may set forth with the fairest prospects of success on the great task that lies before him and grow up

to prove himself a worthy successor of his revered grandfather, Maharaja Hira Singh.

The Maharani was also told that every consideration befitting Her Highness' rank and position would be given to her at Nabha. She was assured that she could always depend on the help and sympathy of the Governor General and his officers.[1] In this proposition the Maharaja was deliberately made irrelevant.

Lord Irwin could hardly be more persuasive but the Maharani did not as yet feel safe in the changed situation. While invoking her religious and moral duty to her husband, she admitted that she had 'considerable hesitation' in taking the Tikka Sahib to Nabha for reasons of security and safety. Nabha was full of persons who were inimical to the welfare of the Nabha House. She, therefore, wanted the Governor General's approval for living in Dehra Dun and Mussoorie. She could bring up and educate her children, the Tikka Sahib and his four siblings, in consultation with Fitzpatrick, in whom she had full and implicit confidence.[2] The Maharani appears to have accepted the proposition that she was the only relevant party in matters of the Tikka's education and custody.

Both Fitzpatrick and the Nabha Administrator, Wilson-Johnston, were also of the view that the Maharani should not go to Nabha immediately, and that she should stay on at Dehra Dun.[3] Viceroy Irwin wrote to the Maharani that he did not wish to press her to adopt any course of action which she thought was dangerous to the safety of the Tikka Sahib, but added that the fears of Her Highness were groundless. He trusted that she would agree 'some day to the Tikka Sahib being brought up in his own State and among his own people'. For the present, she could continue to live in Dehra Dun and Mussoorie with the children and to arrange for their upbringing in consultation with Fitzpatrick.[4] The installation of Tikka Partap Singh was postponed for the present.

The authorities appear to have used the question of allowance to pressurize the Maharani. Early in March 1928, Fitzpatrick wrote to Sarojini Devi that her allowance was tentatively fixed at 2,500 rupees a month, and of the young Maharaja at 2,000 rupees.[5] The Maharani pointed out that 'His Highness' used to receive a monthly allowance of 25,000 rupees, which had now been reduced to 10,000 rupees. The allowance proposed for her and her children, including the Tikka, was wholly inadequate. A suitable amount was at least 15,000 rupees, the saving from the sum fixed for the Maharaja before his deportation.[6] Fitzpatrick wrote to the Maharani that he could not agree to any increase 'without full details in justification'.[7] The Maharani replied that no detail was asked for when the Maharaja's allowance was fixed at 25,000 rupees a month. There was no reason why the figure should now be cut down: 'I do not wish to argue about this matter any further.'[8] The Maharani knew the importance of her situation.

Fitzpatrick wrote to the Political Secretary, Watson, that the proposed allowances were suggested after discussion with the Maharaja of Patiala, Wilson-Johnston, Sardar Gurdial Singh, the Assistant Administrator of Nabha, and the leading Sardars of Nabha. In Wilson-Johnston's view the allowances fixed were generous. But 'the lady thinks otherwise'. Fitzpatrick thought that her intention was to send the balance to her husband and, thus, defeat the object of the government to stop the Maharaja's anti-government propaganda by reducing the allowance. The Maharani was in regular correspondence with her husband. Fitzpatrick added, however, that the 'critical time' had passed and the Maharani was unlikely to join her husband in Kodaikanal.[9] Watson suggested that the allowance could be revised to 4,000 rupees a month so that the Maharani received the total amount of 6,000 rupees, and not 4,500 rupees.[10] Fitzpatrick had no objection but thought that the Maharani would not feel satisfied. Fitzpatrick hoped that he would succeed in keeping the Maharani from joining the Maharaja with the Tikka.[11]

Sir Chimanlal Setalvad, an eminent barrister and pro-government statesman, saw Watson on 29 May 1928 and mentioned that the Maharani was thinking of visiting her husband for a brief period, leaving her children at Dehra Dun, and that she was willing to take the Tikka Sahib to England for education if the government agreed. Sir Chimanlal went on to add that the amount of 6,000 rupees a month was 'derogatory to her position'. If she gave her word not to send money to her husband, she could be trusted to refrain from doing so. Watson agreed to reconsider the question and put it to the Viceroy.[12] The Viceroy thought that it was not necessary to increase the allowance, but a fund could be created with 15,000 rupees a month; additional grants could be given to the Maharani from this fund according to her needs. There would be no objection to the Maharani taking the young Maharaja to England if she desired, and she could visit the Maharaja at Kodaikanal but without the young Maharaja.[13]

At this juncture, Fitzpatrick received a telegram from the Maharani that she was about to leave for Kodaikanal with the whole of her family.[14] He reached Mussoorie on 25 June 1929 and spent three days mostly in conversation with the Maharani and her advisers: C. S. Ranga Iyer and Durga Prasad, a former Vakīl of the Maharaja. The Maharani's father, Sardar Prem Singh, and her brother, Sardar Ranbir Singh, were also there for 'frank and friendly' discussions. Consequently, the Maharani decided to cancel her plans and to reconsider her decision. Fitzpatrick offered to carry her letter to the Viceroy, or she could go personally to Simla for an interview. Fitzpatrick made it absolutely clear:

> To go to Kodaikanal with her children in defiance of the Viceroy's wishes and advice would be sheer folly and selfishness and bound to do harm to her husband and children.

This friendly advice was little short of a threat.

On the question whether or not the Maharaja's case could be reconsidered if she and her children kept away from him, Fitzpatrick expressed his own opinion:

> If she followed our advice and devoted herself to the upbringing of her children until the minor Maharaja attained an age suitable for his joining a public school in England (she had said she wanted to enter him at Eton or Harrow when he was 12 years of age) it might be found possible to allow her husband to accompany her to England, provided his conduct in the interval was such as to satisfy the Government that his heart was really changed and that no detriment was likely to result from his association with the boy during holidays.

The Maharani said that she would think and talk things over, and decided for the present to remain in Mussoorie with the children.

On the question of allowances, Fitzpatrick suggested to the Maharani that the entire amount of 15,000 rupees a month could be credited to a fund and she could have unconditional control over 6,000 rupees, but for abnormal expenditure it would be necessary to have Fitzpatrick's approval. The advisers of the Maharani welcomed the scheme but she was very firm. All that Fitzpatrick could get from her was 'her word of honour as a lady' that the allowance of 15,000 rupees a month would be spent only on herself and her children and the amount unspent would be saved for the younger children. Fitzpatrick reported:

> We have now an opportunity of climbing down gracefully by accepting her word of honour and thus ending a situation which is most objectionable and liable to be misunderstood.

The Maharani and the children were living with her parents, which was undignified for the Nabha state and unfair to her only brother, Sardar Ranbir Singh, whose patrimony was thus being eaten away.[15]

In her letter to the Viceroy, the Maharani underscored that 'as a Hindu wife I would first share the sorrows and troubles of my wronged husband'. If the Tikka was kept away from his father, it would add to the punishment already meted out to him 'on the groundless and unfair charge that he was disloyal to His Imperial Majesty the King-Emperor'. The Maharani hoped to have an early opportunity to make His Excellency's acquaintance.[16] The Viceroy appreciated her feelings, but harped on the welfare of the young Maharaja. Every care should be exercised in fitting him for the very responsible position as the ruler of Nabha. The Maharani should understand the Viceroy's reluctance to modify the advice he had already conveyed through Fitzpatrick. 'But I shall be very glad to talk things over with you, should you see your way to pay a visit to Simla.' Other subjects like the future arrangements for the Maharani and the younger children could be discussed at that time.[17] A copy of this letter was sent to Fitzpatrick.[18] The first round had gone well for the paramount power.

The Issue of Education of the Minor Maharaja

Towards the end of June 1928, Maharaja Ripudaman Singh sent a cable to the Labour MP Graham-Pole in London, asking him to save the situation by taking 'all necessary steps to secure immediate restoration to me of my wife and five children'.[19] At the end of July, the Secretary of State sent a telegram to the Viceroy that Major Graham-Pole wanted to visit India to consult the Maharaja of Nabha as his solicitor.[20] The Viceroy replied a week later that there was no probability whatever that any useful purpose would be served by his visit to India. It would be better to dissuade him from carrying out his intention.[21] A telegram from the 'Maharaja of Nabha' for Maharani Sarojini Devi, sent wrongly to Nabha, indicated that she was thinking of going to Kodaikanal.[22] Two weeks later, Miss Dickinson, the governess, informed Fitzpatrick that the Maharani would leave for Kodaikanal in about three weeks. Her idea was to spend the cold weather in Kodaikanal and proceed to England in the spring. Fitzpatrick was inclined to think that the Maharani earnestly wanted to join her husband, and there was no point in making any further protest: it would be 'undignified and useless as all that can be said has been said'. He was confident, however, that she was keen to educate her son in England and to do so she must eventually appeal to the government. That would be the time to dictate terms.[23]

Viceroy Iwrin wrote a private letter to the Secretary of State, the Earl of Birkenhead, explaining the situation briefly:

> It seems probable that, if she carries out her intention, the ex-Maharaja will soon grow weary of the extra expense which her presence and that of her children will entail; and the Maharani herself is likely to suffer a further disillusionment after a brief sojourn at Kodaikanal. She appears to be anxious that the young Maharaja should go to England for his education next spring, and in this case she will have to apply to Government for assistance which ought to give us an effective opportunity of coming in. My information about the lady leads me to believe that she is genuinely anxious to do the best for the boy, and to work with Government, but also very naturally anxious not to incur criticism as a disloyal wife. But I shall be surprised if, as time goes on, the interests of her son do not loom larger for her than anything else.[24]

This letter could assure the Secretary of State that there was nothing to worry about the Nabha affairs.

However, the illness of Tikka Partap Singh, who had been 'fretting over his father', induced Maharani Sarojini Devi to seriously consider joining her husband with all the children. She wrote to the Viceroy that her visit to him depended on the release of her husband without whom she could not avail herself of the Viceroy's kind invitation. If His Excellency was pleased to release him she would certainly accompany him and have the pleasure of meeting Lord and Lady Irwin.[25] Lord Irwin did not take long to reply to this letter. All that he said was: 'I have received Your Highness' letter of 27 August 1928. I regret to learn of the decision at which your Highness has arrived.'[26] The brevity of this letter and its tone conveyed an unmistakable disapproval. Fitzpatrick was informed that if the Maharani decided to join her husband at Kodaikanal with her family, her own allowance was to be discontinued.[27]

Meanwhile, Sir Chimanlal Setalvad tried persistently to persuade the Political Secretary to the Viceroy that the Tikka might be allowed to go to Kodaikanal for a short time as a compromise. Finally, it was made absolutely clear that the Maharani must choose between her husband and her son now or later. The minor Maharaja would not be allowed to go to Kodaikanal. Watson did not recommend the use of force to prevent the Maharani from taking the minor Maharaja to

Kodaikanal, but he felt sure that she was not so foolish as to defy us: 'If she did so she would be given to understand clearly that whatever might be the result of her visit there would be no question of concessions either to her or the Maharaja.'[28] The Maharani proved not to be so foolish as to defy the wishes of the government. The bureaucrats won the second round.

Bhagwan Das of the CID reported that the Akali papers threatened to start agitation if the minor Maharaja was removed from the influence of his parents. The *Akālī* of 7 August 1929 stated that the Maharani of Nabha had already received a letter about the appointment of a Christian tutor to the young Maharaja, and there was a proposal to send him to one of the Chiefs' Colleges, which had gained unenviable reputation. This scheme might have been devised by the Maharaja of Patiala to divert attention from him. The *Akālī* was obviously informed of the correspondence that had been passing between the Maharani and Fitzpatrick. 'All the correspondence appeared to have been passed by her to the Maharaja, and his agents were constantly in touch with the Akali circles', said the CID report.[29]

The *Akālī* of 26 August 1929 asserted that whatever was done against the Nabha family had been done with the help of Maharaja Bhupinder Singh and in consultation with him. The bureaucracy was trying to place the Tikka 'under the influence of itself and Christians'. The 'house of Nabha would permanently go out of Sikhism' with the steps now proposed to be taken. The Sikhs would not tolerate it. The struggle for getting justice done to Nabha should not be considered to have ended. The Sikhs had not forgotten what happened to Maharaja Dalip Singh. The Tikka had already been separated from his father, and the intention of the government was to separate him from his mother too. She should have the full charge of the Tikka and give him whatever education she liked.[30]

On 6 September 1929, the Viceroy sent a telegram to the Secretary of State in response to his telegram of 2 September, in which the question of 'amelioration of conditions attaching to ex-Maharaja's internment' was raised. This question was intimately linked with the education of the minor Maharaja. The Maharani was in regular correspondence with the Maharaja at Kodaikanal about the Tikka's education and improvement in the Maharaja's situation. It was absolutely necessary that action in the matter should depend on satisfactory settlement of the question of education. It was essential to keep the boy away from the evil influence of his father, and if concessions were made unconditionally the Maharani might take the boy with her to Kodaikanal. Then it would be extremely difficult to get him away without resort to force, and forcible measures 'would arouse agitation of a serious nature, and perhaps even among loyal Sikhs, and most certainly among disaffected classes of Sikhs'.[31]

Watson told Sir Chimanlal on 17 November that the government would be willing to give the Maharaja an enlarged sphere of liberty by letting him go to Madras during the cold weather if the Maharani was willing either to take the young Maharaja to England at once for his education or to place him at one of the Chiefs' Colleges other than Lahore. The concession given to the Maharaja could be withdrawn in the event of his 'misbehaviour'. If neither of these two courses was acceptable to the Maharani then 'we had fully determined to take the boy ourselves, appoint a guardian for him and send him to one of the Chiefs' Colleges except Lahore'. The Viceroy was going to write to the Maharani on these lines and to tell her lawyer so that he could use his influence to make the lady 'reasonable'.[32]

On 19 November 1929, Lord Irwin wrote to Maharani Sarojini Devi about the education of the minor Maharaja:

> If Your Highness is ready to fall in with my wishes either by taking the boy to England at once or completing arrangements for placing him at a Chiefs' College in consultation with my Agent in the Punjab States, then I should be prepared to consider granting to your husband, the ex-Maharaja, greater freedom of movement and allowing him to spend the cold weather in Madras, subject of course to his continued good behaviour.

The Viceroy very much hoped that the Maharani would meet the wishes of the government.

> If however you are unwilling, I must make it plain, that in view of the fact that your son is now 10 years old, I shall be constrained to take other measures in the discharge of my responsibility for his education.

This was followed by the Viceroy's telegram to the Secretary of State that 'it would be worthwhile offering ex-Maharaja's conditional transfer to Madras during the winter months in consideration for cooperation of Maharani in education of her son, thus avoiding possible necessity for adoption of forcible measures to remove him from under her charge'.[33]

On 10 January 1930, Maharani Sarojini Devi wrote to Lord Irwin that her feeling from the outset was that education of the Tikka was 'the sacred duty of his own parents'. What had absorbed all her thoughts and feelings was her husband and the father of their children. The settlement of the question of her husband 'shall settle all other questions automatically'. She had strong and valid objections against her children going to any Chiefs' College in India. She hoped that the requirements of the situation would be met adequately if she were to send the Tikka to the Woodstock College in Mussoorie 'where I also had partly received my education before proceeding to England for further studies'. The institution was under a European management. The boy would be under her personal supervision as well.[34]

Lord Irwin had a long interview with the Maharani on 10 March 1930. She appealed to his sense of justice for fair treatment of her husband who was passionately loyal to the British Crown. The Viceroy told her that the Maharaja's attitude was very different in his relations with the Government of India. Nevertheless, 'if we reached agreement about the education arrangements for her son', he was willing to accord greater liberty to the Maharaja within the Madras Presidency, subject to his good behaviour. The Maharani was now thinking of St Joseph's College at Naini Tal for the education of the Tikka. The Viceroy favoured England, but he was willing to give a trial to the Maharani's proposal. He attached importance to an English tutor for his 'friendly' influence upon the boy's character and his future feeling towards the government. Furthermore,

> We should be willing to give her the additional Rs. 9,000 a month as from the time that we reached agreement about the educational arrangements, and on the understanding that she did not make the money available to her husband.

The Maharani readily accepted this proposition. She asked whether it would not be possible 'for her and him and all the family to go to England forthwith'. The Viceroy was doubtful 'whether this would be feasible'. She wanted to know if she would be allowed to take the boy and the other children to see their father in December. She was willing to give any assurance about returning to Dehra Dun and Mussoorie in March 1931.[35]

In reply to a private letter from the Labour Secretary of State, W. Wedgwood Benn, Irwin clarified in August 1930 that the qualification of good behaviour for the Maharaja's 'enlargement' had not been fulfilled. Fitzpatrick's enquiry into the *Indictment* had revealed objectionable activities of the Maharaja, and it was not possible 'to grant him any concession'. In fact, the Viceroy was thinking of reducing his allowance at this time.³⁶ In September, Maharani Sarojini Devi again raised the issue of the release of her husband.³⁷ Lord Irwin gave a categorical reply to the Maharani.

> I can hold out no hope whatever that the ex-Maharaja will be reinstated in the position which he has forfeited. His release from detention is also at present impossible, and any question of relaxation of the existing conditions of his detention will have to depend upon the extent to which he can satisfy Government that he would not misuse it.

Lord Irwin then expressed his fervent hope that the young Maharaja would take his rightful place upon the gaddī of his ancestors 'after he had received that careful training for which we are both striving'.³⁸

Another interview between the Viceroy and Maharani Sarojini Devi took place at Dehra Dun on 26 October 1930. He had already made up his mind to allow 15,000 rupees a month but not to give arrears. The bureaucracy still suspected that the money given to the Maharani would be used by the Maharaja for his own political purposes. With regard to the Maharaja's position, the Viceroy repeated that when his conduct no longer gave the government any cause for complaint, a new situation would arise in which he would be glad to consider the possibility of his 'enlargement', though he could never contemplate his return to Nabha. Irwin assured the Maharani that she had no cause to fear molestation from Patiala and that her husband's only course of wisdom was to drop his anti-Patiala activities. The whole interview was quite friendly and the impression gathered by the Viceroy was that the Maharani was genuinely anxious to do her best for the Tikka and that she was putting up requests on behalf of her husband 'with no great conviction'.³⁹ This change in the Maharani's attitude came about after the failure of the indictment of the Maharaja of Patiala.

Public Entry of the Minor Maharaja in Nabha

For about a year and a half a few individuals in India and England tried to intercede on behalf of Maharaja Ripudaman Singh, such as K. V. Ramaswamy Iyengar, Sir Chimanlal Setalvad, Vijiaraghavachariar, and A. Fenner Brockway (an anti-war activist and Labour MP), but without any result.

On 28 February 1932 Fitzpatrick reported that the senior Maharani and the Tikka were in Lahore to discuss the possibilities of their visit to Europe. The Maharaja had been sending her reply-paid telegrams from Kodaikanal, complaining of her relations with the government and entreating her to join him. She was 'much worried' and had come to the conclusion that time had come for 'finally breaking with him'. Fitzpatrick could hardly contain his satisfaction at this 'very desirable development'. He knew very well that it was the result of 'patient and sympathetic effort' of four years.[40] Writing to the India Office early in March about the intended visit of the Maharani of Nabha with the minor Maharaja Partap Singh and his uncle, Sardar Ranbir Singh, Fitzpatrick underlined its importance: 'This means a final break with the ex-Maharaja—a consummation for which we have long hoped and worked and I should like Her Highness to be well pleased with her visit.' The Fitzpatricks were to travel with her. He asked the political ADC to arrange for Her Highness' attendance at all the Court and society functions to which ruling princes were asked and include his wife and himself in those which he thought suitable.[41]

The Maharani and the minor Maharaja returned to India in September 1932. The visit to England had been most successful. Their Highnesses were particularly pleased at being privately received by Their Majesties at the Buckingham Palace. They were received at Bombay with the usual ceremony on behalf of the Nabha Council of Regency by Sardar Bahadur Gurdial Singh, Home Member. He escorted them to Dehra Dun from where they proceeded to their residence in Mussoorie. Fitzpatrick felt gratified:

> This is the first occasion since the accession of the minor Maharaja that Her Highness has recognized or had dealings with the Council and it augers well for her future relations with the minority administration.

Sardar Bahadur Gurdial Singh was gratified and reassured by his friendly reception at Bombay, because he had been charged with disloyalty to the Maharaja 'owing to his having cast in his lot with our administration'.[42]

The Maharani's visit to England was important in another way too. Considerable anxiety and inconvenience had been caused to her by the emissaries of the Maharaja who shadowed her. The Maharani was so alarmed that the aid of the Scotland Yard was sought through the India Office. Their discreet enquiries revealed that two men had been employed by a private enquiry agent at the instance of the Tikka's father to follow him and the Maharani for the purpose of seeing with whom they associated but not to cause any harm to either of them. The Maharani was most anxious now that no relaxation was granted to Maharaja Ripudaman Singh. 'In fact she regarded Kodaikanal as dangerously near and had more than once mentioned Burma as a more suitable residence for the ex-Maharaja.'[43] She finally cut the Gordian knot and agreed to Partap Singh's visit to Nabha to hold a Darbar against the known wishes of her husband.[44]

Almost five years after the detention of his father, the young Maharaja made a public entry into Nabha on 14 February 1933. He was accompanied by Fitzpatrick and Diwan Gyan Nath, President of the Council of Regeney. The entire town was 'en fete' and the route from the railway station to the fort was most tastefully decorated with triumphal arches, flags, buntings, and mottoes of welcome. The young Maharaja came in a motor car with Fitzpatrick sitting on his left and Diwan Gyan Nath in front. On the day following, the Maharaja held Darbar in the old Diwān Khāna where his ancestors had held Darbars. In addition to the leading officials and non-officials of the state, the Darbaris, jāgīrdārs, *biswedārs* (persons entitled to a share in the produce from land owned by another), zaildārs, and lambardārs attended in large numbers. The President of the Council of Regency read an address of welcome in which the surplus budgets of the state were highlighted. In the afternoon the young Maharaja visited the samādh of his grandfather and the other royal samādhs in Nabha. On 17 February, he reviewed the Nabha troops when the artillery fired a salute of 13 guns and the state flag was unfurled. On 18 and 19 February, shooting was arranged for the young Maharaja in two of the Nabha Bīrs (reserved forests). On 25 February he visited the Jind Field Trials at Sangrur, where the Maharajas of Patiala and Jind were delighted to meet him and performed the sarwārna ceremony. The newspaper reports refer to the meeting of the three Maharajas at Sangrur as a memorable event 'in the history of the Phulkian States'.[45]

Criticism of the Maharani in the Press

The *Khālsā* of Lahore struck a note of criticism, expressing the view that during the minority administration, the management of the state should be either in the hands of the Maharani herself, who was 'an enlightened and a cultured lady', or in the hands of an eminent Sikh instead of Diwan Gyan Nath. A Sikh prince should be brought up in an atmosphere consistent with his religious principles. The cases of the Sikh states of Patiala, Kapurthala, Jind, and Kalsia demonstrated that the neglect of this principle had led to disaster. No Sikh could feel proud about them. The *Khālsā* was not happy about the meeting of Maharaja Partap Singh with the Maharajas of Patiala and Jind. Everyone knew what kind of Sikhs they were. The Tikka should not follow in their footsteps; he should preserve the tradition of Nabha as the 'Guru's House'.[46]

An article in the *Akālī Samāchār* of 1 March 1933 was more comprehensive in criticism. It talked of the treachery, deceit, and fraud of the Maharani of Nabha towards her husband as a painful episode for the entire country. Maharani Sarojini Devi was referred to as the second Rani Jindan of the Sikh Panth. In fact, she behaved worse than Rani Jindan, who had done no wrong at least in the lifetime of her husband. At the instigation of Maharaja Bhupinder Singh, she had returned to Nabha along with the Tikka Sahib to be received by the disloyal officers of the state, like 'Gurdialu' (Sardar Bahadur Gurdial Singh, Home Member). 'Even if the whole world had betrayed the Maharaja, it was not proper for the Maharani to betray her dear husband, who was passing the days of his misery in exile.' She had abandoned the 'self-respecting jewel of the Sikh Panth' and taken residence in his palaces. The *Akālī Samāchār* denounced the Sikh leaders who had pledged themselves before the Akal Takht to the cause of the Maharaja of Nabha and abandoned it subsequently on account of their greed and dishonesty. All this had happened primarily due to the intrigues of the Maharaja of Patiala.

This 'highly offensive' article was brought to the notice of Diwan Gyan Nath who wrote to the Secretary to the AGG that a scurrilous attack had been made on the Maharani of Nabha and the Maharaja of Patiala with the object of bringing both the Houses 'into hatred and contempt with the Sikh population, both inside and outside the Phulkian States, and to excite disaffection towards them'. As the Nabha Darbar was unable to take any action against this paper, the Council of Regency requested the AGG to address the Punjab Government on this subject so that an appropriate action was taken against the management of the *Akālī Samāchār*. Diwan Gyan Nath hoped that deterrent action would be taken urgently in this case in view of 'the close co-operation shown by the Nabha Administration consistently with the Punjab Government in the suppression of political agitation and of undesirable movements subversive of law and order'.[47]

On instruction from Maharani Sarojini Devi, a cutting from the *Pāras* of Lahore, dated 23 April 1933, was brought to the notice of Diwan Gyan Nath.[48] As a lead article on the Maharaja of Nabha and his wife, it underlined the senior Maharani's infidelity towards her husband and her regrettable excess of freedom. The senior Maharani had defied her husband and turned faithless and treacherous towards him, snatching from him his dear child. She went to Nabha against her husband's wishes and joined hands with his worst enemies. Equally indefensible were the life of unrestricted freedom and the course of fearlessness which she had pursued after her separation from the Maharaja. Whereas the Maharaja was a strict adherent of Indian culture, the Maharani was behaving like English women. The writer of the article exhorted the Sikh Panth to do something 'to show the right path to this defiant woman' who had betrayed her husband and brought disgrace on a Sikh royal family. The whole issue involved the honour of 'that beloved leader of the Sikhs, who in spite of having been deprived of his crown and Gaddi, was still a servant of the Panth and a beloved of the Sikh Nation'. The writer pointed out that the senior Maharani was instigated by Fitzpatrick, who had encouraged her to desert her husband to give Western education to her son. His role as a responsible British officer was deplorable. It was the duty of the highly placed officers of the Government of India 'to extricate Tikka Sahib from the clutches of the Maharani and hand him over to the Maharaja who may make suitable arrangements for his education'. The increasing tension between the father in exile and the son on the throne was not conducive to the good of the state.[49]

The Punjab Government thought that this article was probably inspired by Maharaja Ripudaman Singh, who was known 'to have spent in the past large sums on propaganda of this nature'. The most effective means of stopping such articles was to warn the Maharaja that if they continued to appear the government would have to consider the question of reducing his allowance. For doing this, however, it was necessary to establish the connection between the Maharaja and the articles appearing in various papers. At the same time, detailed information on visitors to Kodaikanal could be collected to strengthen the suspicions against the Maharaja in order to justify the case for reducing his allowance.

'Objectionable' articles appeared in the *Desh Darpan* too. It was edited by Niranjan Singh, who at one time was a personal servant (*nafar*) of Maharaja Ripudaman Singh and was married to the widow of Maharani Sarojini Devi's brother. This appeared to confirm the view that such articles were inspired by the Maharaja of Nabha.[50] On 9 May 1933 the Council of Regency passed a resolution with regard to the 'propaganda of a scurrilous nature in a section of the Vernacular Press against the ruling house of Nabha'. It stated that articles of this nature had begun to appear since the return of the Maharani and the young Maharaja to Nabha. The specific examples of the *Akālī Samāchār* and the *Pāras* were cited. The Council members had no doubt in their mind that the person responsible for this propaganda was Maharaja Ripudaman Singh, as suggested by the Punjab Government. The resolution underlined that the young Maharaja's return to the state had been welcomed by its Sikh and non-Sikh subjects and by the Sikhs of the Punjab. The only person who could feel sore in this situation was the Maharaja, whose hopes of reviving the Nabha question had vanished. Nothing had incensed him more than the return of the Maharani and the young Maharaja of Nabha against his will. 'Moreover, the defection of the Maharani Sahiba and the young Maharaja from his cause leaves the ex-Maharaja as an isolated individual with no support even from his family in his foolish notions regarding the justness of his case.' It was suggested that the present campaign was motivated by a feeling of revenge; it was also an attempt to create sympathy among the Sikhs for his lost cause. The Maharani in her anxiety for future peace wisely permitted her son to meet the Maharaja of Patiala to obviate the feud going down to another generation. However, the Maharaja of Nabha regarded the Maharaja of Patiala as his inveterate enemy. That the article in the *Akālī Samāchār* was orchestrated by him was evident from the contemptuous term 'Bhupa' used for Maharaja Bhupinder Singh. This was 'a pet word' of Maharaja Ripudaman Singh.

The articles published in the *Desh Darpan*, edited by Niranjan Singh, left no doubt that this was done 'at the bidding of his master'. Indeed, the *Desh Darpan* owed its existence to the Maharaja and it had been created by him to further his propaganda. Since it was not possible to launch prosecution against the managers and editors of the vernacular papers concerned, the only effective way of stopping the campaign was to cut off the source which fed the newspapers. The Council requested the AGG to approach the Government of India for reducing the allowance of Maharaja Ripudaman Singh. The conditions in which the allowance was originally given and subsequently reduced had changed further by his disloyal activities. As a political detainee, he was entitled only to a reasonable subsistence allowance. Therefore, the Council requested that the position might now be reexamined and his allowance reduced to a sum which would suffice for his legitimate requirements. The Council further requested that arrangements might be made for the secret censorship of all correspondence of the Maharaja, and for the supply of information on all persons who met him at Kodaikanal from time to time.[51]

The 'Nabha Number' of the *Desh Darpan* was published on 9 July 1933, with a few poems contrasting the position of the Maharaja of Nabha as the ruler of a state and a prisoner in Kodaikanal. Unlike Maharaja Bhupinder Singh, he refused to humiliate himself before the enemy and subserve the bureaucracy. The only fault of the Maharaja of Nabha was his love for the True Guru and the Panth. He was the flag-bearer of freedom. He was a born patriot, and the government was determined to ruin him sooner or later. He was held responsible for the Akali and the Babbar Akali movements. The government used the Maharaja of Patiala as their tool to force the Maharaja of Nabha to abdicate. The Jaito Morcha was launched to get the Maharaja reinstated but the Akali leaders eventually compromised with the government. Maharani Sarojini Devi betrayed him to safeguard the interests of her son. Looking upon her son as the Maharaja, she did not join her husband. Against his wishes, she went to England and, without his knowledge, to Nabha. Apart from a few fearless papers, none had condemned the Maharani's actions. The well-wishers of the Maharaja were threatened as his agents. The Khalsa Panth should not have betrayed Maharaja Ripudaman Singh after its pledge before the Guru.

In connection with the 'Nabha Day', a diwān was held in Calcutta at which a poem addressed to the Khalsa Panth depicted the plight of the Maharaja of Nabha, the injustice done to him, and the need for his restoration. An article in prose called for help to those who had suffered banishment for the cause of the Maharaja. The senior Maharani did not care about them because of their sympathy with the Maharaja. It was the duty of the Panth to care for these 'live-martyrs'. The 'Nabha Jilawatan Parwar Sahaik Committee' (Committee for Aiding the Nabha Family in Exile) should be given all possible help. Another article described the sad situation of the Maharaja in exile and asked the Panth not to ignore this issue any longer. In the frightening hills of Kodaikanal not even an animal of the Punjab could be seen. The Panth should remember its pledge to support the cause of the Maharaja. There was also a cartoon in the *Desh Darpan* bringing the Maharaja of Patiala into ridicule. A poem entitled 'His Master's Voice' referred to the Maharaja of Patiala as 'Dhuta Bhup' who was at the root of the whole problem as a tool in the hands of his British masters.[52]

Another article published in the *Desh Darpan* of 3 August stated that the Government of India were going to put restrictions on the correspondence of the Maharaja and his interviews on the plea that he had written some letters to his well-wishers in England against Lord Willingdon and the Political Department of the Government of India. The Maharaja of Patiala was bent upon ruining him utterly because he had not bent before the Maharaja of Patiala in spite of all his excesses.

Diwan Gyan Nath did not succeed in getting the Maharaja's allowance reduced. The Nabha administration began to keep record of the visitors from the Nabha state to Kodaikanal and proclaimed that no Nabha subject should visit Maharaja Ripudaman Singh without prior permission from the state authorities. The Government of India began to keep a record of the visitors to Kodaikanal and to censor the correspondence of the Maharaja.[53] The Nabha administration under the Council of Regency appears to have become more hostile to Maharaja Ripudaman Singh than ever before. This could be a reflection of the changed attitude of Maharani Sarojini Devi towards her husband.

Notes

1. India Office Records (IOR) (microfilm), R/1/1/1996, File no. 694-P (secret) / 1927, copy of letter from the Viceroy to the Maharani Sahiba of Nabha, handed over to her by the AGG at Dehra Dun on 19 February 1928.
2. IOR, R/1/1/1996, no. 694-P(S)/1927, Maharani Sarojini Devi to Lord Irwin, 22 February 1928.
3. IOR, R/1/1/1996, no. 694-P(S)/1927, AGG J. A. O. Fitzpatrick's report.
4. IOR, R/1/1/1996, no. 694-P(S)/1927, Lord Irwin to Maharani Sarojini Devi, 27 February 1928.
5. IOR (microfilm), R/1/1/1719, File no. 97-P (secret)/1928, AGG to the Maharani of Nabha, 9 March 1928.
6. IOR, R/1/1/1719, no. 97-P(S)/1928, the Maharani of Nabha to the AGG, 19 March 1928.
7. IOR, R/1/1/1719, no. 97-P(S)/1928, AGG to the Maharani of Nabha, 26 March 1928.
8. IOR, R/1/1/1719, no. 97-P(S)/1928, the Maharani of Nabha to the AGG, 5 April 1928.

9. IOR, R/1/1/1719, no. 97-P(S)/1928, Fitzpatrick to C. C. Watson (Political Secretary to the Government of India), 10 April 1928.
10. IOR, R/1/1/1719, no. 97-P(S)/1928, Watson to Fitzpatrick, 26 April 1928.
11. IOR, R/1/1/1719, no. 97-P(S)/1928, Fitzpatrick to Watson.
12. IOR, R/1/1/1719, no. 97-P(S)/1928, note by Watson on his meeting with Sir Chimanlal Setalvad on 29 May 1928.
13. IOR, R/1/1/1719, no. 97-P(S)/1928, verbal message by B. J. Glancy to Fitzpatrick, recorded on 13 June 1928.
14. IOR, R/1/1/1719, no. 97-P(S)/1928, B. J. Glancy's note, dated 23 June 1928.
15. IOR, R/1/1/1719, no. 97-P(S)/1928, Fitzpatrick to B. J. Glancy, 29 June 1928.
16. IOR, R/1/1/1719, no. 97-P(S)/1928, Maharani Sarojini Devi to the Viceroy, 2 July 1928.
17. IOR, R/1/1/1719, no. 97-P(S)/1928, Lord Irwin to the Maharani of Nabha, 11 July 1928.
18. IOR, R/1/1/1719, no. 97-P(S)/1928, W. G. Neale to Fitzpatrick, 14 July 1928.
19. IOR R/1/1/1764(2), copy of a cablegram from the ex-Maharaja of Nabha to Major Graham-Pole, dated 29 June 1928.
20. IOR, R/1/1/1719, no. 97-P(S)/1928, telegram from Secretary of State for India to Viceroy, dated 31 July 1928.
21. IOR, R/1/1/1719, no. 97-P(S)/1928, telegram from Viceroy to Secretary of State, dated 6 August 1928.
22. IOR, R/1/1/1719, no. 97-P(S)/1928, letter from the AGG's office to B. J. Glancy, 26 July 1928.
23. IOR, R/1/1/1719, no. 97-P(S)/1928, Fitzpatrick to Glancy, 11 August 1928.
24. IOR, R/1/1/1719, no. 97-P(S)/1928, extract from a private letter from the Viceroy to the Earl of Birkenhead (Secretary of State for India), dated 23 August 1928.
25. IOR, R/1/1/1719, no. 97-P(S)/1928, Maharani Sarojini Devi to Lord Irwin, 27 August 1928.
26. IOR, R/1/1/1719, no. 97-P(S)/1928, Lord Irwin to the Maharani of Nabha, 6 September 1928.
27. IOR, R/1/1/1719, no. 97-P(S)/1928, Neale to Fitzpatrick, 10 September 1928.
28. IOR, R/1/1/1719, no. 97-P(S)/1928, 'Polindia' to the Viceroy in Camp.
29. IOR, R/1/1/1719, no. 97-P(S)/1928, note by Bhagwan Das, dated 20 August 1929.
30. IOR, R/1/1/1719, no. 97-P(S)/1928, report from Sub-Inspector Dhian Singh.
31. IOR, R/1/1/1764(2), telegram from Viceroy to Secretary of State for India, dated 6 September 1929.

32. IOR, R/1/1/1764(2), Watson's note on his interview with Sir Chimanlal Setalvad, dated 17 November 1929.
33. IOR, R/1/1/1764(2), Lord Irwin to the Maharani of Nabha, 19 November 1929.
34. IOR R/1/1/1896, Maharani Sarojini Devi to the Viceroy, 10 January 1930.
35. IOR R/1/1/1896, Lord Irwin's notes, dated 10 March 1930.
36. IOR (microfilm), R/1/1/1881, File no. 390-P (secret)/1930, G. Cunningham to Wilberforce-Bell, 12 August 1930, with an extract from a letter of Secretary of State to Viceroy.
37. IOR, R/1/1/1881, no. 390-P(S)/1930, Maharani Sarojini Devi to the Viceroy, 10 September 1930.
38. IOR, R/1/1/1881, no. 390-P(S)/1930, Lord Irwin to the Maharani of Nabha, 20 September 1930.
39. IOR, R/1/1/1881, no. 390-P(S)/1930, Lord Irwin's note of the Maharani's interview with him, dated 26 October 1930.
40. National Archives of India (NAI), New Delhi, Crown Representative Records (CRR) (microfilm), Accession no. 14, Reel no. 9, File no. 182-P (secret)/1932, Fitzpatrick to Watson, 28 February 1932.
41. NAI, CRR, Reel no. 9, no. 182-P(S)/1932, Fitzpatrick to Colonel S. B. Patterson (Political ADC, India Office), 7 March 1932.
42. NAI, CRR, Reel no. 9, no. 182-P(S)/1932, Fitzpatrick to Glancy, 28 September 1932.
43. NAI, CRR, Reel no. 9, no. 182-P(S)/1932, Fitzpatrick to Glancy, 15 October 1932.
44. PSA, Patiala, PCRNS Records, File no. 29, extract from the *Shujaat*.
45. PSA, PCRNS Records, no. 29, extracts from *The Hindustan Times*, dated 16 Feb. 1933; *Central India Times*, dated 22 Feb 1933; *Civil and Military Gazette*, dated 23 February 1933; *The Tribune*, dated 2 March 1933.
46. Punjab State Archives (PSA), Patiala, President, Council of Regency Nabha State (PCRNS) Records, no. 29, extracts from *The Khālsā*, dated 16 February and 2 March 1933.
47. PSA, PCRNS Records, no. 46, translation in English and transcription in Urdu of an article from the *Akālī Samāchār*, dated 1 March 1933.
48. PSA, PCRNS Records, no. 46, note dated 4 March 1933 and confidential letter of Diwan Gyan Nath to Secretary to the AGG, 4 March 1933.
49. PSA, PCRNS Records, no. 49, letter from A. G. Dix to Diwan Gyan Nath, 25 April 1933, with enclosures.
50. PSA, PCRNS Records, no. 49, cutting from the *Pāras* of Lahore, dated 23 April 1933, and its translation in English.
51. PSA, PCRNS Records, no. 46, Diwan Gyan Nath to C. L. Griffin, 9 May 1933.
52. PSA, PCRNS Records, no. 46, resolution passed by the Council of Regency on 9 May 1933.

53. PSA, PCRNS Records, no. 46, cuttings from the *Desh Darpan*.
54. PSA, PCRNS Records, no. 46, Diwan Gyan Nath to Griffin, 2 September 1933; translation of the article published in the *Desh Darpan* of 3 August 1933; its transcription in Urdu and the original cutting; note by Diwan Gyan Nath, dated 25 September 1933.

13

THE NABHA ISSUE IN THE HOUSE OF COMMONS

Nabha affairs figured in the House of Commons from time to time, beginning with the issue of the Anand Marriage Act in 1911–12. An important round of questions appeared in the House of Commons in 1928 when Maharaja Ripudaman Singh was taken to Kodaikanal as a political prisoner. The second round lasted longer, from 1934 to 1938. All these years the Maharaja was at Kodaikanal under detention. The Members of Parliament who tried to get concessions for the Maharaja belonged mostly to the Labour Party. They found at the end that the Government of India could not be induced to change the decisions it had taken.

When Maharaja Ripudaman Singh was taken to Kodaikanal, the Imperial Legislative Assembly happened to be in session. Sardar Gulab Singh gave notice of a motion of adjournment for the purpose of discussing the arrest and deportation of the Maharaja. He argued that Ripudaman Singh was no longer a Maharaja of any state. Therefore, the House should discuss his detention in British India. The Foreign Secretary, Sir Denys Bray, contended that the motion could not be taken up because no resolution could be moved in regard to any matter affecting the relations of the government with any prince or chief under the suzerainty of His Majesty, or relating to the affairs of any such chief, or to the territory of any such prince or chief. Maharaja Ripudaman Singh was a prince or chief under the suzerainty of His Majesty when action was taken with regard to him, and it affected the administration of the territory of 'the Present Prince or Chief'.

Diwan Chaman Lal put forth the view that international law recognized that the relations of suzerain and vassal disappeared in certain situations, as in the present. The Maharaja of Nabha could no longer be considered a vassal of the British Government. S. Srinivasa Iyengar supported the view that Ripudaman Singh was not a prince or chief at the time of his arrest and deportation. Therefore, the motion was fully in order. Arthur Moore contended that the proposition was absolutely untenable because any discussion of the fate or fortunes of the ex-Maharaja of Nabha concerned the relations of the Government of India with 'the existing Maharaja of Nabha and the State of Nabha'. Pandit Madan Mohan Malaviya ridiculed this contention and argued that the Maharaja could not be denied 'the ordinary courtesy and protection which the laws of this land give to every subject of His Majesty'.

However, Vitthalbhai J. Patel, President of the Assembly, supported the view that the House could not discuss the motion without raising a debate on the relations between the Government of India and the ex-Maharaja of Nabha, who since his deportation had 'ceased' to be a prince or chief. The subject matter of the motion might not contravene the letter but it did contravene the spirit of rule 23. He went on to give the ruling:

> I know that during the last two years attempts have been made several times to raise the debate on Nabha affair in some form or other, and I have always disallowed any such debate. I hold, therefore, that in the particular circumstances of the case I should withhold my consent to the making of the motion.[1]

No hopes of any redress could be expected from the legislative bodies in India. The matter was regarded as outside their purview.

Early in April 1928, the Madras Government reported to the Government of India that the Maharaja was corresponding with the Labour Members of Parliament in England and the Swarajist leaders in India. Certain nationalist leaders had met him at Kodaikanal, which might lead to some undesirable agitation in his favour.[2] C. S. Ranga Iyer, member of the Legislative Assembly and author of *Father India*, was said to have been specially engaged in negotiating with the Maharaja to expose the wickedness of the Government of India. Efforts were being made to work up an agitation in England too, and an appeal had been made to the *Daily Herald* for support.[3]

The First Round of Questions

Indeed, questions were raised in the British Parliament in connection with the arrest and internment of Maharaja Ripudaman Singh, presumably as the outcome of his correspondence with Labour Members in England.[4] The Secretary of State for India sent a telegram to the Viceroy that the questions to be raised in the Parliament for 17 April 1928 related inter alia to 'reasons for arrest and detention of ex-Maharaja of Nabha', and whether any charges had been communicated to him, and whether any period for his detention had been fixed. The communiqué of 19 February 1928 did not provide enough information. The Secretary of State wanted to know if he could use the explanation given in the Viceroy's telegram of 10 October 1927. He also wanted to know if 'explanations in general terms could be supported by any explicit instance of disloyal activities'.[5]

The Viceroy sent a prompt reply. The reasons for the detention of the ex-Maharaja of Nabha should be confined to the communiqué of 19 February. If necessary, the general terms in the first paragraph of the Viceroy's telegram of 10 October could be mentioned: attacks on the Government of India and the Maharaja of Patiala, encouragement of the Akali movement, and of disaffection in Nabha. It should also be pointed out that the ex-Maharaja had been plainly committing a breach of the terms on which he was permitted to sever his connection with his state. 'Beyond this I would not go.'

The ex-Maharaja had been officially informed of the facts stated in the communiqué of 19 February immediately after his apprehension, and no period for his detention at Kodaikanal had been fixed. The Maharani was invited to take the young Maharaja to Nabha for his installation but she had chosen to stay at Dehra Dun for the present with her children. The Maharani had, however, agreed to her children being educated under the supervision of the Agent to the Governor General.[6]

The Secretary of State informed the Viceroy of further questions to be answered in Parliament. The Maharaja of Nabha had been arrested under Bengal Regulation III of 1818, which was a Regulation of the Government of India: Why were questions related to this matter forbidden in the Indian Legislative Assembly? Was the ex-Maharaja regarded as a foreigner and, if so, was there anything to prevent his moving for a writ of habeas corpus in a High Court in India for his release, or applying to Privy Council? Was Regulation III of 1818 applicable to the ruling princes or to a prince or chief under the suzerainty of His Majesty? What was the case against the ex-Maharaja, and was it proposed to bring any action in any Indian court? If not, for how long did they intend to deprive him of his liberty without any charge being brought against him? On what grounds could the separation of the ex-Maharaja from his wife and five minor children be defended? Had the ex-Maharani been induced or urged to write or sign any document since his arrest and to what effect?[7]

In reply to all these questions, the Viceroy said that it was presumed that Regulation III of 1818 applied to the Maharaja. He was a subject of an Indian state under the suzerainty of His Majesty. When he severed his connection with his state, he ceased to be a ruling prince. It was not considered necessary to make any pronouncement of deposition in February 1928. He was merely deprived of his rights and dignities. It was not proposed to bring any action in an Indian court. No orders had been passed enjoining separation of the Maharaja from his wife and children. The Maharani had not been induced or urged to sign any document. She had expressed her desire to remain at Dehra Dun for the present with her children in response to the Viceroy's suggestion that she might go to Nabha for the installation of her son.[8] It is interesting to note that the Viceroy had merely presumed that the legal points concerning Ripudaman Singh's detention had been verified with the Legislative Department. The points in question were referred to the Legislative Department for verification after the reply had been sent to the Secretary of State. In the opinion of the Legislative Department, the 'real' deposition had taken place in 1923.[9]

The information and suggestions from the Government of India guided the Under Secretary of State for India, Earl Winterton, in his responses to the questions raised in the House of Commons by the Labour Members in April 1928. Earnest Thurtle, a senior member of the Party who had taken interest in the Maharaja's case earlier also, wanted to know the reasons for the Maharaja of Nabha's arrest and whether any charges had been communicated to him and any period for his imprisonment without trial had been fixed. Winterton replied:

> A condition subject to which the ex-Maharaja of Nabha was permitted in 1923 to sever his connection with the Nabha State was that he would remain subject to the obligations of loyalty and obedience to the British Crown and the Government of India which are imposed on the rulers of Nabha by the Sanad granted to them in 1860. It was also a condition that should the Maharaja fail to fulfil any of the obligations then imposed upon

him, the Government of India would hold itself free to annul or modify any of these conditions. It was after having satisfied themselves that the ex-Maharaja had repeatedly taken part in disloyal activities since his departure from Nabha and having clearly warned him of the consequences that the Government of India deprived him of his title, rights and privileges as Maharaja, and took the action against him referred to by the hon. member. He was informed on his apprehension of the reasons for his detention for which no period has been fixed.

Thurtle argued that no definite charge had been formulated against the Maharaja and he was not being tried. 'Does the noble Lord not think that any man is entitled to have the charges brought against him formulated so that he may have an opportunity of clearing himself?' Winterton replied that the ex-Maharaja had actively engaged in a propaganda associated with notorious agitators, and spent considerable sums on press campaigns in several provinces. In so doing, he had broken the engagement he gave to the Government of India in 1923. Thurtle insisted that it was contrary to the British conception of justice to keep him indefinitely in prison without any trial at all. Winterton stuck to his position, simply reiterating that he was informed on his apprehension of the reasons for his detention, for which no period had been fixed. Mardy Jones, who was a specialist on India, wanted to know whether arrest and detention without any charge had not caused considerable dissatisfaction in India, especially in the Sikh community, of which the Maharaja was the reputed leader. Earl Winterton replied with the characteristic imperialist slant that the only dissatisfaction caused in India had been 'among the notorious and disloyal agitators'.[10]

In the adjournment debate on the following day, Mardy Jones called the attention of the House to the arrest of the Maharaja of Nabha on 19 February and his deportation to south India. The warrant for his arrest was issued under Regulation III of 1818. Its use in the twentieth century was barbaric. No charge was made against the Maharaja and there appeared to be no intention of placing him on trial. Earl Winterton's insinuation that the only dissatisfaction caused in India had been among the notorious and disloyal agitators was 'entirely untrue'. The question was raised in the Legislative Assembly not by notorious and disloyal agitators but by 'some of the most prominent and respected leaders of Indian political opinion'. A motion for adjournment of the House was made by Sardar Gulab Singh. Another man to protest strongly against the action of the

Government of India was Srinivasa Iyengar, who was President of the Indian National Congress in 1926. Another national leader to protest was Pandit Malaviya. Yet another was Lajpat Rai, the leader of the Nationalist Party. Even Sir Hari Singh Gour, who was reputed to be with the government, protested very strongly that this action was illegal. It was evident that there was 'a considerable and growing feeling in India about the injustice of this action'.

Mardy Jones went on to say that the Chamber of Princes at Delhi, like the Legislative Assembly, was powerless to deal with the case because the Government of India opposed its discussion in India. 'They were afraid to face the music and sheltered themselves behind the technicality that the Parliament of India has no jurisdiction over the native States and princes.' The British Parliament, in any case, was responsible for the good governance of British India. It was the duty of the Government of India to prove and not merely to assert, that the Maharaja had been disloyal to the Crown.

> His chief crime appears to have been what is regarded as a virtue in any Britisher. He has refused consistently blind obedience to the political agents of the Viceroy. For the last 20 years he has been persecuted for his independence of mind, and his frank aid of the Nationalist cause in India.[11]

In other words, action against the Maharaja Ripudaman Singh was taken essentially due to his political inclinations and refusal to yield to bureaucratic pressure.

Mardy Jones urged the British Government to reconsider their attitude and make up their mind to state the definite charges of disloyalty they had against the Maharaja and grant him the elementary right of British justice—a fair and open trial. He expected Earl Winterton to answer all his questions. Winterton replied to all the seven questions raised by Jones. The first question was: 'The Maharaja of Nabha having been arrested under Regulation III of 1818, and that being a Regulation of the Government of India, why are questions with regard to the matter forbidden in the Indian Legislative Assembly?' Winterton said that the President of the Assembly had given his ruling on the question. He was not actuated in any way by the attitude of the government. The second question was: 'Is the ex-Maharaja regarded as a foreigner, and, if so, is there anything to prevent his moving for a writ of *habeas corpus* in the High Court in India for his release, or applying to the Privy Council?' Winterton replied that the powers of the High Court in India as to habeas corpus did not apply to persons detained under the Bengal Regulation, and, therefore, the ex-Maharaja could not make an application.

The third question was: 'Will the Under-Secretary of State for India say whether he considers that Regulation III of 1818 is applicable to ruling Princes or to a prince or chief under the suzerainty of His Majesty?' Winterton replied that the ex-Maharaja ceased to be a ruling prince when he severed his connection with the state in 1923. There was, therefore, no question as to his deposition in February 1928. The fourth question was: 'Will the Under-Secretary inform the House of the case against the ex-Maharajah and whether it is proposed to bring any action in any Indian Court?' Winterton said that the Government of India had evidence that the ex-Maharaja had been flagrantly and continually violating the obligation of continued loyalty to the British Government, which he voluntarily gave in 1923, violating thereby the sanad that was given to the ruler of Nabha in 1860. He had been actively engaged in propaganda and spent considerable sums in press campaigns in several provinces; and he had held meetings and demonstrations in various places to arouse public empathy in his favour. All these acts constituted a breach of the undertaking given in 1923. It was not proposed to bring any action against the ex-Maharaja in an Indian Court of Law.

The fifth question was: 'How long is it intended to deprive him of his liberty without any charge being brought against him?' Winterton said that the ex-Maharaja was informed of the facts stated in the communiqué of 19 February 1928. No period had been fixed for his detention, which depended on his future conduct. The sixth question was about the separation of the ex-Maharaja from his wife and five minor children. Winterton replied that the Government of India had passed no order enjoining separation from his wife and children. The Maharani was free, if she so chose, to visit him in his place of detention and to take her children with her. Jones retorted: 'Is there room for them to stay there?'

The last question was: 'Has the Maharanee been induced or urged to write or sign any document since the arrest of her husband, and to what effect?' The answer was that the Maharani had not been induced or urged by the Government of India to sign any document. Winterton added that he had answered all the questions fairly fully in the short time at his disposal. Mardy Jones remarked that many of the replies given were misleading and untrue, and hoped that there would be a further opportunity to discuss the matter. 'The point is, why do you not give this man the opportunity to face the statements which you are making, and rebut them if he can?'

On 26 April, Thurtle asked the Under Secretary of State for India whether the Maharaja of Nabha was regarded by the Government of India as a foreigner or as a British subject, or whether he would define his present status. Winterton's reply simply was that the ex-Maharaja was the subject of an Indian state under the suzerainty of His Majesty.[12] On 30 April, Thurtle asked whether the Government of India or the Secretary of State had any evidence of disloyalty to the Crown on the part of the Maharaja of Nabha. He got the reply that the Government of India were satisfied from evidence in their possession that the ex-Maharaja had repeatedly taken part in disloyal activities since his departure from Nabha. Finally, Thurtle asked if the Noble Lord would be good enough to answer the specific question as to whether 'this ex-Maharaja has been guilty of disloyalty to the crown'. Earl Winterton retorted: 'That is exactly the question which I have answered.'[13]

We can see that all the answers given by the Under Secretary of State for India, including some wrong or evasive statements, were supplied to him by the Government of India. The British Indian bureaucracy was able to speak to the British Parliament through Earl Winterton. The perceptions and decisions of the Government of India were reinforced by the Under Secretary of State for India.

The Second Round

After the Fitzpatrick Enquiry and the installation of Tikka Partap Singh on the gaddī of Nabha in 1933, Maharaja Ripudaman Singh was convinced that London was far more important than Delhi. Early in 1934, he wrote to Sardar Sant Singh, Member, Imperial Legislative Assembly, who was in London:

> Though I am not a lawyer but as a student of History I know that the final authority in the matter lies in London and not in Delhi.

The Maharaja recalled a memorable speech of Lord Morley in the House of Commons in which he said that Parliament was responsible for the good governance of India and the Viceroy carried on the administration under his orders and instructions as the Secretary of State for India. In the case of succession in Bhopal, the Secretary of

State, Lord Birkenhead, had reversed the orders of Viceroy Reading. In another case, a suspended chief was reinstated by a proclamation of His Majesty, the King.[14]

Maharaja Ripudaman Singh decided to concentrate on White Hall to seek justice. Early in May 1934, he engaged a young Bar-at-Law, A. H. Chowrryappah, to secure for him 'relief and full justice'. As spelt out in the Maharaja's letter, Chowrryappah was to work for (*a*) the return of his state and of all movable and immovable properties to him and (*b*) adequate compensation for all his unjust suffering since 1923. Chowrryappah was to secure, first, the pre-internment position and status in each and every respect and, after that, the restoration of the state. His immediate objective was to secure the refund of money 'arbitrarily and unjustly' deducted from the Maharaja's allowance since 1923, with interest or at least without prejudice to arrears due to the Maharaja since his internment.[15]

Chowrryappah sailed for England in June 1934 when the Maharaja was giving his careful consideration to the 'revised draft', presumably of a representation.[16] Three weeks later, he advised Chowrryappah 'under no circumstances' to court 'a negative or unfavourable reply in the Parliament, from the White Hall or otherwise' as that would do 'more harm than good'.[17] Early in August, the Maharaja made the order of objectives clear once again: First arrears of payment then restoration of status-quo-ante, and then freedom, and restoration.[18] Because of the crucial importance of the Darbar held by the young Maharaja Partap Singh in Nabha, Maharaja Ripudaman Singh wanted Chowrryappah to find out if Sir Samuel Hoare, Secretary of State for India, had given assurance, as it was rumoured, to Maharani Sarojini Devi in 1932 that the Maharaja would never be released. It was said that the Maharani had gone to Nabha in 1933 only after securing that assurance from Sir Samuel.[19]

Working for the Maharaja in England from May to October 1934, Chowrryappah got in touch with the Political Department of the India Office, and met Sir Samuel Hoare, Lord Willingdon (who was then on leave from India), R. A. Butler, who was Under Secretary of State for India, and several Members of Parliament, both Labour and Conservative, including Rev. George Woods and H. K. Hales. This exploration led Chowrryappah to believe that initiative in connection with the case of Maharaja Ripudaman Singh was to come from India. He came to India to have 'prolonged interviews' with the heads of the Political Department in New Delhi, and with Sir Eric Mieville, Private

Secretary to the Viceroy.[20] Besides meeting Mieville on 5 December 1934, he met Wingate, Joint Secretary in the Foreign and Political Department, on 14 December.[21]

During Chowrryappah's meeting with Corfield on 6 March, he was told that the government had received 'a similar verbal representation' about seven months back that restrictions on the Maharaja should be relaxed, but there did not seem to be any reason to comply with the request unless something new could be adduced that would lead the government to reconsider the position. Chowrryappah had nothing new to add but wished to know if there was anything against the Maharaja submitting a memorial or representation. He was told that there was no reason against such a representation but it was for the Maharaja to use his own discretion.[22]

H. K. Hales arrived at Kodaikanal on 28 March 1935 and interviewed the Maharaja on three consecutive days. Though a Conservative, Hales had become interested in Nabha affairs and was preparing to help him.[23] In the House of Commons at the beginning of August, Hales asked R. A. Butler, Under Secretary of State for India, whether he was prepared to give the Maharaja of Nabha the opportunity of proving his innocence before an independent tribunal. Butler evaded a direct reply, saying that the circumstances of the Maharaja's detention under Regulation III of 1818 were announced in the press communiqué in India. In a supplementary question Hales asked: 'In the best interests of British justice should not this man be given an opportunity of refuting any charge brought against him?' To this Butler gave the same old answer: 'The ex-Maharaja should make representation to the authorities in India.'[24]

By this time, Chowrryappah was in England again. On his behalf, E. H. Pickering approached Butler, who remembered his last interview with Chowrryappah. Butler was emphatic that there would be no point in Chowrryappah writing about the Nabha case. Pickering was aware that 'representations on behalf of the ex-Maharaja must be addressed to the authorities in India in the first instance'. There was no possibility of the Government of India treating Chowrryappah as the accredited representative of the Maharaja.[25]

A Labour Member Takes a Firm Stand

On 6 May 1936, Rev. George S. Woods, many a time Labour MP 'who had spent his life in serving what seemed to him were good causes', wrote to Butler (with reference to an earlier interview) that he had been assured that the Maharaja of Nabha had not taken part in any 'disloyal activities' since 1928. He had engaged counsel to secure extension of his liberty and the retention of his titles, which was legitimate and not something disloyal. Woods wanted to have evidence of the Maharaja's further disloyalty. If his record since 1928 was free from any taint of 'disloyal' activity, how many more years were needed before his word could be accepted that any extension of the liberty would not be abused? Did not clause 3 of Regulation III of 1818, under which the Maharaja had been interned, contemplate the review of the case every six months? The Maharaja had not conceded the right to be deprived of titles except by the operation of the Government of India Resolution of October 1920 providing for a Court of Arbitration.[26] At the instance of the India Office in 1934 Chowrryappah had approached the Government of India on behalf of Maharaja Ripudaman Singh, but the Government of India were unwilling to take any action. Rev. Woods asked: 'Would it not be possible for Nabha to be given permission to proceed to England direct from Kodaikanal and put his own appeal to the Secretary of State for India?'[27]

The India Office wrote to the Government of India that G. S. Woods, 'one of the most pertinacious of the Members of Parliament who have made personal representation on the subject of the detention of the ex-Maharaja of Nabha', had entered into correspondence with the Parliamentary Under Secretary of State. The India Office wished to know the views of the Government of India regarding the procedure by which representations should be submitted by the Maharaja, and whether 'they would now be prepared to entertain such representations if made to them by him direct'.[28]

Two weeks later, Woods wrote to Butler again that he was concerned about the modus operandi by which action was taken in 1928. Was it one of the conditions agreed to on which the Maharaja severed his connection with Nabha Administration? Or could the action of this nature be taken without regard to the principle of natural justice? Even if there was breach of the Agreement of 1923, the Government of India was not free to have gone back upon its own Resolution, which in law was binding. 'It was precisely for such cases that the formalities of the Resolution [of 1920] were so carefully provided.' The Judicial Enquiry of 1923 was entirely different from the Commission of Enquiry (under the Resolution of October 1920), which ought to have been appointed before the Government of India could have deprived the Maharaja of his titles and dignities. In paragraph 308 of the Montagu–Chelmsford Report, it was left to the discretion of the Viceroy to appoint a Commission with regard to inter-state disputes, but in paragraph 309 there was no such discretion with regard to depriving the ruler of a state of his rights, dignities, and powers.[29] Woods was informed by the India Office before the end of the month that his representations had been brought to the notice of the Government of India with whom rested the action for the 'enlargement' of the Maharaja.[30]

The India Office wrote to the Political Department on 10 July 1936 that there were increasing signs of activity in London on behalf of the Maharaja of Nabha. A barrister and a solicitor were making enquiries from the Legal Adviser on the means of making representations to the Secretary of State by, or on behalf of, the Maharaja. His objective probably was to make his peace with the government to obtain enlargement from Kodaikanal and to have his allowances restored to 25,000 rupees a month.[31] The Political Department wrote to the India Office that there was nothing to prevent the Maharaja from submitting representation under section 5 of Regulation III of 1818, addressed to the Governor General in Council through the District Magistrate of Madurai. After the Governor General had passed orders on this representation, the Maharaja could submit a memorial to the Secretary of State through the same channel, which would be dealt with according to Memorial Rules and could probably not be withheld.[32]

Woods responded to Butler's letter of 17 July by a longish letter on the 24th. He was beginning to feel, he said, that the Government of India had not only been entirely unconstitutional in their treatment of the Maharaja of Nabha, but were also guilty of the very crime which they had ascribed to the Maharaja in 1923:

> The Government of India can not conceive a more insidious form of oppression than the methodical perpetation of injustice in these cases under the cover of legal forms.

The quotation, ironically, is from the communiqué of the government issued on 7 July 1923 to announce the Maharaja's deposition. In the communiqué of 19 February 1928 after his arrest, it was said: 'The Government of India have accordingly been compelled to pass orders that he shall be deprived of title of Maharaja, and of all rights and privileges pertaining thereto.' Butler later maintained that the Maharaja 'had ceased to be in any sense an Indian Ruler' when he was detained under Regulation III of 1818. The contradiction in the two statements apart, could the Government of India deprive a prince of his powers, title, and dignities simply by passing orders to that effect?

Woods went on to say that there was enough evidence to show that the Maharaja was a ruling prince on the day when he was detained. The Foreign Secretary, Sir Denys Bray, referred to the Maharaja as 'a prince or chief under the suzerainty of His Majesty'. The Home Secretary, James Crerar, referred to him as 'the Maharaja of Nabha'. Therefore, the following conclusions were inevitable:

1. His arrest and internment under Regulation III of 1818 was illegal.
2. The deprivation of his powers, title, and dignities, by which it is now sought to justify the application of Regulation III was equally illegal, in as much as he could not be so deprived except under operation of the 1920 Resolution of the Government of India, which is imperative in such cases.

There was yet another matter which could neither be reconciled with justice nor could it be justified. This was the reduction of the income of the Maharaja of Nabha from 25,000 rupees to 10,000 rupees a month. This was a 'new type of fine' which was entirely foreign and repugnant to every canon of British justice. Woods hoped that Butler would discuss the whole matter with the Secretary of State in the light of his letter to come to a satisfactory understanding on some such terms as these: (*a*) removal of detention, with no return to Nabha or the Punjab, (*b*) restoration of personal title, and (*c*) re-establishment of his right to his own income according to pre-1928 basis. The Maharaja had expressed in the past his loyalty to the King Emperor, and Woods believed it would be a good thing if he were allowed 'to come to England and pledge his loyalty to the King'.[33]

Meanwhile, Chowrryappah returned to India to advise the Maharaja to make a representation through the Madras Government. The Maharaja was suspicious that this was intended to be a further humiliation, or a trap 'to get him to acknowledge a lowered status, that of an ordinary citizen'. Therefore, G. S. Woods wrote to Butler if he could give 'a definite assurance that there is no cause whatever for him to be suspicious of your motives in advising this line of action'.[34] Butler replied that the advice given to the Maharaja of Nabha to make use of 'the channels prescribed in the Regulation under which he was interned' was a happy news. The answers given to Woods' enquiries were inspired by no motive other than 'a desire to indicate what would be the correct procedure in the circumstances'.[35]

The Maharaja wrote to Woods that the Government of India was 'as adamant and unrelenting as ever' with regard to his case. For relief and justice he looked only to London. He hammered the point that

> the Secretary of State for India is the head of the Indian Administration in England, and as a member of the Cabinet he is solely responsible to, and represents the supreme authority of, Parliament. The Secretary of State can impose orders on the Government of India. In matters requiring secrecy viz: foreign policy and affairs of Indian States the Secretary of State can act on his own authority without consulting his council.[36]

At the same time, the Maharaja urged upon Chowrryappah the need of sailing to England again. He should try to leave as soon as possible to resume work in London. 'Proceed to England at once', he wrote on the following day.[37]

Woods wrote to Butler on 27 April 1937 that he had been informed that the Maharaja made representation to the Viceroy as suggested by Butler. He hoped that the Maharaja would soon get the reply. He added:

> The more I have considered the present position of the ex-Maharaja the more convinced I am that it is contrary to all standards of British justice.

Woods added further that Chowrryappah was in England and could be consulted for fuller information, if necessary. Would an interview with Lord Zetland, the Secretary of State for India, be of any use?[38]

Chowrryappah informed the Maharaja that he was trying his utmost to expedite instructions from White Hall to Simla. The Maharaja was not satisfied. A friend had written to him that there was need of vigorous action 'in view of the attempts that are being made, I learn, to hasten the consummation of the Senior Maharani's object. She has not been idle in this direction'.[39] 'Things are moving rapidly', wrote Chowrryappah, 'a settlement is likely to be reached very shortly'. But the Maharaja responded by telling him 'not to invite me to live in a fool's paradise'.[40] Before the end of May 1937, the memorial submitted on behalf of the Maharaja was returned to Chowrryappah by the District Magistrate of Madurai.[41]

Early in June 1937, Woods wrote to Lord Zetland, giving the background of his interest in the Maharaja's case. In March 1936, he had approached Butler as it appeared to him that the treatment given to the Maharaja could not be justified in law whether British or Indian. He had great difficulty in believing that 'such things could happen under British Rule'. Butler gave him to understand that there were two alternatives: a constitutional trial or petition by the Maharaja to the Viceroy through the Madras authorities. He advised the latter course, and accordingly a memorial was duly submitted on 25 March 1937. But it was not even acknowledged. Woods' correspondence and conversations with Butler had fully confirmed the strength of the claims of the Maharaja. Woods suggested, therefore, that the Secretary of State should personally interest himself in the case of the Maharaja of Nabha.[42]

Within a fortnight, Lord Stanley wrote to Woods on behalf of the Secretary of State, acknowledging his letter with which a copy of the memorial submitted by the Maharaja was enclosed. All that Stanley added to this mere acknowledgement was:

> The passing of orders upon the memorial is of course a matter within the discretion of the authorities in India, with which the Secretary of State regrets he would not be prepared to interfere.[43]

Woods thanked Stanley for his letter and informed him that the Government of India had refused to correspond with the Maharaja through an attorney, referring to an order of 1928. It was inconceivable that the submission of a memorial to the Viceroy as the representative of the Crown could be regarded as one and the same thing as correspondence with government officers under section 5 of Regulation III of 1818. The Government of India had been entirely unconstitutional from the very beginning. The Regulation was never intended to apply to an Indian prince, and 'it could be proved to the hilt that the status of Nabha at the time of his arrest was that of an Indian Prince'. His internment, therefore, was illegal. He could be deprived of his powers, title, and dignities only under the Government of India Resolution of 29 October 1920, which provides for a Court of Arbitration. When all this had been pointed out to Butler, he sent for Woods and assured him that the case of the Maharaja would be most carefully considered if representations were made to the Viceroy through the appropriate channel.

Woods captured the drift of things:

> If, however, such discretionary powers are abused in this manner, it is evident that no useful purpose will be served by any further approach to

the Government of India, particularly as the same Government of India are apparently responsible both for the illegality and the irregularities in the treatment meted out to the ex-Maharaja of Nabha.

Woods felt very strongly that in these circumstances the Secretary of State, as the constitutional head of the administration in India responsible to Parliament, should intervene and deal with the case on the merits of the memorial that had been submitted.[44]

The Secretary of State did not propose 'to interfere with the decision of the authorities in India upon the Maharaja's memorial'. He, added, however, that the decision of the Government of India 'in no way precludes the Maharaja from submitting himself any representations which he may desire to make to the authorities'.[45] Woods wrote back that Butler had assured him that representations could be made *on behalf of* the Maharaja, which was confirmed by the Private Secretary to the Viceroy, and that was why the memorial was duly submitted. He wished to be enlightened:

> Why, after these explicit directions had been complied with, the memorial should be ruled out of order on the score that it was made 'on behalf' of the ex-Maharaja? Why the elementary right of making representations through Counsel was denied to the Maharaja, and it was insisted that he should himself make such representations?[46]

As in the past, Winterton played with words, making a fine distinction in the words used by Woods and by Butler and the Private Secretary to the Viceroy. They had not 'explicitly said that representations could be entertained if made on behalf of the ex-Maharaja'. What they said was that 'representations by or on behalf of the ex-Maharaja must be made through the appointed channel'. Winterton was sorry if the use of the words 'on behalf of' had given rise to any misunderstanding. 'It is a well known rule in India that memorials, petitions and the like addressed to Government should be submitted and signed by the petitioner. In the present case there would appear to have been no special reason for waiving this rule.' This, however, did not prevent the petitioner from availing himself of legal advice and assistance in the preparation and drafting of his representations.[47] Woods expressed his exasperation and anger in a letter to Chowrryappah. There seemed to be no limit to the subterfuges of the India Office. Words lost their ordinary meanings when used by the India Office. Woods then wanted to know if the Maharaja of Nabha would put his signature to the petition and resubmit it.[48]

The Maharaja's Refusal to Be Treated as an Ordinary Subject

Maharaja Ripudaman Singh did not wish to be humiliated further. Rather than signing and resubmitting the petition, he now thought of engaging a solicitor to obtain some favourable modification of the conditions under which he was suffering. The material needs of a growing family with a shrinking establishment had aggravated his hardship. Ripudaman Singh authorized Chowrryappah to engage Messrs J. H. Milner & Son particularly to approach the India Office, and to obtain such satisfaction as possible.[49]

Major J. Milner, a Labour Member of Parliament who had been a Member of Indian Franchise Committee and later became Lord Milner of Leeds, wrote to Chowrryappah on 30 November 1937 that the India Office contended that the Maharaja had waived any right he might have had to the 'Commission of Enquiry' under Government of India Resolution of 29 October 1920, and that he had put himself in the hands of the Government. They further contended that they had to deport the Maharaja to Kodaikanal because of his conduct between 1923 and 1928. Even after 1928, his action in regard to his first wife had not been good and he had caused some newspapers to write articles against Patiala. Of late, however, the Maharaja's conduct was good. Nevertheless, the British Government was unwilling to prevail upon the Government of India to consider mitigation of the Maharaja's position of their own volition and without asking the Maharaja to submit a memorial. But 'if the Maharaja will submit such a Memorial to the Viceroy they believe it will have favourable consideration'. Any further action appeared to be impossible 'from this end'. Major Milner suggested, therefore, that Chowrryappah should 'strongly advise' the Maharaja to submit a memorial and to sign it himself. He added:

> If you will let me know that the Maharaja is going to accept your advice and sign such a memorial himself, I will then ask the British Government to inform the Government of India that they are favourably disposed to it.

Milner hoped that Chowrryappah would be successful in persuading the Maharaja to sign the memorial. A further mitigation of his position might be possible if the Government of India had no further complaint.[50]

The India Office wrote to the Political Department that Major Milner had been asked to act professionally on behalf of the Maharaja of Nabha and he called to see Lord Stanley. Milner referred to the correspondence between Rev. Woods and Lord Winterton and asked if there were 'any prospects of the ex-Maharaja's case being reviewed by Government without any representation on his part'. Milner was informed that the Secretary of State was not prepared to suggest to the Viceroy the desirability of reviewing the Maharaja's case, but it rested with him to avail himself of the prescribed procedure for making a representation to the Governor General in Council. Major Milner asked whether a representation made on the same lines as Chowrryappah's but signed by the Maharaja would receive consideration. He was informed that there was no reason to anticipate that such a representation would not receive consideration or that it 'would be withheld on formal grounds'.[51]

On 4 January 1938, Woods sent a cable to Chowrryappah to the effect that Under Secretary Butler had personally conveyed Lord Zetland's assurance that if the Maharaja represented through the Collector under 'Regulation Three Miscarriage of Justice. Likewise Deprivation of Dignities without Commission of Enquiry', the Secretary of State would do the needful even if the Government of India was unrelenting. There was no trap and the representation would do no harm to the case. 'DON'T HESISTATE', Woods insisted.[52]

However, Maharaja Ripudaman Singh refused to sign a memorial.[53] He wanted the Secretary of State to review his case without a representation personally signed by the Maharaja. To sign a memorial was to 'depose' himself and become a British subject. He could not barter his princely autonomy by becoming an ordinary subject of the empire for dubious concessions from the government.

Notes

1. India Office Records (IOR) (microfilm), L/P S/10/1024, extract from the Legislative Assembly Debates—'motion for adjournment, arrest and deportation of the ex-Maharaja of Nabha-disallowed', 29 February 1928.

    Vitthalbhai J. Patel was elected President of the Legislative Assembly for the second time in 1928. His attitude was in consonance with that of his leader, Pandit Motilal Nehru, who had resiled already from his earlier position of support for the Maharaja.
2. National Archives of India (NAI), New Delhi, Crown Representative Records (CRR) (microfilm), Accession no. 11, Reel no. 6, File no. 93-P (secret) of 1928, 'Internment of ex-Maharaja of Nabha at Kodaikanal'.

IOR, R/1/1/1717, no. 93-P (S)/1928, H. C. Stokes (from Madras) to Sir John Thompson, 12 April 1928.
3. IOR, R/1/1/1717, no. 93-P (S)/1928, Chief Secretary to Government of Madras to Political Secretary to Government of India, 7 April 1928.
4. IOR, R/1/1/1717, no. 93-P (S)/1928. This is evident from the notes on letters from the Madras Government, dated 19 April 1928.
5. NAI, CRR, Accession no.12, Reel no.7, File no.174-P (secret)/1928, telegram from Secretary of State for India to Viceroy, dated 10 April 1928.
6. IOR (microfilm), R/1/1/1731, File no. 174-P (secret)/1928, telegram from Viceroy to Secretary of State, dated 14 April 1928.
7. IOR, R/1/1/1731, no. 174-P(S)/1928, telegram from Secretary of State to Viceroy, dated 14 April 1928.
8. IOR, R/1/1/1731, no. 174-P(S)/1928, telegram from 'Polindia' to Viceroy's Camp, dated 15 April 1928.
9. IOR, R/1/1/1731, no. 174-P(S)/1928, notes in the Legislative Department, dated 18 April 1928.
10. IOR, R/1/1/1731, no. 174-P(S)/1928, debate in Parliament on 18 April 1928.
11. Printed record of the *Proceedings in the House of Commons in the Parliament House*, pp. 509–14, related to the debate on the ex-Maharaja of Nabha on 19 April 1928 (received through the kind courtesy of the late Mr Piara Singh Khabra, MP).
12. IOR, R/1/1/1731, no. 174-P (S)/1928, debate in the House of Commons on 26 April 1928.
13. IOR, R/1/1/1731, no. 174-P (S)/1928, debate on 30 April 1928.
14. NAI, CRR, Reel 9, no. 105-P(S)-1934, Maharaja Ripudaman Singh to Sant Singh Kapur, 21 January 1934.
15. Punjab State Archives (PSA), Patiala, Chief Minister Nabha State (CMNS) Records, File no. 10419-E, Maharaja of Nabha to A. H. Chowrryappah, 5 May 1934.
16. PSA, CMNS Records, no. 10419-E, Maharaja to Chowrryappah, 30 June 1934.
17. PSA, CMNS Records, no. 10419-E, Maharaja to Chowrryappah, 21 July 1934.
18. PSA, CMNS Records, no. 10419-E, Maharaja to Chowrryappah, 4 August 1934.
19. PSA, CMNS Records, no. 10419-E, Maharaja to Chowrryappah, 11 August 1934.
20. PSA, CMNS Records, no. 10419-E, E. C. Mieville to Chowrryappah, 4 December 1934.
21. PSA, CMNS Records, no. 10419-E, G. Leicester to Chowrryappah, 11 December 1934.

22. IOR (microfilm), R/1/1/2685, File no. 218-P(S)/ 35, note by C.L. Corfield, 6 March 1935.
23. IOR, R/1/1/2685, no. 218-P(S)/35, C. F. Brackenbury of the Madras Government to Political Secretary to Government of India, Foreign and Political Department, 26 April 1935.
24. IOR, R/1/1/2685, no. 218-P(S)/35, questions in Parliament.
25. PSA, CMNS Records, no. 10419-E, R. A. Butler to Pickering, 26 July 1935.
26. Under Resolution no. 427-R, dated 29 October 1920 of the Foreign and Political Department, a Court of Arbitration could be set up for settling the disputes arising between an Indian state and Supreme Government or Local Government, or between two or more Indian states, or in cases where a state was dissatisfied with the ruling or advice of the Supreme Government or its local representatives. For some detail, see S. M. Verma, *Chamber of Princes* (New Delhi: National Book Organisation, 1990), p. 97.
27. NAI, CRR (microfilm), Accession no. 13, Reel no. 8, File no. 101-P(S)/ 1936, G. S. Woods to R. A. Butler, 6 May 1936.
28. NAI, CRR, Reel 8, no. 101-P(S)/1936, India Office to Glancy, 15 May 1936.
29. NAI, CRR, Reel no. 8, no. 101-P(S)/1936, George S. Woods to R. A. Butler, 20 May 1936.
30. NAI, CRR, Reel no. 8, no. 101-P(S)/1936, India Office to Woods, 30 May 1936.
31. NAI, CRR, Reel no. 8, no. 101-P(S)/1936, India Office to Glancy, 10 July 1936.
32. NAI, CRR, Reel no. 8, no. 101-P(S)/1936, telegram from Viceroy to Secretary of State for India, dated 14 July 1936.
33. IOR, R/1/1/2806, File no. 101-P(S)/1936, Woods to Butler, 24 July 1936.
34. IOR, R/1/1/2806, no. 101-P(S)/1936, Woods to Butler, 28 January 1937.
35. IOR, R/1/1/2806, File no. 101-P(S)/1936, Butler to Woods, 3 February 1937.
36. PSA, CMNS Records, no. 10419-E, Maharaja to Woods, 3 February 1937.
37. PSA, CMNS Records, no. 10419-E, Maharaja to Chowrryappah, 7 and 8 March 1937.
38. IOR, R/1/1/2806, no. 101-P(S)/1936, Woods to Butler, 27 April 1937.
39. PSA, CMNS Records, no. 10419-E, Maharaja to Chowrryappah, 30 April 1937.
40. PSA, CMNS Records, no. 10419-E, Maharaja to Chowrryappah, 18 May 1937.
41. PSA, CMNS Records, no. 10419-E, A. R. C. Westlake to Chowrryappah, 27 May 1937.
42. IOR, R/1/1/2806, no. 101-P(S)/1936, Woods to Lord Zetland, 3 June 1937.

43. IOR, R/1/1/2806, no. 101-P(S)/1936, Lord Stanley to Woods, 16 June 1937.
44. IOR, R/1/1/2806, no. 101-P(S)/1936, Woods to Stanley, 7 July 1937.
45. IOR, R/1/1/2806, no. 101-P(S)/1936, Lord Winterton to Woods, 16 July 1937.
46. PSA, CMNS Records, no. 10419-E, Woods to Winterton, 22 July 1937.
47. IOR, R/1/12806, no. 101-P(S)/1936, Exchange between Woods and Winterton, 23 and 29 July 1937.
48. PSA, CMNS Records, no. 10419-E, Woods to Chowrryappah, 3 August 1937.
49. PSA, CMNS Records, no. 10419-E, Chowrryappah to Messrs J.H. Milner & Son, 23 September 1937.
50. PSA, CMNS Records, no. 10419-E, J. H. Milner to Chowrryappah, 30 November 1937.
51. IOR (microfilm), R/1/12952, File no. 235-P(S)/1936, P. J. Patrick to Glancy, 1 December 1938.
52. PSA, CMNS Records, no. 10419-E, telegram from Woods to Chowrryappah, dated 4 January 1938.
53. PSA, CMNS Records, no. 10419-E, Maharaja to Chowrryappah, 7 and 9 February 1938.

14

LAST BID AND THE LAST DAYS

Maharaja Ripudaman Singh turned his attention to the authorities in India again in 1938, and memorials were sent to the Viceroy by central and provincial legislators. Opinion in favour of the Maharaja began to articulate in the Punjab in July 1939. After the outbreak of the World War II, Maharani Gurucharan Kaur decided to go to the north to seek justice from the Government of India. She went to the Punjab too and met Sikh leaders to mobilize support for the Maharaja. The bureaucracy was rather hostile to her. The investiture ceremony of the young Maharaja Partap Singh was hastened and held in March 1941. It was a clear signal that the doors of the Government of India remained closed for Maharaja Ripudaman Singh.

In March 1938, Maharaja Ripudaman Singh sent Chowrryappah to England for the fourth time 'to endeavour to dispence with his signature to any Memorial', and to persuade the India Office to restore the Maharaja to pre-internment position and status.[1] In India, at the same time, C. Vijiaraghavachariar, who lived in Kodaikanal and was a senior lawyer, tried to persuade the Viceroy to remove the long-standing grievances of the Maharaja. The Viceroy's office informed Vijiaraghavachariar on 31 March 1938 that His Excellency was unable to consider representations on behalf of the Maharaja unless they were submitted through 'proper' official channel. This had been made clear to him on various occasions earlier.[2]

Sardar Sant Singh, Member of the Central Legislative Assembly, wrote to Sir Bertrand Glancy, Political Adviser to the Viceroy, on 11 April 1938 that he wanted to see the Political Secretary in connection with the detention of Maharaja Ripudaman Singh. Enclosed with this letter was a memorial to His Excellency Lord Linlithgow. This memorial was signed by Members of the Legislative Assembly representing various communities, interests, and parties. The memorialists had stated that they did not wish to enter into any controversy with regard to the merits of the case. They emphasized that the Maharaja had suffered much and his case might be reviewed. This could be of advantage to both the Maharaja and the government. Sir Bertrand suggested an alternate way in which representation could be made. Sardar Sant Singh sent the re-drafted memorial on 14 April. Again, it was signed by several Members of the Central Legislative Assembly, including Sant Singh himself, Bhai Parmanand, Abdul Majid, Krishna Kant, Madan Mohan Malaviya, B. B. Verma, Hasan Imam, and Abdul Qayyum, among others. The Maharaja had suffered, they said, tremendously in mind, body, reputation, and property. He was suffering from high blood pressure and his health was shattered. Ten years of detention without a trial was a very long period. In the name of humanity and British justice, he should be released from detention. Sardar Sant Singh received the reply on 16 April that it had 'already been made clear to the Maharaja that if he wishes to make any representation, he should do so himself through the proper channel'.[3]

The supporters of Maharaja Ripudaman Singh had various ways of making representations but the bureaucracy had only one answer: the proper official channel prescribed for the common subjects of British India. C. S. Ranga Iyer, Member, Central Legislative Assembly, saw Glancy on 23 May 1938 and talked about the release of Maharaja Ripudaman Singh. Glancy said that the Maharaja had been told repeatedly that 'he must use the correct channel for any representation which he might wish to make'.[4]

B. G. Horniman met Glancy on 8 September 1938 and said that he was interested in Maharaja Ripudaman Singh's welfare because he had contributed generously to the *Indian Daily Herald* launched by Horniman 25 years ago. His first point was that the allowance of 25,000 rupees should be restored. His second point was that the order of internment should be withdrawn. He too was told that the Maharaja could make any representation through the prescribed channel. Horniman said that he would advise the Maharaja to do so. Glancy expressed his doubt about the Maharaja accepting Horniman's advice. Several other persons on numerous occasions had given this advice to the Maharaja but he had not accepted it.[5]

In early October, the Maharaja wrote to C. S. Ranga Iyer to arrange for submission of a public petition to the Viceroy about his case, suggesting that it should be signed by at least one hundred distinguished persons in the United Provinces without distinction of caste and creed. A draft petition enclosed for his guidance referred to the Maharaja having been made a scapegoat in the dispute between Nabha and Patiala. His ruin was brought about by his enemies who succeeded in persuading Lord Irwin to take the still more drastic action of arresting him under the Bengal Regulation III of 1818. The Maharaja's son was proclaimed ruler in his place, and his own allowance was reduced to 10,000 rupees a month. He was still languishing in Kodaikanal in shattered and broken health. An appeal was made to the Viceroy to look into the case as a statesman and restore the Maharaja to freedom and to his state, in the name of fairness, humanity, and justice.[6]

Maharaja Ripudaman Singh's proposal was modified by Ranga Iyer in two important ways: the proposed public petition was to be brief, and it was to be signed by members of the Legislative Assembly and Legislative Council of the United Provinces. The Maharaja approved of the change. The petition now referred to the Viceroy's statement about releasing political prisoners, but nothing came out of this endeavour.[7]

Mobilization of Opinion in the Punjab

Meanwhile, the Sikh Naujawan Society, formed at Lahore for the restoration of the Maharaja, had organized a meeting on 9 July 1939 with the veteran Sikh leader Baba Kharak Singh in the chair and Labh Singh Narang as the main speaker. Both of them had never wavered in their support for the Maharaja.[8] Among the other speakers were Karam Chand, editor of the *Pāras*, Harcharan Singh Sistani, and Pritam Singh Bhatia. They dwelt on the independent attitude of Maharaja Ripudaman Singh as the cause of his unpopularity with the Political Department so much so that he was deprived of his state. The meeting demanded that the Maharaja be restored to the gaddī of Nabha as its rightful owner. The meeting also protested against Tikka Partap Singh who had cut his hair, and demanded that he should not be allowed to occupy the gaddī of Nabha so long as he remained a renegade (*patit*). Baba Kharak Singh appealed to the people to carry on agitation for the restoration of Maharaja Ripudaman Singh.[9]

In November 1939, Pritam Singh Bhatia, General Secretary of the Khalsa Youngmen's Union of Lahore, sent a telegram to the Viceroy requesting him to reconsider the case of the Maharaja of Nabha sympathetically and to reinstate him on his gaddī.[10] Labh Singh Narang, President of the Khalsa Youngmen's Union, forwarded a memorial to the Private Secretary to the Viceroy, requesting His Excellency to reinstate the Maharaja. Included among the signatories were two members of the Central Legislative Assembly: Bhai Parmanand and Maulana Zafar Ali Khan. There was one member of the Legislative Assembly of the North West Frontier Province: Sardar Ajit Singh (Sarhadi). More than a score of the members of Punjab Legislative Assembly signed the memorial, such as Sir Gokal Chand Narang, Malik Barkat Ali, Rai Bahadur Mukand Lal Puri, Mian Abdul Aziz, Sardar Sahib Santokh Singh, Rai Bahadur Lala Gopal Dass, Tikka Jagjit Singh Bedi, K. L. Gauba, Sultan Mahmud, Harnam Singh Sodhi, Girdhari Lal, Nawabzada Muzaffar Ali Khan Qazalbash, Sardar Indar Singh Rais, Sardar Gopal Singh, Sardar Lal Singh, Lala Sita Ram Mehta, Sardar Balwant Singh, Sardar Ajit Singh Rais, Fateh Khan, Mian Noor Ahmad Khan, Chaudhari Jafar Ali Khan, Rai Bahadur Badri Dass, and Muhammad Amin.

This impressive list given in *The Tribune* justified the impression that 'all the Punjabees irrespective of their caste and creed' desired the reinstatement of Maharaja Ripudaman Singh.[11] Barkat Ram Bhalla, who had served the Maharaja for the best part of his life, wrote to the editor of *The Tribune* that a personal interview of the Maharaja with the Viceroy could have been more effective than the memorial. He begged the memorialists and other Punjabis to work hard to arrange an interview.[12] In January 1940 it was reported that Maharaja Ripudaman Singh was ill. Besides fever and cough, his blood pressure was rising and he had several sleepless nights.[13]

The news of the Maharaja's health caused concern to his well-wishers. The All India Akali Conference held at Attari on 8–12 February 1940 resolved that the continued internment of Maharaja Ripudaman Singh at Kodaikanal was wholly unjustifiable and 'urged upon the Government of India to recall forthwith the ban on the Maharaja'.[14] At the end of the conference, Labh Singh Narang wrote to the editor of *The Tribune* that the public sympathized with the Maharaja due to the general belief that he had been wronged because he was ahead of his times and an exception among the Indian rulers. He had suffered enough and it was for the government to accede to the popular demand for the reinstatement of the Maharaja.[15] On 17 February 1940, Baba Kharak Singh, President, Central Akali Dal, Sardar Sardul Singh Caveeshar, President, Punjab Forward Bloc, and more than a hundred other influential and leading citizens of the Punjab who represented various public bodies and organizations appealed to 'the Sikh Nation' to observe 25 February as Nabha Day. The Khalsa had solemnly pledged not to rest till Maharaja Ripudaman Singh was restored to the gaddī of Nabha. Huge sacrifices had been made to redeem this pledge and the Khalsa were prepared to make more sacrifices, if necessary. For the present, the movement for the reinstatement of the Maharaja was purely constitutional. All the Panthic organizations should observe the Nabha Day and pass the resolution that the continued internment of the Maharaja was beyond justification of any kind.[16]

Baba Kharak Singh presided over the Nabha Day meeting of the citizens of Lahore under the auspices of the Khalsa Youngmen's Union. The Maharaja's internment was attributed to his love for freedom, religion, and the nation. It was resolved that he should be restored to the gaddī. It was also resolved that Tikka Partap Singh, who had become a renegade by cutting his hair, should not be installed on the gaddī of the Sikh state of Nabha. Yet another resolution expressed sympathy with the exiles of Nabha, who had been punished for expressing support for the Maharaja, and demanded the restoration of their confiscated property to them.[17]

Two meetings were held inside the Nabha state on the 'Nabha Day': one at Jaito and the other at Gumti Khurd. The gathering at Jaito was reported to be small, and the man who presided over the meeting had no influence. At Gumti Khurd, the meeting was held in the Gurdwara under the chairmanship of a local Akali. Resolutions were passed at both the meetings, requesting the government to release the Maharaja and to reinstate him. The state authorities thought that there was no need of a repressive action for this 'mild agitation'. Steps were taken, however, to make people aware that action or speech designed to secure the restoration of the Maharaja to the gaddī of Nabha ipso facto involved 'disloyalty to the present Maharaja'. And disloyalty constituted 'sedition' and would be regarded as such by the state authorities.[18]

Maharani Gurucharan Kaur Comes to the North

Maharani Gurucharan Kaur, whom the Maharaja had married during his stay at Dehra Dun, had joined him a few months after his arrest in February 1928. According to the records of Kodaikanal Municipality, their first girl child was born on 21 May 1929 at the Conservatory House, and named Vijaya. The second child, a male, was born on 16 March 1931 at the house called 'Manorma', where the Maharani's parents were residing at that time. Named Jasmer Singh after the Maharaja's mother, Jasmer Kaur, he came to be called 'Tikka Jasmer Singh' in the family. Registered as 'Prince Shamsher Singh', the third child was born on 20 August 1932 at the house called 'Corrie'. The fourth child was 'Princess Shamsher Kaur' (later called 'Princess Charanjit Kaur'), born at 'Corrie' on 25 March 1934. The mother's name was recorded in the Municipal register as 'Maharani Gurucharan Kaur'. The youngest child was 'Prince Fateh Singh', born at 'Corrie' on 11 April 1935.[19] With her two daughters and three sons, the Maharani decided to come to Delhi in October 1939 to seek justice from the Government of India.

Maharani Gurucharan Kaur met the Political Secretary to the Viceroy as well as his Political and Military Advisers in January 1940 but only to get the stock response that unless sent through the local authorities, the former Maharaja's request could not be considered. While the bureaucrats were struck by the Maharani's dignified bearing, good looks, perfect English, and her strong religious views and feelings, Ogilvie, formerly the acting Administrator of Nabha, told the Political Secretary that 'sooner she goes back to Kodaikanal the better'.[20] The authorities probably anticipated the welcome she would get and feared that her presence would give momentum to the agitation for the Maharaja's release and restoration.

Maharani Gurucharan Kaur began her visit to the Punjab from the holy city of the Sikhs. Accompanied by her two daughters and three sons, she went to Amritsar on 9 April 1940 to pay homage to Sri Darbar Sahib. Master Tara Singh, Sardar Bahadur Hukam Singh, and other Akali leaders were present at the railway station to receive her. She offered 250 rupees at the Golden Temple and 125 rupees at the Akal Takht, and received a saropā.[21]

At the Lahore Railway Station on 10 April, a rousing reception was accorded by a cross-section of political leaders to 'Her Highness Maharani Gurucharan Kaur of Nabha'. Prominent among those who received her at the railway station were the Congress leaders Dr Satyapal, Sardar Ujjal Singh, Sardar Sardul Singh Caveeshar, Shri Virendra, Sardar Amar Singh of the *Sher-i Punjab*, Shaikh Sirajuddin Paracha, and Lala Kidar Nath Sehgal. A very large number of Sikh women were also present. The Maharani and her children were profusely garlanded amidst the shouts of 'Sat Sri Akal'. Labh Singh welcomed the royal family on behalf of the Central Khalsa Youngmen's Union. A few days later, she visited the nearby historical Gurdwara Dehra Sahib, where she was received with enthusiasm. Jathedar Achhar Singh narrated the history of the Nabha agitation and the members of Guru Nanak Sewak Sabha expressed strong opposition to the installation of the patit Tikka on the gaddī of Nabha. After receiving saropās, the Maharani and her children visited the samādh of Maharaja Ranjit Singh.[22]

On 20 April 1940, a ladies' meeting was held in honour of 'Maharani Gurucharan Kaur of Nabha' at the YMCA Hall, Lahore.[23] On 27 April, a reception was held in the Town Hall gardens of Lahore in her honour. Over 200 prominent citizens of the city, representing different communities, had signed the invitation. More than 400 guests responded, including some Europeans. Labh Singh garlanded 'Maharani Gurucharan Kaur'. The welcome address by Kirpal Singh, Secretary, Sri Guru Singh Sabha, referred to the sacrifices made by the Sikhs for the restoration of the Maharaja of Nabha. Among the other speakers were the Bishop of Lahore, Baba Kharak Singh, Mahashe Krishna, K. L. Gauba, Lala Duni Chand, Shanno Devi, Tikka Jagjit Singh, Gyani Sher Singh, K. L. Rallia Ram, Sardar Amar Singh of the *Sher-i Punjab*, and Karam Chand of the *Pāras*. All the speakers supported the claim of the Maharaja to be set free and to be restored to his gaddī. Baba Kharak Singh offered to lead a morchā, if necessary. Maharani Gurucharan Kaur thanked the speakers in English, and hoped that 'the Government would see its way to release the Maharaja whose health was getting from bad to worse'.[24]

The public meeting organized by the Central Khalsa Youngmen's Union at Lahore on 26 May 1940 was well attended. The first resolution passed condemned the continued internment of Maharaja Ripudaman Singh at Kodaikanal and demanded his immediate release and reinstatement. The second resolution demanded that the patit Tikka should be deprived of his right to succession.[25] An all-India conference opened on 8 June 1940 under the presidentship of Baba Kharak Singh. Maharani Gurucharan Kaur performed the flag hoisting ceremony in the presence of a large gathering. She and her children were given a great ovation. On 9 June, a resolution was passed by the conference urging the Government of India to reinstate the Maharaja without further delay, for otherwise, the Panth would be forced to launch a morchā. A photograph published in *The Tribune* showed the Maharani addressing the conference, with all her children at the centre of the stage.[26]

However, in a meeting at Amritsar, organized by the SGPC and the Shiromani Akali Dal to observe the 'Ghallughara Day' (in memory of the Sikhs massacred in the battle of Kup in 1762) on 26 May, resolutions were passed against the installation of the patit Tikka and the 'Pakistan scheme'. The beardless rulers of Jind and Kapurthala also came in for a share of the general censure. But there was no resolution on the restoration of the Maharaja of Nabha.[27] The Akali Shahidi Conference held on 8 June 1940 at Lahore under the presidentship of Sardar Sant Singh also passed similar resolutions. It was reiterated that the patit Tikka should not be installed on the gaddī of Nabha; the attention of all the Sikh Maharajas was invited to the urgent need of giving Sikh character to their administrations, and the renegade Sikh rulers were advised to take *amrit* (initiation of the double-edged sword) again to become true Sikhs.[28] As a member of the Central Legislative Assembly, Sant Singh had been a strong supporter of Maharaja Ripudaman Singh, but he made no reference to his restoration now.

Given the attitude of the SGPC and the Akali Dal, the two most influential Sikh organizations, the political activity in favour of Maharaja Ripudaman Singh could not go far. Nevertheless, the Central Khalsa Youngmen's Union organized another 'Nabha Day' at Lahore on 9 July 1940 to commemorate the anniversary of Maharaja Ripudaman Singh's 'deposition' in 1923. The resolution passed on this occasion urged the government to release him and to reinstate him in Nabha. The Union was keen to keep alive the agitation in favour of Maharaja Ripudaman Singh's return and reinstatement. Its Working Committee resolved to convene a meeting of all Sikh organizations in the first week of September 1940 for the purpose of discussing the issue.[29] Even the Sikhs of Peshawar in North West Frontier Province passed a resolution against the continued internment of the Maharaja and urged upon the government to reinstate him, demanding, at the same time, that the 'Patit Tikka' should be removed from the gaddī.[30] On 26 July 1940, the Working Committee of the Central Khalsa Youngmen's Union reviewed the situation regarding the Nabha agitation and felt fully satisfied that the whole of the Panth was in support of the demand for the release and reinstatement of the Maharaja. It was proposed, therefore, that a representative gathering of the whole

Panth should take a decision regarding the future course of action in the first week of September.[31]

The Changed Context of Sikh Politics

The government was not much perturbed over expressions of support for Maharaja Ripudaman Singh. In January 1940, its Intelligence officers had anticipated that the biggest political party of the Sikhs, the Shiromani Akali Dal, would drop out of the agitation spearheaded by the breakaway groups and individuals opposed to Master Tara Singh, most notably Baba Kharak Singh. It was hoped that the Akalis would be deterred also by the charge that they had been bought by the Maharaja. This, in fact, had been the only way the government and its collaborators tried to explain the goodwill for him over the years. Moreover, in their assessment, despite the general concern about 'Tikka' Partap Singh's renegade status, the Sikhs by and large did not think that the government would reinstate his father.[32]

This assessment was proved right when on 24 August 1940 Master Tara Singh and S. Sampuran Singh met the Punjab Governor, Bertrand Glancy, on behalf of the Akalis. They told him that their party had 'definitely come to the conclusion that they must co-operate with the Government in War efforts'. They knew that this would involve a break with the Congress. The two leaders raised three points in connection with the Nabha state. One of these was 'whether it would be possible for government to make a pronouncement that in future no one who had shaved his beard should be allowed to become the Ruler of a Sikh State'. Glancy said politely that such a pronouncement could not be made, but the government could bring their influence to bear on any young Sikh ruler to prevent his departing from Sikh principles. He told them in confidence that efforts were being made to persuade the young Maharaja of Nabha to grow his beard and that any agitation designed to bring this about was likely to defeat its own object. The second point they made was that an Administrator or Regent in a Sikh State under Minority Administration should invariably be a Sikh. They pointed out that the Administrator of Nabha, Raja Gyan Nath, had removed the words 'Akāl Sahāī' from the Nabha state seal. Glancy promised to look into this matter. Master Tara Singh and Sampuran Singh also pleaded that some of the Akalis externed from the Nabha state in 1923 were allowed to return to the state even though they were still unwilling to give any guarantee of good behaviour in future.

Glancy promised to make enquiries.[33] The Akali leaders remained concerned with what they regarded as the larger interests of the Panth in a changed situation.

The Shiromani Akali Dal under Master Tara Singh saw the war as an opportunity for strengthening the position of the Sikhs in British India by offering Sikh support to the government in its war efforts. On this issue he broke with Mahatma Gandhi and the Congress before the end of 1940. Master Tara Singh was the foremost Akali leader to bless the Khalsa Defence League, formed in January 1941 under the leadership of Maharaja Yadvindra Singh (succeeded 1938) of Patiala, to mobilize Sikh resources in support of the war.[34] Apparently, the new Maharaja of Patiala, Yadvindra Singh, was not hostile to Maharaja Ripudaman Singh but he was keen to support the British, and to have the young Maharaja Partap Singh, the acknowledged successor of Maharaja Ripudaman Singh, on his side.

An issue that was even more important for the Akalis than the defence of India was the so-called Pakistan Resolution passed by the All India Muslim League at Lahore in March 1940, proposing an autonomous state in a contiguous area in the north-west of India. The idea of Pakistan appeared to carry the implication of permanent Muslim domination in the Punjab. Whereas the Congress leaders were rather indifferent to the Pakistan Resolution, the Akalis, who had been feeling exercised over the Communal Award (1932) giving statutory majority to Muslims, became increasingly concerned with the implications of Pakistan. How to oppose creation was fast becoming their central political concern.[35] In this situation, Nabha could not possibly remain a major issue for them.

Response of the Bureaucracy

Maharani Gurucharan Kaur's political activities began to irritate the bureaucrats. The Resident, C. P. Skrine, felt unhappy that she used the title of 'Maharani', and the people and the press too looked upon her as the 'Maharani of Nabha'. Efforts were made by his office to dig out evidence to disprove her marriage to the Maharaja, but nothing was really discovered to refute the fact.[36] She was eventually told by the Resident that the cause of the Maharaja's release had not been helped by her association with 'venal Sikh agitators' and other anti-government elements. He advised her to return to Kodaikanal and persuade the Maharaja to submit a proper memorial through proper channels and under his own signatures.[37]

Apparently, insistence on the prescribed procedure had only been a way of warding off the Maharaja's supporters, without ever intending to release him. The real position of the government came out in Bertrand Glancy's response to the President and Secretary of the Khalsa Young Men's Union, Labh Singh Narang and Pritam Singh Bhatia. They met Glancy in August 1940 to seek the Maharaja's release from internment. After a tirade against his alleged maladministration, the Governor came to the real point that the government feared that his 'intrigues' and anti-government activities would be intensified if he was set free. Glancy then appealed to their sentiment as good Sikhs. He said that any activity on behalf of Maharaja Ripudaman Singh would seriously undermine the position and authority of his son who would shortly hold a very important position in the Sikh community. Glancy added that the young Maharaja would grow his hair 'as soon as medical advice permitted him to do so'.[38]

The government's position regarding Nabha was made absolutely clear in the Viceroy's orders of November 1940 conveyed to Maharani Gurucharan Kaur. She was informed that no representation relating to the Maharaja could be entertained except his own memorial through the Madras Government; that her claim to the title of 'Maharani' could not be recognized as her 'husband was no longer a Maharaja'; and that the Viceroy accorded sanction to the payment of 1,000 rupees per mensem for her maintenance, together with her children, and for the payment of her debts, on the condition that she would refrain from 'undesirable activities'. The sum of 1,000 rupees was to be deducted from the monthly allowance of Maharaja Ripudaman Singh. This allowance was liable to deductions up to 300 rupees a month by the Nabha Darbar. However, no guarantee could be given to the Maharani that Maharaja Partap Singh (actually his mother, Maharani Sarojini Devi) would be bound by this decision of the Viceroy 'in respect to the allowance after he assumes his powers'. At any rate, the state would not allow any other facilities or funds to her. She was given no option to accept or reject the allowance sanctioned. 'Failing instructions from you as to the disposal of the money', informed Woods-Ballard, Secretary to the Resident, 'it will be credited to your account with the Nabha Darbar, and utilized to settle proved claims from hotels, etc. against you. The balance will be allowed to accumulate until you claim it'.[39] To clinch matters, the Imperial Bank of Delhi was instructed that with effect from the remittance due on 1 December 1940, the Bank should remit only 9000 rupees to the account of 'Sardar Gurucharan Singh' with the National Bank of India at Madras.[40]

The decision of the Government of India not to recognize Gurucharan Kaur as a Maharani was unjust and untenable from the very beginning; their decision to allocate 1,000 rupees to her out of the allowance of Maharaja Ripudaman Singh was unilateral as well as mischievous. It would not be wrong to infer that, among other things, the bureaucrats did not wish to offend Maharani Sarojini Devi who was cooperating with the authorities in every way and whose hostility towards Maharaja Ripudaman Singh and Maharani Gurucharan Kaur was known to them.

In January 1941, the Resident suggested to the new Political Adviser to the Viceroy to hasten the investiture of Partap Singh who otherwise did not seem to be ready yet to shoulder the responsibilities of rulership.[41] On 5 March 1941, an auspicious day chosen by the state astrologer, he was invested with ruling powers, with E. B. Wakefield, President of the Council of Regency, as his Chief Minister to act as his 'guide, philosopher and friend'. In return, Maharaja Partap Singh proudly placed all the human and material resources of his state, along with half of its gross annual revenues for the year 1941, and his own services at the disposal of the Crown. The ceremony of investiture was 'entirely satisfactory' from the viewpoint of the government.[42] The state and its resources were to remain under bureaucratic control even after conferment of ruling powers on its Maharaja.[43]

The formal ceremony of Maharaja Partap Singh's investiture made it clear to all and sundry that Maharaja Ripudaman Singh was never to come back to Nabha. Though all doors were closed on Maharani Gurucharan Kaur, she held on to her vow not to return to Kodaikanal until she had secured concessions for her husband and her children.

The End

After the departure of Maharani Gurucharan Kaur, things had begun to go from bad to worse, and the health of the Maharaja began to deteriorate more visibly. Dr Prasaman remained in the employment of the Maharaja from June 1930 to July 1940. Mirza Gharoor Beg, a Yunānī Hakim, was engaged first in 1936–7, and then from 15 July 1940 to 14 December 1942. According to an old servant, during the last few months of his life, the Maharaja was often seen in delirium due to high fever. All alone, he died of renal failure on 14 December 1942. He was cremated rather unceremoniously in a local park which had no memorial or even a notice at the spot. His ashes were taken to Nabha to be deposited near the *marhīs* (small structures at the place of cremation) of his father and mother.[44]

For the paramount power the name of Maharaja Ripudaman Singh was better forgotten. In the Nabha state, however, there were still his well-wishers who wanted him to be remembered. Through the efforts of the son of Lala Bishan Das, the Maharaja's English tutor and later a minister, a college was established at Nabha in the name of Ripudaman Singh. It was significant that he was remembered by his original name and title as the ruler of Nabha.

Niranjan Singh Talib of Nabha, who had known Maharaja Ripudaman Singh for long, had remained with him at Dehra Dun for five years and at Kodaikanal for three years before going to Calcutta for bringing out the *Desh Darpan* as a Punjabi daily. He was himself a fighter in the struggle for India's freedom. He was in the Montgomery Jail in 1942 when its *daroghā* (superintendent) came to tell him: 'Your Maharaja has passed away.' As President of Punjab Pradesh Congress and a Member of Parliament in 1975, Talib advocated the setting up of a memorial for the Maharaja whose life was devoted to the service of the country and the Sikh Panth.[45]

Notes

1. Punjab State Archives (PSA), Patiala, Chief Minister of Nabha State Records (CMNS Records), No. 10419-E, Maharaja to Chowrryappah, 7 and 9 February 1938.
2. IOR, R/1/13109, Political Department, No. 331-P(S)/1938, 'Activities on behalf of the ex-Maharaja of Nabha', Vijiaraghavachariar to the Viceroy, 16 March 1938 and its reply.
3. IOR, R/1/13109, No. 331-P(S)/1938, correspondence between Sant Singh and Glancy.
4. IOR, R/1/13109, No. 331-P(S)/1938, Glancy's note of his interview with Ranga Iyer, 25 May 1938.
5. IOR, R/1/13109, No. 331-P(S)/1938, Glancy's note of his interview with B. G. Horniman, 8 September 1938.
6. PSA, Patiala, President Council of Regency Nabha State (PCRNS) Records, File no. 230, Ripudaman Singh to C. S. Ranga Iyer, 4 October 1939, with copy of draft of the letter to Lord Linlithgow.

7. PSA, PCRNS Records, no. 230, Maharaja to Ranga Iyer, 20 October 1939, draft of representation to His Excellency.
8. As noticed earlier, as the President of the Shiromani Akali Dal, Baba Kharak Singh had toured through the Punjab states and inspired resolutions in support of the Maharaja. Even in July 1923, Labh Singh had moved a resolution after 'a strong and stirring speech' in a large gathering at Montgomery that the Shiromani Gurdwara Prabandhak Committee and the Central Sikh League be requested to take up the issue of Nabha to bring about the restoration of Maharaja Ripudaman Singh.
9. *The Tribune*, 11 July 1939, p. 2.
10. *The Tribune*, 23 November 1939, p. 13.
11. *The Tribune*, 11 December 1939, p. 12.
12. *The Tribune*, 2 January 1940, p. 12.
13. *The Tribune*, 12 January 1940, p. 7.
14. National Archives of India (NAI), New Delhi, Crown Representative Records (CRR) (microfilm), Acc no. 10, Reel no. 5, File no. 11(19)-P(S)-1940.
15. *The Tribune*, 12 February 1940, p.12.
16. *The Tribune*, 19 February 1940, p. 7.
17. *The Tribune*, 26 February 1940, p.7.
18. Fortnightly Report for 15–29 February 1940. File no. 11(19)-P(secret)/1940, Fortnightly Report for 1–15 March 1940.
19. Information for this paragraph has come from the birth certificates of the children of Maharaja Ripudaman Singh and Maharani Gurucharan Kaur, obtained by the authors from the Kodaikanal Municipality.
20. NAI, CRR, Acc no. 9, Reel no. 4, File no. 27(33)-P(secret)-39, representation of Sardarni Gurucharan Kaur. NAI, IOR (Microfilm), R/1/1/3539, File no. 15(4)-P(secret)/1940, note of an interview between DMO (Brigadier Molesworth) and H.H. Sardarni Sahiba Gurucharan Kaur, wife of ex-Maharaja of Nabha at 17 York Road, New Delhi on 25 January 1940.
21. *The Tribune*, 10 April 1940, p. 7.
22. PSA, PCRNS Records, File no. 440C. IOR R/1/1/3518 (microfilm), File no. (27)-P(S)/1940, Secret Report by the Central Intelligence Officer, Lahore, 15 April 1940.
23. PSA, PCRNS Records, no. 440C, cuttings from *The Tribune*, 11, 22 April 1940.
24. PSA, PCRNS Records, no. 440C, an extract from *The Tribune*, 27 April 1940.
25. *The Tribune*, 31 May 1940, p. 6.
26. NAI, CRR, Acc. no. 10, Reel no. 5, File no. 11(19)-P(S)/1940. This file also contains the photograph of the family appearing in *The Tribune*.
27. NAI, CRR, Acc. no. 10, Reel no. 5, File no. 11(19)-P(S)/1940, resolution of the SGPC.

28. NAI, CRR, File no. 11(19)-P(S)/1940, Fortnightly Report, 1-15 June 1940.
29. NAI, CRR, Acc. no. 10, Reel no. 5, File no. 11(19)-P(S)/1940, Acc no. 11, Reel no. 5, Fortnightly Reports, July 1940.
30. IOR, R/1/1/3518 (microfilm), File no, 11(27)-P(S)/1940.
31. NAI, IOR, R/1/1/3539 (microfilm). File no. 15(4)-P(S)/1940, cutting from *The Tribune*, 27 July 1940.
32. NAI, IOR, R/1/1/3518, File no. 11(27)-P(S)/1940, W. D. Robinson's Report, 30 January 1940; also NAI, IOR, R/1/1/3518, File no. 11(27)-P(S)/1940, 'Sikh Affairs', 27 January 1940.
33. IOR, R/1/1/3518 (microfilm), File no. 15(4)-P(S), 1940, Glancy's note of 24 August 1940.
34. For a discussion, see J. S. Grewal, *Master Tara Singh in Indian History: Colonialism, Nationalism, and Politics of Sikh Identity* (New Delhi: Oxford University Press, 2017), pp. 230–6.
35. Indu Banga, 'The Demand for Pakistan and Sikh Politics at Cross Roads', in *The Punjab Revisited: Social Order, Economic Life, Cultural Articulation, Politics, and Partition (18th-20th Centuries)*, edited by Karamjit K. Malhotra (Patiala: Punjabi University, 2014), pp. 292–328.
36. PSA, Patiala, PCRNS Records, File no. 440C. Woods-Ballard to Wakefield, 28 April 1940; Wakefield to Woods-Ballard, 2 May 1940; Woods-Ballard to Wakefield, 24 May 1940; note by the Home Member, Council of Regency, and others; correspondence between the Chief Police Officer, Nabha and the Managers of *The Tribune*, the *Aslī Qaumī Dard*, the *Akali te Pardesi*', and *The Civil and Military Gazette*.
37. NAI, IOR, R/1/1/3539, no. 15(4)-P(S)/1940, Skrine to Glancy, 10 July 1940, with a note on his interview with Maharani Gurucharan Kaur.
38. NAI, IOR, R/1/1/3539, no. 15(4)-P(S)/1940, Glancy's note of 6 August 1940.
39. NAI, IOR, R/1/1/3539, no. 15(4)-P(S)/1940, The Viceroy's order was conveyed to 'Sardarni' Gurucharan Kaur on 10 November 1940 by Woods-Ballard, Secretary to the Resident.
40. NAI, IOR, R/1/1/3539, no. 15(4)-P(S)/1940, E. B. Wakefield to the Agent, Imperial Bank of India Ltd., Delhi, 19 November 1940.
41. NAI, IOR, R/1/1/3539, no. 15(4)-P(S)/1940, C. P. Skrine to Sir Francis Wylie, 16 January 1941.
42. NAI, IOR, R/1/1/3539, no. 15(4)-P(S)/1940, Political Department to C. P. Skrine, 12 February 1941; Skrine to Sir Kenneth Fitze, Secretary to the Viceroy, 11 March 1941; Skrine's Address on 5 March 1941; Speech of Maharaja Partap Singh of Nabha on 5 March 1949.
43. PSA, Patiala, PCRNS Records, File no. 440C, Confidential D.O. no. 67/67-C, 9 August 1941, addressed to Major B. Woods-Ballard.
44. PSA, Patiala, Chief Minister of Nabha State Records (CMNS), File no. 10419E.

45. Niranjan Singh Talib, 'Desh Bhagat te Panth Prast Maharaja', *Kaumī Ektā* (New Delhi, February 1975), pp. 7–10. It may be added that Talib's father was an ahlkār of Nabha in the time of Maharaja Hira Singh. Talib himself was a school student at the time of the Delhi Darbar of 1912, and was among the four boys who lifted the robe of Maharaja Hira Singh.

IN RETROSPECT

The House of Nabha was descended from Chaudhri Phul, whose eldest son, Tiloka, was initiated by Guru Gobind Singh into the Khalsa order in 1706. Tiloka's son extended his territorial jurisdiction and his grandson, Hamir Singh, founded the town of Nabha in 1755, which came to serve as the capital of the state. He remained closely associated with the Khalsa across the Sutlej and probably did not formally accept Ahmad Shah Abdali's suzerainty. However, his son and successor, Jaswant Singh (1783–1840), felt obliged to accept British 'protection' in 1809. The latter's son, Devinder Singh (1840–6), was not keen to help the British during the Sikh War, which cost him his throne, and Nabha lost one-fourth of its territory. Ironically, while the deposition, arrest, and exile of Raja Devinder Singh to Mathura by the British were a source of embarrassment for Hira Singh (1871–1911), they were a source of inspiration for Hira Singh's son, Ripudaman Singh (1912–23). On the third birthday of the heir-apparent, Partap Singh (b. 1919), Ripudaman Singh got Raja Devinder Singh especially eulogized in a celebratory poem entitled, *Partāp Ude*.

Hira Singh, who was made Maharaja in the Imperial Darbar of 1911, appears to have left a mixed legacy for his successor. The British appreciated Hira Singh's dignified cooperation, especially his readiness to send the Imperial Service Troops of Nabha for service of the paramount power. In view of his efficient administration, the Political Agent was instructed not to interfere in his internal affairs. By the beginning of the twentieth century, he was virtually the leading ruler among the 36 princely states of the Punjab (among the Phulkians the Patiala ruler was a minor and the Jind ruler was hard of hearing).

Hira Singh was one of the five rulers chosen by Viceroy Curzon to represent the princely order on the coronation of Edward VII in 1902. Like some Rajput rulers, Hira Singh would not eat with the British, whether at Nabha or on the occasion of the Viceregal Darbars, and appeared only for a toast towards the end.

Initiatives as the Tikka

Significantly, Hira Singh preferred his only son and heir (Tikka) to be educated at home rather than sent to one of the Chief's Colleges, which were meant to Westernize the scions of the ruling families, encourage social conformity, and inculcate unquestioning loyalty to the British empire.

Tikka Ripudaman Singh had two tutors and both of them belonged to Nabha. The first, Bhai Kahn Singh, was associated with the Lahore Singh Sabha and its programme of radical reform in religious and social life of the Sikhs. He later became well known as a Sikh scholar. He was entrusted with the Tikka's establishment in 1887 when the latter was barely four years old. The Tikka learnt the *Guru Granth Sahib*, and he was educated in statecraft and politics through traditional texts. The other tutor, Lala Bishan Das, a graduate from Forman Christian College, Lahore, was the Headmaster of a government school in Dera Ismail Khan when he was called back to Nabha to be the Tikka's tutor for English. Lala Bishan Das was closely associated with the Arya Samaj and the nationalists like Harkishen Lal. Bishan Das developed a lifelong association with Ripudaman Singh, serving him in different capacities. Influenced deeply by both his tutors, Ripudaman Singh began his public life without the advantages or disadvantages of having been educated in a public school or Chiefs' College.

At the age of 21, Tikka Ripudaman Singh took the initiative to write to the Lieutenant Governor of the Punjab to get the idols in the precincts of the Golden Temple removed as this was against the tenets of the *Guru Granth Sahib*. He also added that a 'Sikh possessing force of character' (by which he meant a Singh Sabha reformer) should be appointed to the 'most sacred and responsible post' of the *sarbarāh* (manager). The idols were finally removed after a long enquiry by the district administration. There had been considerable counter-pressures from the moderate Sikhs and orthodox Hindus, who elicited the support of Raja Hira Singh.

At Nabha in 1906, Lady Minto noticed a marked contrast between the father and the son. Raja Hira Singh was 'a typical Indian Ruling Chief of the old school'; the Tikka, on the other hand, was 'rather sympathetic with modern and moderate school of Indian politicians'. In recognition of his father's steadfast loyalty, he was made Additional Nominated Member of the Imperial Legislative Council from December 1906 to October 1908. As evident from the tenor of his speeches and questions, he responded favourably to the prevailing anti-government climate in Calcutta. Initially, he quoted some well meaning British statesmen themselves to give constructive suggestions. Gradually, he began to criticize the British authorities directly for their policies and measures in several areas of governance.

A strong patriotic strain and social concerns were evident in Ripudaman Singh's speeches and questions. Responding to the changing situation of the first decade of the twentieth century, he touched upon a wide range of subjects of an all-India character: for example, racial discrimination in the judicial and police administration; restricted entry of Indians in the higher civil and military administration; change in the opium and liquor (excise) policy; the system of education and neglect of free compulsory education; inadequate provisions for public health; export of grains during famines; and lack of improvement in the condition of women. He also expressed concern about the conditions of Indians in the Transvaal colony in South Africa. Ripudaman Singh pleaded for respect for the treaty rights of princes and non-interference in their administration. He was strongly in favour of trial of a prince, if necessary, only by his peers as was the practice in England. He favoured the idea that expenditure on the Imperial Service Troops should be in proportion to the resources of a state.

Like Gokhale, Ripudaman Singh voted against the Seditious Meetings Bill as vague and likely to be misused. He opposed the Newspapers (Incitement to Offences) Bill on the argument that the government should first identify the causes of discontent and remove them. Conciliation rather than coercion was a better remedy in his view. He was critical of the Civil Procedures Bill on several grounds, and was opposed to separate electorates for Muslims. His effort to use parliamentary language barely concealed his brusqueness, which offended the British Members of the Council, shocked its princely members, and surprised the other Indian Members. Eventually, the questions raised by him began to be disallowed. The Governor

General conveyed his displeasure to Raja Hira Singh over the conduct of the Tikka. Hira Singh apparently felt helpless as his son would not heed his advice.

Ripudaman Singh was able to convince some British Members of the Council about the need for legislation for the Anand ceremony of marriage among the Sikhs. He mobilized public opinion in its favour among the Sikh intellectuals, professionals, and the Singh Sabha reformers. Despite opposition from some quarters, he was allowed to introduce the Bill in October 1908, but his term was not extended to pilot it. Sunder Singh Majithia, leader of the moderate and pro-government Chief Khalsa Diwan, was nominated to steer the Bill. The Tikka resented this very much not only as a matter of his personal honour, but also because his original proposal was whittled down.

Ripudaman Singh went to England in 1910–11, ostensibly on health grounds, but actually to pursue the matter of his re-nomination on the Council. Among others, he contacted James Keir Hardie, founder of the Labour Party and Member of Parliament, whom he might have met during Hardie's visit to Calcutta or Lahore in 1907. After Hardie's persistent efforts and protracted correspondence with the Secretary of State, Edwin Montagu, then the Under Secretary of State for India, admitted in Parliament in May 1912 that Tikka Sahib was the 'real author' of the Anand Marriage Bill and that 'the entire credit of its inception and introduction, and for its being finally passed into law' was due to him. In response to a specific question from Hardie, which had been decided upon in consultation with Ripudaman Singh, Montagu stated that it was not for want of confidence that Tikka Sahib could not steer the Bill. 'His term simply expired.' Ripudaman Singh took this explanation as an apology and a kind of victory over the government, but the authorities were not amused. From the government's point of view, he was 'a most unsatisfactory person', and was likely to be 'troublesome as a ruler'. Governor General Minto had already indicated in a private letter to the Secretary of State: 'Between you and me I certainly would not have reappointed the Tikka Sahib to the Legislative Council under any circumstances.'

The restraint with which the Secretary of State and the Governor General had dealt with Ripudaman Singh was at least partly due to a new orientation in the paramount power's relations with the princes. The interventionist policy had reached its apogee under Lord Curzon (1899–1905), with 3 rulers deposed, 63 placed under some kind of temporary British control, and restriction imposed on foreign travel of princes. However, the growing political extremism and revolutionary terrorism in the wake of the partition of Bengal had obliged the government to reorient its relations with the princes as a counterpoise to extremist politics of the educated middle class. The new policy announced by Minto at Udaipur in November 1909 assured the princes that their treaty rights would be protected and there would be minimum of interference in their internal affairs. A generally accommodating stance towards them was encouraged subsequently by Minto's two successors and also by King George V. At the Delhi Coronation Darbar in December 1911, the King had renewed the assurances given by his father, King Edward VII, and grandmother, Queen Victoria, that the 'rights, dignity and honour of native princes would be protected' by the Imperial Government.

Resistance as the Maharaja

The Tikka was in England when Maharaja Hira Singh passed away on 25 December 1911. Sailing immediately for India, Ripudaman Singh landed in Bombay on 14 January, and proceeded by train to Nabha. He walked barefoot from the railway station to the spot where his father had been cremated. He invoked his late father's forgiveness and his blessings for a successful rule. He declared state mourning for a year. On 24 January, Ripudaman Singh held a Darbar, and the due ceremonies of dastār-bandī were performed in the presence of the *Guru Granth Sahib*. He went on the assumption that he came into full powers with the ceremonies performed according to the established usage of his House.

However, the Lieutenant Governor, Louis Dane, and the Political Agent insisted on a formal installation and investiture, which had been evolved towards the end of the nineteenth century. Ripudaman Singh maintained that his right to succeed and rule ante-dated British paramountcy, and it was inherent and flawless. Moreover, the sanads of 1860 and 1862 entitled him to be 'the *de facto* and *de jure* Ruler' of his state immediately upon his father's death, and no other ceremony of installation and investiture by the British was required. Significantly, he engaged Sir Eardley Norton, the well-known pro-Congress barrister from Madras, to draft his correspondence with the government. Eventually, the Government of India felt obliged to concede Ripudaman Singh's essential point that the ceremony of installation was held in his own Darbar, the representative of the government seated to his left. Their insistence on a formal ceremony of installation and investiture was trivialized when Ripudaman Singh held his own Darbar on 20 December 1912 and came, wearing his own necklace, sarpech, and sword, the supposed emblems of royalty, which were to be conferred by the representative of the paramount power. The Maharaja was able to resist encroachments upon his rights but this controversy did not augur well for his relations with the Punjab authorities, who began to talk of his removal.

The next 10 years were marked by a growing tension between Ripudaman Singh and the government on several counts. Interpreting the sanads literally and looking upon himself as the head of a sovereign state, he maintained that he would accept only that advice from the Political Department which appealed to reason and did not encroach upon his internal autonomy. He ignored the objections of the Political Department to the use of a crown on his Coat of Arms. Unlike the other Phulkian rulers, Ripudaman Singh declined the honour of receiving the outgoing Lieutenant Governor, Louis Dane, and of playing host to his successor, Michael O'Dwyer. Far more outrageous from the viewpoint of the bureaucracy was Ripudaman Singh's response during the World War when some native princes offered all they had, their entire revenues, their jewellery, and their personal service. The Maharaja of Patiala surpassed all the princes in his enthusiasm, and was ahead of all the Punjab rulers in sending men and materials. He was rewarded rather generously for his services. Ripudaman Singh, on the other hand, did the minimum required to fulfil his treaty obligations. He offered help in money, horses, and houses for use as hospitals directly to the Viceroy, bypassing the provincial authorities. He managed to get the Imperial Service Troops of Nabha rejected for active service. Consequently, he was the only Indian ruler not included in the honours list for the war effort.

Ripudaman Singh offended the government in many other ways. His indifference towards apprehending the Ghadarites in 1914–15 in his territories was particularly galling to O'Dwyer. Ripudaman Singh personally and financially supported the founding of the Benares Hindu University set up at the initiative of Madan Mohan Malaviya, the veteran Congressman. Ripudaman Singh sat through the special enquiry to go into the Martial Law imposed by Michael O'Dwyer, and even made an effort to have him impeached for the Punjab wrongs, including the Jallianwala Bagh massacre. The Maharaja also presided over a session of the Tilak School of Politics at Massourie, and contributed towards the Tilak Swaraj Fund. He had engaged a pro-Congress Chief Minister like Purushottam Das Tandon and continued to support a pro-Congress paper like the *Bombay Chronicle* of B. G. Horniman, an Englishman, who was later deported to England for his close association with the Congress. Ripudaman Singh was known to be on good terms with a zealous revolutionary like Raja Mahendra Pratap, and the nationalist leaders like Gopal Krishan Gokhale and Lala Lajpat Rai.

Even more alarming for the government were Ripudaman Singh's close links with several radical Sikh reformers, called the tat Khalsa or Neo-Sikhs in the CID reports. He financed radical Sikh papers such as the *Sikh Review* and the *Akali*, and patronized well-known Sikh reformist institutions such as the Panch Khalsa Diwan, Bhasaur, Sikh Kanya Mahavidyalayà, Firozpur, and the *derā* (establishment) of Sant Attar Singh at Mastuana. After the founding of the pro-Congress Central Sikh League in 1919 and the Shiromani Gurdwara Prabandhak Committee (SGPC) and the Shromani Akali Dal in 1920, he is known to have taken a keen interest in their activities and provided funds. On the Nankana Day on 5 April 1921, he declared official mourning in the state in the memory of those Akalis who had lost their lives in the massacre at Nankana. All offices in Nabha were closed, and the Maharaja himself wore a black turban and slept on the floor.

Even when the Punjab bureaucrats were not happy with Ripudaman Singh's general sympathy with individuals, institutions, and movements antithetical to the government, they could not find fault with his administration, which could be termed progressive. He modernized the administration of Nabha, which had already been put on a sound footing by his father, as admitted by the British themselves. Ripudaman Singh now introduced a central secretariat with different ministries, reorganized the judicial, police, and revenue administration, and established a Legislative Council. He took steps towards better health and sanitation facilities in Nabha, and attempted to introduce electrification. Early in his rule, emulating Sayajirao of Baroda, he had introduced free primary education in the state.

In the Princes' Conferences convened during and after the war, Ripudaman Singh reiterated his insistence on the respect for treaty rights. He was quick to react to any proposal that was likely to erode the autonomy of the princely states. He maintained that furnishing of statistics to the paramount power by the states should be regarded as their internal matter and not a political obligation. He also pleaded for transparency of procedures and exhibited a dignified stance of independence in his speeches. In the inaugural meeting of the Chamber of Princes in February 1921, he suggested that in the absence of the Viceroy, a prince rather than a senior British official should preside over the meeting. He sought division on the participation of the 'lesser' states in the Chamber, which could not possibly be appreciated by the Viceroy. Significantly, Ripudaman Singh had actively contributed towards the October 1920 Resolution for setting up a Court of Arbitration with princes as members for settling disputes between states, or between them and the paramount power. Ironically, in his own case, Ripudaman Singh was denied such a court.

Until about the middle of 1921, Ripudaman Singh had been able to retain initiative vis-à-vis the government. In his administrative reforms and reorganization, he emulated the progressive states like Baroda and Mysore. It is not unlikely that the small princely states had begun to look upon him as the champion of their political rights. He was widely respected among the Sikhs for his views on religion and his advocacy of radical reform. He was generally well regarded for supporting nationalistic causes. One single thread that ran through Ripudaman Singh's public career till then was the direct or indirect resistance to the government, with a strong sense of patriotism.

Deposition

It is possible to discern three strands in this rather complex resistance: as a prince, as a Sikh, and as an Indian. As a native prince, Ripudaman Singh took a historical, even literal and contractual, view of the sanad rights and customary practices. Despite the Political Department invoking 'usage' and 'political practice' and interpreting the sanads in favour of the paramount power, he continued to insist on their original meaning and intent, often to the exasperation of the bureaucracy. As a Sikh, Ripudaman Singh passionately subscribed to the Sikh tenets and worked for the introduction and enactment of the Anand Marriage Act. He also lent support to the movement for the restoration of the outer wall of the Gurdwara Rakabganj in Delhi. His genuine support for radical reform of Sikh practices and institutions and advocacy of such reform incurred the hostility of the Punjab Administration and Patiala. His involvement in Akali politics was not due to his rivalry with Bhupinder Singh of Patiala. This is a superficial and inadequate view of Ripudaman Singh's ideological position and public career. His self-identification as a Sikh, his invocation of treaty rights, and glorification of Raja Devinder Singh's recalcitrance against the British were easily assimilated into a nationalist stance. His pride in the past glory of India and the superiority of its culture underpinned his critique of colonial rule in the Imperial Legislative Council. Taking interest in diverse issues and activities regarded as anti-British in character and spirit, Ripudaman Singh played a dangerous game for almost a decade and a half before he was finally trapped by the paramount power.

All the representatives of paramount power—the Viceroy, the Punjab Administration, and even the Home Government—had been unhappy with Ripudaman Singh since the beginning of his public career. But the government could neither openly disregard the sanads of Nabha nor easily establish Ripudaman Singh's disloyalty. After a CID enquiry was instituted in September 1921 to 'collect' evidence of his seditious activity, the zealous Agent to the Governor General, in collaboration with the resourceful Prime Minister of Patiala, ensured that the recurrent disputes between Nabha and Patiala were escalated to a point of no return, so as to afford an opportunity to the paramount power to intervene. In October 1921, the Secretary of State, Edwin Montagu (who, as the Under Secretary of State, had been obliged in 1912 to offer an explanation in Parliament for not renewing Tikka Ripudaman Singh's term on the Council) advised Viceroy Reading to rely on Patiala in this project.

Maharaja Bhupinder Singh of Patiala was the anti-thesis of Maharaja Ripudaman Singh. Educated at the Chief's College, Lahore, and carefully groomed by the British for loyal and unstinted cooperation, he had become their biggest collaborator. Foremost among the princes in war effort and later as Chancellor of the Chamber of Princes, he was known in British circles for his lavish hospitality and penchant for pomp. He willingly accepted the advice of the Political Officers and befriended them with his generosity. Unlike Ripudaman Singh, he was least interested in administrative and social reform, and was actually indifferent to the tenets of Sikhism or the issue of Sikh identity. Even his credentials as a Sikh were publicly questioned by some Akali leaders. At any rate, he had no qualms about cooperating with the government in undermining the Akali movement, or in publicly opposing the Congress programme. In return, the British would overlook his gross administrative and financial mismanagement, miscarriage of justice, criminal acts, and rather exceptional appetite for sensual gratification. Later on, when the All India States' People's Conference clamoured for his removal, the government bailed him out through a farcical enquiry. This was partly a reward for his having provoked and sustained petty territorial disputes with Nabha, and then backing the government efforts by relentless propaganda, intimidation, and bribes to ensure treachery on the part of the Nabha officials.

By the time the decision to chastise Ripudaman Singh, with crucial support from Patiala, was finally taken, the Akalis had formally joined the non-cooperation movement, and the mainstream nationalism led by Mahatma Gandhi was at its height. Its abatement after the Chauri Chaura incident in early 1922 encouraged Viceroy Reading to neutralize Ripudaman Singh altogether and make an example of him as an assertive prince. Bhupinder Singh of Patiala was encouraged to become more aggressive and unrelenting. Ripudaman Singh's repeated demand for a Court of Arbitration under the Resolution of October 1920 to resolve the disputes between Nabha and Patiala was brushed aside by the Viceroy. Instead, he invoked the idea of the 'King's Peace' in the English Common Law, probably for the first time, to set up a commission of enquiry. A British judge with impeccable imperialist credentials was appointed to conduct the enquiry, counsels were disallowed, procedures were tailored, and laws were interpreted according to the needs of the moment. Strategy continued to be evolved amidst hectic exchange of views and advice from the Secretary of State down to the AGG, who projected Ripudaman Singh as 'a danger to the whole of India'. As expected, Justice Louis Stuart came up with a suitable report that, though legally untenable, was used to intimidate and coerce Maharaja Ripudaman Singh to abdicate.

Ironically, Ripudaman Singh's forced deposition brought him to the centre stage of Sikh politics. The initial demand of the Akalis, which led to the Jaito Morcha (1923–5), was for his restoration, and it was never formally abandoned. Its echoes were heard in the Congress sessions and in the British Parliament. Successive questions raised by the Labour Members of Parliament regarding the legality of Ripudaman Singh's deposition, impropriety of separating him from his son, and inhumanity of his detention without trial were parried by the Tories. On his part, Ripudaman Singh continued to fight his proxy battles against the paramount power and its collaborators, articulating his criticism of its policies towards the princes and the people. On the plea of 'disloyalty' and disobedience, the government decided to send him to Kodaikanal in the south as a political prisoner under the archaic Bengal Regulation III of 1818. It was an extraordinary measure that was invoked where 'danger' to the empire was certain but 'conviction' through judicial process was not.

Ripudaman Singh continued to maintain that he could not be detained under a Regulation meant for British India. Moreover, he had been denied hearing by a Court of Arbitration. He refused to sign a petition addressed to the Governor General and send it through the Collector of Madurai like an ordinary subject of British India. He would not barter away his inherent right or compromise his legal position to buy his freedom.

As a matter of fact, Ripudaman Singh's failure in this unequal fight might have been structurally inevitable. On the ground, in India, he was pitted against diehard imperialists like Michael O'Dwyer, J. P. Thompson, Malcolm Hailey, Louis Stuart, and the hostile Agents to the Governor General—A. B. Minchin and James Fitzpatrick. They all subscribed to the imperialist ideology of the Tories and actively worked for it in their official and private capacities. For them there was no higher morality than holding on to the empire. The brief interludes of the Labour and the so-called National Government could neither make a dent in the outlook of the India Office in Britain nor influence the working of the Political Department in India. The men on the spot acted as the watchdogs of the empire. Both Minchin and Fitzpatrick took care of the necessary manipulations on the ground, and even influenced decisions in crucial ways. They were the kingpins of the political charades called the Stuart and Fitzpatrick 'enquiries'—one geared to corner Ripudaman Singh and the other to extricate Bhupinder Singh of Patiala. In fact, Fitzpatrick put the blame on Ripudaman Singh for the damaging *Indictment* of Patiala, published by the All India States' People's Conference. While Ripudaman Singh excited the prejudice and paranoia of these men, Bhupinder Singh boosted their ego and fed their greed. Both Minchin and Fitzpatrick saw no contradiction between the defence of the empire against a disloyal adversary like Ripudaman Singh and acceptance of gratification from a loyal collaborator like Bhupinder Singh. Collectively, the British bureaucrats worked for dividing the two princes and collaterals and also the Sikhs in general and the Akalis. From the Viceroy down to the AGG, the British also manipulated to separate Ripudaman Singh from his wife, Maharani Sarojini Devi, and their son, Tikka Partap Singh. Later on, efforts were made to create a rift between Ripudaman Singh and Maharani Gurucharan Kaur when she came to the north to make a last bid for her husband's release and restoration.

In a Nationalist Perspective

Despite all odds, Ripudaman Singh had been able to raise and consistently pursue issues that were significant for the future. He advocated trial by peers and protection of treaty rights and defended internal autonomy of princely territories, eventually obliging Viceroy Reading to openly counter this position through his well-known letter to the Nizam of Hyderabad in 1926. Earlier, Ripudaman Singh had obliged Viceroy Hardinge to review the procedures and ceremonies used for the installation and investiture of princes. Ripudaman Singh's insistence on transparency of procedures and rights of the 'lesser' states in the Chamber of Princes could potentially alter the rules of the game for the paramount power. Far more significant were the issues springing from Ripudaman Singh's Sikh identity, like proper use and management of Gurdwaras, proper utilization of public charities and endowments, promotion of denominational education, and recognition of Anand Marriage. In fact, he came to be regarded as the father of the Anand Marriage Act (1909). As a nominated Member of the Imperial Legislative Council, he pleaded earnestly for wide-ranging administrative and economic reforms and social changes of all-India importance. As a ruler, he did attempt to translate some of his concerns into practice. It may not be far too wrong to say that through his government and politics Ripudaman Singh bridged 'Indian India' with British India.

Interestingly, in their political attitudes, administrative reforms, and social concerns, there were palpable similarities between Ripudaman Singh and his senior contemporary, Maharaja Sayajirao III of Baroda (1875–1939), who ruled over a 'major' state with much larger territory and resources and higher ranking among the princes. In fact, Baroda came next to Hyderabad in precedence and had a 21-gun salute against the 13-gun salute of Nabha. In his politics and administration, Ripudaman Singh, however, was not deterred by the small size of his state or its ranking in princely order.

Both Sayajirao and Ripudaman Singh made deliberate attempts to modernize their states by introducing administrative, judicial, and legislative reforms, which the British did not always relish. In their own ways, both favoured radical educational and social reform, and both were invited to preside over the National Social Conference, which met alongside the Indian National Congress, Maharaja Sayajirao in 1904 and Tikka Ripudaman Singh in 1909. They took men of known nationalistic sympathies into the state service and shielded 'extremists' and even 'seditionists' in their territories.

On another plane, and deeply conscious as they were of the deposition of their predecessors, both the princes invoked the letter and spirit of the engagements of their Houses with the paramount power and jealously guarded their autonomy. Not servile in their general attitude, they were the least keen to entertain the local representatives of the government. Rather, both preferred to deal directly with the Crown. The two shared an aversion also for ceremonial dress and rituals of the empire. Sayajirao's uncourtly conduct towards the King Emperor in the Delhi Darbar in 1911 and Ripudaman Singh's resistance against the rituals of installation and investiture in 1912 led to an open demand in the British circles for deposition of the former, and murmurings among the Punjab officials about its desirability in case of the latter. If the bureaucracy viewed their stance of independence, tenacity, and initiative as inconvenient and obstructive, both were defended and supported by James Keir Hardie, a strong critic of the imperialists in the British Parliament.

The outbreak of the World War I saved Sayajirao from the almost impending deposition and brought him closer to the government, but Ripudaman Singh got singled out as the only prince who was not keen to help in the war effort. Seasoned and more circumspect, Sayajirao appears to have made a strategic retreat after 1914, which was the 39th year of his reign. His activities during and after the war show 'a tendency to go along' or have 'peace with the Raj at all cost', according to his grandson and biographer, Fatesinghrao Gaekwad. Sayajirao's involvement in the Princes' Conferences and later in the inaugural meeting of the Chamber of Princes was more of a ceremonial and formal nature. Subsequently, like the rulers of the other major states, he stayed away from the Chamber, which was dominated by the middle-ranking states such as Bikaner and Patiala. Ripudaman Singh at that time was in his thirties and full of ideas. He was enthusiastic about the use of the Princes' Conferences and the Chamber of Princes for improving the position of the princes vis-à-vis the paramount power. As things turned out, there was not much scope for any thawing of relations between the government and Ripudaman Singh, whose strong ideological predilections drew him into the vortex of the post-war politics in the province and the country.

It can nevertheless be argued that given the anxiety of the government to use the princes as a counterpoise to the extreme form of nationalism represented by the Akali, Khilafat, and non-cooperation movements, and an earlier volte face in their attitude towards Sayajirao, Ripudaman Singh's predilections too could have been tolerated or overlooked. But a particular historical conjuncture in the early 1920s worked against him: the princes were becoming vocal, the Akalis remained irreconcilable, and the Congress was in disarray after the withdrawal of non-cooperation. In view of Ripudaman Singh's insistence on the autonomy and rights of princes per se and overt sympathies with Akali politics, it was feared that he might become a symbol simultaneously of resistance among the princes and the Sikh masses, with dangerous implications for the loyalty of the Sikh soldiers. Action against Ripudaman Singh could restrain the other outspoken members of the princely order. His removal would most certainly make way for the Maharaja of the much larger Sikh state of Patiala, who was the most enthusiastic princely collaborator, to influence the politics of the Sikhs along desirable lines.

The real reason behind Ripudaman Singh's deposition was not lost on his contemporaries in India and Britain. Mardy Jones, who was among a dozen Labour MPs who interceded on his behalf, maintained that 'his chief crime' was 'his independence of mind and his frank aid of the Nationalist cause in India'. Several of the leading papers in India regarded his dispute with Patiala as merely a pretext to penalize Ripudaman Singh for what *The Tribune* called his 'sturdy independence'. *The Nation* suggested that the government was actually afraid of his 'progressive political tendency' and expected that his removal would serve as 'a deterrent to the Rajas and Maharajas similarly inclined'. Writing in the Nabha Number of the *Akali*, dated 9 September 1923, the Punjab Congress leader, Dr Saifuddin Kitchlew observed:

> The Maharaja of Nabha is not one of those rulers who consider it essential for their existence to support every measure of the Government. He had in him the spirit of a true patriot, citizen and ruler and exhibited his independent views and fair-mindedness on every occasion.

On Nabha Day in Delhi on 17 September, Dr Kitchlew put Ripudaman Singh's 'offence' rather succinctly: 'He wished well of the country and was not afraid of anybody except the Akal Purakh.' A clue to his studied opposition to the British empire lies in his strong sense of patriotism arising both from his Sikh and Indian identity.

1. Maharaja Hira Singh (1871–1911)

2. The Coat of Arms of Nabha, with a crown at the top

* We gratefully acknowledge the sources of photographs: the Nabha Foundation, New Delhi, India, for nos 1, 2, 11–15; Gurjot Singh Galwatti, 'Riyasat-E-Nabha', for nos 6–7 (from Bagrian Estate Illustrated, in his personal possession) and no. 9 (acquired by him from Sukhmanjit Singh); and the Punjab Digital Library, Chandigarh, India, for no. 10. Four photographs are from public domain: no. 3 from http://tribuneindia.com; nos 4–5 from http://sikh-heritage.co.uk; and no. 8 from http://royalcollection.org.uk. We are thankful to Professor Reeta Grewal and S. Gurjot Singh Galwatti for their help in locating these photographs and their sources.

3. Raja Hira Singh with Tikka Ripudaman Singh

4. Seated, left to right: Raja Hira Singh, Tikka Ripudaman Singh, and Bhai Kahn Singh Nabha. Standing, left to right: Sardar Nihal Singh and Munshi Faiz Bakht

5. Seated, left to right: Tikka Ripudman Singh, Lord Curzon, Raja Hira Singh, and Dunlop Smith (1903)

6. Maharaja Ripudaman Singh outside the Nabha Fort after *dastār bandī* (coronation)

7. Seated, left to right: Bhai Arjan Singh Bagrian, Maharaja Bhupinder Singh of Patiala, and Maharaja Ripudaman Singh of Nabha. Standing, left to right: Raja Gurdit Singh of Retgarh and Bhai Kahn Singh Nabha

8. Maharaja Ripudaman Singh with his courtiers

9. Maharaja Ripudaman Singh and his infant son, Tikka Partap Singh, seated on a hunted tiger

10. The young Maharaja Partap Singh at the time of his installation (1928)

11. A signed portrait of Maharaja Ripudaman Singh at Kodaikanal (September 1929)

12. Maharaja Ripudaman Singh and Maharani Gurucharan Kaur with their children at Kodaikanal

13. Maharani Gurucharan Kaur and her children with Sardar Kharak Singh and others

14. Maharani Gurucharan Kaur and her children with Master Tara Singh and others

15. Maharani Gurucharan Kaur in conversation with Master Tara Singh at his residence in Amritsar

GLOSSARY

achkan	Indian long coat
ahlkār	an agent; an official
Akāl Sahāi	under the protective care of the Immortal; may God be our helper
Akali	a staunch follower of Guru Gobind Singh; equated with the Nihang in the early nineteenth century; in the twentieth century, initially a volunteer to take over Sikh Gurdwaras and afterwards a member of the Shiromani Akali Dal
akhand pāṭh	an uninterrupted reading of the *Guru Granth Sahib*
amrit	initiation of the double-edged sword
ardās	a prayer; a formal and collective prayer of the Sikhs, noticed by the author of the *Dabistān-i Mazāhib* in the seventeenth century; probably going back to the time of Guru Nanak
Baisakhi	the festival held on the first day of the month of Baisakh
bairāgī	a renunciate; generally, a Vaishnava
begār	unpaid or forced labour
benāmī	property registered in the name of a person other than the real owner
bhog	conclusion of the reading of the *Guru Granth Sahib*, followed generally by singing of hymns and always by an *ardās*; enjoyment of worldly pleasures

biswedār	a person entitled to a share (lit. one-twentieth part) in the produce from land owned by another
chaudharī	the acknowledged head of a clan who acted as an intermediary between the brotherhood and the state, generally with jurisdiction over a number of villages; a headman of a group of villages for collecting revenues on behalf of the government; the office was generally hereditary
chaukī	an outpost
chaukidār	a watchman
dafedār	an officer of infantry or cavalry, commanding a small body of men
Darbar	a royal court; the court of a king; the court of the Guru; also used for the Harmandar Sahib at Amritsar, and the Gurdwara at Tarn Taran
daroghā	a superintendent or head of a department
dastār-bandī	lit. tying of turban; the custom of *dastār-bandī* after the death of the head of the family in the Punjab entailed the tying of turban as the symbol of succession; coronation
dastūr-al-'amal	the long-standing rules of practice
deodhī	entrance to an establishment
derā	encampment; a religious establishment
dharmarth	charitable grants
dīwān khāna	a hall of audience
dīwān	public meeting
Dīwān	an officer; the person holding the position next to that of the ruler, a chief minister
Dīwān-i Sadr	a chancellor; the chief court
doim darje ka arzinavis	second-grade petition writer
duādashī	the twelfth day of the moon
farmān	an injunction, an order; a royal order
gaddī	lit. a cushioned seat; a throne; the seat of the head of a religious fraternity
granthī	a professional reader of the Granth; the person in charge of a Gurdwara
Gurdwara (*gurdwārā*)	'the door of the Guru'; the Sikh sacred space where *kīrtan*, *kathā*, and *ardās* are performed and community meal is cooked and eaten by all

Glossary

Guru (*guru*)	a religious teacher; an epithet used for the founder of Sikhism and each of his nine successors; the Granth Sahib and the Sikh Panth are also given the status of the Guru
Guru Granth	the Sikh scripture, compiled by Guru Arjan in 1604 (containing the compositions of the first five Gurus and a number of *bhaktas*, *sants*, and Sufis) and authenticated by Guru Gobind Singh, with the compositions of Guru Tegh Bahadur included. Now known as the *Guru Granth Sahib*
hakīm	a physician in the Unani (Greek) system of medicine
hartāl	to stop work in protest
hukamnāma	a written order, used generally for the letters of the Sikh Gurus to their followers
imdādī	auxiliary
ishtihār	advertisement; a public notification
'itar	perfume
ittila'nāma	a proclamation
izzat	honour; social repute; good name
jāgīr	an assignment of land revenue for rendering salary
jāgīrdār	the holder of a *jāgīr*, who is entitled to collect revenues from a given piece of land in lieu of service to the state
jarrāh	a surgeon
jathā	a group, a band
jathedār	the leader of a band
kār sewā	physical labour; an act of service; used specially for digging out mud from the *sarovar* at the Golden Temple, Amritsar
karhā parhsād	sacramental food distributed in Gurdwaras to all persons present, generally prepared with equal quantities of wheat flour, sugar, and ghee
khādī	home-spun cloth
Khāngī Kārobārī	the household department
kharīta	an exalted communication
khil'at	a dress of honour, containing articles of costume generally numbering 3 to 21, including arms or

	horses, and bestowed by a superior on an inferior as a mark of distinction
kirpān	curved sword
kīrtan	singing of hymns
Kuka	a member of the Namdhari sect of the Sikhs who were known for their shrieks (*kūks*) during a *kīrtan*
Lambardār (Namberdār)	the village headman in the colonial Punjab, earlier called *muqaddam*
langar	a kitchen for the community; an open kitchen for charity; a community meal; generally, a feature of the Sikh sacred space for congregational worship
lāthī	a long stick
lāvān	a composition of Guru Ram Das in which the metaphor of marriage is used for conveying a spiritual message, and which is now used for the Sikh marriage ceremony in which each of the four stanzas are recited for each circumambulation of the *Guru Granth Sahib* by the bridegroom and the bride
māfidār	grantee, holder of revenue-free land
mahkma	department
mandī	a grain market
marhīs	small structures at the place of cremation
masnad	throne
morchā	an agitational struggle used metaphorically for a nonviolent agitation over a specific issue or a number of issues
murāsila	letter
musāhib	companion; associate; a courtier
nafar	servant
nām	name
nazar	an offering, in cash or kind, to a superior; a kind of tribute
nāzim	the governor of a province; an administrator of a primary division (*nizāmat*) in Nabha
Nāzim Nahr	superintendent of canals
nazrāna	offering of a gift to a superior; the tribute paid by a vassal; also paid by an official on a regular basis or on special occasions

nizāmat	an administrative unit
pahul	water used for initiating a person as a Sikh (*charan pahul*) or a Singh (*khande ki pahul*)
pālkī	a palanquin, a litter
pān	betel leaf
Panth	literally a path; the people following a particular path; collectively the followers of the Gurus; the Sikh community
pardah	veil or seclusion
pargana	a small unit of administration
parkarmā	the circumambulatory path on all four sides of the tank around the Harmandar Sahib; also the path around the Harmandar Sahib, called the inner *parkarmā*
parshād	food or sacred food
pāṭh	reading; reading of the *Guru Granth Sahib*
patit	renegade
pāṭhī	professional reader of a religious book
pātshah	a ruler, a king, an emperor; used generally for the Mughal rulers instead of *sultan*; used metaphorically for the Sikh Gurus
patwārī	a village accountant; there could be one *patwārī* for several villages; the keeper of revenue records of a village
pujārī	the attendant of a shrine; a Brahman priest who conducts rituals
rāgī	a singer, particularly of the hymns of the Sikh scripture
Riyāsat	state; principality
roznāmcha	daily diary
sabhā	a society or an association
sahāyak (*sahaik*)	lit. supporter; in aid
samādh	a structure raised over a spot of cremation in honour of an important person, whether secular or religious; the counterpart of a mausoleum
samitī	a volunteer body
sanad	an affidavit; a written document possessing legal validity; royal ordinance or any deed or grant or certificate from one in authority; a formal document recording agreement between two parties

sangat	an assembly; a religious congregation; a congregation of Sikhs; the collective body of Sikhs at one place
sarbarāh	a manager, an officer
sarkār	an administrative unit for law and order; one who is at the helm of affairs, a person in authority, a ruler; popularly used for a government
saropā	lit. from head to foot; the robe of honour in Mughal times, consisting of a large number of articles of dress from the head to the feet, including arms and horses; in Sikh practice, a simpler robe of honour, now even a single shawl, or a piece of cloth symbolic of honour
sarpech	a jewelled headband worn over the turban
sarwārna	cash rotated round the head of a person and given in charity for his safety
satyāgraha	non-violent resistance
shabad	lit. the word; a hymn; verse from the *Guru Granth Sahib*
shahīdī	the act of becoming a martyr; martyrdom in the Sikh tradition
shikār	hunting; the chase; a prey; game
shuddhī	purification; used for reconversion to the Hindu fold in the late nineteenth and early twentieth centuries
sūtak	the deemed state of a woman's impurity during childbirth and menstruation
swadeshī	a movement in favour of using Indian goods and institutions; implying rejection of British goods and institutions
swarāj	self-rule; self-government
Tahsīldār	the officer in charge of a *tahsīl* for the collection of revenue, with some executive and judicial powers
tat-Khālsa	the staunch Khalsa; a radical Singh reformer of the early twentieth century
thāna	a police post
Tikka	heir apparent; the eldest son of a ruler
toshākhāna	a storehouse; a treasure-house
vāk	an 'order' taken from the *Guru Granth Sahib*

vakīl	an authorized representative; an agent or a deputy; an envoy
yog	union with the Supreme Being through austerities and meditation
zail	circle
zaildār	circle officer; an officer over a number of village headmen under the British

SELECT BIBLIOGRAPHY

Unpublished Official Records

Cambridge University Library, University of Cambridge, UK

Crewe Papers, 'Tikka Sahib of Nabha', I/3(12) (1911–12)

India Office Records (IOR), British Library, London, UK

Microfilms, Manuscripts, and Records

1915, R/1/1/1024, Simla Records, Foreign and Political Department, nos 78–80
1916, MSS Eur E 264/17
1917–18, L/P and S/10/217 (Confidential), Reel nos 22, 33, and 164 (Political)
1918, R/1/19/602, Foreign and Political Department nos 1–18
1923, R/1/29/32, File no. 628-P (Secret)
1923, R/1/29/53, File no. 838-Political (Secret)
1923, L/P and S/10/1022, Register no. 3607
1923, R/1/29/26, File no. 583-Political II-(Secret)
1923, R/1/1/1375(1), File no. 628(3) Political
1924, Judicial J&P (S) 264/24
1924, 281(S), 1079
1924, R/1/1/1518(I), Reel no. 32
1924, R/1/29/77, File no. 14-P (Secret)
1924, R/1/1/1520, File no. 64 (17) Political
1924, Eur E 236/26, vol. IV, nos 8 (6 March), 17, 22, 25, and 76b
1924, Eur E 238/7, vol. V, nos 9 and 22
1924, Eur E 238/26, Reading Collection, vol. IV, no. 286

1924–5, R/1/1/1526, File no. 64(27)-P (Secret) of, Government of India, Foreign and Political Department, Serial nos 1–2
1926, L/P and S/10/1027
1926–7, R/1/1/1525
1927, R/1/1/1635, File no. 404-P (Secret)
1927, R/1/1/1696, File no. 694-P (Secret)
1927, R/1/1/1707 (a), Foreign & Political Department, File no. 752-P
1927, R/1/1/1707 B, File no. 752-P (Secret)
1927–28, R/1/1/1729
1928, R/1/1/1996, File no. 694-P (Secret)
1928, R/1/1/1727, File no. 155-P (Secret)
1928, L/P S/10/1024
1928, L/P and S/1028, Register no. 5370
1928, R/1/1/1717, File no. 93-P (Secret)
1928, R/1/1/1719, File no. 97-P (Secret)
1928, R/1/1/1721, File no. 99-P (Secret)
1928, R/1/1/1727, File no. 155-P (Secret)
1928, R/1/1/1731 File no. 174-P (Secret)
1928, R/1/1/1732, File no. 175-P (Secret)
1928, R/1/1/1756, File no. 253-P (Secret)
1928, L/P S/10/1024, 29 February, extract from the official report of the Legislative Assembly Debates
1928–9, R/1/1/1764(2)
1930, R/1/1/1896
1930, R/1/1/1981 File no. 390-P(Secret)
1930, R/1/1/1881 File no. 390-P(Secret)
1930, L/P and S/10/100028, Reel no. 37, Register no. 6832
1931, R/1/1/2133, File no. 319-P(Secret)
1935, R/1/1/2685, File no. 218-P(Secret)
1936, R/1/1/2806, File no. 101-P (Secret)
1936, R/1/12952, File no. 235-P (Secret)
1938, R/1/1/13109, Political Department File no. 331-P(S)
1940, R/1/1/3518, 11(27)-P(S), File no. 440C
1940, R/1/1/3539, File no. 15(4)-P (Secret)

National Archives of India (NAI), New Delhi, India

1909, Anand Marriage Act, (Legislative Department)
1911–15, Hardinge Papers
1922, 22 February, Home/Political, No. D95-Pol
1923, Home/ Pol, 5/II
1924, 19 February, Extract From the Legislative Assembly Debates, vol. IV, no. 14

1924, Home/Pol & KW File 320K
1928, Crown Representative Records (CRR), Accession no. 11 (microfilm), Reel no. 6, File no. 93-P (Secret)
1928, CRR, Accession no.12 (microfilm), Reel no.7, File no.174-P (Secret)
1930, CRR, Punjab States, Accession nos 7 and 13, Reel no. 2, File no. 115- P (Secret), Part I
1930, CRR, Accession no. 8 (microfilm), Reel no. 3, File no. 390-P (Secret)
1930, CRR, Punjab States, Accession no. 7 (microfilm), Reel no. 2 File no. 115-(2), P(Secret), Foreign and Political Department
1932, CRR, Accession no. 14 (microfilm), Reel no. 9, File nos 182 P (Secret), and 105-P (Secret)
1934, CRR, Accession no. 8 (microfilm), Reel no. 3, File no. 366-P (Secret)
1936, CRR, Accession no. 13 (microfilm), Reel no. 8, File no. 101-P(Secret)
1940, CRR, Accession no. 10 (microfilm), Reel no. 5, File no. 11(19)-P (Secret)
1940, CRR, Accession no. 9 (microfilm), Reel no. 4, File no. 27(33)-P(Secret)-39
Foreign Department, Native States, no. 321/6, 322/6
Halifax Collection, Accession nos 3885, 3890, 3895, 3940, 1930
Home Department, Political Branch, 1924, File no. 401
'Papers Relating to Anand Marriage Act VII of 1909 (Legislative Department)'

Nehru Memorial Museum and Library (NMML), New Delhi

All India Congress Committee (AICC), G-19, File no. 19/1927.
AICC (Supplementary), File no. 56, items 240, 241, 247–8, 249 (Home D/2505 Poll), 253–4, 262, 268

Punjab State Archives (PSA), Chandigarh, India

1905, 30 March; 20 and 27 April; I, 8, and 16 May; 5–8, 10, 12 and 15 June; I July; 14 October; 20 November, nos 668/12 Confidential

Punjab State Archives (PSA), Patiala, India

1911, June, Proceedings, Foreign Department–Secret 1, nos 30–2
Nabha Affairs 1912–1917
1912, PGR (Punjab Government Records), 'Installation',1 April; 9 May, 3, 6, and 25 June; 4 and 19 July; 6 August; 20 and 30 September, 8, 9, and 28 October; 22 November, 3, 5, and 20; and 22December
1913, PGR, 'Installation', 2 January; 5 February; and 27 February
1912, PGR, File nos 6, 291, Pol. N.S
1913, PGR, Political Department, Annual File nos 2, 3, 4, 6, 152-C, 261 and 291

1913, PGR, Foreign Department, Annual File no. 4.2
1914, PGR, Political Department, Annual File nos 2, 11, 30, 31, and 36
1916, PGR, Political Department, File no. 2
1916, Punjab Government Civil Secretariat: 'Procedure at Installation and Investiture', Annual File no. 20
1917, January, Proceedings Punjab Government Political Department, nos 62 A and 62 E
1921, February, Chamber of Princes Archive, *Proceedings of the Chamber of Princes*
1922, Diwan and Chief Secretary, Nabha State Office (DCNS) Records, 2–4, 10–11, 13, 17–19, May 1922
1923, President Council of Regency Nabha State (PCRNS Records), 24 September and 9 October, File no. 1 C, 14, 60, 168, 203/C, 381 and Postscript
1924, File no. 937 E
1927, Administrator of Nabha State (AONS) Records, 19 September, File no. 3530-E
1929, File no. 523/E
1930, Delhi Record-4, 4, 22, 29 August, File no.115-(2), Political Secret, Government of India, Foreign and Political Department
1933, PCRNS Records, 1 May, File nos 29, 46 and 49
1934, 1935, 1937, 1938, Chief Minister of Nabha State (CMNS) Records, File no. 10419-E
1939, PCRNS Records, File nos 230
1940, PCRNS Records, File no. 440C
1941, File no. 440C, Confidential D.O. no. 67/67-C
1942, CMNS Records, File no. 10419E (Part B), 'Claims relating to Kodaikanal'
PCRNS Records, File no. 8702 E
Administrator of Nabha State (AONS), File nos 225 and 10002 E
Miscellaneous Papers, Imperial Service Troops 8 Front, vol. VI, with File 90A
Patiala Government, Ijlas-i-Khas Office, 'Patiala's Complaints against Nabha of Violation of Sovereignty'

Contemporary Newspapers and Periodicals

Akali
Akali te Pardesī
Amrita Bazaar Patrika
Bande Matram
Khalsa Advocate
'Men of the Day', *May Fair and Town Topics*, 20 July 1911.
Pioneer, The
Punjābī Bhain

Sikh Review, The
Times, The (London)
Tribune, The

Contemporary Published Sources

Ahluwalia, M. L., ed. *Select Documents of Gurdwara Reform Movement 1919–1925: An Era of Congress–Akali Collaboration*. New Delhi: Ashoka International Publishers, 1985.

Aitchison, C. U. *A Collection of Treaties, Engagements and Sanads Relating to India and Neighbouring Countries*, vol. VIII. Calcutta: Government Printing, 1909.

Gauba, K. L. *The Rebel Minister: The Story of the Rise and Fall of Lala Harkishen Lal*. Lahore: Premier Publishing House, 1938.

Griffin, Lepel H. *The Rajas of the Punjab*. Patiala: Languages Department, Punjab, 1970 [1870].

India's Contribution to the Great War. Calcutta: Government of India, 1923.

Indictment of Patiala (Being a Report of the Patiala Enquiry Committee Appointed by the Indian States' People's Conference), 1930.

Iyer, S. Ranga. *Diary of the Late Maharaja of Nabha*. Lucknow: Indian Daily Telegraph, 1924.

Josh, Sohan Singh. *Akali Morchon ka Itihas*. New Delhi: Peoples Publishing House, 1974 (translated from Punjabi).

Lee-Warner, Sir William. *The Native States of India*. London: Macmillan & Co., 1910 [1899].

Leigh, M. S. *The Punjab and the War*. Lahore: Punjab Government, 1922.

Mary, Countess of Minto. *India: Minto and Morley 1905–1910*. London, 1934.

Mitra, H. N. *The Indian Annual Register*, 1928, vol. XX, part ii. New Delhi: Gyan Publishing House, 1990 (reprint).

Mitra, H. N. and N. N. Mitra, eds. *The Indian Annual Register: An Annual Digest of Public Affairs of India (1919–1928)*. New Delhi: Gyan Publishing House (reprint).

Nehru, Jawaharlal. *Jawaharlal Nehru: An Autobiography*. New Delhi: Oxford University Press, 1982 (reprint).

O'Dwyer, M. *War Speeches*. Lahore: Government Printing, 1918.

———. *India as I Knew It, 1885–1925*. London: Constable & Company, 1925.

Prinsep, Henry T. *Origin of the Sikh Power in the Punjab*. Patiala: Languages Department Punjab, 1970 [1834].

Proceedings of the Chiefs' Conference. Delhi, 1917.

Proceedings in the House of Commons in the Parliament House, pp. 509–14, related to the debate on the ex-Maharaja of Nabha on 19 April 1928 (received through the kind courtesy of Mr Piara Singh Khabra, MP).

Proceedings of the Chamber of Princes, held at Delhi in February 1921, Chamber of Princes Archive, PSA, Patiala.

Proceedings of the Council of the Governor General of India Assembled for the Purpose of Making Laws and Regulations. Vol. XLV: April 1906–March 1907. Calcutta, 1907. Vol. XLVI: April 1907–March 1908. Calcutta, 1908. Vol. XLVII: April 1908–March 1909. Calcutta, 1909. Vol. XLVIII: April 1909–March 1910. Calcutta, 1910.

Punjab States Gazetteers. Vol. XVII A. *Phulkian States: Patiala Jind and Nabha 1904.* Lahore, 1909.

Ripudaman Singh, Tikka. *Presidential Address to the All India Social Conference.* Lahore, 1909.

Sahni, Ruchi Ram. *Struggle for Freedom in Sikh Shrines.* Amritsar: SGPC, n.d.

Sever, Adrian, ed. *Documents and Speeches on the Indian Princely States*, vol. II. Delhi: B. R. Publishing Corporation, 1985.

Singh, Bachan. *Sikhs and Idols: A Reply to the Raja of Nabha.* Lahore: Civil and Military Gazette Press, n.d.

———. *Na Ham Hindu Na Musalman: Nabha Da Uttar ate Khandan* (Punjabi). Amritsar: Wazir Hind Press, n.d.

Singh, Bhai Kahn. *Gurshabad Ratnākar Mahānkosh: Encyclopaedia of Sikh Literature* (Punjabi). Patiala: Languages Department Punjab, 1974 (reprint).

———. *Ham Hindu Nahīn* (Punjabi). Amritsar: Singh Brothers, 1995 (reprint).

Singh, Bhai Sahib Randhir. *Jail Chitthian.* Ludhiana: Bhai Randhir Singh Trust, 2010 (14th impression).

Singh, Ganda, ed. *Some Confidential Papers of the Akali Movement.* Amritsar: SGPC, 1965.

Singh, Kirpal. *Hardinge Papers Relating to Punjab.* Patiala: Punjabi University, 2002.

Singh, Master Tara. *Meri Yad* (Punjabi). Amritsar: Sikh Religious Book Society, 1945.

Speeches by the Marquis Lansdowne, Viceroy and Governor General of India 1884–1894. Calcutta: The Standard Press, 1895.

Syngal, Sardar Munnalal. *The Patriot Prince, or the Life Story of Maharaja Ripudaman Singh of Nabha Who Died as a Martyr.* Ludhiana and Delhi: Doaba House, 1961.

The Legislative Assembly Debates. vol. IV, Part I and II: 30th January 1924 to 18th February 1924. Delhi: Government Central Press, 1924.

Truth about Nabha. Amritsar: Shiromani Gurdwara Prabandhak Committee, 1923.

Tupper, C. L. *Indian Political Practice*, vol. I. New Delhi: B. R. Publishing Corporation, 1974 [1895].

Secondary Works

Books

Allen, Charles and Sharada Dwivedi. *Lives of the Indian Princes*. Mumbai: Eeshwar, 1998.

Arora, A. C. *British Policy towards the Punjab States 1858–1905*. Jalandhar: Export India Publications, 1982.

Arora, Anju. *The Princely States: British Paramountcy and Internal Administration 1858–1948 (A Case Study of the Kapurthala State)*. New Delhi: National Book Organisation, 2001.

Ashton, S. R. *British Policy towards the Indian States 1905–1939*. New Delhi: Select Book Service Syndicate, 1985.

Banga, Indu. *Agrarian System of the Sikhs: Late Eighteenth and Early Nineteenth Century*. New Delhi: Manohar, 1978.

———, ed. *Five Punjabi Centuries: Polity, Economy, Society and Culture*. New Delhi: Manohar, 2000 [1997].

Bhagwan, Manu. *Sovereign Spheres: Princes, Education and Empire in Colonial India*. New Delhi: Oxford University Press, 2003.

Bridge, Carl. *Holding India to the Empire* (The British Conservative Party and the 1935 Constitution). London: Oriental University Press/Asian Studies Association of Australia, 1986.

Caine, Barbara. *Biography and History*, Theory and History Series. Hampshire, UK: Palgrave Macmillan, 2016 [2010].

Cannadine, David. *Ornamentalism: How the British Saw Their Empire*. London: Penguin Books, 2001.

Chandra, Bipan, Mridula Mukherjee, Aditya Mukherjee, K. N. Panikkar, and Sucheta Mahajan. *India's Struggle for Independence 1857–1947*. New Delhi: Penguin Books, 1989 [1988].

Chatterji, Basudev. General Editor. *Dictionary of Martyrs: India's Freedom Struggle (1857–1947)*. Vol. I, Part II, *Delhi, Haryana, Punjab and Himachal Pradesh (1920–1947)*. New Delhi: Indian Council of Historical Research/Manak Publications, 2012.

Chudgar, P. L. *Indian Princes under British Protection: A Study of Their Personal Rule, Their Constitutional Position and Their Future*. Chandigarh: Sameer Prakashan, 1976 (first Indian reprint).

Collet, Nigel. *The Butcher of Amritsar: General Reginald Dyer*. London: Hambledon Continuum, 2005.

Copland, Ian. *The British Raj and the Indian Princes: Paramountcy in Western India 1857–1930*. Bombay: Orient Longman, 1987 (reprint).

———. *The Princes of India in the Endgame of Empire 1917–1947*. Cambridge: Cambridge University Press, 1997.

———. *The State, Community and Neighbourhood in Princely North India, c. 1900–1950*. New York: Palgrave Macmillan, 2005.

Cunningham, Joseph Davey. *History of the Sikhs: From the Origin of the Nation to the Battles of Sutlej*. Delhi: S. Chand & Co., 1955 [1849].

Datta, V. N., and S. C. Mittal, eds. *Sources on National Movement*. New Delhi: Indian Council of Historical Research/Allied Publishers, 1985.

Deol, Gurdev Singh. *Sardar Sundar Singh Majithia: Life, Work and Mission*. Amritsar: Khalsa College, n.d.

Ernst, Waltraud and Biswamoy Pati, eds. *India's Princely States: People, Princes and Colonialism*. Delhi: Primus Books/Routledge UK, 2010.

Farooqi, Mian Bashir Ahmed. *British Relations with the Cis-Sutlej States 1809–1823*. Patiala: Languages Department Punjab, 1971 (reprint).

Fisher, Michael. *Indirect Rule in India: Residents and the Residency System 1764–1858*. Delhi: Oxford University Press, 1991.

Gaekwad, Fatesinghrao P. *Sayajirao of Baroda: The Prince and the Man*. Bombay: Popular Prakashan, 1997 [1989].

Grewal, J. S. *History, Literature, and Identity: Four Centuries of Sikh Tradition*. New Delhi: Oxford University Press, 2011.

———. *Master Tara Singh in Indian History: Colonialism, Nationalism, and Politics of Sikh Identity*. New Delhi: Oxford University Press, 2017.

———. *Recent Debates in Sikh Studies: An Assessment*. New Delhi: Manohar, 2011.

———. *The Sikhs: Ideology, Institutions and Identity*. New Delhi: Oxford University Press, 2009.

———. *The Sikhs of the Punjab*, The New Cambridge History of India, II.3. Cambridge: Cambridge University Press, 2014 [1990].

Grewal, J. S., and Veena Sachdeva. *Kinship and State Formation: The Gills of Nabha*. New Delhi: Manohar, 2007.

Grewal, J. S., Harish K. Puri, and Indu Banga, eds. *The Ghadar Movement: Background, Ideology, Action and Legacies*. Patiala: Punjabi University, 2013.

Hasrat, Bikrama Jit. *Anglo-Sikh Relations 1799–1849: A Reappraisal of the Rise and Fall of the Sikhs*. Hoshiarpur: V. V. Research Institute, 1968.

Heimsath, Charles H. *Indian Nationalism and Hindu Social Reform*. Princeton, New Jersey: Princeton University Press, 1964.

Herrli, Hans. *The Coins of the Sikhs*. New Delhi: Munshiram Manoharlal, 2004 [1993].

Hill, John. *Maharajas in the Making: Life at the Eton of India 1935–40*. Sussex, England: The Book Guild Ltd, 2001.

Hyde, H. Montgomery. *Lord Reading: The Life of Rufus Isaacs, First Marquess of Reading*. London: Heinemann, 1967.

Jeffrey, Robin, ed. *The People, Princes and Paramount Power: Society and Politics in the Indian Princely States*. Delhi: Oxford University Press, 1978.

Jog, N. G. *Lokmanya Balgangadhar Tilak*. New Delhi: Publications Division, Government of India, 1974 (reprint).

Johnston, Hugh J. M. *The Voyage of the Komagata Maru: The Sikh Challenge to Canada's Colour Bar*. Vancouver: UBC Press, 2014 (expanded and rev. edn.).

Jones, Kenneth W. *Socio-Religious Reform Movements in British India*. The New Cambridge History of India, III. 1. Cambridge: Cambridge University Press, 1989.

Judd, Denis. *Lord Reading: Rufus Isaacs, First Marquess of Reading, Lord Chief Justice and Viceroy of India, 1860–1935*. London: Weidenfeld and Nicholson, 1982.

Keen, Caroline. *Princely India and the British: Political Development and the Operation of Empire*. New Delhi: Viva Books, 2013.

Kohli, Sita Ram. *Sunset of the Sikhs Empire*. Edited by Khushwant Singh. New Delhi: Orient Longman, 1967.

Kooiman, Dick. *Communalism and Indian Princely States: Travancore, Baroda and Hyderabad in the 1930s*. New Delhi: Manohar, 2002.

Kumar, Ravinder, ed. *A Centenary History of Indian National Congress (1885–1985)*, vol. II. New Delhi: AICC (I)/Vikas, 1985.

Mahajan, Ganeshi. *Congress Politics in the Punjab (1885–1947)*. Shimla: K. K. Publishers and Distributers, 2002.

Malhotra, Karamjit K. *The Eighteenth Century in Sikh History: Political Resurgence, Religious and Social Life, and Cultural Articulation*. New Delhi: Oxford University Press, 2016.

———, ed. *The Punjab Revisited: Social Order, Economic Life, Cultural Articulation, Politics, and Partition (18th–20th Centuries)*. Patiala: Punjabi University, 2014.

Malhotra, S. L. *Gandhi and the Punjab*. Chandigarh: Panjab University, 2010 [1970].

Manor, James. *Political Change in an Indian State, Mysore 1917–1955*. New Delhi: Manohar, 1977.

McLeod, John. *Sovereignty, Power, Control: Politics in the States of Western India (1916–1947)* (first South Asian Edition). New Delhi: Decent Books, 2007.

Metcalf, Thomas R. *Ideologies of the Raj*. The New Cambridge History of India, III. 4. New Delhi: Cambridge University Press, 2010 [1995].

Morgan, K. O. *Keir Hardie: Radical and Socialist*. London: Phoenix, 1997.

Owen, Nicholas. *The British Left and India: Metropolitan Anti-Imperialism, 1885–1947*. Oxford: Oxford University Press, 2007.

Panikkar, K. M. *British Diplomacy in North India: A Study of the Delhi Residency 1803–1857*. New Delhi: Associated Publishing House, 1968.

———. *Indian States and the Government of India*. London: Martin Hopkinson, 1932.

Pathik, B. S. *What Are Indian States?* (With an Introduction to the Study of the Problem of Indian States and the Real Conditions of their People). Ajmer: Rajasthan Publishing House, 1928.

Patil, S. H. *The Congress Party and Princely States*. Bombay: Himalaya Publishing House, 1981.

Porter, Barnard. *Critics of Empire: British Radicals and the Imperial Challenge.* London: I. B. Tauris, 2008 (reprint).
Pugh, Martin. *Speak for Britain! A New History of the Labour Party.* London: The Bodley Head, 2010.
Ramusack, Barbara N. *The Indian Princes and Their States.* The New Cambridge History of India, III.6. Cambridge: Cambridge University Press, 2008 [2004].
———. *The Princes of India in the Twilight of Empire: Dissolution of a Patron–Client System, 1914–1939.* Columbus: Ohio State University Press, 1978.
Rao, C. Hayavadana. *The Indian Biographical Dictionary 1915.* Madras: Pillar & Co., 1925.
Reid, Alistair J., and Henry Pelling. *A Short History of the Labour Party.* New York: Palgrave Macmillan, 2005 (12th edn).
Roy, Mihir Kumar. *The Princely States and the Paramount Power, 1858–1876: A Study on the Nature of Political Relationship between the British Government and the Indian States.* New Delhi: Rajesh Publications, 1981.
Rudolph, Susanne Hoeber, and Lloyd I. Rudolph. *Essays on Rajputana: Reflections on History, Culture and Administration.* New Delhi: Concept Publishing Company, 1984.
Sarkar, Sumit. *Modern India 1885–1947.* New Delhi: Macmillan, 2003 (reprint).
Sen, S. P., ed. *Dictionary of National Biography*, vols I–IV. Calcutta: Institute of Historical Studies, 1972–4.
Shankar, Prabha Ravi. *The British Committee of the Indian National Congress, 1889–1921.* New Delhi and Chicago: Promila and Co. Publishers in association with Bibliophile South Asia, 2011.
Singh, Ganda. *Ahmad Shah Durrani: Father of Modern Afghanistan.* Bombay: Asia Publishing House, 1959.
———, ed. *Hukamnāme: Guru Sāhibān, Māta Sāhibān, Banda Singh, ate Khalsa ji de* (Punjabi). Patiala: Punjabi University, 1967.
Singh, Harjeet. *Faith and Philosophy of Sikhism.* New Delhi: Gyan Publishing House, 2009.
Singh, Joginder. *A Short History of Namdhari Sikhs of Punjab.* Amritsar: Guru Nanak Dev University, 2010.
Singh, K. Natwar. *The Magnificent Maharaja: The Life and Times of Maharaja Bhupinder Singh of Patiala 1891–1938.* New Delhi: Harper Collins Publishers India, 1998.
Singh, Pardaman. *Lord Minto and Indian Nationalism (1905–1910).* Allahabad: Chugh Publications, 1976.
Singh, Pritam. *Bhai Kahn Singh Nabha: Pichhokar, Rachna te Mulankan* (Punjabi). Amritsar: Guru Nanak Dev University, 1989.
Singh, Surinder. *Sikh Coinage: Symbol of Sikh Sovereignty.* New Delhi: Manohar, 2004.

Singh, Vir, ed. *The Life and Times of Raja Mahendra Pratap*. Delhi: Originals (Low Price Publications), 2005.
Sinha, Aruna. *Lord Reading, Viceroy of India*. New Delhi: Sterling Publishers, 1985.
Sitaramayya, B. Pattabhi. *The History of the Indian National Congress*, vol. I, 1885–1935. Bombay: Padma Publications, n.d.
Tuteja, K. L. *Sikh Politics (1920–40)*. Kurukshetra: Vishal Publications, 1984.
Vaikuntham, Yallampalli, ed. *People's Movements in the Princely States*. New Delhi: Manohar, 2004.
Verma, S. M. *Chamber of Princes (1921–1947)*. New Delhi: National Book Organisation, 1990.
Vidyarathi, Devinder Singh. *Bhai Kahn Singh Nabha, Jiwan te Rachna* (Punjabi). Patiala: Punjabi University, 1987.
Walia, Ramesh. *Praja Mandal Movement in East Punjab States*. Patiala: Punjabi University, 1972.
Zaidi, A. M. and S. G. Zaidi. *Encyclopaedia of the Indian National Congress*, vols VIII and IX. New Delhi: Indian Institute of Applied Political Research/S. Chand & Co., 1980.

Articles in Edited Volumes

Banga, Indu. 'The Demand for Pakistan and Sikh Politics at Cross Roads'. In *The Punjab Revisited*, edited by K. K. Malhotra. Patiala: Punjabi University, 2014, pp. 292–328.
Caveeshar, Sardul Singh. 'The Sikh Kanya Mahavidyala Ferozepur'. In *The Singh Sabha and Other Socio-Religious Movements in the Punjab, 1850–1925*, edited by Ganda Singh. Patiala: Punjabi University, 1973 [1937].
Cohn, Bernard, S. 'Representing Authority in Victorian India'. In *An Anthropologist among the Historians and Other Essays*, edited by Bernard Cohn. Oxford India Paperbacks, New Delhi: Oxford University Press, 2006 (reprint).
Grewal, J. S. 'Agrarian Production and Colonial Policy in Punjab'. In *India's Colonial Encounter: Essays in Memory of Eric Stokes*, edited by Mushirul Hasan and Narayani Gupta. New Delhi: Manohar, 1993, pp. 293–308.
Malik, Ikram Ali. 'Muslim Anjumans and Communitarian Consciousness'. In *Five Punjabi Centuries*, edited by Indu Banga. New Delhi: Manohar, 1997 (2000).
Ramusack, Barbara N. 'Incident at Nabha'. In *The Punjab Past and Present: Essays in Honour of Dr Ganda Singh*, edited by Harbans Singh and N. Gerald Barrier. Patiala: Punjabi University, 1996 [1976].

Journal Articles

Hyslop, Jonathan. 'The World Voyage of James Keir Hardie: Indian Nationalism, Zulu Insurgency and the British Labour Diaspora 1907–1908'. *Journal of Global History*, vol. I, no. 3 (2006): 343–54.

Singh, Harbans. 'Maharaja Ripudaman Singh—His Involvement in Popular Causes'. *The Panjab Past and Present*, vol. IV, no. 2 (October 1970).

Singh, Harjot [Oberoi]. 'From Gurdwara Rikabganj to the Viceregal Palace—A Study of Religious Protest'. *The Panjab Past and Present*, vol. XIV, no. 1 (April 1980).

Singh, Mohinder. 'Akali Involvement in the Nabha Affair'. *The Panjab Past and Present*, vol. VII, no. 2 (October 1971).

Singh, Surinder. 'Nabha State Coinage'. *Panjab University Research Bulletin* (Arts), vol. XXI, no. 1 (1990).

Talwar, K. S. 'The Anand Marriage Act'. *The Panjab Past and Present*, vol. II, no. 2 (October 1968).

Proceedings of History Conference

Singh, Mohinder. 'Abdication of Maharaja Ripudaman Singh of Nabha'. *Proceedings Punjab History Conference*, Eighth Session, Patiala: Punjabi University, 1973.

Dissertations

Kaur, Deepinder. 'Maharaja Ripudaman Singh of Nabha'. MPhil diss., Punjabi University, Patiala, 1981.

Kuldeep. 'Modes of Colonial Control: A Case Study of Nabha under Maharaja Hira Singh, 1871–1911'. MPhil diss., Panjab University, Chandigarh, 2006.

———. 'Paramountcy and Patiala, 1900–1947'. PhD diss., Panjab University, Chandigarh, 2008.

Pall, Sheena. 'The Sanatan Dharm Movement in the Colonial Punjab: Religious, Social and Political Dimensions'. PhD diss., Panjab University, Chandigarh, 2008.

INDEX

Abdali, Ahmad Shah 2, 301
Adamson, Harvey 36
administration of Nabha 98–101; divisions of 95; education system 97, 99; expenditure on hospitals and dispensaries 99; judicial administration 94, 99; Legislative Council for 98; under Maharaja Hira Singh 93–7; under Maharaja Ripudaman Singh 98–101; manual for 93–4; Nāzim (governor) 94; octroi department 96; police circles 94; revenue collection 17, 94; state capital 96; strategy of Government of India 163; Tahsīldārs 94; units of administration 94; village administration 94–5; Zaildārs (circle officers) 95
Agent to the Governor General (AGG) 106, 201; threats held out by 76, 150–4
agricultural development in native states 96, 102–3
Aitchison, Charles xiii, 24
Aitchison College, Lahore 25, 201

Akal Infantry of Nabha 169–70
Akali 307
Akali Dal. *See* Shiromani Akali Dal
Akali jathā 152, 182, 184
Akali movement (1920–5) xviii–xix, 119, 147, 164, 172, 222, 226, 237; anti-government activities 121; culmination of 181; Gandhi and 189; Jaito Morcha 160, 166–70; on management of Gurdwaras 173
Akali Sahayak Bureau 187–8
Akālī Samāchār 256–8
Akali *satyāgraha* 186
Akali Shahidi Conference 292
Akāl Sahāi 101, 293
Akal Takht 167, 256, 290; Jathedār of 168
All India Akali Conference 288
All India Congress Committee (AICC) 187, 194
All India Social Conference 39, 47n59
All India States' People's Conference 221–4, 230, 233, 239, 310; Enquiry Committee of 233
Amritsar, Treaty of (1809) 5
Anand Marriage Act (1908) 36–9, 42, 208, 264, 304, 308, 312

ancestors and predecessors, of Ripudaman Singh (Appendix 1A) 19
Anderson, G. B. 73, 87
Andrews, C. F. 190
Anglo-Sikh War (1845–6) 75, 120, 301
annual allowance, of Maharaja 146
anti-Akali organizations, formation of 172
anti-British movements 93, 106–13
army of Nabha State 14, 71, 97; auxiliary 94
Arya Samaj 25, 29, 36, 302
Atkins, C. H. 49, 50–3, 55–6, 58–9; 64; letter of Maharaja Ripudaman Singh to 55
Atma Ram, Lala 73, 77, 98
Autobiography (of Jawaharlal Nehru) 181, 185
Azad, Maulana Abul Kalam 187

Babbar Akali movement 202, 259
Barnes, G. C. 11
begār 225–7
Benares Hindu University 112, 306; Ripudaman Singh's donation to 112
Bengal Regulation III of 1818. *See* Regulation III of 1818
Benn, W. Wedgewood 240, 252
Bhagwan Singh, Raja (1864–71) 11–13, 26, 96, 222–3, 232
Bharpur Singh, Raja (1846–63) 8–11, 16, 26, 75
Bhatia, Pritam Singh 287, 288, 295
Bishan Das, Lala 27, 98, 105, 297, 302
Bhopal, succession in 271–2
Bhupinder Singh of Patiala (1900–38) 65n12, 111, 118, 162, 202, 235, 250; bomb factory charge 224–6 of 238; indictment of 225–8; letter to Viceroy Irwin 232; Patiala under 223; relation with Maharaja Ripudaman Singh 25, 49, 103–6, 118, 162–3, 202, 205, 223, 238, 250, 256, 258, 309, 310
Birdwood Committee 172
Birkenhead, Earl of 200, 249, 272
Bombay Chronicle 194, 198n48, 307
Brahmo Samaj 25, 27
Bray, Denys 264, 276
British Administrator of Nabha xvi, 8, 29, 161, 166, 172, 190, 206
British Crown 167; obligations of 'loyalty and obedience' to 211; supremacy of 202
British Indian empire xi, 230, 264, 302
British justice 32, 277, 286
British Parliament 40, 170, 229, 234, 266, 269, 271, 310, 313
British Revenue Law 96
Broadfoot, Major 7–8
budgetary provisions for railway passengers 34
Butler, R. A. 272–9, 281

Canning, Lord 10–12, 16
Caveeshar, Sardul Singh 110, 201, 205, 224, 228, 234, 289, 290
Central Khalsa Youngmen's Union 291; Working Committee of 292
Central Legislative Assembly 286, 288
Central Sikh League 110–11, 119, 150, 189, 202, 307; founding of 307; resolution in support of the Maharaja 152
Central Sudhar Committee of Amritsar 175
Chamber of Princes xiii, xv, 103, 231, 269, 308–9, 312–13
Chand, Karam 287

changes introduced by Ripudaman Singh 98–101
Chatterjee, P. C. 73, 98
Chauri Chaura incident (1922) 190, 310
Chelmsford, Lord xv, 82–3, 102
Chief Khalsa Diwan 25–6, 28, 38, 109–10, 208, 304
Chiefs' Colleges xiv–xv, 200, 250–2
Chowrryappah, H. 272–4, 276–7, 279–81, 285
Christian Marriage Act (1872) 37
Cis-Sutlej States 8, 10–12, 53
Civil Disobedience campaign 187–8, 192
Collection of Treaties, Engagements and Sanads Relating to India (1865) xiii
Commission of Enquiry 202, 215, 231, 281; under Resolution of 1920 232
Committee for Aiding the Nabha Family in Exile. *See* Nabha Jilawatan Parwar Sahaik Committee
compensation, to Patiala 146
Congress Khilafat Swaraj Party. *See* Swaraj Party
Council of Regency 8, 10–11, 15, 163, 239, 254–7, 260, 296
Court of Arbitration 125–6, 274, 278, 308, 310–11
Craik, H. D. 174, 205
Crewe, Lord 40–3
Criminal Intelligence Department (CID) 43, 86, 119
Criminal Procedure Code 182
Crump, Leslie M. 84–5
Curzon, Lord xiv, 14, 30, 97, 302, 304
custody, issue of 244–8; monthly allowances 247

Dalip Singh, Maharaja 250
Daljit Singh, Raja 109
Dane, Louis 37–8, 40–1, 43, 48, 51, 54, 57, 60, 84, 305; letter of Maharaja Ripudaman Singh to 60
Das, Bhagwan 122, 140, 204, 250
dastār-bandī (coronation) ceremony 48–52, 54, 57, 64n2, 305
Dehra Dun: Mussoorie Electric Tramway Company 99; removal of Ripudaman Singh to 199, 207
Delhi Darbar xviii, 300n45, 313
Dera Ismail Khan 27, 302
Desh Darpan 257–60, 297
Devi, Sarojini (Maharani of Nabha) 112, 156, 239, 244–5, 248–9, 251, 253, 256–7, 260, 272, 295–6, 311; criticism in the press 255–60; on education and custody of minor Maharaja 245; letter to Lord Irwin 251; Lord Irwin's letter to 244; monthly allowance 245, 247; telegram from 'Maharaja of Nabha' for 248; visit to England 254
Devinder Singh, Raja (1840–6) 7–8, 75, 120, 301
divisibility of sovereignty (dual sovereignty), principle of xiii
Diwān-i Ām (Red Fort), Delhi 103
Dufferin, Lord xiv, 14
Duke of Connaught 103, 112
Dunlop-Smith, James 15, 30, 40–1, 202–3
Durand, Mortimer xiii, 12–13

early life and education, of Ripudaman Singh 23–8; birth 23; English education 27; first birthday 24; learning of Gurmukhi 24; learning of Sikh scripture 26; political education 27; salute of 17 guns 24; salute

of 21 guns 23; Singh, Kahn 26; tutors 26
economic nationalism 34
education: Anglo-Sikh education 25; 'communally-safe' modern education 25; denominational 33; female education 97; under Maharaja Hira Singh 97; Mayo, Lord 43n7; of minor Maharaja 248–53; moral and religious training 33; neglect of free compulsory education 303; primary education 33, 99; public school education 25; Ripudaman's policy on 33–4; Western 25
Edward VII, King 14, 17, 302, 305
Explosive Substances Bill 31

Fenton, M. W. 37
foundation of Nabha State 1–18
Fitzpatrick, James 221, 228, 246; as Enquiry Officer 229–32, 271; ex parte enquiry 233; farce of 232–8; insinuation against Nabha 236; operation crisis management
Foreign Jurisdiction and Extradition Act (1879) 17

Gaekwad, Fatesinghrao xviii
Gaekwad, Sayajirao III of Baroda xiv, 312
Gandhi, Mahatma xv, 32, 181, 310; article on 'Sikh Awakening' 189; and Nabha issue 189–95; and the Akalis 181, 188–9, 192–4; non-cooperation movement 190, 197n33; policy of non-intervention xv; release from jail 181, 191; visit to Golden Temple 194
Gangsar Gurdwara 169, 191–3
George V, King 17, 52, 238, 305

Ghadar movement 106–7, 306
Ghadar Party 107, 210
Ghosh Rashbeary 31
Gidwani, A. T. 169, 182, 185–7
Glancy, Bertrand 230, 240, 285–6, 293–5
Gokhale, Gopal Krishna 30–1, 41–2, 303, 307; friendship of Ripudaman with 30
Golden Temple (Amritsar) 28, 120, 156, 190; management of 110; removal of idols from 302 (also see Harmandar Sahib)
Gour, Hari Singh 269
Governor General in Council 5, 60, 72, 82, 170, 175, 275, 281
Grand Commander of the Order of the Indian Empire (GCIE) xviii, 14
Grand Commander of the Star of India (GCSI) 14
Griffin, Lepel 15
Gurdon, B. E. M. 70–1, 73, 77, 81, 84
Gurdwara Rakabganj (Delhi) 109, 308; association of Ripudaman Singh with 110; movement for restoration of the wall of 110
Gurdwara Tibbi Sahib 169
Guru Gobind Singh, 1, 20n4, 24, 26, 152, 301
Guru Granth Sahib 24–9, 48, 101, 166, 168–9, 302, 305
Guru ka Bagh Morcha 190
Gwalior, Maharaja of 82

habeas corpus, writ of 266, 269–70
Hailey, Malcolm 109, 171–2, 174, 176, 188, 194–5, 207–9, 215, 311
Hales, H. K. 272–3
Ham Hindu Nahīn (1898) 27
Hamir Singh, Raja 2, 20n7, 301
Hardie, James Keir 41, 113, 304
Hardinge, Lord 7, 14, 51, 64, 72, 82, 86, 312

Harmandar Sahib. *See* Golden Temple
Hindu Hitkari Sabha 29
Hira Singh, Maharaja (1871–1911) 13–18, 203, 301, 304; administration of 93–7; army of Nabha under 97; death of 104; leadership of the Phulkians 104; loyalty to the Crown 15; restoration of the Nabha territory 16
His Highness, title of xiii
historians' view of Ripudaman Singh xix–xx
historiography: of individual princes, xvii–xvix
Hoare, Samuel 272
honours, system of xiii
Horniman, B. G. 194, 198n48, 207, 286
House of Commons 42, 170, 204, 234; communiqué of 19 February 1928 266; on evidence against Maharaja's disloyalty 274; first round of questions on Nabha 266–71; Labour Members stand on Nabha affairs 273–9; on Maharaja's refusal to be treated as an ordinary subject 280–1; on Nabha affairs 264–81; pronouncement of deposition 267; on reasons for detention of ex-Maharaja of Nabha 266; second round of questions on Nabha affairs 271–3
House of Lords 173–4

Ijlās-i Khās 94
Ilbert Bill controversy 32
Imam, Ali 83, 129
Imam, Hasan 125, 286
Imperial Advisory Council 33
Imperial Bank of Delhi 296

Imperial Cadet Corps 33
Imperial Legislative Assembly: representation to Sir Alexander Muddiman 175, 264, 271, 286
Imperial Legislative Council (ILC) 11, 29–36, 58; Anand Marriage Act (1908) 36–9; committee to inquire into Sikh agitation 171; Ripudaman Singh membership of 56, 303; Sikh members of 173, 176
Imperial Service Troops xiv, 14, 104; of Nabha 80–1, 86, 97; Ripudaman Singh's opposition to expenditure on 33; during World War I 71
Imperial War Conference (1918) xviii
indemnity, payment of 129, 144
India Defence League 139n62
India Office
Indian Civil Service 145
Indian Court of Law 270
Indian Daily Herald 286
Indian Empire Society 88n1, 139n62
Indianization of the services, demand for 34
Indian National Congress xv, xix, 30, 39, 56, 98, 110, 181, 206, 269, 313; Amritsar Conference 187; Civil Disobedience campaign 187–8; Congress–Akali dialogue 181; Gauhati Session of 194; Gaya Session of 191; resolutions in support of Ripudaman Singh, 191, 194; resolution demanding complete independence xix; Swarajist interlude 181; Varanasi Conference 186; Working Committee of 188, 190
Indian Relief Fund 71
Indictment of Patiala, The 221, 225–8, 230, 232, 234, 236, 237
indirect rule, notion of xvi

Indore Enquiry 201
installation and investiture: for exercise of ruling powers 54; formal recognition, principle of 54; Government of India policy on 56, 62; by inheritance 55; installation-cum-investiture ceremony 61–3; as matter of right 48–52; modification by Paramount Power 63–4; procedure of 1871 51, 54; Viceroy's ruling of 19 July 1912 on 56–8
inter-state disputes 126, 275
Irwin, Lord 200, 232, 244, 249, 251; interview with the Maharani 252
Iyengar, S. Srinivasa 194, 265, 269
Iyer, C. S. Ranga 247, 265, 286–7
Iyer, Ramaswamy C. P. 233

Jaito Morcha (1923–5) 188, 259; Akali movement and 160, 166–70; Nehrus and 181–7; for restoration of Ripudaman Singh 63, 160–2, 165, 173, 181, 188, 193, 195, 287, 292; 310
Jallianwala Bagh massacre (1919) xviii, 69, 87n1, 88n2, 112, 306
Jasmer Singh, Tikka 290
Jaswant Singh, Raja (1783–1840) 2–7, 9, 16, 20n4, 75, 301
Jeji, Harchand Singh 225–6, 235–6
Jind, Raja of 2, 9, 11, 16, 104, 127
Jones, Mardy 268–70, 314
judicial administration of Nabha 94; under Maharaja Ripudaman Singh 99

kār sewā 120, 150
Kaul, Daya Kishan 116n44, 117n55, 120, 124, 125, 129, 134, 163, 226
Kaur, Gurucharan (Maharani of Nabha): departure from Kodaikanal 296; marriage 285; political activities of 289–93, 294; recognition by Government of India 296; visit to Punjab 285, 290
Kaur, Jagdish (Maharani of Nabha) 141, 210
Kaur, Jasmer 23, 290
Keir Hardie, James 41–2, 304, 313
Khalsa College 46n57, 110
Khalsa Defence League 294
Khalsa order 1, 301
Khalsa Panth 113, 120; Ripudaman support to 113
Khalsa Youngmen's Union of Lahore 288–9, 291–2
Khan, Khan Munawwar Ali 73, 98
khil'at (robe of honour) 7, 9, 11–12, 51–3, 57–8, 60
King George V 14, 18, 40, 238, 305; Maharaja's tribute to 52
King's Peace, idea of 126–7, 129, 130, 135, 310
Kitchlew, Saifuddin 169, 314
Kodaikanal, removal of Ripudaman Singh to 199, 210–16, 264, 294
Kuka movement 120
Kukas. *See* Namdharis
Kup, battle of (1762) 292

Labour Party 41, 170, 264, 267, 304; members of 112, 204–5, 265, 267, 280, 310, 314
Lahore Darbar 7
Lahore shooting case 32
Lahore Singh Sabha 25–6, 99, 302
Lake, General 3–4
Lal, Chaman 170, 204–5, 265
Lal, Harkishen 112, 176, 182, 302
Lansbery, George 170
Lansdowne Hospital, Nabha 96–7
Lansdowne, Lord 14, 24, 97
Lawrence, John 12

Linlithgow, Lord 286
Longowalia, Bhagwan Singh 222–3, 232
loyalty and obedience, issue of 75, 79, 149n8, 154, 203, 211–12, 240, 267

Maclagan, Edward 172
Madras Presidency 214, 252
Maftun, Diwan Singh 225–6
Mahendra Pratap, Raja xix, 112, 210, 219n38, 307
Mahrajke Sikhs 6
Majid, Abdul 286
Majithia, Sunder Singh 38, 40–1, 43, 46n57, 110, 304
Malaviya, Kapil Deva 183; friendship of Ripudaman with 30
Malaviya, Madan Mohan 30, 98, 112, 286, 306
Malerkotla, Nawab of 127–9, 222
Martial Law 112, 306
Mayo, Lord xiii, 14, 43n7
Messrs J. H. Milner and Son 280, Milner, J. H. 280–1
Metcalfe, C. T. 4
Mieville, Eric 272–3
Minchin, A. B. 106, 119–34, 141–57, 160, 163–4, 167, 185, 239, 311
minor Maharaja, of Nabha. *See* Partap Singh, Tikka
Minto, Lord xv, 5, 6, 9, 16, 29, 40, 203, 305; conciliation, policy of 82–5
Mohammadan Anglo-Oriental Conference. *See* Aligarh movement
Montagu–Chelmsford Report 275
Montagu, Lord 41–2, 118–19, 304, 309
Moore, Arthur 265
Morley, Lord 271
Mudki, battle of (1845) 8
Mutiny of 1857 xi, 8, 107

Nabha Conference (21 January 1928) 215
Nabha Council of Regency 254, 257, 260
Nabha Darbar 18, 52–3, 57, 73–6, 78, 86, 94, 101–2, 105–9, 124, 134, 154, 256, 295
Nabha Day (25 February) 165, 259, 289, 292, 314
Nabha Jilawatan Parwar Sahaik Committee 259
Nabha Morcha 172
Nabha Mutual Benefit Marriage Fund 81
Naib Nāzims 94
Namdharis 21n34
Nankana Sahib tragedy (1921) 111, 119, 189–90
Narang, Labh Singh 109, 287–8, 295
Nātak Bhāvārth Deepikā (1897) 27
Nath, Diwan Gyan 260
National Social Conference 39, 47n59, 313
native princes xvi, 305–6, 308
Nathu Ram, Lala 98
natural justice, principle of 274
nazrāna 5, 9–10
Nehru, Jawaharlal 181–8, 195n1
Nehru, Motilal 181–3, 185, 187, 191, 194, 195n2, 281n1
Newspapers (Incitement to Offences) Bill (1908) 31, 303
Nizam of Hyderabad xv, 202–3, 223, 312
non-cooperation movement 190, 310, 314
non-interference in state affairs, policy of xv
Norton, Eardley 56, 66n33, 76–7, 82, 135, 305

Ochterlony, David 4–6, 20n9; proclamation of 3 May 1809 5

O'Conner, Scott 213
O'Dwyer, Michael 64, 68n50, 69–87, 107, 120, 306; Government of India and 102, 105; interference in Maharaja's domestic affairs 84; Maharaja's letter to 69, 74; Maharaja's stance of independence 84; Martial Law imposed by 306; political ideology of 87n1; special report on sedition at Lohatbadi 108; tension with Ripudaman Singh 69, 71–80, 84, 105, 112, 306, 311
Ogilvie, C.M.G.; orders prohibiting political meetings 161, 163–5, 290; Ogilvie, G. D. 141, 150, 163
opinion in Punjab: in favour of Maharaja 285; mobilization of 287–9
opposition and resistance, Maharaja's attitude of 101–3

Pakistan Resolution (1940) 294
Pakistan scheme 292
Pal, Bepin Chandra 30
Panch Khalsa Diwan, Bhasaur 208, 307
Panikkar, K. M. 188
Panthic conference, Patti (1913) 109–10
Panth Sewak 119
Paramountcy, historiography of xvi–xvii; practice of xi, xii, 53, 77, 305, 309
Paramount Power xix, 50, 76, 104; Agreement of 1923 199; doctrine of unfettered paramountcy 202; Maharaja's stand against 53–6; on installation and investiture of ruling princes 63–4; princely states under xi, xii, 53, 305; rationalization of xi–xvi; relations with princely states xvi, 16, 32; representatives of 309; Ripudaman Singh resistance to 199, 305–8; on Tikka's education 199–201; working of 43, 50, 62, 63–4, 77, 202, 235
Parmanand, Bhai 286
Partap Singh, Maharaja/Tikka 244, 285, 289, 296, 301; custody, issue of 199–201, 244–8; education of 199–201, 246, 248–53; installation on gaddī of Nabha 271; investiture of 296; public entry of 253–5; renegade (*patit*) status 291–3, 295; visit to samādh of his grandfather 255
partition of Bengal (1905) xv, 30, 305
passport, request for 209
Patel, Vallabhbhai J. xvi, 265
Patiala Darbar 101, 105, 119, 122–4, 126, 129–30, 134, 142, 149n7, 155, 162, 168, 223, 224, 228, 234
Patiala, Maharaja Bhupinder Singh of 2, 9, 129, 199, 255, 309–11; and anti-Patiala propaganda 228; Bhupinder Singh (1900–38) 65n12, 111, 118; compensation/indemnity by Nabha State 144, 146; 'Dhuta Bhup' 259; formulation of charges against 222–5; Patiala Enquiry Committee 221, 224, 233, 235
Patiala–Nabha dispute 70, 103–6, 119, 122, 287
patron–client relationship xix
Peel, Lord 147, 173–4
Pehdani firing, case of (1922) 135
Petrie, David 205, 207, 210, 216
Pherushahr, battle of (1845) 8
Phul, Chaudhari 1, 6, 11, 13, 301
Phul dynasty 162
Phulkian rulers 29, 103, 306

Phulkian States 64, 94, 256; under control of Government of India 106; map of 3
Pickering, E. H. 273
Political Agent 6–7, 9, 24, 27, 30, 49–50, 52–4, 58–60, 64, 70–3, 77–8, 80–2, 86, 101, 105; appointment of 15–16
political movements, repression of ix, 106, 191
political practice, principle of 56, 308
political prisoners 176, 199, 236, 264, 287, 311
Praja Rakshak Committee of Nabha 162
Prasad, Durga 247
Prevention of Seditious Meetings Bill 31
princely states, hierarchy of xiii
Princes' Conference (1916) xv, 83, 307, 313
Princes Protection Act 228, 230, 231
Privy Council 266, 269
propaganda, for defamation of Ripudaman Singh 165
Provisional Government of India 112
Public Works Department 96, 109
Punjab Alienation of Land Act (1900) 96
Punjab Congress 224, 314
Punjab Legislative Council 124, 176
Punjab Riyasati Praja Mandal 222–4, 222–33, 236, 239
'Punjab School' of administration 87n1
Punjab states, political awakening in 222–5
Punjab States Shiromani Darbar 222; objectives of 222

racial discrimination 32, 303
Rai, Lala Lajpat 30, 112, 120, 211, 269, 307

Ramgarhia, Sunder Singh 190
Ranade, Mahadev Govind 47n59
Ranjit Singh, Tikka 6–7
Rao, Narasinga 122–3, 141, 150
Reading, Lord 118–19, 130, 164, 167, 201, 223, 310; reply to representation of Ripudaman Singh 170; Ripudaman Singh's letter to 167
Reform Act 185
Regulation III of 1818 xiv, 213, 215–16, 266–70, 273, 275–6, 287, 311; arrest of Maharaja under 267–9
reinstatement, of Maharaja of Nabha: agitation/movement for 287, 289, 292; Akali Dal support to 160; Birdwood Committee on 172; changed context for 293–4; Congress–Akali dialogue for collaboration on 181; counter-propaganda against 162–3; demand for 160, 289; Jaito Morcha for 166–70, 181; legislation without 175–7; Legislative Assembly, views on 170–5; resolution on 292; response of the bureaucracy on 294–6; Sikh Naujawan Society for 287; Sikh organizations' demand for 162–6
religious neutrality, policy of 33
removal, of Maharaja of Nabha 105, 308–12; conditions for 148–9; counter-proposal, imposition of 142–6; under duress 140–57; grounds for (*See* grounds for deposition, of Maharaja); under military escort 154–7; new conditions imposed by the Secretary of State 146–50; pronouncement of 267; proposals for voluntary

dissociation 140–2; protest against 161; reactions in Nabha on 160–2; resolutions against 161–2; settlement for 145–6, 150; threats held out by AGG 150–4
Resolution of October 1920 125–6, 274, 276, 278, 280, 310
Richards, Erle 36
Ripudaman Singh, Maharaja(1883–1942) 258, 301; accession as the Maharaja 1, 42; ancestors and predecessors of 19; confrontation with the government 39–43; death of 296–7; early interest in affairs of the Sikhs 28–9; fall of 130; initiatives as the Tikka 302–5; letters to newspapers 201–2; on management of Gurdwaras 35; memorial to the viceroy 76–81; monthly allowance of 245, 247, 295; in nationalist perspective 312–14; refusal to be treated as an ordinary subject 280–1; self-identification as a Sikh 309; sense of allegiance to the King Emperor 59; stand on right to succession 56; succession to his father's position 48; support to British Empire during World War I 70–6; on true facts of his abdication 167; Viceroy's memorandum delivered 81–2
Rivaz, Charles 28
Riyasat 204, 230
Riyasati Praja Mandal 222–4, 232–4, 236, 239
Round-Table Conference 83, 237
royal knighthoods xiii

Sadr Adālat 94
Sanad of 1860 xi, 9–11, 52–3, 75, 122, 309
Sanatan Dharm 25, 44
Santanam, K. 182
Sapru, Tej Bahadur 233
Sarabha, Kartar Singh 108
Scindhia, Mahadaji 2–3
Scotland Yard 254
Secretary of State: concern over case of Nabha 85–7; new conditions for removal of Maharaja 146–50; Viceroy's telegram to 87, 231, 251, 266
sedition, charge of 289
Seditious Meetings Bill 31, 303
Setalvad, Chimanlal 246, 249, 251, 253
Shafi, Muhammad 101
shahīdi jathā 169, 185, 188
Sheth, Amritlal 233–4
Shiromani Akali Dal 111, 166, 172, 211, 293, 307; Congress–Akali dialogue 181; under Master Tara Singh 294; nonviolent activities of 187; Ripudaman Singh's political connection with Akalis 147; as unlawful association 168, 187
Shiromani Gurdwara Prabandhak Committee (SGPC) 111, 121, 152, 162, 307; and Central Sudhar Committee of Amritsar 175; charges of sedition and conspiracy against 166; communiqué on Nabha issue 172; Executive Committee of 165, 168, 190; Ghallughara Day (26 May) 292; Guru ka Bagh Morcha 190; jathās to perform akhand pāṭh 166; nonviolent activities of 187; resolution against removal of Maharaja 162, 164; on Ripudaman Singh's restoration 165, 174; *Truth about Nabha* 165; as unlawful association 168, 187; Working Committee of 173, 221, 224, 292

Sikh community 35, 38, 110, 121, 165, 171, 186–7, 268, 295
Sikh Gurdwara Committee 185
Sikh Gurdwaras Act (1925) 160, 176, 194
Sikh identity 27, 309, 312
Sikhism, tenets of 309
Sikh Kanya Mahavidyalaya, Firozpur 47n60, 307
Sikh Marriage Act. *See* Anand Marriage Act (1908)
Sikh Nation 77, 168, 209, 257, 289
Sikh nationalism 210
Sikh Naujawan Society 287
Sikh reformers, Maharaja links with radical 307
Sikh Review 110, 307; Ripudaman financial support to 110
Sikh Sudhar Committee 174
Sikh Sudhar Sangat 175
Simon Commission 215
Simon, John 112
Singh, Amar 2, 225–6, 235, 290–1
Singh, Arjan, of Bagrian 36, 38, 48, 100, 105, 110, 122, 124, 130, 173, 238
Singh, Bakhshish 73, 81, 98, 104–5, 135, 155, 224–6, 235
Singh, Balbir 199
Singh, Bhai Kahn, of Nabha 26, 46n57, 302; *Ham Hindu Nahīn* (1898) 27; *Nātak Bhāvārth Deepika* (1897) 27]
Singh, Bhai Randhir 108–10
Singh, Chanda 111, 119
Singh, Daulat 172
Singh, Gulab 264, 268
Singh, Gurucharan 208, 296
Singh, Hazura 73, 98, 208
Singh, Kharak 111, 190, 211, 225, 287, 289, 291, 293, 298n8; political activity of 222
Singh, Lal 223–4, 235
Singh, Niranjan 169, 257–8, 297, 300n45
Singh, Raja 173–4
Singh Sabha movement 25–6, 34, 36, 99, 291, 304
Singh, Sant 271, 285–6, 292
Singh, Sardar Bahadur Gurdial 98, 153, 166, 238, 254, 256
Singh, Sodhi Hira 199–200
Singh, Yadvindra (Maharaja of Patiala) 294
Skrine, C. P. 294
socio-religious reform xvii, 25
Stanley, Lord 278, 281
state oppression, protest against 163
States' Peoples' Conference xix, 221–4, 230, 233–4, 239, 310–11
States' People's Movement xv
Stuart Enquiry 237–8, 310; failure of attempts at reconciliation 126–30; and Government of India 119–22; grounds for deposition of Maharaja 118; against Nabha 130–5; parallel political enquiry 122–6; secret enquiry against Nabha 119–22
Stuart, Louis 310
Sukarchakia, Ranjit Singh (1780–1839) 4–5
Supplementary Lahore Conspiracy Case 109
suzerain–vassal relationship xi
swadeshī 30, 34
Swaraj Party 191
swarāj (self-government) 30
Syngal, Munnalal xix, 132, 134–5

Tandon, Purushottam Das 81, 98, 307
tat Khalsa 29, 46n57, 108–9, 307
Taylor, R. G. 12–13

Temperance Societies 34
territorial sovereignty 123, 130
Thakker, Amritlal V. 224
Thikriwala, Sewa Singh 222
Thomas, George 2–3
Thompson, J. P. 101, 120, 122, 124, 126–34, 138n55, 141–6, 155, 205–7, 211, 311
Thurtle, Earnest 267, 271
Tilak, Bal Gangadhar 30
Tilak School of Politics 112, 120, 306
Tilak Swaraj Fund 307
Tippar Chand, Lala 73, 76, 98
Tribune, The 35, 39, 160, 162, 177n1, 185, 188, 189, 205, 206, 207, 288, 292, 314

usage, concept of xiii

Victoria, Queen xiii, xvi, 14, 33, 305
Vijiaraghavachariar, C. 253, 285
Vincent, W. H. 120
voluntary dissociation, proposals for 140–2

Wakefield, E. B. 296
Watson, C. C. 70–1, 227–8, 230–1, 236–40, 246, 249, 251
Wedgewood, Josiah 112
White Hall 272, 277
Wilberforce-Bell, H. 226–7, 236
Wilson-Johnston, J. 154, 157, 165, 168–9, 174, 182–3, 185, 199–200, 212, 216, 223, 245–6
Winterton, Earl 267–71, 279, 281
women upliftment, Ripudaman's efforts for 33, 39
Wood, J. B. 83
Woods, George S. 272–4, 276
World War I xv, 69; outbreak of 110; political issue on Nabha State offers on 70–6
World War II 285

Yakub, Muhammad 122, 124, 127, 131–3, 155
Yunānī dispensaries 97

Zamindara Association 222
Zetland, Lord 277, 281

ABOUT THE AUTHORS

J.S. Grewal, formerly professor and vice-chancellor, Guru Nanak Dev University, Amritsar, India, and director and later chairman, Indian Institute of Advanced Study, Shimla, India, has published extensively on the historiography of medieval India and the Punjab and Sikh history. His most recent books published by Oxford University Press are *The Sikhs: Ideology, Institutions, and Identity* (2009), *History, Literature, and Identity* (2014), and *Master Tara Singh in Indian History* (2017).

Indu Banga, professor emerita, Panjab University, Chandigarh, India, and formerly professor of history, Guru Nanak Dev University, Amritsar, India, has authored/edited over 15 books on agrarian, urban, institutional, social, and cultural history of medieval and modern India and the Punjab, including *Agrarian System of the Sikhs* (1978), *Five Punjabi Centuries* (2000), *The City in Indian History* (2005), and *The Ghadar Movement* (conjoint, 2013).